启真馆 出品

第 一 辑

CHINESE
HUMANITIES
VOL.1, 2019

彭国翔 主编

浙江大学出版社
ZHEJIANG UNIVERSITY PRESS

目　录

一　研究论文

二、书评论文

三、书评

一　研究论文

METAPHOR AND TRANSLATION

张隆溪

(City University of Hong Kong)

We may not notice that metaphor and translation have some kind of a hidden relationship with one another until we explore the linguistic and conceptual roots of these words. That relationship or affinity is brought home in the German word for translation—*übersetzen*—which translates the Latin *translatio* and, through it, the Greek word *metapherein*, that is, metaphor.[1] Literally, *übersetzen*, like *metapherein*, means to carry something across, and in the case of translation, something is carried over from one language to another, hence to translate. Metaphor, on the other hand, indicates a similar act of transference (*Übertragung*), as it is a figure of speech in which a word or phrase signifying one thing is used in place of another to suggest some degree of likeness or equivalence. In the use of a metaphor, the connotative semantic value is carried over from one term to another insofar as the two terms can be linked together by connotation, some semantic similarity or conceptual affinity. When we think about the etymologies of these words, we may realize that both metaphor and translation operate in a similar manner, for both are transference of semantic values from one term to another, or from a term in one language to a similar term in a different language. I would argue that to recognize the *modus operandi* of metaphor and translation as acts of transference can also help us understand the nature of translation and thereby to clarify the often-debated issue of translatability or, perhaps more significantly, untranslatability, particularly in intercultural studies. In this essay, I shall discuss these issues by referring to texts in

---

1 See Paul de Man, "The Epistemology of Metaphor", in Sheldon Sacks (ed.), *On Metaphor* (Chicago: University of Chicago Press, 1979), p. 15.

the Chinese tradition and texts of European literature, that is to say, texts that are radically different and thought by some as incommensurable. Such a deliberate choice of radically different texts purports to challenge the argument of untranslatability and to illustrate the point I try to make about translation as an act of intercultural communication, in which what is sought and can be reasonably achieved is some degree of equivalence, but not total identity.

Metaphor as Transference

The use of a metaphor can be very effective in conveying a complex idea as it displaces that idea and all its abstractness with a concrete image in a graphic and memorable form. That is why metaphorical expressions are important for poetry as a particular form of language, in which concrete images are far more prevalent than abstract notions. That is also the reason why Roman Jakobson chose metaphor to characterize the poetic or aesthetic function of language.[2]

Let me illustrate the point by quoting some lines from Robert Frost's famous poem "The Road Not Taken":

I shall be telling this with a sigh
Somewhere ages and ages hence:
Two roads diverged in a wood, and I—
I took the one less traveled by,
And that has made all the difference.[3]

Here the poet speaks of choosing a road in a wood, but as readers, we understand him as speaking of dealing with options or alternatives in life, because we typically think of a poem as a structure of symbolic meanings, as a text that means more than what it literally says. In this poem, then, the image of taking or not taking a particular road is a metaphorical way of saying that once

2 See Roman Jakobson, "The Metaphoric and Metonymic Poles", in Hazard Adams (ed.), *Critical Theory since Plato*, rev. ed. (New York: Harcourt Brace Jovanovich, 1992), pp. 1041–1044.

3 Robert Frost, "The Road Not Taken", in Richard Poirier and Mark Richardson (eds.), *Collected Poems, Prose, and Plays* (New York: The Library of America, 1995), p. 103.

we make a choice and decision in life, that choice or decision will have irreversible consequences for all subsequent choices or decisions available to us. The abstract idea of making choices in life thus comes out clearly in the concrete and vivid image of taking a crucial step at a crossroads. Facing the dilemma of diverging roads or forking paths is in fact a recurrent literary motif, a metaphor of the necessity and challenge of making choices.

In Western literature, "the Choice of Heracles" is probably the earliest example of such a literary motif, "the first true personification allegory in the West."[4] According to Xenophon, the story was written by the fifth-century BCE sophist Prodicus, and Socrates recounted that story in a dialogue when he was discussing the rigorous training of virtue and the temptation of vice. "Wickedness can be had in abundance easily: smooth is the road and very nigh she dwells," says Socrates. "But in front of virtue the gods immortal have put sweat: long and steep is the path to her and rough at first; but when you reach the top, then at length the road is easy, hard though it was."[5] It is in this context that Socrates mentioned Prodicus' story and described Heracles as "passing from boyhood to youth's estate," that is the young hero "went out into a quiet place, and sat pondering which road to take," upon which two beautiful women, personifications of virtue and vice, approached him and offered him the choice of different roads.[6] From Prodicus and Xenophon to a well-known *Tatler* essay by Joseph Addison, to Handel's musical interlude, and to numerous modern variations and children's stories, the Choice of Heracles has been a popular story in the West, as it effectively dramatizes the anxiety of choice—not only choice of a moral character, but also the anxiety of knowing that once a choice is made, possibilities offered by other choices are closed or lost. Only in the surreal world of a fantastic story like Borges' "Garden of Forking Paths" can all the imaginary possibilities be kept simultaneously open, but to have all choices taken, just like to have all paths followed, is so mind-boggling that the imaginary garden of forking paths becomes a total mystery, "an indeterminate heap of contradictory drafts," "a labyrinth of symbols," possible only in the pages

4 Jon Whitman, *Allegory: The Dynamics of an Ancient and Medieval Technique* (Cambridge, Mass.: Harvard University Press, 1987), p. 22.
5 Xenophon, *Memorabilia*, II.i.20, trans. E. C. Marchant. Loeb Classical Library 168 (Cambridge, Mass.: Harvard University Press, 1997 [1923]), p. 93.
6 Ibid., II.i.21, p. 95.

of a fantastic tale.[7] In real life, the anxiety of choice is truly great because temporality and life itself are experienced as linear and irreversible, and once you take the decisive step and move forward, it would be impossible to return to the original moment or condition.

In great literature that holds a mirror up to nature, temporality carries with it the same burden of choice as tragic consequences. In commenting on *Macbeth* as a play about prophesy and temporal consequences, Frank Kermode remarks that "nothing in time can, in that sense be *done*, freed of consequence or equivocal aspects. Prophecy by its very forms admits this, and so do plots. It is a truism confirmed later by Lady Macbeth, 'What's done cannot be undone.' The act is not an end."[8] We can cite many more examples of the same literary motif or conceptual metaphor because facing a crossroads happens to be one of the most common metaphors with which we think about challenges, possibilities, and decision-makings in life. "Basic conceptual metaphors are part of the common conceptual apparatus shared by members of a culture," as George Lakoff and Mark Turner argue. "We usually understand them in terms of common experiences."[9] I would emphasize the word "common," because here both the structure of the domain to be understood, i.e., making choices in life, and the domain in terms of which we understand it, i.e., facing a crossroads, are common experiences shared not just by members of one culture, but people across cultures. That is to say, the basic conceptual metaphor of facing a crossroads can be found not just in Western literature and culture, but also in the East across different literatures and cultures.

In the Chinese tradition, we have the famous image of the philosopher Yang Zhu who "wept when he saw bifurcating roads that could lead to either south or north."[10] The striking image of a wise man weeping at a crossroads

---

7 Jorge Luis Borges, "The Garden of Forking Paths", trans. D. A. Yates, in Donald A. Yates and James E. Irby (eds.), *Labyrinths: Selected Stories and Other Writings* (New York: Modern Library, 1983), pp. 24–25.

8 Frank Kermode, *The Sense of an Ending: Studies in the Theory of Fiction* (Oxford: Oxford University Press, 1967), p. 86.

9 George Lakoff and Mark Turner, *More than Cool Reason: A Field Guide to Poetic Metaphor* (Chicago: University of Chicago Press, 1989), p. 51.

10 He Ning何宁, *Huainanzi Jishi* 淮南子集释 [*Huainanzi with Collected Annotations*], 3 vols. (Beijing: Zhonghua Book Company, 1998), 3: 1230. All translations from the Chinese are mine.

certainly dramatizes the anxiety of making difficult choices, and this image becomes a recurrent one often alluded to in Chinese literature. For example, the great Tang poet Li Bai (701—762) writes:

> How difficult the journey, how difficult and hard!
> Numerous are crossroads, but where's my way ahead?
> Yet time will come when the wind will break the waves,
> And I—I'll hoist the sails and set off to the sea![11]

Many commentators read the difficult journey as a metaphor for the difficult and treacherous situations the poet faced in social and political life, which is surely part of the textual meaning. The journey is difficult, however, not just because roads are treacherous, but also because there are numerous crossroads that make choices and decision-making risky and perilous. The idea here is not so different from the one in Robert Frost's poem quoted above. This and the other classical Chinese texts we shall discuss later have no connection with texts in the West either by contact or by influence, but the very non-connectedness is in itself a powerful testimony to the sharedness of basic human experiences and the common structure of conceptualizing those experiences metaphorically across cultures and cultural differences.

On the conceptual level, the above quotations from different literary works are all variations of the same basic metaphor that replaces the concept of making choices in life with one of the most common and concrete human experiences—that of facing a crossroads. In using such a basic conceptual metaphor, we have the benefit of seeing complex ideas unfold in concrete and easily comprehensible images, but at the same time, we must also realize the difference between the metaphor and the idea it symbolically represents. Strictly speaking, making a choice is not facing a crossroads or taking a step forward on the road. Metaphor, in other words, does not tell us directly what it is only suggesting indirectly. As Northrop Frye says:

11　Li Bai李白, "Xing Lu Nan" 行路难 [Difficult Journey], in *Li Taibai Quanji* 李太白全集 [*Complete Works of Li Bai*], 3 vols., ed. Wang Qi 王琦 (Beijing: Zhonghua Book Company, 1977), 1: 189.

Thus the metaphor turns its back on ordinary descriptive meaning, and presents a structure which literally is ironic and paradoxical. In ordinary descriptive meaning, if A is B then B is A, and all we have really said is that A is itself. In the metaphor two things are identified while each retains its own form. Thus if we say 'the hero is a lion' we identify the hero with the lion, while at the same time both the hero and the lion are identified as themselves.[12]

Frye sees metaphor as almost the prerogative of poets, but a major point Lakoff and Turner make is that basic conceptual metaphors are everywhere in language, in ordinary as well as the poetic usage of language, and therefore great poetry is a whole lot closer to our daily language than we may have realized. "The basic metaphors are not creations of poets," Lakoff and Turner argue; "rather, it is the masterful way in which poets extend, compose, and compress them that we find poetic."[13] There are only a small number of basic conceptual metaphors in any given language, but great poets can make innovative variations of such basic metaphors and give us new and unforgettable expressions. A metaphor, as Aristotle observes, is "the application [to something] of a name belonging to something else...according to analogy."[14] Some analogies are obvious, while some are not, and poets are especially capable of discerning the unexpected analogy or likeness between two names and forming a metaphorical relation. So Frye is absolutely right in emphasizing the poetic quality of extraordinary metaphors, for Aristotle also held that "to make metaphors well is to observe what is like [something else]," and that the capability of sharp observation, that inborn capability that "cannot be acquired from someone else," is "an indication of genius."[15] In other words, we all use metaphors, but great poetic metaphors are very special, almost unique, indicative of the talents of a literary genius.

The not so obvious analogy or likeness between the tenor and the vehicle of a metaphorical expression makes a poetic metaphor striking and attractive, but the two names connected by the metaphor are also remarkably differ-

---

12 Northrop Frye, *Anatomy of Criticism: Four Essays* (Princeton: Princeton University Press, 1957), p. 123.

13 Lakoff and Turner, *More than Cool Reason*, p. 54.

14 Aristotle, *Poetics* 57b7, trans. Richard Janko (Indianapolis: Hackett, 1987), p. 28.

15 Ibid., 59a7, p. 32.

ent, thus confirming the point Frye makes, that metaphor is not strictly logical, and that in a metaphorical expression the two terms identified *with* one another remain separate *as* themselves. For all the poetic vividness and brilliance of the analogy, making a choice is not taking a step at a crossroads after all. The two terms, choice and crossroads, domain A and domain B, are not and cannot be really identical. In fact, the brilliance of a poetic metaphor largely depends on the discrepancy between the two domains, for the pleasure of a poetic metaphor lies in the revelation of brilliant, but totally unexpected connections between two domains that are otherwise radically different.

Here perhaps the concept of transference in psychoanalysis may offer some additional help for our understanding of the way metaphor works. Freud speaks of the "distortion through transference," for he defines transference as a patient's strong resistance to the doctor's treatment by distorting their interpersonal relationship and making "the object of his emotional impulses coincide with the doctor." [16] According to Freud, all root causes of a patient's neurosis are deeply hidden in the unconscious and are erotic in nature, and these unconscious impulses manifest themselves not "in the way the treatment desires them to be, but endeavour to reproduce themselves in accordance with the timelessness of the unconscious and its capacity for hallucination." [17] To put it simply, transference in psychoanalysis indicates a case of misidentification, a patient's projection of his or her unconscious and ultimately erotic impulses onto the doctor who is not the person to whom those impulses were initially intended. In this sense, then, the domain A and the domain B, the original object of the patient's impulses and the analyst, are not at all identical, though under the circumstances of a therapeutic analytic session, the patient will always find some similarities and affinities between the two.

In the light of transference as Freud discussed, then, we may understand that what links the two domains together in a metaphor can only be partial similarity or equivalence, not total identity. Metaphor is always transference of one term to cover another, but it only covers part of the semantic field of the second term, perhaps an essential and important part, but only a part nonetheless.

---

16 Sigmund Freud, "The Dynamics of Transference", trans. James Strachey in vol. 12 of *The Complete Psychological Works of Sigmund Freud* (London: The Hagarth Press, 1958), p. 104.

17 Ibid., p. 108.

It always makes a part to stand for the whole. Giambattista Vico characterizes the nature of metaphor as just such a partial coverage or overlapping based on a sort of poetic logic. "Synecdoche became metaphor," says Vico, "when people raised particulars to universals or united parts to form wholes." [18] Following Vico, Ernst Cassirer puts it even more clearly. In logical conceptualization, there is a tendency of "concentric expansion over ever-widening spheres of perception and conception," that is to say, making ever more careful and minute distinctions from genus to species, from the whole to the parts.[19] In mythicolinguistic thought, however, "exactly the opposite tendency prevails. Every part of a whole is the whole itself; every specimen is equivalent to the entire species," says Cassirer with regard to the nature of metaphor. And this, in effect, is "the principle which might be called the basic principle of verbal as well as mythic 'metaphor'—the principle of *pars pro toto*."[20] In rain-making rituals, for example, water is sprinkled on the ground or poured on red hot stones where it is evaporated with hissing noise. In both rituals, says Cassirer, their true magical sense lies in the fact that "the rain is not just represented, but is felt to be really present in each drop of water."[21] The same principle of *pars pro toto* can be applied to the Christian ritual of the Eucharist, in which bread and wine are symbolically identified with Christ's body and blood. But a drop of water is not really rain, and the ritual brean and wine can only symbolically represent Christ. In reality, the part is not the same as the whole, and there is always a difference or disparity between the idea or object and its metaphorical displacement. As Frye has reminded us, metaphor joins two terms together, but the two terms remain separate as themselves.

The study of metaphorical formulation is not just an achievement in Western scholarship. In modern Chinese scholarship, the erudite scholar Qian Zhongshu (1910—1998) has developed a similar principle of the formation of metaphors based on his reading of Chinese classics and a great number of European texts. He calls it the principle of the "two handles and multiple sides of metaphors." What this means is that a metaphor may have either a positive or a nega-

---

18 Giambattista Vico, *New Science*, trans. David Marsh (Harmondsworth: Penguin, 1999), p. 161.

19 Ernst Cassirer, *Language and Myth*, trans. Susanne K. Langer (New York: Dover, 1953), p. 90.

20 Ibid., pp. 91–92.

21 Ibid., p. 93.

tive connotation, can be approached from different angles, and may carry a multiplicity of meanings. It is so because a metaphor only partially overlaps with what it symbolically signifies. For instance, the reflection of the moon in water is a fairly common image used metaphorically in Buddhist texts as well as in Chinese literary works. As a metaphor, the moon reflected in water may carry a positive meaning to suggest the intangible mystery of the ultimate truth or Way, something delicately beautiful and difficult to reach; but it may also have a negative meaning to imply the vanity of vanities, the futility or emptiness of the ephemeral world. Qian Zhongshu explains such a multiplicity of meanings by looking at the basic relationship between the two terms in a metaphorical formulation, and locates the origin of such multiplicity in the multiple natures, capabilities, functions and effects of things themselves and a metaphor's different intended uses. He writes:

> Metaphors all have two handles and many sides. Things are all one to themselves, but they are not limited to having but one nature and one capability, nor are they restricted to producing but one function or one effect. Because of the different intentions or perspectives of their users, metaphors may have very different significata even if their denotatum is the same. Therefore the image of an object can stand alone and yet respond to a multiplicity of situations, constant to itself while changing in transformation.[22]

As Qian Zhongshu points out, translators of Buddhist texts in China had long realized the multiple functions of metaphors. Fa Yun (1086—1158), a Buddhist monk in the Southern Song dynasty, has made some interesting remarks on metaphor and translation. He points to the multiple sides of metaphors by raising such rhetorical questions: "When snow-capped mountains are made a metaphor for elephants, who can blame them for lacking tails and trunks? When the full moon is made a metaphor for the human face, how can one expect it to have eyes and eyebrows?" Qian quoted some lines from Christiana Rossetti's poem "Sing-song": "A pin has a head, but no hair; / A clock has a face, but no mouth

---

22 Qian Zhongshu 钱锺书, *Guan zhui bian* 管锥编 [*Pipe-Awl Chapters*] (Beijing: Zhonghua Book Company, 1979), p. 39.

there; / Needles have eyes, but they cannot see," etc., and he comments that these lines and Fa Yun's rhetorical questions "are words that speak of the same mind."[23] Indeed, when we speak of the face of a clock or the moon as a face, we are drawing an analogy between a round and flat shape and a human face, but ignoring all the other details that do not overlap or fit in. The point is, again, that metaphor is only a partial displacement of that which is being expressed metaphorically. To say that making a choice is like facing a crossroads is not to identify choice with crossroads completely, but to suggest some similar attributes or qualities between the two domains. What we appreciate in a metaphor is thus not total identity, but equivalence, and good metaphors are always capable of showing us hidden similarities of seemingly unrelated things in a surprising and sudden revelation, a sort of poetic epiphany that teaches us a new way of looking, a whole new perspective from which we may discern the secret connections of things in a symbolic universe. Metaphors are bridges across which we see the connections and affinities of different things and diverse objects.

The Problem of (Un) Translatability

Translation, the act that turns the alien and unintelligible into the familiar and knowable, is also a metaphorical bridge and has always served as the indispensable mediation between the vast unknown world and whatever is our claim to knowledge. This is so because much of what we know beyond our limited direct experience owes to translation, both in the narrow sense of renderings from foreign sources and in the broad sense of understanding. As transference, however, translation always entails some sort of transformation, modification, and change. In that sense, then, nothing is beyond or outside the mediation of translation, for everyone, everything changes, and language, as George Steiner argues, offers a linguistic model of all changes, "the most salient model of Heraclitean flux. "[24] Since language is always changing in time, understanding language is also always a hermeneutic process, an act of internal translation; so

---

23 Qian Zhongshu 钱锺书, *Guan zhui bian* 管锥编, p. 41.

24 George Steiner, *After Babel: Aspects of Language and Translation* (Oxford: Oxford University Press, 1975), p. 18.

much so that our effort to understand language, or simply our effort at understanding, is already translation. Much of our culture is transmitted through just such a process: "In short, the existence of art and literature, the reality of felt history in a community, depend on a never-ending, though very often unconscious, act of internal translation. It is no exaggeration to say that we possess civilization because we have learnt to translate out of time."[25] Here translation is of course understood in a broad sense, but it is so because translation in the narrow sense is exemplary of all the intellectual activities of mediation and understanding. "'Translation', properly understood," Steiner continues to say, "is a special case of the arc of communication in which every successful speech-act closes within a given language. On the inter-lingual level, translation will pose concentrated, visibly intractable problems; but these same problems abound, at a more covert or conventionally neglected level, intra-lingually...In short: *inside or between languages, human communication equals translation*."[26] In effect, we learn by reading about the foreign and about our own historical past, and much of what we read is translation, in both the narrow and the broad sense of the word.

To put it simply, we educate ourselves through translation. That is why the German concept of *Bildung*, i.e., education or self-cultivation, was fundamentally related to the idea as well as the project of translation in the German Enlightenment and Romanticism. *Bildung* is the dialectic process of going beyond the limitation of the self to encounter and experience the foreign, and returning to a new self educated and enriched in that encounter and experience. Translation, or in German *Übersetzung*, the transferring of oneself to the position of the Other, is thus inherently part of the idea of *Bildung*. As Antoine Berman observes, *Bildung* is "*closely connected with the movement of translation*—for translation, indeed, starts from what is one's own, the same (the known, the quotidian, the familiar), in order to go towards the foreign, the other (the unknown, the miraculous, the *Unheimliche*), and, starting from this experience, *to return to its point of departure*."[27] Given its importance for educa-

---

25 Steiner, *After Babel*, pp. 30–31.
26 Ibid., p. 47.
27 Antoine Berman, *The Experience of the Foreign: Culture and Translation in Romantic Germany*, trans. S. Heyvaert (Albany: SUNY Press, 1992), p. 46. Emphasis is the original text.

tion and cultivation, then, translation has always worked, though certainly with varying degrees of success in making it possible for us to know and understand what is distant from us in time and space, and in making communication possible among different linguistic and cultural communities.

And yet, we often hear claims and even fundamental arguments about linguistic and cultural untranslatability. Many writers and poets claim that translation is impossible. Cervantes has Don Quixote denigrating translation in a famous simile, "translating from one language into another, unless it be from one of those two queenly tongues, Greek and Latin, is like gazing at a Flemish tapestry with the wrong side out: even though the figures are visible, they are full of threads that obscure the view and are not bright and smooth as when seen from the other side."[28] But Don Quixote is a comic figure Cervantes loved to ridicule, and one can hardly take what he says as a sensible opinion representing the author's view. Many, especially poets, have indeed talked about untranslatability, and romantic poets infatuated with the ideas of uniqueness and originality are particularly prone to such views. Coleridge, for example, sees untranslatability as the hallmark of good poetry, for it is "the infallible test of a blameless style; namely, its *untranslatableness* in words of the same language without injury to the meaning." [29] Shelley also speaks of "the vanity of translation" in a well-known passage:

> Hence the vanity of translation; it were as wise to cast a violet into a crucible that you might discover the formal principle of its colour and odour, as seek to transfuse from one language into another the creations of a poet. The plant must spring again from its seed or it will bear no flower—and this is the burthen of the curse of Babel.[30]

A famous remark—"Poetry is what gets lost in translation"—is attributed to Robert Frost, but Stanley Burnshaw argues that this remark is not meant to disparage the value of translation. The poet simply emphasizes the uniqueness

---

28 Miguel de Cervantes, *The Ingenious Gentleman Don Quixote de la Mancha*, trans. Samuel Putnam (New York: The Modern Library, 1949), II.lxii, p. 923.

29 Samuel Taylor Coleridge, *Biographia Literaria*, eds. James Engell and W. Jackson Bate, 2 vols. (Princeton: Princeton University Press, 1983), 2: 142.

30 P. B. Shelley, "A Defense of Poetry", in Adams (ed.), *Critical Theory since Plato*, p. 518.

of poetic expression and the impossibility of their replacement by any other words; thus, Frost's remark should read, according to Burnshaw, "*The poetry of the original* is the poetry that gets lost from verse or prose in translation."[31] If we understand translation as transference and partial displacement of the original, we should have no problem agreeing with Frost's view, because having the original lost or displaced in another language is precisely what happens in translation. The displacement, however, generates its own effect, which can and should be equivalent to that of the original. But there are many other articulations of the idea of untranslatability, particularly of that of poetry. Emily Apter's book, *Against World Literature*, is a recent example.[32] Such claims of untranslatability, says Berman, "is perhaps an inevitable dialectical turning-back by which late Romanticism seeks to affirm in its way the absolute autonomy of poetry."[33] But the examples of Cervantes and Frost indicate that this view is not limited to romantic poets alone. The irony is, however, that claims of untranslatability, like many other kinds of claims and views, are often disseminated through translation; moreover, those who consider translation impossible often attempt at translation anyhow. Thus despite his overt pronouncement, Shelley, for example, did translate poetry, that of Homer, Dante, and Calderón, into English. In the Chinese tradition, complaint about translation also has a long history. Kumarajiva, the great fifth-century translator of Buddhist sutras, famously compared translation to "feeding people with chewed-up rice." He was commenting on the unsatisfying, diluted meaning of complicated Buddhist concepts in Chinese translation, but Kumarajiva proceeded to translate nonetheless and made valuable contributions to the development of Buddhism in China by finding Chinese equivalents for original concepts in Sanskrit. Here is what we see often happened in history: in spite of all the talk of untranslatability, translators have always worked in quiet and self-effacing humility to help bring new ideas, concepts, theories, literary and artistic expressions, scientific and technological novelties from one culture to another. And in doing so, they help change the way we think and live and thereby make great contributions to the profound trans-

---

31　Stanley Burnshaw, *Robert Frost Himself* (New York: George Braziller, 1986), p. 123.
32　See Emily Apter, *Against World Literature: On the Politics of Untranslatability* (London: Verso, 2013).
33　Berman, *The Experience of the Foreign*, p. 119.

formation of the world and its various cultures. Indeed, we cannot imagine the world as we know it without the benefit of translation.

In a narrow and restricted sense, we all know that certain words and expressions are untranslatable because what exists in the source language may not exist or may not have a close equivalent in the target language. Many idioms, puns, set phrases, jokes, and technical terms are in this sense untranslatable. In such cases, transliteration and loan words are useful ways to solve the problem. This is, however, not the unique problem in translation, because the growth of language has always been a case of catachresis, that is, a process of borrowing from the existing vocabulary to signify what is new and unnamed. When we say a "footnote," or "the eye of a needle," or "the head of the mountain," we are already using metaphors and translating an outside phenomenon into the language of our own body. This is true especially of abstract notions and concepts. As Vico observes, the "property of the human mind is that, when people can form no idea of distant and unfamiliar things, they judge them by what is present and familiar." [34] He further noticed "the fact that in all languages most expressions for inanimate objects employ metaphors derived from the human body and its parts, or from human senses and emotions." [35] This seems to be the common principle of etymology in all languages. In an ancient Chinese text, the appended words to the *Book of Changes*, we find a remarkably similar formulation of the same principle, where it is said that the ancient king Paoxi invented hexagrams by observing the configurations of heaven and earth and by imitating the pattern of traces left by birds and animals on the ground. "By taking hints near at hand from his body and farther away from external things, he created hexagrams to make the virtue of gods comprehensible and the nature of all things known in signs."[36] That is to say, language and its vocabulary are largely metaphorical; they grow by borrowing from their own stock, as it were, by transferring the meaning of one word to another. Thus words are taken out on loan not only between languages, but within the same language as well.

If we recall the point made earlier in my discussion of the relationship

---

34 Vico, *New Science*, p. 76.

35 Ibid., p. 159.

36 *Zhouyi zhengyi* 周易正义 [*The Correct Meaning of the Book of Changes*], 74b, in Ruan Yuan 阮元 （ed.), *Shisan jing zhushu* 十三经注疏 [*Thirteen Classics with Annotations*], 2 vols. (Beijing: Zhonghua Book Company, 1980), 1: 86.

between metaphor and translation, we may realize that the idea of untranslatability is largely based on a fundamental misunderstanding of the nature of translation. To recapitulate, metaphor is only partial substitution and displacement, the saying of one thing by means of another, and so is translation. "A metaphor with the name 'A is B' ", as Lakoff and Turner point out, "is a mapping of part of the structure of our knowledge of source domain B onto target domain A."[37] Replace the word "domain" with "language," and we have a pretty good description of what happens in translation. If a metaphor is the mapping or transference of part of the structure of our knowledge of a source domain onto a target domain, translation is likewise the transference of part of the structure of a source language onto that of a target language. Just as we cannot demand total identity in a metaphorical expression, it would be pointless to require that translation produce an exact replica of the original.

In his famous essay, "The Task of a Translator," Walter Benjamin makes the statement that "no translation would be possible if in its ultimate essence it strove for likeness to the original."[38] This is not to say that translation should not be true to the original or that free paraphrasing should pass as good translation. What this means is that translation is a re-creation of the original, an equivalent expression in the target language of what the original text says in the source language. Benjamin, however, is speaking on a metaphysical level rather than the level of technical considerations of translation as practice. Deeply rooted in Jewish mysticism as well as German philosophical idealism, Benjamin conceived of translation not as a mere rendering of an original foreign work, but as the attempt to articulate what no work in the original can articulate, what he calls the intention of all languages or the "pure language." As Berman comments, Benjamin's idea of the task of the translator "would consist of a search, beyond the buzz of empirical languages, for the 'pure language' which each language carries within itself as its messianic echo. Such an aim, which has nothing to do with the ethical aim, is rigorously metaphysical in the sense that it platonically searches a 'truth' beyond natural languages."[39] In Benjamin's own

---

37 Lakoff and Turner, *More than Cool Reason*, p. 59.
38 Walter Benjamin, "The Task of the Translator," *Illuminations*, trans. Harry Zohn (Glasgow: Fontana, 1973), p. 73.
39 Berman, *The Experience of the Foreign*, p. 7.

words, it is this mystical pure language that links all languages together. "Languages are not strangers to one another," says Benjamin, "but are, a priori and apart from all historical relationships, interrelated in what they want to express." [40] What all languages want to express is a deep intention, "the intention underlying each language as a whole—an intention, however, which no single language can attain by itself but which is realized only by the totality of their intentions supplementing each other: pure language. While all individual elements of foreign languages—words, sentences, structure—are mutually exclusive, these languages supplement one another in their intentions."[41]

For Benjamin, then, it is into this pure language that the translator tries to translate, rather than trying to produce a likeness to the original. It is also in this pure language, almost as the Word of God, that he finds the absolute legitimacy of translatability. As he says, "The translatability of linguistic creations ought to be considered even if men should prove unable to translate them."[42] In Benjamin's metaphysical conceptualization, then, translation becomes a creative or a re-creative act that brings out what is intended but not articulated in the original. In a passage that is highly poetical, he describes the translator's re-creation:

> In translation the original rises into a higher and purer linguistic air, as it were. It cannot live there permanently, to be sure, and it certainly does not reach it in its entirety. Yet, in a singularly impressive manner, at least it points the way to this region: the predestined, hitherto inaccessible realm of reconciliation and fulfillment of languages. The transfer can never be total, but what reaches this region is that element in a translation which goes beyond transmittal of subject matter. This nucleus is best defined as the element that does not lend itself to translation.[43]

This is a difficult passage, but here we may get at least two things clear out of Benjamin's highly metaphysical argument. One point is that texts are translatable despite all difficulties and actual cases of untranslatable words and

---

40 Benjamin, *Illuminations*, p. 72.
41 Ibid., p. 74.
42 Ibid., p. 70.
43 Iibd., p. 75.

sentences, because translatability is rooted in the very nature of all languages and their shared intentionality. The other point is that adequate translation preserves, paradoxically, "the element that does not lend itself to translation." To put the second point in plain language, we may say that the translator should not domesticate the foreignness of the foreign text, but to allow that foreignness to come through in the translation. "It is the task of the translator," says Benjamin, "to release in his own language that pure language which is under the spell of another, to liberate the language imprisoned in a work in his re-creation of that work."[44] The translation is not judged by the original, but the "pure language" underlying the original, to be released in the translation.

We can better understand this paradox of translatability and the fundamental resistance to translation by going back to the idea of *Bildung* discussed earlier. If the concept of *Bildung* indicates an edifying process of self-cultivation, a process of going beyond the self to experience the foreign and to learn from that experience, then the foreign becomes valuable precisely at the point where it keeps its foreignness as an irreducibly different system, from which one can learn something new and valuable. Insofar as translation works, then, it should keep that irreducible foreignness of the foreign text intact, rather than reducing it to the domestic banality. As Berman argues, to overly domesticate a foreign text is the mark of bad translation: "A bad translation I call the translation which, generally under the guise of transmissibility, carries out a systematic negation of the strangeness of the foreign work."[45] So here we have the dialectic quality of translation: what can be translated must at the same time be kept irreducibly foreign, but again, it is precisely the foreignness of a foreign work that calls for translation and makes a good translation possible. We educate ourselves as individuals and as cultures through translation, and it is the foreign, the new, the unfamiliar, or whatever we do not yet know and understand, that calls for translation in the first place. That is to say, we translate because we want to know something new and foreign, and it is therefore the task of the translator to retain the foreign concepts and values in the translated text even though linguistically the translator has already rendered the foreign language into our own. In effect, we are asking the translator to provide a text that can

---

44 Benjamin, *Illuminations*, p. 80.
45 Berman, *The Experience of the Foreign*, p. 5.

give us, even though in translation, an equivalent experience of directly encountering the foreign. This is the reason, as Northrop Frye puts it memorably, "why the humanists have always insisted that you don't learn to think wholly from one language: you learn to think better from linguistic conflict, from bouncing one language off another."[46] It is in that sense and on that theoretical level that we learn to appreciate the value of translation as an experience of the foreign.

---

46 Northrop Frye, *The Educated Imagination* (Toronto: Canadian Broadcasting Corporation, 1963), p. 50.

Confucianism and the Inadvertently Interpersonal Universe: Sacred Humanity Beyond Personhood

Brook Ziporyn 任博克

(University of Chicago)

Why Care About Chinese Metaphysics:
Sacred Personhood Without Monotheism[1]

In Plato's *Phaedo,* there is a remarkable tableau in which Socrates reports having heard someone reading from a book of Anaxagoras in the marketplace, proposing an idea that changed his life and set the agenda for his future philosophical vocation—and, as it turned out, the philosophical agenda for quite a lot of human thinking for the next two millenia. It was the suggestion that the first cause or principle of all things was not, as previously suggested, water or fire or air, but something called *noûs*—intelligence. The nature of this concept was derived from its everyday usage as something that belongs to a conscious mind, involved in consciously planning and arranging things to accord with the values held by that mind. This particular aspect of experience was now elevated to the position of first principle. I regard this as the defining moment by which we can understand what is so special and so important for global philosophy about Chinese metaphysics: a tradition of systems of thought in which nothing like this idea was ever a serious contender.

For this idea what was to become the mainstream philosophical tradition of Greece and, later, of Christendom: the initial shot of monotheism and all the

---

1 This essay continues a line of thought presented in more general terms in "The Importance of Being God-less: The Unintended Universe and China's Spiritual Legacy", *Journal of Chinese Philosophy* 41: S1 (December 2014) 686–708.

permutations of post-monotheism that have been so decisive for the formation of what has been called "Western thought"—*even when* it tried to break away from it into the opposite forms of thinking, and even though it was succeeding in doing so. For what leaps to the eye in this astonishing passage in the *Phaedo* is five concepts that are brought into a fateful encounter: 1) the Good, 2) consciousness, 3) causality, 4) purpose and 5) unity. The key unspoken premise behind Socrates' enthusiasm here is a certain experience of conscious willing, identifying with the aspect of oneself which *knows in advance what it wants*, and tries to achieve it through *efforts* of which it is also *fully aware*. *Purpose*, as something conceived clearly in the mind before an action is undertaken, is implicitly privileged here, considered without ado to be what actually makes things happen. The assumption is that whenever something happens, it is due to an intelligence choosing for it to happen. The Good—that is, a single purpose—lies at the source of all being, gives being to beings, and is what makes things as they are. The shorthand we will be using for this idea in all its permutations to come is *noûs* as *arché*.

Purpose, Infinity and God in the Roots of Western Metaphysics

Arché is a Greek word meaning "beginning, origin, source" with the derivative meanings of "what is first," "having priority" and "ruling." It is the Greek root of English words like "hierarchy," "archangel," "patriarch," "archetype." The Latin equivalent is *principium*, "principle." Philosophy is said to begin in Greece when Thales suggested that *water* was the *arché* of all the other elements (fire, air, earth): water came first, and was in some way what underlay and explained them all. All the others *came from*, *were made of*, *were moved by*, and/or *returned to* water. Thales' student Anaximander proposed *apeiron*, the boundless, infinity, as the origin. *Apeiron* appears to be related to primal chaos, to randomness, to lack of definition and boundary and order. As we shall see, the status of *apeiron*, raw infinity, is a bone of contention, for the term will be usurped into a new and contrary meaning by Anaxagoras, striking the beginning of the proto-theistic tradition.

Early Chinese cosmogonies follow a similar trajectory, starting with *water* origin stories (e.g., in the recently excavated text *taiyi sheng shui* 太一生水) but quickly settling into what comes to be mainstream Daoist motifs which point to the formless, the boundless, the indeterminate as the only possible source of the determinate. *Dao*, originally a word for order and purpose, for the articulated boundaried guidance of a *path*, is seized on by the Daoism in a new *reversed and ironic* sense, as I've argued elsewhere, to indicate this formlessness, purposelessness and orderlessness that is the real source of all orders and purposes. Chinese speculation of all schools continues on this basis in various complicated ways, developing a variety of ways to relate the boundless to the bounded, the indeterminate to the determinate, the orderless to the ordered—but almost without exception remaining grounded in the fundamental primacy of the indeterminate.[2] What is interesting about pre-Socratic Greek thinkers, in contrast, is how thoroughly the suggestion of raw infinity, the formless randomness as the origin of all things, is rejected, neglected, and sometimes transformed. Anaximenes, allegedly a student of Anaximander, transforms it right away: not the raw infinite, but the most infinite concrete element is now put forward as the *arché*: air, which could be regarded as condensing into concrete things and dissipating back into air when they perish. Thus far we have an analogue in China, in the theories of *qi* as the first stand-in for the formless *Dao*. But hereafter the two traditions radically part ways. Herakleitos suggested that the *arché* was fire. Air or fire or water are the kind of physical candidates for *arché,* for the first principle giving the most basic explanation of things that annoy Socrates in the passage quoted above. New dimensions begin to emerge with Empedocles' suggestion of something other than the material elements as the ultimate principle, Love and Hate, and the Pythagoreans suggestion of harmony or

---

2 The apparent exception of Cheng-Zhu Neo-Confucianism and its derivatives is, in my view, still really a variant of this: the Great Pivot (*taiji*太极), which defines determinate order and is primary, is itself a form of indeterminacy between the contrasted determinations of *yin* and *yang*, and for Zhu Xi, following Zhou Dunyi, is itself formless and in that sense undifferentiated in itself (*wuji*无极), though admittedly an effort is made here to distance this idea from a completely indeterminate formlessness—the result of which is, however, not to make the ultimate principle determinate in the manner of a consciously arranging choice-making, but rather a relegation of all apparent conscious arranging to an ontologically secondary role, even on the cosmic level, and with it a redefining of what determinateness actually is, moving it even further away from the determinacy of conscious purposive action. For a discussion of Zhu Xi, see my "Zhu Xi on the Consciousness and Unconsciousness of the Mind of Heaven and Earth: Cross-Cultural Considerations of Ontological Theism and Atheism in Honor of the Work of Professor Donald Munro", in *Festschrift for Professor Donald Munro* (CUHK: forthcoming).

proportion as the *arché*. But the big break, according to Socrates in this passage—and to his pupil Plato and his pupil Aristotle—is Anaxagoras. Anaxagoras says that none of those finite material elements can be the *arché*. Nor can *apeiron*, the raw infinite of Anaximander, be the *arché*. It is *noûs*, intelligence, that is the first principle.

Noûs is sometimes translated "mind," but a modern reader needs to be wary about this translation. We sometimes speak of "consciousness" or "awareness" as mental functions, or even as the essence of mind. But this sort of detached awareness, a kind of allowing of whatever presents itself, is not what *noûs*-means. *Noûs* is specifically *intelligence*, connected to the idea of *understanding* as opposed to merely perceiving, and *good sense* or *sensibleness* in activity, as opposed to foolish, aimless, reckless or random behavior, or unthinking openness to events as they transpire, or daydreaming, or playful whimsy—even if any of the latter is conscious. *Noûs* is thus not consciousness, but *a specific kind* of consciousness. It does the kinds of things that are accomplished by *thinking*, of *planning*, of *designing*. In its simplest and most direct meaning, it is mind in its purposive, active mode, when it is trying to figure something out or is guiding the actions of the body. It is mind in command, mind as guide, mind as arranger and optimizer and disposer, mind as active doer with long-term plans and unity of purpose over time. It is mind that asks and answers the question, "What should I do now to make things better, to achieve my goal, to maximize my effectiveness?" It is mind as purposive designer. It is mind with problems to solve, work to do, things to work out. It is mind acting purposively, doing what makes the most sense to attain its goal, maximizing effectiveness. This is why Socrates immediately sees this as an explanatory principle: if *noûs* is *arché*, then the explanation of why anything is so is because *it is best for it to be that way*. It is that way because the intelligence that runs the world thought it would be good for it to be that way. It exists because it was wanted, because it fit the plan, because it had a specific job to do. It is the agent which coordinates means to ends. This is a particular model of mind, perhaps rooted in a particular experience of mind in a particular kind of self, prioritized and privileged as the model of all effectiveness and the origin of all being. It is in this particular sense that it joins together the five concepts mentioned earlier: 1) a concept of the Good, 2) consciousness, 3) causality, 4) purpose and 5) unity. It is the *controlling conscious selfhood* writ large.

Design Versus Infinity:

Two Rival Explanations for the Intricacy of Existence

One fairly straightforward way of touching on what is at stake here, when we look at the historical record of the emergence of this idea in ancient Greek thought, as a struggle between *raw infinity* and *purpose*. For *infinity* as an explanatory principle is initially the marker of what we might call the atheist approach to metaphysics—atheist not in the sense of denying the existence of the gods, plural, but in the eschewal of the premises behind the concept of a single big G God, the kind that can be conceived as the creator or arranger or controller or judge of the world. This "atheist" approach goes all the way back to Anaximander's *apeiron* but further develops in the thought of the atomists, of Democritus and the Epicureans: it is the *alternative* to design, to control, to *noûs*, mind. As David Sedley summarizes, "The atomist universe is infinite, consisting of infinite void housing an infinite number of atoms. That in turn means that worlds must form not only where we are but elsewhere too: there could be no explanation of how in infinite space just one region, or even a merely finite plurality of regions, had been specially privileged in this regard. Not only, therefore, is there a plurality of worlds, but the same calculation yields the result that there be infinitely many of them."[3] The later Roman Epicureans, Sedley tells us, inherit this Democritean idea of "the extraordinary power of infinity," and speak explicitly of it as the "*visinfinitatis*": it is rooted in what Epicurus called *isonomia*, "distributive equality." [4] Infinity is here singled out as a positive force, as an actual reason for things being as they are.

For here is where the ancient battle begins: what explains the world we see around us? Why is there something rather than nothing? Where do these amazing things come from? What made them? How do things so desirable as those we desire and so beautifully put together come to be? The Anaxagorans, the Platonists, later the monotheists and Stoics, and in his own subtler way even Aristotle, say that it is due to it being *good* in some way; all but the last-named take

---

3 See David Sedley, *Creationism and Its Critics in Antiquity* (Berkeley: University of California Press, 2007), p. 138.

4 Ibid., pp. 155–166.

this to mean that some *purpose-bearing mind or mindlike entity made them this way*. They were designed to be this way; they are the way they are because of *noûs*. The atomists, on the other hand, strike what will become the distinctive atheist alternative: given infinite time and space, it would require something to *prevent* any particular configuration from appearing, *and appearing infinitely many times*. What makes them is infinity itself, which is just a positive name for a negative: it is a way of naming the absence of limits, the failure of any limits, the fact that nothing is there to provide a reason why anything should be any one way rather than another, to exclude any possible outcome. Infinity in this sense is the same thing as formlessness, the impossibility of restriction to any finite shape, or set of shapes, or determinate definite characteristics. A God-less universe is, in the absence of any reason making it otherwise, an infinite one, infinitely productive and infinitely diverse. In its simplest form, as we find it here, this is something like the "monkeys at a typewriter" idea—infinite monkeys typing randomly for eternity will eventually write every one of Shakespeare's plays. The ancient atomists used the image of grains of sands forming shapes on the windswept beach. The more unlikely or absurd this seems, the more one is under appreciating the real extent of infinity. The more one allows infinity to be infinite, the more its power is felt. The more distinctly one senses the infiniteness of infinity, the more secure one feels in the groundedness of any particular form in formlessness. The sense of infinity and the sense of trust in infinity are directly proportional to one another. They appear together, and they grow together. To see one is to see the other. The less you assume about what may steer or limit or constrain existence, the bigger your sense of infinity is; the bigger your sense of infinity, the more tightly you experience it to be compressed into the very structure and being of each unlikely finite thing.

This general way of thinking perhaps feels vaguely comfortable to moderns, because it is more or less the line of explanation behind Darwinian natural selection (an idea somewhat foreshadowed in Empedocles's idea of what Sedley calls "the creative power of accident," [5] though not yet given there the status of ultimate explanatory principle as it has for the atomists). Given enough time, everything happens. Chance and infinity *can* do the same work which we are tempted to attribute to design and purpose. Chance and infinity are both

---

5 See Sedley, *Creationism and Its Critics in Antiquity* p. 60.

mere names for the *absence* of a principle, the absence of a limiter, rather than being any actually constraining law or principle themselves. But already in the "power of infinity" we have a contemplation of this absence as something that, precisely as absence of any constraint, has the decisive creative power that we experience in things.[6]

Now it is true that God too will come to be called "infinite." It is perhaps by now hard to realize just how counterintuitive this claim would initially have been. For *prima facie*, although we are used to hearing that God is infinite, the idea of God is directly in conflict with the idea of infinity. The monotheist claim that God is infinite is a daring coup, a usurpation of the enemy's territory—and one that attempts to foreclose forever the idea of the creative power of raw infinity, the purpose-generative power of purposelessness. God is mind-as-cause, and mind here is construed not as awareness but as intelligence, as choice, as purpose, as preference for the good: but preference is necessarily beholden to finitude. The essence of purpose and choice and preference is *the exclusion of the non-chosen, the non-preferred, the non-fulfillment of the purpose.* God, intelligence as cause, is from the first the exaltation of finitude and exclusion over infinity and inclusiveness. And yet it is true that we find, in the

---

6 The God and proto-God party looks at the birds of the field and sees, at its source, a mind that wanted to make them, and did so; perhaps also a love of them, care for them, surveillance of them and how well they do the job they were made to do (which might just be the job of knowing and loving and praising their maker). Some in this party even think that the very hairs on our heads are numbered (Matthew 10: 30, Luke 12: 7), as if the mind of God is a vast countinghouse where everything must be precisely accounted for. Above all, what we are seeing as we see these little sparrows hopping innocently around is the manifestation of a purpose, of intelligence: they were made *in order to* accomplish some specific goal. The atheist party, looking at these little lifeforms, see rather a concentrated concretion of *chance*, of *purposelessness*, of *non-intentionality*, of *infinity*, of *formlessness*. These very forms are infinity itself—the absence of God, the absence of purpose, the absence of any definiteness—walking and jumping and chirping. They are the antithesis of number. The hairs on our heads are not numbered; they are the very presencing forth of numberlessness, of the failure of all number, of infinity. On this view, if you look at an eyeball or a sparrow and think, "How unlikely! How redolent of the maker's hand! Because how else could so intricate a thing come to be?" You are losing touch with the vastness of time and space, blotting them out of your consciousness, closing yourself to the infinity of openness that necessarily extends outward from any locus. To do this requires *work*: infinity is the default. A concentrated effort and considerable ingenuity is required to come up with a conception of anything that would limit infinity, that would make it unlikely that any particular thing could exist, which would reduce the scape of infinite agentless creativity, and instead attribute things to the specific direction of a mind. God is, as we are tempted to say, a conspiracy against infinity.

opening shot of the theistic view of the world, in Anaxagoras' proposal of *noûs* as the cause of all things, the assertion that *noûs* itself is what is "unlimited" (*apeiron*), i.e., "infinite." Yet it is also "unmixed" with anything else. Indeed, the notion of *noûs* is precisely this seemingly impossible combination of "separation" with "unlimitedness." With the older idea of *apeiron* in mind, this seems to be a brazen and palpable contradiction, right from the beginning. For Anaximander's *apeiron* was precisely what was *common* to all diverse things, copresent to all of them, separate from none, and thus having no special nature of its own. Raw infinity is not separate from anything—if it were, it would have to exclude that thing, and *ipso facto* would not be infinity. But somehow Anaxogoras' attempts to find in the idea of intelligence, mind, *noûs*, a daring combination of what have hitherto been *opposites*: infinity and separateness. How?

In Sedley's translation, Anaxagoras is reported to assert:

> The other things share a portion of each, but intelligence [noûs] is something infinite and autonomous, and is mixed with no thing, but it alone is by itself. For if it were not by itself, but were mixed with something else, it would share in all things, if it were mixed with any of them—for in each thing a portion of each is present, as I have said earlier—and the things mixed with it would prevent it from controlling any thing in such a way as it does in being alone by itself.[7]

This is as close to a smoking gun for the creation of the creator as we are likely to find. Already it is all there: mind is not awareness but intelligence, and this is the *controller* of all things, and it is for this reason that it must be *separate* from them, *beyond them* in some sense. Mind must be separate because mind must stand above all things, so as to be their controller rather than being controlled by them. Already, it seems, only two possible relationships between mind and non-mind, between conscious self and world, between intentional mind and unintentional body, are imaginable: "controlling" and "being controlled". Relinquishing control is thought to have no other meaning than being controlled. Hence mind must be unmixed with anything else, must stand completely above anything it relates to, and must always remain in control.

---

7 Sedley, *Creationism and Its Critics in Antiquity* pp. 11–12. Italics added.

But why is this controlling intelligence then "infinite"? How, indeed, can it be intelligent (and hence exclusive of the unintelligent) and unmixed (and hence apart from and non-present in things) and yet be unlimited or infinite? Sedley's interpretation suggests that this notion of infinity is in fact an idiosyncratic way of talking about precisely about this unmixedness, this transcendence itself. He explains Anaxagoras' idea as follows:

> The stuffs that our bodies are made of either are (on my preferred inter-
> pretation), or at least include, pairs of opposite properties like hot and
> cold, wet and dry. For intelligence to be "mixed" with these would be
> for it itself to have a certain temperature, a certain degree of moistness,
> etc. And that would make intelligence subject to physical change, so that
> it could be acted upon by matter, being for example heated and dried in
> summer, cooled and dampened in winter, when the reality is that it itself
> controls matter. To say that intelligence is unmixed is thus Anaxagoras'
> way of saying that, despite being present in living things, it is in itself nei-
> ther hot nor cold, neither wet nor dry, and so on for all the pairs of per-
> ceptible opposites. In short, to call intelligence unmixed is his way of say-
> ing that it is free of physical properties.[8]

Intelligence is "unlimited" in the same way: it cannot be limited to either hot or cold, because it must be unrestricted to either *so as to be able to control them*. For the controller and the controlled are assumed to be mutually exclusive, whatever is characterized by the qualities of the controlled, then, cannot be a controller. The idea of spontaneous order is completely lacking in this conception. Whatever is ordered is not the orderer. But to be ordered is to be definite, to remain within certain fixed boundaries. So the controller must be beyond all possible boundaries: infinite. Unmixed and infinite here mean the same thing: it means to be unrestricted to any finite thing so as to stand above it and be unaffected by it, so as to be instead the arranger and controller of it, as is required by the notion of *noûs* not as awareness but specifically as *intelligence*—which is to say, precisely as choice-maker, as purpose-monger, as excluder.

This is the key point. For it is indeed possible to think of mind as infinite

---

8 Sedley, *Creationism and Its Critics in Antiquity* p. 12.

in a way that may feel superficially similar if we do not keep our eye on the main issue of *purpose* and *exclusion*. But God is infinite mind precisely as infinite purpose and infinite personality: occupying all of time but not all of space and not all of being. Personality is a unification on the model of purpose and accountability, and hence stands opposed to its otherness, which it excludes from its essence, producing a contingent relationship between the self and any non-self. Infinity proper is rather unity in the sense of inseparability, where there is always more than whatever is so far imagined, but whatever more there is necessarily also included—a relation of inclusion of its necessary otherness.[9] God is infinite in the form of projection into the future forever, continuity of means and ends, of will and purpose, of accountability and control. This temporal infinity is a kind of oneness, a binding together of moments, but in the special form in which this is done by a conscious accountable controller: the mode of accountability and control, of joining purposes to instruments. It is non-necessary infinity, the infinity of "freedom" in precisely the sense Spinoza will deny: God is an infinite mind in control of the world, which his infinity makes necessarily finite. The world is literally required to be finite by the conception of God, and put into a state of subordination to purpose, now made into *infinite purpose*, an *infinite personality*, *which is* a prima facie contradiction in terms.

9 It is true that in a Hartshorne/Whitehead sense personality is a oneness that is a society of actual occasions, including non-personal ones, and thus can be said to incorporate othernesses. But besides the fact that this is a highly alternative account of personality, more Buddhist than classical theist, it must be noted that it is only a personality to the extent that the elements of society are *not yet* integrated, and *as opposed to* what is not integrated. That is, because the integration is not necessary, it is a choice; but it is not necessary only to the extent that we are looking at the elements in the phase of not-yet-being integrated. Similarly, there is a choice about what and how to integrate in the world and in the future, and this means one-as-opposed-to-another is what is operative. The process God is personal only insofar as it has choice and preference, and it has these only to the extent that it has a non-necessary relation to whatever elements it may integrate into the society which is itself. It is personal only to the extent that we are considering the othernesses as not integrated into itself.

Four Types of Theism and Atheism:
Alternate Models of the Purpose/Purposeless Relation

The problem of Western metaphysics is the problem of God, and this problem, we start to see, is largely a question of our relation to purpose. God as in any way personal, as an intelligence, as in any way active in time, is first and foremost a controller, modeled on a certain mode of experiencing our own attempts at control and our own ways of unifying our actions as means toward an end. For as we will explore in detail below, a personality is a center of control, of commitment to continuity through time, enabling in itself and others the relations of accountability, of responsibility, of evaluation, of choice. A personality is a locus of purposes, of selective response shaped according to interest and need and desire, and the ability to compare and connect current states and alternate outcomes to an intended purpose.

Indeed, it is in the idea of purpose as the ultimate ontological category that the idea of God lives and breathes even when the word "God" is absent. A lot of people in the last few thousand years seem to be obsessed with something called "purpose"—especially with people having a purpose, actions having a purpose, life having a purpose.

Why does everyone care so much about having a purpose? The reason is in one sense self-evident: because the idea of purpose is part of the definition of what it means to want anything, and wanting things is what we living beings are all about.

Living beings have needs and desires. To be not only alive but also conscious means sometimes having awareness that what we want is not what we have—wanting some things that are not immediately available. So to be conscious and alive seems to require that we have some degree of a "goal versus means" mentality: since I can't stop wanting what I want and it's also not here, I am compelled to ask myself how to get it. What I want is the goal; how I get it is the means. And this seems to be the matrix of the idea of purposeful action: we do *this* "in order to" attain *that*.

Some have concluded from the definitional inescapability of this structure whenever we wonder what to do, or what is good, or how to go about something, that therefore, purposefulness must reveal to us the essence of what we desire when we desire, of what is desirable as such. Purpose is locked into the very definition of goodness, and from there loaded into the very definition of being. On this view, purpose is the unsurpassable source and goal of all things that happen. Radicalized, literalized, absolutized, this is the marrow of the monotheistic idea.

Others have concluded that purposefulness is a kind of narrow foreground illusion endemic to our particular form of desiring and perception, a *by-product* rather than the *source* or *goal* of conscious animal life, which cannot be the real ultimate root of goodness or the real ultimate source of what happens.

Some of these consider it still the best thing there is, and wish there were more of it, and try to enhance it as much as possible. I call them secular atheists.

Some of these, though, think purpose is an epiphenomenon of purposelessness and that therefore, it must always play a secondary rather than a primary role in our understanding of ourselves and our world, and in our way of being in the world. These folks think that to prioritize and absolutize purpose will distort our understanding about what is really the best part of us and of the world, and how to have there be more of it—*even the "best" part as defined by purposes, and even though no definition of "best" can make any sense without some reference to purpose.*

We can thus sketch something like a Venn diagram with some surprising connections. Roughly, we can identify four models of the relation between the ultimate character of the cosmos and the relative valuing of the aspects of human existence:

1. Emulative Theism. This is the Socratic idea that the universe is ultimately guided by conscious purposes, and the best part of human beings is the consciously purposeful part, their moral rationality which should rightfully guide their behavior. The universe is guided by clear conscious knowledge of the Good (including also the True and the Beautiful, perhaps), and humans should also be consciously guided by their own rational recognition of the Good. Conscious control is what it's all about, both at the macrolevel and at the microlevel, for both the world and human beings. The slogan here might be: "Knowledge is virtue, for it is what makes us most godlike."

2. Compensatory Theism. This position goes with a more acute sense of the unknowability of God, of his inaccessibility to precise human knowledge, of

the gulf between creator and creature. God is still stipulated to have a clear conscious knowledge of the Good and thus a clear conscious purpose, and that, the mind of God, is still the best thing there is, the standard of all value. But human beings can never really know God's plan, and thus they must piously accept that even what does not seem good to their own conscious knowledge might be something that God regards as good, and thus might be something that really *is* good. Humans need to transcend their own conscious purposes, their narrow purposivity. Whatever happens in the end must be good, so the right attitude to the human being is to humbly surrender to the will of God, to give up trying to adjudicate or know what the good is, to let God take them where he wishes, even if at the moment it seems terrible to the humans themselves. That means, though, that while it is still recognized in principle that conscious knowledge of the good and conscious control are the ultimate standards of real value, for a human being it is just the opposite that is the highest possible state: the complete abrogation of conscious control, the surrender to what is beyond one's own consciousness and values, in the faith that this is however the way to accord with Someone's conscious control. Control is still what it's all about, the only thing with any real value. But now the control that matters is not mine, but Thine. The world is purposeful, and for that very reason we must not be purposeful ourselves, but allow ourselves to be driven wherever the wind of the spirit listeth. "Not my will but thine be done" might be the watchword of this stance in its purest form, although in practice we no doubt almost always find it combined with the previous Emulative Theist stance, which strives to find out about and incorporate the will of God. Everyday theism is usually somewhere on the spectrum between these two pure extremes, engaged in mixing them according to a schema of the "the wisdom to know the difference" between what is in my control and what is in God's control, as the Alcoholic's Anonymous prayer has it. But wherever we place the marker between faith and works, whichever way we combine the two, we find the same ultimate evaluative stance: purpose, control, is what it's all about. It's just a question of what's in whose control, mine or God's.

3. Compensatory Atheism: here the idea is that the world itself is purposeless, there is no conscious controller guiding it toward the good, and for that very reason we humans must step up our own efforts at conscious control, at the determining of values, at purposeful activity. We must create our own val-

ues, order our societies, and cultivate our gardens. This is the attitude of some early Confucians like Xunzi, Legalists like Hanfeizi,[10] of most atheist secular humanism in the modern world, arguably in secular collectivist utopianisms like Bolshivism, and in its most extreme and self-aware individualistic form in movements like existentialism. Note that here as in all the previous cases, what is really valuable is still conscious control as such. That's still the best thing there can possibly be, the sole standard of value. Like Emulative Theism but unlike Compensatory Theism, though, the best aspect of the human being is his conscious purposively controlling aspect. That was true for the Socratic Emulative Theists, but untrue for the pious Compensatory Theist mystics, for whom the best aspect of the human being was his faith, his ability to renounce his own conscious control and his own purposes.

4. Emulative Atheism. Here, finally, we have an entirely different alternative. The universe is purposeless, not under anyone's control, not directed toward any conscious goals, but it is here also true that the best aspect of *human* experience is also purposeless, not under anyone's control, not directed to any conscious goals. Here as in Compensatory Theism, the best aspect of the human being is seen to be a renunciation of his commitment to his own conscious control, to his own purposes as he knows them. So this position shares the view of the Compensatory Atheist about the nature of the cosmos, but shares the view of the Compensatory Theist about what the best aspect of human experience is: the abandonment of beholdenness to one's own conscious purposes and controls. And it is unlike all three of the above positions in that it alone views conscious purposes and controls per se as less "valuable" than purposelessness and non-control, not just for humans but for the cosmos as a whole. The most valuable aspect of anything is the unconscious, purposeless, uncontrolling and uncontrolled aspect, and wisdom consists in understanding the purposeless, and understanding the rooting of our purposes and their fulfillment in the purpose-

---

10 Hanfeizi's case is complex and interesting, because though he believes the universe to be purposeless, and advocates the value of purpose and purpose alone for human beings, he develops an elaborate reading of the *Daodejing* to show how apparent purposelessness, as deployed by a ruler, can be extremely useful for the purposes of the ruler. So we have a kind of intricate interesting: humans must be as unlike the purposeless cosmos as possible, but to accomplish this they have to sometimes pretend to be very much like the purposeless cosmos. Nor is Hanfeizi wrong to see a complex intertwining of purpose and purposelessness in the *Daodejing*.

less. It goes without saying that, since "value" itself is defined by its relation to purposes, this will entail some interesting intellectual challenges and a non-dismissive attitude toward paradoxes to flesh out. This is what I call "atheist mysticism."

Emulative Theism is like Compensatory Theism in that both posit a purposive consciousness running the cosmos. Emulative Theism is like Compensatory Atheism in that both see conscious control as the best aspect of humanity and the principle of all ethics. Compensatory Theism and Compensatory Atheism are direct opposites, having neither aspect in common. Emulative Theism and Emulative Atheism are likewise direct opposites. But note that Compensatory Atheism and Emulative Atheism are alike in both seeing the cosmos as meaningless, purposeless, not run by a consciousness, so both are atheist, and yet in their view of human life, Compensatory Theism and Emulative Atheism are alike in seeing the best aspect of human life as its passing beyond its obsession with its own conscious purposive control, so both are mystics. Hence Emulative Atheism is what I call the atheist mysticism.

If the watchword of Emulative Theism is perhaps "Reason is divine, and knowledge is virtue," that of Compensatory Theism is "Not my will but thine be done," and that of Compensatory Atheism is "We must cultivate our own gardens," the watchword of Emulative Atheism in its purest form is something that we search for in vain in Western thought. This is where China becomes so indispensible. For it in Chinese thought alone we find the purest and most unequivocal exemplars of deep mystical emulative atheism. A good candidate for a representative is the description of Zhuangzi found in the 33rd Chapter of the eponymous book:

> Blank and barren, without form! Changing and transforming, never constant! Dead? Alive? Standing side by side with heaven and earth? Moving along with the spirits and illuminations? So confused—where is it all going? So oblivious—where has it all gone? Since all the ten thousand things are inextricably netted together around us, none is worthy of exclusive allegiance. These were some aspects of the ancient Art of the Course. Zhuang Zhou [Zhuangzi] got wind of them and was delighted. He used ridiculous and far-flung descriptions, absurd and preposterous sayings, senseless and shapeless phrases, indulging himself unrestrainedly

as the moment demanded, uncommitted to any oneposition, never looking at things exclusively from any one corner.[11]

Note that the uncertainty and directionlessness of the world and of the
mind go so far that even the uncertainty of the world is not something known—
indeed, even the godlessness of the world is not known. It's just question after
question, an open door even to "the spirits and illuminations"—i.e., all manner
of non-empirical spiritual beings, but not to the firm establishing of any one of
them as discernibly in control, or of the absence of any one or of all of them as
the standard for setting a single goal, as a consciously graspable signpost of purpose. It is purpose itself and conscious knowing itself and control itself that are
dismissed here, for both the universe and the person.[12]

The idea of a personal creator God, a purposeful mind that stands at the
origin of all existence and all value, is above all the deification of the idea of
purpose. With the idea of the monotheistic God, purpose becomes the source
and end and meaning of all things; purposelessness becomes by definition the
thing most to be despised and minimized. The idea of God means that purpose
is the ultimate, the highest, the privileged and eternally unsurpassable category
at the root of all things. Purpose stands at the beginning of all actuality as its
source, and purpose stands at the end of all activity as its goal.

The privileging of the idea of purpose creates a mode of relating to the
world in which, literally by definition, no possible experience can be intrinsi-

---

11 Brook Ziporyn, translator. *Zhuangzi: The Essential Writings with Selections from Traditional Commentaries* (Indianapolis: Hackett Publishing, 2009), p. 123.

12 We should perhaps call this "Isomorphic Atheism" rather than "Emulative Atheism," since the latter term implies the paradoxical attempt to imitate the purposeless, which would itself be a purposive endeavor. Indeed, because purpose is actually ineradicable, is built-in to the entire framework in
which the issue can be raised, i.e., the question of values, what we actually always end up with in Emulative Atheism is some combination of the purposive and the purposeless, of the conscious and the non-
conscious, of the controlled and the uncontrolled; what matters is simply that the purposeless, unconscious and uncontrolled is the ultimate term, stands at both the source and the goal. (Contrast this
to Compensatory Theism, where we always end up with a combination of two kinds of control, mine
and God's, since I must at least willingly consent to my surrender to faith for it to count as my own
faith, but to leawe no place at all for the purposeless, the truly uncontrolled.) Conscious controlling
purposes may and even must be construed as a means in some form, as playing some role, but the
ultimate goal or reference point or regulative ideal that informs all purposes is here purposelessness,
the uncontrolled, the non-conscious as the real locus or at least source of being and of value.

cally worthwhile. Once we accept the idea that accord with a pre-existent purpose is what makes something count as good, or for what makes things exist, we have condemned ourselves to an eternal regress of dissatisfaction. This is the most obvious problem that arises when we prioritize the idea of purpose. If A's purpose is B, what is B's purpose? What is the purpose of the total whole, A plus B? Is it C? What is C's purpose? D? And so on. It would seem that once we have started asking this question, we cannot stop until we come to the largest whole or the ultimate destination. But what is the purpose of the whole or the destination? What is the purpose, the meaning, the point of, say, the universe, or human happiness, or a future utopia? What is the purpose of pleasing God? What is the purpose of God? This is a mirror image of a problem that comes with making causality ontologically ultimate: if "to be" is to be caused by something prior, what causes the prior thing, and its prior thing?

The idea of God is engineered precisely to avert this infinite regress of purposes, as much as to avert the infinite regress of causes: the idea is that somewhere along the line there must be something which is "its own purpose," something valuable in itself, or else the entire chain of purposes becomes meaningless. The only problem is that the very definition of value as purpose makes the very idea of "valuable in itself" inconceivable and impossible. This is a little ironic, since the whole problem only emerges because purpose has been absolutely prioritized in this way. Purpose creates the disease, and the deification of purpose is offered as the cure.

To pull off this cure, the first link and the final link in the chain must be defined as radically different from all the others, since all the others are caused by something prior and lead to something later, which are the usual definitions of being and of purpose. But the first term and the last term cannot have being and purpose in the ordinary sense, so they must exist and be purposeful in some radically other way. The first and the last are typically conflated in theories like this, combined into one. This first and last term has to be something that can somehow mysteriously be its own cause, unlike any other being, and just as mysteriously, it must have value or purpose or meaning just in itself, also unlike any other being. Ordinarily, things are by definition what have causes and purposes beyond themselves; this one has neither. If this non-caused and non-externally-purposed thing, this anti-thing, is removed, all purposes and all causes collapse. It must radically subordinate all the finite meanings and purposes in the chain: they have all of their purpose solely because of this mysterious item which is claimed somehow to have "purpose in itself ." All things must then be aligned from top to toe to serve this final end, or otherwise fail in attaining their purpose, as cogs in this grand plan. They must not have other purposes, but only the ones that derive from and also lead to the purpose-giver. From here we get the idea that all knowable things were specifically made for a specific purpose, whose sole meaning was to serve the purposeful designs of something or Someone that is itself not purposeless but somehow purposeful while violating the usual definition of purpose. So, Someone creates all things with the purpose of knowing, praising, loving, serving, obeying Him.

Alternately, one may try to identify some experiences that we actually do feel to be intrinsically worthwhile, to be ends-in-themselves, that are thus experienced as breaking out of the structure of subordination of present means to future ends. Unfortunately, this privileging of certain experiences over others, regarding some as intrinsically worthwhile and others as worthwhile only to the extent that they serve the first group, will *again* have the consequence of committing us to the idea of purpose as the most important aspect of existence. This seems to be what we have in the humanistic aftermath of formerly monotheistic cultures—i.e., cultures that have long regarded purpose as the ultimate category of all existence. Secular atheists in these cultures, which today compete with God-cultures for dominance of the globe, are generally themselves very much in the thrall, with a slight modification, of the main thing about God-cultures: the obsession with subordinating all existence to purpose as what matters most. In the secular Compensatory Atheist version, purpose no longer stands at the beginning of existence, but it still stands at the end of all actions and as the standard of all value. The purposeful aspect of ourselves is still regarded as the best and most important aspect of ourselves. When God drops out of the picture, the obsession with purpose becomes one or another form of hedonism, whether of the crude type where we work in order to enjoy, earn in order to spend, endure in order to indulge, or else of the more refined type, where we esteem only certain achievements—cultural, social, artistic, technological, moral—and enslave all experience to their service, where life is considered good when we consciously know what we want and make attaining that good the purpose of our actions. In either case, the structure is the same: X exists "for the sake of" Y. Subordination is the name of the game. Conscious purpose still ends up dominating everything.

To find a true alternative to all of these impasses, we must turn to ancient Chinese philosophy. For there we discover that there is another way to approach this problem, proceeding from the other end: by questioning the very structure of meaning, or purpose, or value, itself—the value of value, the point of things having a point, the purpose of having purposes as such. Though it pops up here and there in other places, its main source is the Daoist, and as we shall see in a more complicated way also the Confucian, thinkers of ancient China, which was one of the few literate cultures that was not under the thumb of some form of the crushingly ubiquitous God-generating paradigm, the worship of purpose as the best thing about human life and what it would be best to discover at the root of all existence.

I'm referring to the concept of *wuwei*, literally "non-action," but signifying more specifically "effortless action," which is to say, "non-deliberate action," or to put the point more sharply, "purposeless action." This means action that does not proceed from a conscious embrace of a goal in advance, action that happens "spontaneously," or with no experience of doing it for any reason at all—not even "for itself." It is a critique of the idea that purposes as such—ideals, values—are the most basic thing about either goodness or existence. It begins with a critique of having any values or ideals or indeed, therefore, any ethics at all. The Daoist concept of Dao is the *ne plus ultra* of purposelessness, the precise opposite of the concept of God, which is the *ne plus ultra* of purpose.

Before getting frightened about the alleged "nihilism" of this ("nihilism" being the alarmist term often used by purpose-driven people to slander the denial of the ultimacy of purpose), we must notice one hugely consequential point. Purpose by definition *excludes* the purposeless: to have a purpose is precisely to prefer one outcome over others, and to strive to whatever extent is possible to eliminate that unwanted outcome: wanting something is wanting to get the wanted thing and to avoid whatever is not that thing (though of course I may at the same time also have other, conflicting wants—each structured however in exactly the same way). But this relationship is not symmetrical: purposelessness does not exclude purpose. On the contrary, it includes, allows—and on the Daoist account, even generates—purpose. Not one purpose, however: many purposes, perhaps infinite purposes, a surfeit of purposes, all of which remain embedded in a larger purposelessness, but not contradicted or undermined by it.

The structure of purpose, and hence of person, is such as to exclude: it is specifically a choice, an either/or, beholden to a conception of goodness, whether individual or universal, which necessarily means the exclusion of something. Even if we make some room for the impersonal or the non-exclusive or the purposeless, a monotheist cosmos will be one in which personality, purpose, dualism must win in the end, must be the ultimate. The purposeless must be subordinated to the purposeful. But purposelessness subordinated to purpose is no longer purposeless: it becomes instead instrumental to purpose, pervaded completely by purpose. So a monotheist cosmos is one that ultimately forecloses entirely purposelessness, inclusiveness, non-duality, the non-personal.

The reverse, however, is not true. Purpose is precisely the attempt to exclude whatever does not fit the purpose, but purposelessness is what is by definition not contravened by any possible outcomes. Purposelessness makes no choices; it excludes nothing. It is rather precisely the allowing of unforeseen, uncontrolled, unpredetermined outcomes. Purposelessness is openness. It allows. That means it allows *also* purpose, many purposes; it cannot exclude even purpose, and it is what escapes the control of any single purpose, what splays any given attempt at monolithic control, what opens up any one purpose to alternate purpose. Purposelessness is the fecund matrix from which purposes arise, the allowing of both any given purpose and all other purposes and the further fecund purposelessness that escapes the control of any of them. The personal seeks to subordinate the impersonal; indeed, the personal really is just the attempt to subordinate the impersonal, to completely subdue it into an instrument. But the impersonal allows both the personal and the impersonal. The question is which means and which are ends, which are categories which are only ultimate insofar as purposiveness is ultimate, since they are aspects of the idea of purpose. If the purposeful and personal is the ultimate end, all the impersonal is reduced to a means to reach the purposeful. But if the purposeless and impersonal is ultimate, although it will allow also the purposeful to arise, this will not ultimately be a means to an end, but will be the purposeless allowing itself to be a means to any given non-ultimate purpose for as long as that purpose obtains, and also, to that purposeful being, the allowing of the purposeless to serve its purpose and to find new purposes, indeed to make a purpose of finding the purposeless if it wishes. From the point of view of purpose and the personal, which is undeniably our starting point and necessarily a part of any discussion, any thought, any viewpoint, the personal and purposeful itself is a self-cancelling means to an end that lies beyond it: purposefulness is a means to reach the end of purposelessness—but it is construed in these purposeful terms only from the point of view of the purposefulness, the non-ultimate means which are not even ultimately means at all. Purpose transcending purpose is an additional way the ultimacy of purposelessness manifests itself. Personality as a means to reach into the surrounding impersonality is now an additional meaning of personality. Not the exclusion of personality or purpose, which is impossible, but the multiplicity and non-ultimacy of all persons and all purposes.

Confucianism

The most vivid locus of the concept of *wuwei*, non-deliberate activity with no explicit goal as the ultimate source of cosmic activity and as both the most valuable and the most efficacious state of human activity, would then seem to be the ancient "Daoist" thinkers, Laozi and Zhuangzi. This is, as it were, the ground zero of Emulative Atheism. Dao does nothing and yet all things are done. The sage does nothing and thus leaves nothing undone. Heaven and Earth are not humane: to them all creatures are disposable sacrificial effigies made of straw. The sage is not humane: to him all creatures are disposable sacrificial effigies made of straw. (*Daodejing* 5, and passim) The Dao has no intention, does not play the lord or master, knows nothing and is never known, and *therefore* does its bounty flow to all creatures, as we shall see in a moment.

However, the *ultimacy* if not the centrality of *wuwei*, this hallmark of ultimate godlessness, is the one point shared by theoretical Daoism and Confucianism and, later, even Chinese Buddhism. All see the world as something that comes into being without the intervention of anyone's intention, without any plans or purposes, and each in its own way sees what is best in human experience as some manifestation of that same effortless unintentional purposelessness in us. Indeed, strictly speaking, we must trace the concept of *wuwei* first to Confucian sources. The *locus classicus* is a single ritual-political reference in the *Analects*, "Is not Shun someone who ruled without any effortful action? (*wuwei erzhi*无为而治) He simply made himself respectful and faced south, that is all." (15: 5) The sage-king Shun is here depicted as placing himself in his ritually proper position as emperor, and doing so with the proper ritual attitude of respect. This is probably to be understood as referring to the non-coercive organizing power of ritual, referenced elsewhere in the text. In 2: 1, we are told that "one who rules with virtue (*de* 德, virtuosity) is like the North Star: it simply occupies its place and all the other stars turn toward it." Virtue here is ritual virtuosity, attained mastery of the received ritual system, internalized to the point of grace and effortlessness, believed to come with certain attitudes in the person and effects in the world. Truly internalized ritual mastery is depicted as having an automatic charismatic effect on others who are also operating within that shared traditional ritual system. We see effortlessness manifest on both sides of the relation here: the ruler does no more than take his position, with the respect for that position and for the other positions in the system that is considered by Confucians to be the essence of internalized and thus effortless mastery of the system, and the others, without thinking about it or having to make efforts to overcome contrary inclinations, respond, organizing themselves spontaneously around him. The implications are spelled out a few lines later in the text, which links ritual and virtuosity (virtue) explicitly and contrasts them favorably with "government" (*zheng*政) and "punishment" (*xing*刑), i.e., penal law, as two alternate ways a ruler might bring order to the people. The coercive method of punishment and threat, combined with explicitly formulated statutes and controls, incentivizes the people to avoid the punishments, but without any internalized feeling of shame in failing to comply, as long as they are not caught. "Shame" here means a feeling that one has failed to live up to a standard that one recognizes and has made one's own, that one has internalized as a standard of worth, as one would feel shame in failing to accomplish a task for which one had trained and to which one had aspired. It also presupposes that this failure will mean loss of status and recognition in the system of other social agents sharing membership in this system. This internalized sociality and its power to incentivize action, the threat of loss of recognition and belonging, are key to the ritual form of social organization, the form of orderly social grouping offered as an alternative to law and control and punishment. Leading the people with virtuosity and organizing them with ritual brings to the people their own internalized sense of shame, allowing them to correct themselves, literally "come into the grid" (*ge*格), and to assume their own positions in the same system of ritual that the ruler inhabits and internalizes with *wuwei* mastery. (2: 3) The next item in the *Analects* describes a process by which this *wuwei* mastery of traditional ritual, which allows one both to follow one's own desires with no sense of effort and to elicit order-producing responses from others equally effortless, is attained, through long and sustained practice and effort. (2: 4) The model nearest to hand for understanding this conception is perhaps that of learning a skill: one practices for a long time, having to consciously and purposefully pay attention to every movement, correcting and coercing oneself, subjecting oneself to executive conscious control—with the goal of finally reaching a state where one can forget what one is doing, because one has internalized it and is doing it so well. Such skill entitles one to membership in good standing in a mutually recognizing society of practitioners who share this skill and the values it embodies. The added dimension of spontaneous response to this attained spontaneity has been illuminatingly compared to the sort of response we see, for example, in a handshake.[13] If (and *only* if) the person in front of me has been trained in the same cultural ritual system as myself, he will understand my action of lifting my hand in front of him, and without thinking, without naming it, without controlling it even himself, his own hand will rise to grasp mine. This is the magical responsiveness of ritual—and it presupposes a shared tradition. The content of that tradition need not be entirely rational or explicable or even consciously known: what matters is that it is shared, it is presupposed, and it is internalized, and thus that it works, and works unreflectively.

The seeming curmudgeonly insistence on an irrational inherited system of ritual as the sole source of order, with its profound traditionalism and conservatism, is thus framed actually as a protest against the idea of *coercion* and *deliberate control coming from a single source* as the only possible form of order. Obviously, neither of these alternatives is about freeing the individual from social control: it is assumed that we need some sort of social organization, that this requires some sort of power of normativity and sanction, and that punishment and ritual are the only alternatives to anarchy. But even if we were to assume that social control is a kind of necessary evil (a view not shared by the Confucians), we can say that from the point of view of non-coercion, Confucianism is one long argument that ritual is the lesser of the two evils. This system of cultural forms and traditions, of presupposed accepted usage is, I have

---

13 See Herbert Fingarette, *Confucius: The Secular as Sacred* (New York: Harper and Rowe, 1972).

argued elsewhere,[14] like the grammar of a language: something that is inherited from pre-thematized cumulative traditions, neither created by nor in the control of any one individual center of power, and neither produced nor run according to any specific designs. It is picked up from always-already existing practices, tweaked and focused and amended little by little, only rarely, and regrettably, requiring conscious purposive interventions. Certain people have more authority than others in enforcing ritual or grammatical aberrations when they are regarded as having gone astray, and there may be contention and deliberate regulation employed in making these corrections. But this is in its nature a post-facto intervention, and one that is regarded not as the true source of ritual—until, that is, we get to the fully Compensatory Atheist ritual theory of Xunzi (and even there, the source of order is no single consciousness). In the *Analects*, ritual, like grammar, has no single creator or controller. Like grammar, it is normative but unformulated, and not imposed *ex nihilo* at any point in time. It has no single source: no one is credited with creating it wholesale. Rather, the picture we are generally given is of virtuosic sages and sage-kings who add and subtract to it in minimal ways, forming a communal cumulative system of always-already functioning rules, as much descriptive as prescriptive. Those sages and kings are to ritual what genius writers are to the grammar of the language they work in: through this effortless internalization of the grammar, which was objectively never created or formulated on purpose and which has now become purposeless and effortless for them subjectively, they can make new sentences to serve any purpose — the purposelessness of grammar enables infinite meanings and intentions to be expressed.

Here we see the crucial structure: purposelessness enables infinite purposes. In exceptional cases, these virtuosos can even create new forms that may resonate enough into the future to slightly tweak the grammar itself, as a particularly striking Shakespeare or Goethe phrase might do in English or German, respectively. A virtuoso might deliberately use improper grammar, against a massive background of effortless correctness, for a particular effect in a particular time and context, and this would *ipso facto* make that irregular usage legitimate and effective, perhaps even becoming a precedent, becoming part of correct usage in the future. But no one can make up a grammar or a language

---

14 Brook Ziporyn, *Ironies of Oneness and Difference* (Albany: State University of New York, 2011).

ex nihilo and make people speak it and follow its rules. That would by definition involve coercion and enforcement, for it would require dropping their unreflectively prior ways of speaking and replacing them with new, more "rational" ones. The point of this weird preference for ritual over law is precisely that ritual is mainly unintentional; the small tweaking that constitutes the sole possibility of reform in this context is always concerned only with that surface that is going astray, resting on a massive pre-reflective understanding of the social fabric. As with a grammar, corrections are only possible on the basis of an assumed prior massive correctness: one has to be able to understand the correction in some language before one can correct one's language accordingly.

We can perhaps begin to see how the idea of a controlling consciously purposeful deity begins to get de-incentivized in the context of this general ritual view of the continuity of deliberate and non-deliberate activity, with the deeper role always granted to the non-deliberate. The Confucian tradition was certainly deeply interested in rooting a sense of human ethical normativity into the universe somehow, making human values and purposes feel firmly rooted, non-quixotic, and at home, as it were, in the cosmos. This makes it all the more remarkable that, even when presented with the opportunity for a broadly theistic solution to this challenge in the form of Mohism—which energetically propounded the idea of a single universal ruling deity, very conscious, equally concerned with all humans, constantly watching, relentlessly interested in legislating and enforcing human ethical behavior with clear-cut norms and punishments and rewards—the Confucian tradition literally defines itself in staunch opposition to it, beginning with Mencius (4th century BCE) and continuing throughout its history of over two millennia thereafter. To be a Confucian is, quite literally, to reject the idea of Heaven as a *fully* anthropormophic moral deity who micromanages justice in the universe. And yet the majority of Confucian systems do want a universe that sanctions human values, a cosmos that is even often characterized ontologically above all by its relation to *ren*仁, humaneness (the word is as closely cognate with the word for "human" *ren*人 as the English "humane" is to "human"). But because the essence of human experience is here assumed to be centered not in the planning, separable consciousness but in the spontaneous reciprocal interpersonal responsivities, the idea of Heaven as a separate mind in unilateral control was felt again and again to be actually *at odds* with a humane/human cosmos: an anthropomorphic God, an intentional mind with absolute unilateral power, would make the universe inhospitably inhuman. Instead, Confucianism gravitated from almost its first steps toward a truly narrativeless Heaven which, even when still overseeing the world in some way and lending its weight to some particular tendencies in human affairs over others (enough to still be claimed as a partisan in political struggles), was quickly divested of both speech and deliberate world-creation, of unilateral and identifiable interventions, and was not at all interested in micromanaging rewards and punishments for individual human behavior either before or after death. Already for Confucius, Heaven did not speak, and operated by some means other than the issuing of explicit orders or laws either to humans or to the rest of the cosmos, though this does not prevent him from making occasional references to Heaven as a support and sponsor for his particular cultural mission in some vague way. By the time the Neo-Confucians of the 10th century divested the Heavenly deity also of any non-metaphorical existence, what is most surprising is that there was no one in the literateintellectual tradition who seemed to find this the least bit surprising, shocking or troubling.

For this resistance to a unilaterally and exclusively controlling deity is not something merely incidental to the tradition, but a key structural concomitant of the very ethical ideals it hopes to encourage and the cosmological vision it requires to sustain them. Spontaneous continuity and responsive reciprocity become ultimate; the disjunctive aspects of personality as controller and choice-maker become, both for the natural world and for humans, an always-present-but-always-surpassed mode in the broader fabric of a larger spontaneity. The status of Heaven in the *Analects* and *Mencius* is admittedly a highly contentious and problematic topic. I have elsewhere stated and argued for my view that Heaven in those two texts is a metonym for the locus housing a collective group of forces, both personal and impersonal, like "Hollywood" or "The White House," one that includes both purposeless aspects and diverse purposes which can be temporarily summed as a specific overall collective purpose when linked to some specific human alliance or interest, but which is neither purposive nor purposeless through and through, and where the purposeful is certainly not the ultimate source of either being or value.[15] This view is controversial, however, and our purposes here are served just as well by the accepted view

---

15 Ziporyn, *Ironies of Oneness and Difference.*

that Heaven in these early Confucian texts is indeed a supreme and purposeful personal deity, but not the creator of the world, and one who operates through some means other than those suggested by the Mohists, i.e., not through close control, intervention, supervision, command, explicit standards and injunctions, and punishment of individual behavior. The Confucian Heaven is envisioned as ruling in the same way the Confucian sages rule: through *wuwei*. Confucius' most extensive comment on the nature of Heaven in the *Analects* gives us the earliest *locus classicus* of Emulative Theism turning into Emulative Atheism:

> Confucius said, "I want to speak no words at all." Zigong said, "If you, master, spoke no words, how would we disciples be able to tell others about you in the future?" Confucius said, "What words does Heaven speak? And yet the four seasons move along through it, all things are generated through it. What words does Heaven speak?" (*Analects* 17:19)

> 子曰:"予欲无言。"子贡曰:"子如不言, 则小子何述焉?"子曰:"天何言哉? 四时行焉, 百物生焉, 天何言哉?" (《论语·阳货篇19》)

Confucius wants to be like Heaven, but what Heaven is like is that it says nothing, gives no orders, makes no commands, and yet moves the world along and generates all things. Its efficacy, apparently, is not due to what it says, or by telling anyone to do anything: it is not due to *control*. In other words, it is *wuwei*, just like Shun sitting on his throne in the center of the ritual system: acting purposelessly, and thereby attains his purpose. Rather than seeking to compensate for this dearth of control by taking control, Confucius wants to be like heaven and get things done by non-doing: as Heaven accomplishes the circular motion of the seasons, the production of life, without direct interference, Confucius would like to accomplish the ritual ordering of society in the same way. This is the format of Emulative Theism—man should be like God—but on the cusp of transforming to Emulative Atheism. For in this case, unlike the monotheist case, the deity to be emulated is not *more* purposive and controlling than us, but *less* so. We relinquish direct control not to allow Heaven to take control, but to be more efficacious through being less controlling, as Heaven is. Heaven is arguably not quite fully purposeless yet here, it is true: the specification of its effects in making the seasons flow and making all things grow suggests at least a tilt in the direction of some outcomes rather than others. Heaven has no specific command structure or controlling purpose, perhaps no deliberate activity, but it might still be construed here as having a preference for life over death, for flow over stagnation, and in this very early version of the idea there is room for taking it to be conscious of this preference, which it accomplishes through its own silent charisma, though there is certainly no need to draw this conclusion from the text. The Daoists will subsequently accuse Confucian *wuwei* of being a sham: it claims to get things happening through ritual alone, but if the expected response fails to come, it "rolls up its sleeves" and forces the intended result (*Daodejing* 38). Its *wuwei* thus ends up being a thin sugar-coating for the punishment-based type of control it ostensibly rejects, which is always there at the ready to do the dirty work if and when the non-coercive ritual attempt fails. The reason for this, however, is not that the Confucians do not embrace the ideal of non-deliberateness, but that they do not follow through on it: the Daoists try to radicalize it. The issue is whether or not there is in fact an unstated specific goal informing the apparent non-striving, whether there is an unspoken teleology hidden beneath this veneer of goal-lessness. To the extent that there is, apparent non-coercion and effortlessness is still not thoroughgoing, and is vulnerable to the Daoist critique. The extent to which the effortless Confucian cosmos counts as a real teleology will continue to be a vexed issue in Confucianism; we will see it explicitly addressed in a moment in the thought of Zhu Xi, the formulater of Neo-Confucian orthodoxy 17 centuries later, who offers an ingenious solution that remains true to the spirit of *wuwei* while putting a distinctive Confucian normativity into play at the same time. But it is clear already in the *Analects*, the first properly Confucian text, that we are already moving in the direction, and dangerously close to, the full-blown purposelessness of *wuwei* as it comes to be understood in the Daoist texts, which are soon to follow.

However we may wish to place the case of Heaven in the earliest Confucian texts, we certainly see a clear and forceful example of God-less religiousness developed in the Confucian metaphysic found by the time we reach the end of the Warring States, in the "Xicizhuan" 系辞传 to the *Zhouyi*周易. This text accepts and adapts the Daoist idea of a universe and universal creative process that acts with no ethical intentions—the "Heaven and Earth are not Benevolent" idea of *Daodejing* 5 (*tiandi buren*天地不仁)—but changes the human consequence of Daoism (i.e., the *Daodejing*'s further claim that the sage is also not benevolent, i.e., *shengren buren*圣人不仁) by adding that the sage, on the contrary, *does* have ethical intentions and concerns. The question is how to relate these two. We see this adaptation clearly expounded, along with the key response to Daoism, in the following central passage of the mature Confucian God-less metaphysic:

> The alternation of *Yin* and *Yang* in equal measure—this is called Dao. Whatever continues this is called "the Good." What completes it is called "inborn human nature." The benevolent see this Dao and call it "benevolence"; the wise see this Dao and call it "wisdom"; the ordinary folk use it every day and yet are not aware of it. Thus the way of the exemplary man is rare indeed. It manifests as benevolence, [but] is concealed in [all] those uses [of the ordinary folk]. It drums the ten thousand things forward and yet does not worry itself as the sage must…[16]

This is the key Confucian contribution to the problem: the universe is indeed *thoroughly wuwei*, and is neither created by nor for any particular intention or value. And yet the highest human values, defining the role of human effort, human *youwei*, are those that stand in a unique relation to that *wuwei*: they *continue* it. Value is here still rooted in valuelessness, purpose in purposelessness; the two now form the inseparable halves of a single whole which alone accounts for human values and purposes. The Dao is not good, and doesn't try to be good or want the good; but it is the basis of good. Good is the continued existence of the *Yin-Yang* relationship, which is neutral, neither benevolent nor wise, but "can be seen" as either benevolent or wise, in some sense contains aspects of what, if selectively viewed, can be seen as a source or instantiation of both benevolence and wisdom. The crucial move is a slight tipping of emphasis in the direction of the ethical, for the function of Dao here is "revealed" in

---

16 一阴一阳之谓道，继之者善也，成之者性也。仁者见之谓之仁，知者见之谓之知。百姓日用
而不知，故君子之道鲜矣。显诸仁，藏诸用，鼓万物而不与圣人同忧……——《周易·系辞上》

benevolence, but "concealed" in all other functions. That is, all things express Dao, the neutral process of mutually counterbalancing alternating *Yin* and *Yang*, in some way, but benevolent human activity expresses it in the most direct or complete way. There is an undeniable privileging of human values here, but carefully and ingeniously positioned as both rooted in something real in the operation of the cosmos and as describable in that way only in relation to posterior human activities and ethical feelings, which themselves emerge unintentionally from that pre-ethical process, though rooted in it.[17]

But there are many ways to get to this conclusion, found in the subsequent permutations of the key elements of the Confucian orientation. In one way or

---

17 Indeed, the entire *Yin-Yang* conception on which this text is based is constructed from the interplay of two key metaphors, drawn from observations about the origin of life, in its vegetable and animal forms. Both are emphatically anti-intentional. Vegetable life emerges due to atmospheric cycles (diurnal, seasonal). Animal life emerges due to sexual reproduction. Both of these are root metaphors for the life-giving structure of the *yin-yang* relationship. Atmospheric cycles means day/night, hot/cold, etc. Crops grow only because of the cycle of day and night, of light and dark, and of hot and cold over the course of the year. It is the proper *balance* or *relation* between these two that makes the harvest possible. The same is true of the creative power of the sexual relation of male and female; again we have a balanced relation between two opposed poles which accounts for the origin of things. Note that in both cases, the source of being is 1) non-monolithic, involving more than a single agent, and thus not a matter of unilater command or control, and 2) an unintentional by-product of a spontaneous relation rather than an intended creation (most obvious in sexual reproduction). In sum, *Yin* and *Yang* are just a minimal assertion of "there is something intelligible there, against a background of what it is not." We must emphasize that they are not to be thought of as "first principles" that require anything to be made-so, but rather the lack of any such principles, again as the "Law of Averages" is the lack of any law. Note also the resistance to an overriding order set of mutually consistent laws implied by the fact that the *Yi* system is rationalized divination, an intrinsically case-by-case endeavor geared to changing circumstances and addressed to the specific projects and desires of specific participants in those situations, as opposed to rationalized *mythology*, which typically attempts a global explanation for why the world is as it is, for its constant characteristics. It is no accident that this metaphysics and its "principles" are attached not to a univocal myth, but to a fortune telling book: thoroughgoing situationalism and particularism, not a universal order but an order vis-a-vis each particular time, place, observer and *desire/purpose* (rather than one overridding purpose). Mythology, rationalized, produces God-steered religion and metaphysics. Divination, rationalized, produces God-less religiousness. What we end up with are not global laws laid down once and for all by an intentional lawgiver, but rather rough and ready tendencies which are traceable but not strictly reducible to any formula. The text thus insists, "The transformations simply go where they go; no essential norms or rules can be made for them." (*wei bian suo shi, buke wei dianyao* 唯变所适，不可为典要)

another, this special status of man, as one who can uniquely "form a triad with Heaven and Earth" (*yu tiandi can*与天地参)[18] or as receiver of the most excellent (*xiu*秀), aligned (*zheng*正) and/or numinously efficacious (*ling*灵) *qi* of Heaven and Earth, would become a staple of most Confucian metaphysical systems. But we can see here that it is to be carefully distinguished from the *imago dei* idea in God-centered traditions, which asserts not only a specially exalted role for man, but an isomorphism between the human mind and the mind of the creator which gives a special ontological status to human ideas and ideals as tapping into and accurately instantiating the ultimate source of the being of things via a close imaging or imitation of some kind. The Confucian systems, in contrast, fulfill the religious intent and psychological role of this idea, rooting human awareness and activity in a transformative relationship to the creative source of all things, but in entirely different ways. For this creative source is itself the *wuwei* production of all forms of *youwei*, not a *youwei* source. The relation of human purpose to this ultimate source is thus not the relation of one purpose to a higher purpose that it must submit to or emulate or renounce itself to serve, but of purpose itself to the raw infinite power of purposelessness.

One route was what we saw above in the case of Confucius himself: the ideal man resembles Heaven specifically in his eschewal of any explicit rules, commands, laws, or indeed any specific invocation of Heaven. Confucius instantiates Heaven in his creative timeliness; he is most like Heaven when he says, "There is for me nothing definitely permissible or impermissible" (无可无不可, *Analects* 18: 8); Heaven is not the source of definiteness and rule, but the transcending of them, unifying them not in a cumulative whole forming a system of purposive intention fulfilled in purposive action, but in the inseparability of alternate times, roles, situational responses, as Heaven has its four seasons but is not a cumulative higher unity of the four seasons. Heaven is the timely application of each season in turn, and the unobstructed transition from one to the other when appropriate, rather than a static totality of the four seasons resolved into a higher unity. This is the ethical ideal embodied in Confucius, his participation in the creative work of Heaven. This is still seen as entailing the

---

18 The phrase is found in the "Jingjie" 经解 in the *Liji*礼记 applied to the emperor, but in the *Zhongyong* 中庸 in the same collection, it is applied to human beings generally, at least in their potential for sagehood. The same idea appears in a slightly different form in the *Xunzi*.

generation of desired ethical results, but as we've seen in the "Xicizhuan" passage just quoted, the anti-control atheism at the heart of the tradition incentivizes the creation of explanations of this value as a continuation of a pre-value natural process, rather than an emulation of an eternal value. By being beyond bias, as Heaven is, with nothing permissible or impermissible, one continues the work of Heaven—and the specific bias for this is the Good, the human bias of the good over the evil. This ingenius asymmetry appears as a distinctive stance of the tradition again and again throughout its history. We can thus begin to see the significance of the Confucian tradition's consistent resistance to the idea of an ultimacy of a divine personality exerting intentional control: it is symptomatic of an ethical structure that resists the ultimacy of intentional control and exclusion in general, and with it the ultimacy of the disjunction and discontinuity of being and of values that come with intentional control.

The same problem is approached in another way in what is generally described as the central issue in the first generations of Confucian theory after Confucius himself, the conflict between Mencius and Xunzi over human nature. This is not well-described simply as a crude contrast between the alleged views that some agreed-upon entity called human nature "is good" or that it "is bad". Rather, the issue is how best to characterize the kind of continuity and discontinuity between human moral sentiments and social values on the one hand, and the non-moral spontaneities of affect and desire from which they sometimes emerge on the other. Both assume that the *youwei* of deliberate moral effort is both preceded and, in some form, succeeded by the *wuwei* of spontaneity: one starts out making an effort, and ends up internalizing the moral practice to the point of making it effortless. The model is again of learning a skill: one practices until one gets good at it and it becomes effortless. Both sides also see some form of effortlessness and non-deliberation as the cosmic condition that precedes this taking up of moral effort, both within and outside of the human self. The question is how precisely to conceive the relation between the prior effortless purposelessness, the purposive effort, and the achieved purposeless effortlessness at the end. When Mencius says human nature is good, he means only that a certain subset of the spontaneous unplanned unmotivated responses human beings are born with can, under certain conditions, be selected out, cared for, cultivated, nourished and grown to become what are later identified as full moral virtues. Looking back from the accomplished moral virtues, a continuity with that specified subset of spontaneous human responses can be traced, which provides a guideline for which of the mass of spontaneous responses to the world are thus to be singled out for cultivation. The deliberate activity is thus given a mediating role: its function is to select and care for certain spontaneous aspects of the self and the world, thus deprioritizing other spontaneous impulses equally inborn in human beings. All of these spontaneous impulses, those chosen to be nourished as seeds of morality and those demoted and starved or at least subordinated in this process, are from Heaven, and are extensions of the spontaneity of Heaven. At the other end of the process, the Heaven-like spontaneity is to be recovered in the accomplished moral virtues themselves, in their non-deliberate application, in the behavior of sages and the unpremeditated responses that people will have to that behavior, like the stars rotating around the North Star in the *Analects*. We go from *wuwei* through *youwei* to accomplished *wuwei*. The presence of these spontaneous inclinations in the human being is in some sense due to Heaven. If Heaven were thought of here as deliberate, and had deliberately implanted these spontaneous inclinations in man as part of Its own deliberate plan, then we would have (divine) deliberate activity leading to (human) spontaneous activity, supplemented by further (human) deliberate activity—which then, oddly, is consummated not in maximally godlike deliberate activity, but instead in spontaneous virtue. The result would be a mix of Compensatory and Emulative Theism, with the former put in the ultimate position (Heaven alone has the prerogative of deliberate activity, which is the true value, while man must know his place and be merely *wuwei*). It seems quite clear, however, that Mencius places ultimate value on *wuwei*, as Confucius did. It lies at both the beginning and end of the process: Heaven does not speak, does not act deliberately, and its efficacy in ensuring that mankind has these particular spontaneous inclinations is an *outgrowth* of its own spontaneous growths and actions, not a deliberate choice or bestowal with a moral intent: man's spontaneous goodness is in continuity with some aspect of Heaven's own spontaneity. When final sagely spontaneity is again attained, one has come to resemble Heaven all the more.

Hence Mencius says, "To fully plumb one's own mind is to know one's Nature, and to fully plumb one's Nature is to know Heaven. Thus by preserving our own minds and nourishing our own natures, we serve Heaven. Then it makes no difference whether we live long or die young. We cultivate ourselves and await either outcome, thus establishing ourselves in our destinies." (7A1) To know the spontaneity in oneself is to know Heaven, and to nourish that spontaneity is to serve Heaven, without any interest in the control of external events or punishment and reward. Our own spontaneous goodness—i.e., that subset of our spontaneous impulses that can be retrospectively identified as being what is being continued and developed in those actions that our own human social values recognize as good—is the sole decisive revelation of any basis of goodness in Heaven, with which it is in constant continuity. Least of all is Heaven anything like *noûs*, as Socrates describes it in the *Phaedo*: intelligently arranging things in order to attain its good purpose, choosing the good over the bad through its ability to think. In fact, Mencius tells us explicitly that "thinking," (*si*思)—a term which implies also *seeking* and *choosing*—is exactly what distinguishes Heaven from Man. Heaven does *not* think; it is rather Man who has to think—and what he thinks about and seeks and chooses is how to be more like Heaven precisely in its non-seeking, non-choosing, non-thinking:

> If those in lower ranks have no way of getting to those with power in higher ranks, the people can never be put in good order. There is a way to get to those in positions of higher ranks: one who is not trustworthy with his own friends of the equal rank will not be able to get to those of higher ranks. There is a way to gain the trust of one's friends: if one fails to please one's parents in serving them, one will not be trusted by one's friends. There is a way to please one's parents: if in looking into oneself one finds oneself insincere (bucheng不诚), one will be unable to please one's parents. There is a way to become sincere: if one does not understand what is good (i.e., what one truly wants, integrated into all one's desires), one cannot become sincere. Thus being sincere (*chengzhe*诚者) is the way of Heaven; thinking how to become sincere (*si chengzhe*思诚者) is the way of man. There has never been someone who is perfectly sincere who fails to move others, and someone who is completely insincere can never move others at all. (4B12)

> 居下位而不获于上，民不可得而治也。获于上有道，不信于友，弗获于上矣。信于友有道，事亲弗悦，弗信于友矣。悦

亲有道，反身不诚，不悦于亲矣。诚身有道，不明乎善，不诚
其身矣。是故诚者，天之道也；思诚者，人之道也。至诚而不
动者，未之有也；不诚，未有能动者也。(《孟子·离娄章句上》)

Mencius is talking here about ways in which various levels of a structure interact. The assumption is that some of these have more power and some have less: the "higher" and the "lower." The primary example is a human society or organization. Mencius is here describing his ideal of spontaneous organization: how to get the parts of this nested hierarchical structure to interact harmoniously but without coercion—how to get the various levels to interact. He thinks it has something to do with "sincerity": something inner and effortless in particular actors is what makes other actors respond to them in a way that is equivalent to a non-controlling, non-coercive form of order, allegedly to the benefit and satisfaction of both parties. This is extended to a model for how the observed order of the cosmos comes about—things like the movement of the skies and the turning of the seasons. It is possible to read Mencius as combining a notion of a non-moral Heaven with a Heaven-derived internal imperative for humans to be moral, as Franklin Perkins has convincingly shown: it may be that the will of Heaven is for each thing to follow its own nature, which in the case of humans alone is to strive to be moral and social, without implying that Heaven's own global intentions are for a moral or harmonious cosmos in any way that accords with those values provided by Heaven for human behavior alone. Human values can still be rooted in a Heavenly imperative without implying that Heaven has any moral intentions for the cosmos considered globally, or that it makes any promises that events in the universe will turn out in a way that is morally satisfying to those Heaven-instilled moral values rightfully embraced and developed by humans.[19] But even if we take the more traditional view that Mencius sees the working of the cosmos as exemplifying some sort of value that bears a closer relation to human values, it will have to be one that does not entail precise micromanaged moral justice: as we saw in *Mencius* 7A1 above, a morally exemplar person cannot expect Heaven to reward him, even when he has realized his own Heavenly nature to the utmost. The exter-

---

19 Franklin Perkins, *Heaven and Earth Are Not Humane* [Inidanapolis: University of Indiana Press, 2015].

nal operation of Heaven is not humanly moral in that sense. At most, as in the "Xicizhuan," the human values can be understood as a *continuation and extension* of the value-free natural operations of the seasons and the sky as the preconditions of life, which can be read *retrospectively* as exemplars of a sort of efficacy that has values to human beings, once human beings embrace values, which they must and which is in accordance with *their* Heavenly nature. The operations of Heaven and the rough-and-ready approximate cosmic ordering it accomplishes are enough to produce life and humans, and these are the preconditions of value. These operations too go smoothly and well because of a kind of "sincerity" in the sense of reliability, persistence and effortlessness, as defined above, which is what makes it an order that emerges not as the result of anyone controlling or commanding anyone else, but through spontaneous response of one member to another. But sincerity is precisely *effortlessness.* It is the lack of any interior division or any external ulterior motive, equally describable as *willing with all one's being* or as *not willing.* But willing with all one's being is just being exactly what one is *without* the intervention of a separate controlling executive function of *noûs.* The word for what Heaven has and Man has to think about obtaining is *cheng*诚, which means "trueness" or "sincerity" or "sustainability," or "reliability," with an implication, writ large in the composition of the character, of integration, coherence, consistency. The idea is that when one's innermost desires and commitments are all of a piece with one's outer words and behaviors, one's words and actions are considered "sincere" and "true to oneself," and thus sustainable without any special effort, without conceiving any specific purpose. It takes effort to pretend, or to maintain a division within oneself, or to recall which of the various spontaneous aspects of the self are to be allowed to show. If one is integrated and consistent, coherent within and without, one need not worry about what to do or say, all of it will express the needed content, effortlessly. This inner coherence or consistency in turn is what has efficacy in producing spontaneous effects in the world. This is true in the human sphere, where sincere behavior is believed by Confucians to "move" others without having to coerce them, and Mencius is clearly claiming that this is in fact the model we should apply when we try to think about how Heaven gets things done. It doesn't think, and it moves others just by means of the inner consistency and integration that is what makes thinking and seeking and choosing unnecessary for it. The expanded parallel passage in the

"Zhongyong" is even clearer on the kind of pre-human value we are entitled to envision here:

> …There is a way to make oneself sincere: if one does not understand what is good, one cannot become sincere. Sincerity is the way of Heaven; making sincere (*cheng zhi zhe*诚之者) is the way of man. To be sincere means to make no effort and yet hit the mark, to take no thought and yet get it done, ambling at ease on the Way of the Mean (*chengzhe bumian er zhong, busi er de, congrong zhongdao*诚者，不勉而中，不思而得，从容中道). Thus is the sage. To make sincere is to choose the good and firmly hold to it (*zeshan er guzhi zhi zhe ye* 择善而固执之者也), to broadly study it, acutely investigate it, carefully contemplate it, and clearly discern it, deeply practice it.

> 诚身有道：不明乎善，不诚乎身矣。诚者，天之道也；诚之者，人之道也。诚者，不勉而中，不思而得，从容中道，圣人也。诚之者，择善而固执之者也。博学之，审问之，慎思之，明辨之，笃行之。[20]

Effortlessness is the way of Heaven. Effort, choice, resolution, preference for the good as an object to be pursued—that is man's job. The Mencian form of Confucianism seeks to find that spontaneity in oneself, that subset of spontaneous impulses that are able of "making oneself sincere," those that, if chosen and held to and cultivated above all the others, can in turn be used to spontaneously integrate both all of those other spontaneous desires and inclinations of the self into consistency with themselves (see *Mencius* 6A14–15, where Mencius describes this process as precisely *si* 思, deliberative thought, the particular role given to man's mind *given* to man by Heaven, but not possessed by Heaven itself— that is, the *wuwei* produces the *youwei*, which then makes purposive choices to arrange the *wuwei* in such a way as to fully express the unbiased purposeless spontaneity original *wuwei*) and beyond that integrating the community spon-

---

20 Wang Guoxuan, trans lator. *Daxue · Zhong yong* 大学·中庸 [*The Great Learning · The Golden Mean*] （Beijing: Zhonghua Book Gompany, 2007）, p. 101.

coercion or obedience. As the "Zhongyong" puts it, "The Way of Heaven and Earth can be fully expressed in a single sentence: they are themselves non-double and thus their generation of things is unfathomable and inexhaustible."[22] They are "non-double" both in the sense that the seeming opposites of Heaven and Earth, as of *Yin* and *Yang*, combine and converge into a single point and thus both form a whole and generate new wholes, as male and female do, and this single non-duplicitous undivided point is the sincerity, the Way of Heaven and Earth, manifest in the innermost unseen center in man, the workings of spontaneity in man behind his generation of all his conflicting emotions and impulses, and this is the generative power that is both beyond comprehension in terms of either of the two extremes, and also inexhaustibly productive. The intentional aspect of Mencius's Heaven seems itself to be one such extension of this pre-intentional process, one to which he grants an authoritative role to be sure, but which is itself rooted in a deeper level of spontaneity from which it gets its real value, the unintentional purposeless "Sincerity" or "Integrity" or "Realness" which is in Heaven more than Heaven itself, which is more profoundly Heavenlike than the intentional, knowing part of Heaven.

The emergent personality emerging from the substratum of the unintentional is emphatically *singular*, both in the still quasi-intentional aspect of Heaven and in the intentional *youwei* aspect of man. But here too, as I have argued at length elsewhere, the sort of singularity at play in this conception is not a dismissal of diversity but a coherence of one-and-many: the model in play is of organization and continuity, in this case ghosts and spirits and rulers and populi which are brought into the orbit of Heaven's activity, forming a continuity with it, expressing it. Heaven's Sincerity is at the center of this interested system of reciprocities, but is also present as all its expressions. Heaven is both personal and impersonal, both intentional and unintentional. The sage too is both personal and impersonal, both intentional and unintentional, both *youwei* and *wuwei*. We can imagine a theological rejoinder on this basis: since we would not therefore say that the sage is not a person, why should we say that Heaven is not a person? And indeed, we do not say so. We say rather that, for early Confucianism, Heaven is both personal and impersonal, and the same is

---

22 天地之道，可一言而尽也。其为物不贰，则其生物不测。(See Wang Guo xuan, *Daxue·Zhong yong*, p. 114.)

true for the sage. The fact that this is even *possible* is indeed our point. Personality as ultimate *excludes* impersonality, just as purpose excludes purposelessness, so the sometimes-attempted theological concept of God as both personal and impersonal shipwrecks on the ultimacy of personality. Where thinkers in the monotheist traditions have attempted to situate the personhood of God on the basis of a deeper transpersonal essence (Pseudo-Dionysus, Eckhart, Boehme, the Schelling of the *Essay on Human Freedom* of 1809), they have risked Plotinian heresy, because here "personal" equates to "purposive," "good-seeking," "intelligent," *noûs*, which defines whatever is not-itself as *ipso facto* evil. Schelling is perhaps the bravest of those who attempt to connect all the dots here, requiring a daring redefinition of evil which, however, does not really escape the basic contours of his tradition: evil ends up still meaning free-will disobeying God's will in favor of its own will. That is not the case in Mencius no matter how singular and how personal his Heaven may be. For here, both Heaven and sage are structured in the typically atheist way: combinations of purposive and purposelessness, of personhood and impersonality, of conscious willing and will-lessness, where the latter of each pair is always the more ultimate in both generative power and value.

Another option in Confucian tradition, found in the full compensatory atheism of Xunzi's "Tianlun" 天论, rejecting any intentional aspect of Heaven altogether, was to assert that man fulfills his role in the triad through his specifically human and non-Heavenlike character, i.e., precisely through his purposive intentionality and effort:

> To accomplish without action, to attain without seeking: this is what is
> called the work of Heaven. Although it is something deep, man need
> apply no thought to it; although it is vast, man need apply no skill to it;
> although it is something precise, it does not bear the application of any
> investigation. This is called not competing with Heaven's work. Heaven
> has its times, earth has its resources, and man has his governing. This is
> what allows him to form a triad with them. To try to form a triad with them
> while giving up that by which one forms a triad is just a confusion.[23]

---

23 不为而成，不求而得，夫是之谓天职。如是者，虽深，其人不加虑焉；虽大，不加能焉；
虽精，不加察焉；夫是之谓不与天争职。天有其时，地有其财，人有其治，夫是之谓能参。
舍其所以参，而愿其所参，则惑矣！（参见梁启雄：《荀子简释》，"天论"；北京：中华书局，
1983 年，页 221）

Here it is not spontaneity that has value; as in Xunzi's famous "Human Nature is Odious," value comes from deliberate activity, from control, from purposive control in shaping things towards an end. This is the shared view of the Emulative Theist, the Compensatory Theist and the Compensatory Atheist generally. But even here, this deliberate activity is understood as having a necessary relation to the spontaneous, to the other members of the triad, Heaven and Earth. Unlike the case of the straight Compensatory Atheist of post-monotheist traditions, where the uncontrolled is simply anti-value to be eschewed as much as possible, here the continuity is forefronted: it is really the totality of the non-deliberate plus deliberate, i.e., Heaven-and-Earth plus Man, that is the creator of value. Man is the finisher, the decisive determinant; but the impossibility of this role in the absence of the non-deliberate is still an essential aspect of this Confucian view of the world. Ultimate value is not in purposive control as such, but in the controlled combination of control and non-control.

Finally, we have perhaps the most influential options for this uniquely human participation in the creative work of the universe, those derived from the "Zhongyong"中庸 and *Zhouyi*周易, the metaphysical climax of classical Confucian metaphysical speculation, adopted in various forms in the Neo-Confucian systems. We have already taken up the *Zhouyi* "Xicizhuan" position, finding it to be an artful crystallization of many trends within the tradition. A key concept of the "Zhongyong" has been alluded to in passing, but a few more words need to be said about its contribution to the atheist metaphysics of Confucianism. This text presents a penetrating attempt to characterize the precise nature of the human relation to the creative process of the cosmos that it continues and completes. Extending the motif presented in *Mencius* 7A1, man's distinctive role here is described as plumbing to the utmost his own nature, which in this case reveals to him not just the Heavenly spontaneity as such, but also the spontaneous inborn natures of other people, and indeed the spontaneous inborn natures of *all things*. One is thereby enabled to "assist in the creative and nourishing work of Heaven and Earth, and form a triad with Heaven and Earth." [24] This adaptation of the Xunzian motif of the triad in combination with the initially quite distinct Mencian motif of "plumbing one's own nature" pro-

---

24 可以赞天地之化育，则可以与天地参矣。(See Wang Guoxuan, *Da xue · Zhong yong*, p. 106)

duces crucial new results. "To plumb the nature" of all things in this way certainly does point to some kind of privileged access to the metaphysical reality of things. This is what sometimes misleads unwary readers into thinking we have here something analogous to the God-centric metaphysical systems found elsewhere in the world, where a special capacity of man's (e.g., imago dei, Reason) allows him to grasp the real nature of things. The question, though, is what this "real nature" is in the two cases, and this differs radically in the God-centric and the God-less worldviews. For the Nature of all things, rooted in Heaven, is stipulated in the "Zhongyong" to be inextricably related to *unknowability*, not just to us, but in principle, in itself, just as we see in the Daoist texts. We see this at both the beginning and the end of the text: the Heavenly nature of all things is inseparable from their "root" in the "inner center which is unexpressed" (*xi nu ai le zhi weifa, weizhi zhong*喜怒哀乐之未发，谓之中), which is the more evident and expressed precisely by being the more hidden and unknown (*mo xianhu yin, mo xianhu wei*莫见乎隐，莫显乎微), and the "scentless, soundless" working of Heaven (*shangtian zhi zai,wusheng wuxiu*上天之载，无声无臭)—what is beyond sensuous apprehension here is not the intelligible as such, the mind of God, but rather the unknowable-in-principle, what is unknowable even to omniscience. Here, however, in contrast to what we find in the Daoist accounts, unknowability is presented as only half the story, the less important half; it is the everpresent ground and enabler of reliable knowledge. This unknowability is what grounds the possibility for a continuity between knowledge of entities which are, as known, distinct and separate: the contrasting emotions of joy and anger, sorrow and happiness, as well as the self, other people, and all other things. For because our own nature and the nature of all other things are *in no case fully determinate*, they are not mutually exclusive; growing from the same pre-determinate root, the unexpressed center, they are inextricable linked to one another, and converge at their deepest point. The human nature we plumb is thus more than just Reason, more than just intelligibility; it is the whole being of man. Most crucially, this means that the whole being of man is even more than just human; it partakes in the nature of all things. It is not because we have Reason that knows those things as objects that we plumb them, but because they, like us, are joined to the totality of other things by the unknowability at the unexpressed center, the convergence points of all apparently separate opposites, that is the generative root of them, the non-mutual-exclusivity which is the unknowable aspect of their nature. Daoist unknowability is repurposed, put in the service of knowledge in the Confucian systems, as valuelessness is put in the service of value in the "Xicizhuan" passage repeatedly cited above. And yet, distinctively, the achieved goal is not the full suppression of the unknowability, effortlessness and valuelessness, not even (quite) in the Compensatory Atheism of Xunzi, but rather their full expression. The text begins with the unmanifest "center" that is neither happiness nor sorrow, neither joy nor anger, the innermost inborn nature that is at once the most unmanifest and the most universally expressed, beyond the reach of intention; here again his conscious effort, his carefulness and attention, are directed toward this pre-intentional indeterminate nature. The text ends by describing Heaven's operations as equally unmanifest in any particular form, achieving its universality in the same way. The sage is himself effortless, beginning and ending (as the text itself does) in the maximally unmanifest, the ultimately unknowable, though with a period of purposively making himself purposeless in between, as again Heaven is "sincere" or "integrated" without thinking (*si*思)*,* without purpose, while man must purposively "make himself sincere" or "integrate himself " by "choosing the good and holding tightly to it." [25] Harmony and Heaven's mandate are themselves reconceived as surface manifestations of this deeper indetermination, which is the ultimate source of both being and value. Purposelessness is the source and end of purpose.

We see some form of these two points in nearly all the later Neo-Confucian systems: 1) the dimension of non-specifiability in the ultimate nature (e.g., as *wuji*无极 in Zhu Xi, or as the denial of pre-existing *dingli*定理 in Wang Yangming); and 2) a view of the nature of things whereby in one sense all things have the same nature but in another sense each thing has its own distinct nature. We can see how this invites affiliation with the *Yin-Yang* cosmology of the *Zhouyi* system. For the primary meaning of *Yin* and *Yang* illustrates this deep unknowability in the known: they mean, essentially, the seen and the unseen, the obvious and the obscure, the foreground and the background, linked to "valued" and "neglected." "Definite" and "vague," are given a formal structure here. This is just a formal statement of the previous point about knowledge: whatever

---

25 诚者，天之道也；诚之者，人之道也。诚者不勉而中，不思而得，从容中道，圣人也。诚之者，择善而固执之者也。(See Wang Gwoxuan, Da xue · Zhong yong, p. 101.)

appears to knowledge is always half-in-darkness. To be knowing something is to not-know half of it. To be known is to be half-unknown. To be knowable is to be half-unknowable. Only thus is there any knowing, or anything to know. It is just that now this is in the service of asserting a kind of authoritative, reliable knowledge, but one which necessarily expands the sense of the knowing self and the self to be known beyond the range of any notion of unity as consistency of purpose and conscious control.

Confucianism may seem to resemble monotheism and its derivatives in that it sees the cosmic pre-human source of generativity in terms that are wholly social and interpersonal, and thus is very willing to see personhood as inexorably rooted in the transcendental realm, leaving no aspect of the universal process unconnected to the purposivity of social, moral man. It wants to reassign the purposeless effortless joy of the spontaneous into the realm of utility to social purposes. In some readings, especially of Neo-Confucianism, this is even in the form we found in quite a few post-monotheist systems: non-negotiability as the inviolability of absolute moral demand. But this is what makes Confucianism especially valuable for any student of metaphysics and morals. What is it that, in spite of this shared commitment to ultimacy of the personal and interpersonal, makes Confucianism different from other systems that grant ultimacy to some form of personhood? The answer is simple: Confucianism has a different idea of what a person is. The Confucian person is both body and mind, reason and emotion, purpose and purposeless, controlled and uncontrolled, *youwei* and *wuwei*. Confucian virtue is intercorporeal as much as it is intersubjective: it is mediated always by *li*礼, ritual, saturated with the givenness of both existing traditional social forms and of bodies which no mind has created *ex nihilo*. This personhood will be different from the personhood of disembodied souls of Platonic shades, and even forever different from the selves of Abrahamic believers in the resurrection of the flesh, in spite of the fact that for these body and mind are also inseparable. In the latter case, body is still under control of and indeed still designed by a mind, still purposefully made—not by one's own mind, but by God's mind. So mind, personhood, thinking, *noûs*, purpose, control are ultimate in all directions, body or mind. Confucian persons are not deliberately-created selves in this sense, and control is not the final category accounting for either their existence or their virtue. They are cultivations of a pre-existing givenness, pruned and guided and nourished and grown in a certain purposive way, so that the purposeless is brought partially into the service of a purpose, as in the body-as-tool conception of monotheism.But the purpose into whose service the purposeless is here pressed is not the purpose at the root of the world, for that is not the kind of world it is: it is not a world created by a mind or by anything mental. The Confucian world does not exist for any purpose. Purpose itself, on the contrary, is a mere foreground part of a larger purposeless process that is its own purpose, and of which the joy of fulfilling any definite purpose is merely a recovered echo. Furthermore, the pinnacle of this virtue restores a condition of *wuwei*, of effortless and purposelessness, where mind is not controlling, where ends-means deliberations have ceased. The origin of the Confucian self is in the *wuwei* transformations of the universal process of generation, has a period of deliberate *youwei* activity and deliberate cultivation in which he tries to attain a balance of the two sides of his nature, the spontaneous and the deliberate.

Mencius 2A2 gives a strong version of this Confucian self-conception, one that would later become canonical. We start with something spontaneous, purposeless, non-human in the very depths of the human: those aspects of man's spontaneous (non-deliberate, *wuwei*) being that, with proper nourishment and environment, if they are not unduly obstructed, if they are cultivated and pruned and trimmed properly, will grow into fully fledged social virtues. These are compared to growing a plant, cultivating a garden: the key metaphor is that we are trying to grow the "sprouts" of virtue. The *youwei*, purposeful aspect of life is this pruning and cultivating and feeding of a *wuwei* purposeless spontaneity. Mencius positions the Confucian way between two extremes: total purposelessness, *lassaiz-faire* of anything goes, which just lets the plants grow however they want, all together with whatever weeds might be there—let's call that the Daoist extreme. On the other extreme, are those people who, like the foolish man of Song, tried to "help their sprouts grow": the growth was too slow and indirect, so he tried to pull up on the sprouts—thereby killing them. That is, he tried to exert total control over the spontaneous side of his nature, to force it to follow his conception of how it should be, to make the body genuinely a tool of the mind. Let's call this the Emulative Theist option. Confucianism, for Mencius, is rather a gentle, patient guiding of the spontaneous by the deliberate, which, when successful, then drops the deliberate altogether, leading back spontaneity, an expanded state of spontaneity, as the spontaneous sprout has not become an equally spontaneous and *wuwei* tree, through the temporary inter-vention of the *youwei* gardener. The source and the goal are still both *wuwei*; the instrumental role of the purposive is self-canceling. The proper role of my consciousness is not to be the leader, the guide, the ruler, the king: it is to be the nourisher, guider, trimmer, facilitator of the maximal productivity of the non-conscious. The proper role of purpose is to nourish the spontaneous, the incom-prehensible, that which acts without knowing why it acts. The proper role of the personal is to nourish the impersonal that is its basis, its root, its living font. This is what knowledge does not know, and can never know. Not just my knowledge, not just human knowledge: what no knowledge in the universe knows is the genuinely spontaneous process of nature.

So when Neo-Confucians assert that the universe is *ren*仁, humane—that the intersubjective affection, and respectful yielding to tradition and to others, and harmonious-clustering-each-in-the-right-place and mutual-recognition and acquired-knowhow (for these are the four Mencian virtues: *ren, li, yi, zhi*仁、礼、义、智—which Neo-Confucians correlate to the four seasons) are the ulti-mate, the real source of all being and value, it means something very differ-ent from a monotheist who makes the interpersonal relation the ultimate onto-logical fact. The monotheist interpersonal relation is the relation between two responsible controllers who exist in a universe in which responsible control is the ultimate ontological fact. The ontological interpersonality of the Confucian cosmos is the relation of persons who are, from the beginning to the end, both purposeful and purposeless, with the purposeless dimension as both the deepest root and as the ultimate development, the source and the end. Confucian per-sons are from the beginning to the end purposeless-purpose-purposeless sand-wiches, so the interpersonality of the Confucian cosmos does not imply the ulti-macy of the purposeful, but the opposite.

AGRONOMY AND PHILOSOPHY IN EARLY CHINA

Roel Sterckx 胡司德

(University of Cambridge)

Historians of early China draw on variety of texts (in addition to material evidence) to study agriculture. Calendrical texts describe seasonal cycles of farm labour;[1] studies of soil, fauna, and flora tend to start with the "Yugong" 禹贡 and then move onto technical chapters preserved in the *Lüshi chunqiu*吕氏春秋 and *Guanzi*管子.[2] For specific terminology, entries in the *Zhouli*周礼 and early lexicons offer a rich source.[3] In addition, administrative regulations related to agriculture are preserved in legal texts.[4] The vast majority of these sources

---

1 These include the much quoted "Qi yue" 七月 in the *Shijing*诗经; the *Xia xiaozheng*夏小正, versions of the *yueling*月令, and the *Simin yueling*四民月令 (*Monthly Instructions for the Four Classes of People*, describing life on a farming estate of a mid-level Eastern Han official). For charts comparing the descriptions of climate and human activity in these sources, see He Xin 何新, *Xia xiaozheng xinkao*夏小正新考 (Shenyang: Volumes Publishing Company 万卷出版公司, 2014), pp. 174–182.

2 Xin Shuzhi辛树帜, *Yugong xinjie*禹贡新解 (Beijing: China Agriculture Press 农业出版社, 1964); Xia Weiying夏纬瑛, *Lüshi chunqiu "Shang nong" deng sipian jiaoshi*吕氏春秋上农等四篇校释 (Beijing: Zhonghua Book Company 中华书局, 1956); Wang Yuhu王毓瑚, *Xian Qin nongjiayan sipian bieshi*先秦农家言四篇别释 (Beijing: China Agriculture Press, 1981).

3 Xia Weiying夏纬瑛, *Zhoulishu zhong youguan nongye tiaowen de jieshi*周礼书中有关农业条文的解释 (Beijing: China Agriculture Press, 1979).

4 These include the statutes uncovered at Shuihudi睡虎地 (Yunmeng county, Hubei province, dating to 217 BCE), where regulations are grouped under the headings of "Agriculture" (*tian*田), "Stables and Parks" (*jiu*厩), and "Granaries" (*cang*仓). Legal texts excavated at Zhangjiashan张家山 (Jiangling county, Hubei province, dating to 186 BCE), confirm that these statutes on agriculture were fairly stable and did not change much in early Han. See Anthony J. Barbieri-Low and Robin D.S. Yates, *Law, State, and Society in Early Imperial China (2 vols): A Study with Critical Edition and Translation of the Legal Texts From Zhangjiashan Tomb No. 247* (Leiden: E.J. Brill, 2015), vol.1, p. 692 ff.

are prescriptive.[5] One of the great merits of Hsu Cho-yun's *Han Agriculture: The Formation of Early Chinese Agrarian Economy (206 B.C.—A.D. 220)*, published in 1980, was to bring together many of these materials,[6] and show that a great deal of information about farming and peasant life is contained in sources other than the later *nongshu*农书 "agricultural treatises."[7] This is especially relevant when it concerns the social and economic background of farm life.

However, scholars have overlooked the fact that the language used to

---

5 An alternative way to classify the sources would be to distinguish between texts that are mainly theoretical and those that draw on farming experience. In China the latter came about only in late Han and early medieval times together with the rise of the landed estate. K.D. White notes how Greek and Roman writings on agriculture differ markedly: "Whereas the Greek contribution to our subject comes mainly from the works of philosophers and men of science, Roman agricultural writing was based from its inception on practical farming experience. See *Roman Farming* (London: Thames & Hudson, 1970), p. 18.

6 Hsu Cho-yun许倬云, *Han Agriculture: The Formation of Early Chinese Agrarian Economy* (*206 B.C.—A.D. 220*) (Seattle and London: University of Washington Press, 1980); *Handai nongye: Zhongguo nongye jingji de qiyuan ji texing*汉代农业：中国农业经济的起源及特性，王勇译 (Guilin: Guangxi Normal University Press 广西师范大学出版社, 2005).

7 *Nongshu* are the most comprehensive and user-friendly source of information on the organisation and transmission of agronomic knowledge in pre-modern China. However the earliest extant agricultural treatise today is Jia Sixie's贾思勰 *Qimin yaoshu*齐民要术 (*Essential Techniques for the Peasantry*), compiled ca. 540 CE. Although the *Qimin yaoshu* contains fragments purportedly dating back to earlier times, few technical texts on agriculture have survived for the Warring States and early imperial period. The only extant farming manual dating to the Han, the *Fan Shengzhi shu*氾胜之书 (*Book of Fan Shengzhi*; late first century BCE), is a relatively short text (approximately 3700 characters). *The Fan Shengzhi shu* is the only one of nine agriculture titles (of which four hawe no purported author) in the *Hanshu*汉书 bibliographic treatise that survives in the *Suishu*隋书 bibliography. See *Hanshu* (Beijing: Zhonghua Book Company, 1962), 30.1742–1743; *Suishu* (Beijing: Zhonghua Book Company, 1973), 34.1010. For translations see Hsu, *Han Agriculture*, pp. 280–294; Shi Shenghan, *Fan Sheng-chihshu. An Agriculturistic Book of China Written in the First Century B.C.* (Peking: Science Press, 1959). The great agricultural treatises of the Song and Ming such as Chen Fu's 陈旉 *Nongshu* 农书 (1149), the more extensive work by the same title by Wang Zhen 王祯 (1313), or Xu Guangqi's 徐光启 *Nongzheng quanshu*农政全书 (*Complete Treatise on Agricultural Administration*; published in 1637) tend to fall back on the *Qimin yaoshu* when quoting or referring to past practice. On the *Nongshu* as a genre and their shifting contents, see Francesca Bray, *Science and Civilisation in China*, vol. VI, part 2 "Agriculture" (Cambridge: Cambridge University Press, 1984); and Bray, "Where did the animals go? Presence and absence of livestock in Chinese agricultural treatises", in Roel Sterckx, Martina Siebert and Dagmar Schäfer eds., *Animals Through Chinese History* (Cambridge: Cambridge University Press, forthcoming), Chapter 6. For a comprehensive bibliographic survey of *nongshu*, see Amano Motonosuke天野元之助（tr. Peng Shijue彭世决 and Lin Guangxin林广信）, *Zhongguo gudai nongshu kao*中国古代农书考 (Beijing: China Agriculture Press, 1992).

describe agricultural life in early China was of itself a much used medium for philosophical, social, and political commentary. Both philosophical and ritual texts contain a repository of information on how to "do" agriculture, how to behave as a farmer, and what people observed when tilling the fields. Much of this appears as figurative language in the form of metaphors and analogies. These often appear in contexts that do not announce themselves as technical or particularly preoccupied with agriculture. Rather than showing that people thought *about* agriculture, figurative language illustrates how the early Chinese thought *through* or *with* agriculture.

Agricultural activity lends itself well for analogies that play on core themes in early Chinese thought: for instance, the generation of things out of some sort of prior state (germination, seeding), the idea of growth and timeliness (e.g. the seasons),[8] and, more generally, the forging of patterns of order (civilisation). Prized values such as dedicated collaborative labour, obedience, productivity and self-sufficiency draw on descriptions of peasant life. This paper explores how agriculture figures in the language of philosophical discourse, and what, if anything, the masters of philosophy can teach us about agriculture and the peasant mode of existence in early China.

There are good reasons to be sceptical about the (truth) value of metaphors and analogies, and claim that they contain little or no useful technical content. Derk Bodde suggested that those who conjured up figurative language were far removed from the world they describe:

> Persons who think of bamboos as "men of moral worth" and of the downward flow of water as an example of the Confucian virtue of propriety (*li* 礼) are unlikely to have much interest either in the growth of bamboo or the movements

---

8 Chinese historians of agriculture tend to highlight notions of "timeliness" and "seasonality" (rather than order and control) as the central contribution of philosophy to agronomy. See e.g. Ni Genjin倪根金, "Zhongguo gudai zhexue sixiang dui chuantong nongye kexue jishu de yingxiang" 中国古代哲学思想对传统农业科学技术的影响, in *Liang Jiamian nongshi wenji*梁家勉农史文集 (Beijing: China Argiculture Press, 2002), pp.448–453. Shi Shenghan notes that knowledge about agriculture in the pre-imperial masters texts remains at the level of "common knowledge" (*changzhi*常知), that is, the seasons (*tianshi*天时) and soil compatibility (*tuyi*土宜). See "Zhongguo gudai nongshu pingjia" 中国古代农书评价, in *Shi Shenghan nongshi lunwen ji*石声汉农史论文集 (Beijing: Zhonghua Book Company, 2008), pp. 330–410 (p. 340).

of water as scientific phenomena. Or even if they have, they are not going to know the methodology necessary to satisfy this interest.[9]

For Bodde, Chinese views of nature are almost exclusively moralistic and he singles out some prominent examples of natural objects and substances that serve frequently as metaphor or analogy: water, jade, and bamboo. Bodde's quest for "scientific phenomena" leaves him irritated. How is it possible, he asks, that centuries later, a twenty-year old Wang Yangming 王阳明 (1492) and his friend still could do no better than to fall ill after days of concentrated study of how bamboos were growing in front of his pavilion? What does it take to get a philosopher to look at bamboo as bamboo?

The opposite of outright scepticism of the value of figurative language is to fall prone to philosophical reductionism and assume that the way in which philosophers (the "schools" or lineages we have pigeonholed them into) think about the world has a direct influence on technical or practical decisions. The following comment in Robert Marks' otherwise excellent survey of Chinese environmental history wades into this zone:

> Two schools developed [in early imperial times] for how to deal with the problems of flooding and silting of the Yellow River, broadly reflecting Confucian and Daoist views. Those with more Daoist leanings argued that the river (mostly) should be allowed to follow its "natural" course, with relatively low dikes built a very long way from the riverbed—basically simply defining a flood plain. Confucians tended to want to build higher dikes to confine the river to a narrower course (much as they wanted to define proper human behaviour). Neither approach proved totally effective over the next two thousand years, but Yellow River dikes did get higher as the silt deposits raised the river bed—until unusually heavy rainfall broke the dikes and flooded the surrounding plain.[10]

To be sure, both Bodde and Marks have a point: the early Chinese rarely

---

9 Derk Bodde, *Chinese Thought, Society, and Science*: *The Intellectual and Social Background of Science and Technology in Pre-modern China* (Honolulu: University of Hawai' i Press, 1991), p. 263.

10 Robert B. Marks, *China*: *Its Environment and History* (Plymouth: Rowman and Littlefield, 2012), p. 89

separated the technical from the moral or philosophical. Explaining "how" to do something is regularly done through metaphor or analogy.[11] Yet, the implication of this then has to be that metaphors and analogies cannot simply, or invariably, be taken as purely literary devices aimed at making a moral or philosophical point. We ought to be open to the idea that figurative language belonged to the normal register of tools used to analyse and describe nature and the management of natural resources (alongside definitions, lexicographical comment, etc.). It also follows then that "as if " or "just as" descriptions may have functioned as regular communicative or didactic devices to convey social and political ideas and perhaps even to transmit a modicum of technical knowledge.

Hardly any aspect of agricultural labour escapes the eyes of early China's masters of philosophy and ritualists: irrigation, seeding and sowing, reaping and harvesting, storing, weeding, etc. In what follows I approach figurative language in a way somewhere in-between Bodde's scepticism and Marks' philosophical optimism. I start from the premise that the technical (or "scientific") and the philosophical (or moralistic and political) are not necessarily mutually exclusive. I will focus on a set of examples that each offer different interpretative possibilities, and show that figural language involving agronomy offers a useful lens into early Chinese socio-political thought and philosophy. At times, it also helps us understand farming practice itself.

Irrigation, Levees, Dikes

Let us start with the flood-fighting Confucians Marks refers to. No element of nature has done more to massage the brain of the masters of philosophy

---

11 I use the terms "metaphor" and "analogy" loosely to denote any kind of figurative or figural language: [Metaphor] "I have a new crop of students" and [analogy] "You should foster your students in the same way as a farmer tends to his crops." I take it in its simplest form as a particular image that serves as a referent to an idea behind the image. Several scholars have thought about the issue at great length. Sarah Allan (*The Way of Water and Sprouts of Virtue*, SUNY Press, 1997) is interested not so much in metaphors as literary or concrete images to illustrate primary philosophical concepts; she believes, with Angus Graham, in the existence of pre-logical conceptual schemes that shape a particular philosophical tradition and the vocabulary it uses. Other scholars such as Edward Slingerland and Christoph Harbsmeier attempt to unveil metaphoric deep structures in the cognitive make-up of Chinese thought or within the lexicon and syntax of the literary Chinese language.

than the handling and mishandling of water. Embankments and flood defences appear frequently as images for ritual guidance and the orderly society (*pace* Karl Wittfogel's hydraulic societies). The following example from the *Liji*礼记 illustrates the idea:

> Ritual prevents the rise of disorder and confusion, like the embank-ments that stop the overflow of water. Therefore he who thinks the old embankments useless and destroys them is sure to suffer from the deso-lation caused by overflowing water; and he who considers the old rules of propriety useless and abolishes them would be sure to suffer from the calamities of disorder.[12]

> 夫礼禁乱之所由生，犹坊止水之所自来也。故以旧坊为无
> 所用坏之者，必有水败；以旧礼为无所用而去之者，必有乱患。

The image is carried through in a *Liji* chapter title, "Fangji" 坊记 ("Record of the Embankments") and throughout this chapter. It starts by stating that "the way of the gentleman may be compared to the dykes" (君子之道，辟则坊与), and then uses expressions such as "framing rites to dyke (= preserve) virtue" (礼以坊德), "embanking someone's desires" (坊欲) and rituals that "serve as dykes for the people" (以为民坊者).[13] The *Lunheng*论衡 paraphrases the above *Liji* passage, concluding that "scholars are the old embankments of *li*礼 and *yi*义"; just as old embankments have become part of the landscape, the *Ru*儒 operate as the unnoticed gatekeepers of moral values:

> Thus if old di kes are discarded as useless, there will inevitably be a flood. If old rituals are discarded as good for nothing, there will inevitably be chaos and disaster. The *Ru* in the world are the old dikes of propriety and righteousness. When they are there they are of no direct use, but their

---

12 *Liji jijie*礼记集解. Edited by Sun Xidan孙希旦 (Beijing: Zhonghua Book Company, 1995), 48.1257 ("Jing jie" 经解).

13 *Liji jijie*, 50.1281. See also Michael Ing, *The Dysfunction of Ritual in Early Confucianism* (Oxford: Oxford University Press, 2012), pp. 31–32, 124–125, 165–166.

absence is fatal.[14]

> 故以旧防为无益而去之，必有水灾；以旧礼为无补而去
> 之，必有乱患。儒者之在世，礼义之旧防也。有之无益，无之
> 有损。

The embankment analogy is widely attested. In *Chunqiu fanlu*春秋繁露, for instance, it helps describe how the sage sets limits to excessive wealth or poverty: "The way of the sage corresponds to the category of levees and dikes. He promulgates regulations and limits, he promulgates ritual restrictions."[15] Embankments and canals area didactic image, they offer a political vocabulary for the notion of preservation and control of resources:

> When fish have water, they swim in it and enjoy themselves, but if (the dikes) break and the water dries up, then they will be eaten by insects. If you strengthen and repair the dikes and embankments and replace the water that leaked out, the fish will be restored and benefit from it. A country has something by means of which it is preserved; people have something by means of which they stay alive. What preserves a state is humaneness and rightness; what keeps people alive is good conduct.[16]

> 鱼得水而游焉则乐，唐决水涸，则为蝼蚁所食。有掌修其
> 堤防，补其缺漏，则鱼得而利之，国有以存，人有以生。国之
> 所以存者，仁义是也；人之所以生者，行善是也。

---

14 *Lunheng jiaoshi*论衡校释. Compiled by Wang Chong 王充 (27–ca.100 CE), edited by Liu Pansui刘盼遂 (Beijing: Zhonghua Book Company, 1990), 10.433 ("Fei Han").

15 *Chunqiu fanlu yizheng*春秋繁露义证. Edited by Su Yu 苏舆 (Beijing: Zhonghua Book Company, 1996), 27.231 ("Du zhi"): 圣人之道众堤防之类也。谓之度制，谓之礼节。

16 *Huainan honglie jijie*淮南鸿烈集解. Edited by Liu Wendian刘文典 (Taipei: The Liberal Arts Press 文史哲出版社, 1992), 9.316 ("Zhu shu"); cf. John Major et al., *The Huainanzi. A Guide to the Theory and Practice of Government in Early Han China* (New York: Columbia University Press, 2010), 339 (9.31).

To be sure, embankments and dikes respond to the need to contain flood-waters; they do not originate from an instinctive "Confucian" desire for order and proper human behaviour: the *Ru*儒 do not build embankments, nor would they know how to do it. Nevertheless, the image of raising levees appears so frequently as a *simile* for the idea of governance through ritual that we must assume that those who used the image were somehow familiar with a hydraulic landscape.[17]

The analogy above tells us little about irrigation or dike-building methods. The ritualist only knows how to restore old rituals. To find out how to deal with old dikes (旧防) we must turn to the *Guanzi*, where it is suggested that dike-building involves social engineering: people are spatially assigned to them for upkeep and defence:

> Each year increase the size of the dikes and plant them with thorns and brambles in order to make their earthwork more secure. Mix in juniper and pussy willows to provide against flooding. From this the people will enjoy such abundance that it will be said to flow like hot lard. Order the poorest people to stand guard on the dikes and everywhere mark out their sectors. The dikes then will never fail.[18]

> 岁埤增之，树以荆棘，以固其地；杂之以柏杨，以备决水，民得其饶，是谓流膏。令下贫守之，往往而为界，可以毋败。

---

17 Another fine analogy between governing people and managing natural resources occurs in the (late 4th—early 3rd century BCE) "Qi fa" 七法 chapter in the *Guanzi*: "Governing the people is like controlling a flood, nurturing them is like feeding the six domestic animals, and employing them is like making use of grass and trees (治人如治水潦，养人如养六畜，用人如用草木)." See *Guanzi jiaozhu* 管子校注. Edited by Li Xiangfeng黎翔凤 (Beijing: Zhonghua Book Company, 2004), 6.111-112 ("Qi fa"). For other examples see *Fayan*法言, 8.25-26; Yang Xiong, tr. Michal Nylan, *Exemplary Figures* (Seattle: University of Washington Press, 2013), p. 135: "From the fact that rivers have their dikes and utensils their molds, we see the ultimate utility of instruction in the rites (川有防，器有范。见礼教之至也)"; and *Yantielun jiaozhu*盐铁论校注. Edited by Wang Liqi王利器 (Beijing: Zhonghua Book Company, 1996), 24.299 ("Lunfei"): "Therefore, when the dams and dikes are kept whole, the people never suffer from floods; when rituals and righteousness are established, the people will not behave disorderly (故堤防成而民无水蓄，礼义立而民无乱患)."

18 *Guanzi jiaozhu*, 57.1063 ("Du di"); cf. W. Allyn Rickett, *Guanzi: Political, Economic, and Philosophical Essays from Early China (2 vols.)* (Princeton: Princeton University Press, 1985—1998), vol. 2, p. 250 .

Here it is suggested that dikes are not simple *man-made* but also *manned* structures. They are populated by and depend on a human presence. Thus the interpretative distance between the image of dikes that form an orderly grid across a populated landscape and the idea of ritual as a mechanism of social control gets tighter. It may not be a simple case of analogy; the observer who witnesses the construction of levees and dikes notices that it involves manipulating both soil and people, both material as well as human labour.

The Well-sweep

On occasions, figural language offers technical insights not found elsewhere. An example of this is the case of the well-sweep (*jiegao*桔槔), a device to bring up water by lowering a bucket into a well by means of a long pole (the so-called sweep).[19] The earliest descriptions of this device are in the *Zhuangzi*庄子, where it occurs twice.

> Zigong had been wandering south to Chu, and was returning through Jin. As he passed (a place) on the southbank of the river Han, he saw an old man who was just about to work in his vegetable garden. He had dug his channels, gone to the well, and was bringing from it in his arms a jar of water to pour onto his garden. Toiling away, he expended a great deal of effort, but with little result. Zigong said to him, "There is a tool (*xie* 械) here, by means of which a hundred plots of soil may be irrigated in one day. With the expenditure of very little strength, the result is great. Would you not like to try it, Sir?" The gardener looked up at him, and said, "How does it work?" Zigong said, "One cuts a lever from wood, heavy behind, and light in front. It picks up the water as quickly as you could do with your hand, as fast as the bubbles on boiling water. Its name

---

19 The best known image of a well-sweep occurs in the 1637 edition of the *Tiangong kaiwu*天工开物. Han murals contain depictions of well-sweeps but most are set in domestic (kitchen or stable) scenes, not in fields or an agrarian setting. See e.g. Zhou Xin 周昕, *Zhongguo nongju tongshi*中国农具通史 (Jinan: Shandong Science and Technology Press 山东科学技术出版社, 2010), pp. 348–349.

is 'well-sweep.'"

The gardener put on an angry look, laughed, and said, "I have heard from my teacher that where there are ingenious contraptions, there are sure to be ingenious affairs, and where there are ingenious affairs, there are sure to be ingenious minds. But, when there is a scheming mind in the breast, its pure simplicity is impaired. When this pure simplicity is impaired, the spirit becomes unsettled, and the unsettled spirit is not the proper residence of the *Dao*. It is not that I do not know (a well-sweep and how it works), but I should be ashamed to use it." Zigong looked blank and ashamed, hung down his head, and did not reply.[20]

子贡南游于楚，反于晋，过汉阴，见一丈人方将为圃畦，凿隧而入井，抱瓮而出灌，搰搰然用力甚多而见功寡。子贡曰："有械于此，一日浸百畦，用力甚寡而见功多，夫子不欲乎？"为圃者仰而视之曰："奈何？"曰："凿木为机，后重前轻，挈水若抽，数如泆汤，其名为槔。"为圃者忿然作色而笑曰："吾闻之吾师：'有机械者必有机事，有机事者必有机心。'机心存于胸中，则纯白不备；纯白不备，则神生不定；神生不定者，道之所不载也。吾非不知，羞而不为也。"子贡瞒然惭，俯而不对。

The second occurrence is in a passage where Yan Hui 颜回 is told that Confucius' way is nearing its end.

Are you then the only one who has never seen a well-sweep? When you pull on it, it goes down, and when you let go of it, it comes up. Because it is pulled by men (human force) and does not pull men around, it can go up and down without committing an offense against men [manipulating

---

20 *Zhuangzi jishi*庄子集释. Edited by Guo Qingfan郭庆藩 (Taipei: Guanya 贯雅文化, 1991), 12.433 ("Tiandi"); tr. Victor Mair, *Wandering on the Way* (Honolulu: Univesity of Hawai' i Press, 1994), p. 111.

or damaging the person who pulls it]. Therefore, the decorum and regulations of the Three August Sovereigns and Five Emperors were not prized because they preserved the status quo, but because they could bring good government. Thus we may compare the decorum and regulations of the Three August Sovereigns and Five Emperors to the hawthorn, the pear, the orange, and the pomelo. Although their flavours are quite different, they all taste good.[21]

且子独不见夫桔槔者乎？引之则俯，舍之则仰。彼，人之所引，非引人也，故俯仰而不得罪于人。故夫三皇、五帝之礼义法度，不矜于同而矜于治。故譬三皇、五帝之礼义法度，其犹柤梨橘柚邪！其味相反，而皆可于口。

The context in which these passages occur is essentially philosophical. In the first fragment, the argument is that tools and technology ("civilization") spoil the purity of experience ("drawing water with jars"). In the second fragment, the idea is that rules and decorum should change over time, and that change and adaptability to circumstances need not be harmful. Just as the well-sweep has no mind of its own and follows the impulse of those who pull and release it, humans should avoid clinging to a strong sense of self and go along with the times. Change can be instigated by humans without it taking control over them.

Yet the narrative is interesting beyond the philosophical point made. First, and most obviously, both passages describe the mechanics of a well-sweep, how to cut the sweep and the method of pulling and releasing it (the story of Zigong instructing the gardener is, if not the only, than certainly the most quoted anecdote or gloss for commentators explaining the graph for a well-sweep). The *Huainanzi*淮南子 contains a reference to it in a passage that contrasts past and primitive techniques with present technological innovation. As in Zhuangzi's gardening encounter, the well-sweep in *Huainanzi*淮南子 is hailed as an alternative for handling jars (*baoweng/zhui* 抱瓮/甀) to draw water.[22] Secondly, these

---

21 *Zhuangzi jishi*, 14.514 ("Tian yun"); tr. Mair, *Wandering*, p.137.
22 *Huainanzi*, 13.422–423 ("Fan lun").

passages also contain clues as to whether or not people were familiar with the device. In the first story, the gardener insists that "it is not that I do not know" (吾非不知); in the second, the interlocutor wonders "are you then the only one who has never seen a well-sweep" (子独不见)? One can take these comments simply as rhetorical overdrive; or should we infer from them that the well-sweep was widely familiar to folk at the time? If the power of an analogy or metaphor rests on the recognition of its imagery, this would be a logical conclusion (although it would still not explain its rare occurrence in texts).

Leaving aside the unanswerable question of what audience these stories might have been directed at, the Zigong passage is also interesting sociologically. Its setting is an encounter between a supposedly knowledgeable person (usually an official, disciple, etc.) and an ignoramus tilling the land, who happens to possess the key to wisdom. The image here is that of seeking recourse to the fields to preserve a sense of integrity. The fields (or wilds野), and the plough, act as a buffer against the tribulations of officialdom, corruption, and moral decay. A similar setting appears in the *Zhuangzi*'s "Tiandi" 天地 chapter:

When Yao was ruling the world, Bocheng Zigao was appointed by him prince of one of the states. From Yao (afterwards) the throne passed to Shun, and from Shun (again) to Yu; and (then) Bocheng Zigao resigned his principality and began to cultivate the ground (辞为诸侯而耕). Yu went to see him, and found him ploughing in the open country (耕在野). Hurrying to him, and bowing low in acknowledgment of his superiority, Yu then stood up, and asked him, saying, "Long ago, when Yao was ruling the world, you, sir, were appointed as one of the feudal lords. Then Yao passed the throne to Shun, and Shun passed it to me, whereupon you, sir, resigned your position as feudal lord, and are (now) ploughing (here) (辞为诸侯而耕). I venture to ask the reason of your conduct." Zigao said, "When Yao ruled the world, the people encouraged one another (to do what was right) without his offering them rewards; they stood in awe (of doing wrong) without his threatening them with punishments. Now you employ both rewards and punishments, and yet the people are not benevolent (今子赏罚而民且不仁). Consequently virtue is on the wane and punishments are on the rise; the disorder of future ages begins with this. Why don't you just go away, sir, and not interrupt my work?" With this he resumed his ploughing with his head bent down, and did not (again) look round (for Yu) (偈偈乎耕而不顾).[23]

The theme of the hermit-plowman recurs elsewhere. Yi Yin 伊尹 delights in the way of Yao and Shun while plowing the fields of the ruler of Xin before responding to King Tang's汤 call to office.[24] Then there is the story of the noble Chu minister Sunshu Ao孙叔敖 (6th century BCE): "Becoming a prime minister and yet not (particularly) happy (about it); returning to plowing (退耕), and yet (not particularly) sad (about it): such was the virtue of Sunshu Ao."[25] Yan Ying 晏婴 (Yanzi) resigns his service to Lord Jing for a period of seven years, when he "withdrew to his humble home, moving east to plow the fields by the sea. Herbs grew beneath the hall and brambles flourished outside his gate."[26]

These narrative settings contrast with descriptions of farm labour as a physical chore and anti-dote to intellectual self-realization. Confucius did not handle the plough himself: officials are there to manage the fields and its farming folk, but they do not work them personally. Shang Yang商鞅, Xunzi荀子and Han Fei韩非 present farm labour as a way to keep people simple of mind and obedient: all a farmer needs to know is farming.[27] "When the gentleman serves in office, he does not farm (君子仕则不稼)," in the words of Dong Zhongshu董仲舒.[28]

Therefore, I would argue that these well-sweep scenes can be read as an implicit criticism of the idea that officials understand what happens on the fields. To speculate further, it is possible that Zhuangzi's gardener's refusal of a well-sweep is a reflection on the alienating effects of increased technical advances and managerial interference in agriculture that had started to take place in the

---

23 *Zhuangzi jishi*, 20.413; tr. Mair, *Wandering*, 107 (modified).

24 *Mengzi*, 5A.7; cf. *Mengzi*, 6B.15.

25 *Shizi*尸子; cf. Paul Fischer tr., *Shizi: China's First Syncretist* (New York: Columbia University Press, 2012), p.140 (63).

26 *Yanzi chunqiu jishi*晏子春秋集释. Annotated by Wu Zeyu吴则虞 (Beijing: Zhonghua Book Company, 1962), 7.482; cf. Olivia Milburn, *The Spring and Autumn Annals of Mr Yan* (Leiden: E.J. Brill, 2015), 2.7.22 (pp. 395–396).

27 See Roel Sterckx, "Ideologies of the Peasant and Merchant in Warring States China", in *Ideology of Power and Power of Ideology in Early China: Studies in Early Chinese Political Thought*, ed. Yuri Pines, Paul Rakita Goldin, and Martin Kern (Leiden: E.J. Brill, 2015), pp. 211–248. Farming as both hardship and pleasure converge in early medieval farmstead poetry.

28 *Hanshu*, 56.2521; *Chunqiu fanlu yizheng*, 27.229.

Warring States period (iron tools that were beyond the reach of common farmers, the introduction of single-ox plowing, etc.). As Albert Galvany has suggested, anecdotes involving trees and vegetal imagery in the *Zhuangzi* draw their metaphorical power from the fact that trees, and the cultivation of trees, were an integral element of what was perceived to be ordered, agrarian society. Tree metaphors therefore should be read in the political context of a society in which the cultivation of wood and the symbolism of trees was important in economic and religious terms.[29] I believe that Zhuangzi's well-sweep encounters are more than just metaphors. We can read them, as historians of science and technology would have it, as indicative of the importance of irrigation or as evidence of advanced techniques in hydrology. Yet, equally, and by contrast, these narratives may represent an implicit criticism of advanced technologies that shift ownership of skill and tools away from the farmer and towards the official.[30]

Planting, Harvesting, Weeding, Soil

Craft analogies make up a large share of agricultural imagery. Planting, sowing, growing, weeding and harvesting appear frequently as metaphors for education, moral cultivation and scholarly or literary achievement. The *Mencius* sets the tone here with arguments on nature and nurture (and/or both) that are steeped in agrarian imagery, from "pulling up seedlings to help them grow" (2A.2),[31] to the lopped-down trees on Ox Mountain (6A.8). In 6A.7, all humans are said to possess the seed of sagehood: "Now, let barley be sown and covered by earth; the ground being the same, and the time of planting also being the same, it grows rapidly, and in due course of time, it all ripens. Though there may be differences in the yield, this is because the fertility of the soil, the nour-

---

29 Galvany, "Discussing usefulness: trees as metaphor in the *Zhuangzi*", *Momumenta Serica* 57 (2009), pp. 71–97.

30 The best chronological overview of officials related to agrarian management is Wang Yong 王庸, *Zhongguo gudai nongguan zhidu* 中国古代农官制度 (Beijing: China Three Gorges Publishing House 中国三峡出版社, 2009), pp. 6–96 (chapters 1 and 2).

31 For the image of humans drawing their energy from food just as plants rely on the soil, and the pulling up of roots causing premature death, see also *Lunheng jiaoshi*, 7.336 ("Dao xu").

ishment of the rain and the dew, and the human effort invested are not the same. Things of the same kind are thus like one another. Why is it that we should doubt this only when it comes to human beings? The sage and we are of the same kind."[32] Humaneness needs to develop through maturity like the five grains develop from the finest seed (6A.19). A gardener who neglects his *wu*梧 and *jia* 檟 trees while nurturing thorns and brambles is an inferior gardener; a person who, unknowingly, nurtures a single finger while neglecting his back and shoulders, is a confused animal (6A.14).[33]

A wide range of similar analogies occur beyond the *Mencius*. Good rulers exploit the most appropriate circumstances for state building, just as a good farmer chooses the most suitable land and plants when the rains are seasonal.[34] Without a strong husbandman crops do not grow; unless a state possesses good writers, its virtues remain hidden.[35] Farmers know that the exuberant growth of grain is due to the natural fertility of the soil, so people ought to understand that abundant literary productions are the upshot of extraordinary talents.[36] Several analogies are variations on the theme that one reaps what one sows.[37] Weeding, hoeing, and harrowing are common images for the elimination of unwanted rivals or subjects; weeds represent unwelcome elements that can overtake regular or normal society.[38]

---

32 Tr. Irene Bloom, *Mencius* (New York: Columbia University Press, 2009), p.125.

33 Tr. Bloom, *Mencius*, 129. For other analogies see *Mencius* 6A.13; 7B.10 (a store of grain to stand for a store of virtue); 7B.32 (neglecting your own fields while going to weed those of others).

34 *Lüshi chunqiu jiaoshi*吕氏春秋校释. Edited by Chen Qiyou 陈奇猷 (Shanghai: Xuelin Press学林出版社, 1995), 14.791 ("Zhang gong").

35 *Lunheng jiaoshi*, 12.539–540 ("Cheng cai").

36 *Lunheng jiaoshi*, 13.581 ("Xiao li"). See also *Lunheng jiaoshi*, 1.10 ("Lei hai")

37 E.g. *Huainanzi*, 18.597 (tr. Major, 728), "Planting glutinous millet will not get you a crop of panicled millet, planting resentment will not be repaid with virtue" (树黍者不获稷，树怨者无报德). See also *Lunheng jiaoshi* 18.780 ("Ziran").

38 For examples of obstructive weeds see *Mencius* 7B.21; *Huainanzi*, 16.537 ("Shuishan"). Weeds appear first as a metaphor in the first two stanzas of "Fu tian" 甫田 (Mao 102): "Do not till too big a field/ Or weeds will ramp it/ Do not love a distant man/ Or heart's pain will chafe you/ Do not till too big a field/ Or weeds will top it/ Do not love a distant man/ Or heart's pain will fret you." The idea here is that one should not exert oneself beyond one's own strength. The poem is quoted in *Yantielun* by the literati who criticize Sang Hongyang's桑弘羊 preoccupation with reaching out to trade with or cultivate frontier regions. See *Yantielun jiaozhu*, 16.208 ("Di guang").

Someone who runs a state or clan looks upon evil relations as a husband-man devotes himself to removing weeds. He cuts down, kills them, collects them, and heaps them up, extirpating their roots so that they may not be able to grow; and then the good grain stretches itself out.[39]

为国家者，见恶如农夫之务去草焉，芟夷蕴崇之，绝其本根，勿使能殖，则善者信矣。

Like the dikes and embankments that signify ritual and order, weeding furnishes the political language for countering dissonance and opposition: "The principle of governing a country consists in removing the noxious and hoeing out the unruly. Only then will the people enjoy equal treatment and find satisfaction under their own roofs."[40] The following passage uses the analogy of weeds to explain obstacles to ritual propriety:

The farmer's weeding is the ridding of that which harms the sprouts. The worthy's ordering is the ridding of that which harms propriety. To contemplate things that do not increase propriety and yet to (still) think them, this is a weed of the mind (心之秽). To speak about things that do not increase propriety and yet to speak of them, this is a weed of talking (言之秽). To do things that do not increase propriety and yet to do them, this is a weed of action (行之秽).[41]

The "Li yun" 礼运 extends the metaphors and explains that ritual and righteousness act like agrarian tools that regulate and control human emotions: "Emotions were the field (to be cultivated by) the sage kings. They cultivated ritual propriety to plough it. They set forth righteousness with which to seed it. They instituted schools to weed it. They considered benevolence the root by which to gather all its fruit and they employed training in music to give repose

---

39 *Chunqiu Zuozhuan zhu*春秋左传注. Edited by Yang Bojun杨伯峻 (Beijing: Zhonghua Book Company, 1995), 50 (Lord Yin, year 6); see also *Dongguan Hanji*东观汉记 (Sibubeiyao ed.), 13.4a.

40 *Yantielun jiaozhu*, 14.179 ("Qing zhong"). See also *Huainanzi*, 16.553 ("Shuishan"), "Governing a country is like hoeing a field. One gets rid of harmful plants; that is all."

41 *Shizi*, 7.1 (tr. Fischer, 92).

(to the minds of learners)."[42]

As in the case of the well-sweep, a description of technique can take up a significant share in the political analogy. A nice example of this occurs in the *Han Feizi* which contains descriptions of political pruning and planting. The efficient ruler manipulates his subjects and ministers like a tree surgeon who keeps wild growth under control:

> He who acts as the ruler of men should frequently stretch the tree but never allow its branches to flourish. Luxuriant branches will cover the gates of public buildings, until private houses become full, public halls empty, and the sovereign deluded. Therefore, stretch out the tree frequently but never allow any branch to grow outward. Any branch that grows outward will obstruct the position of the sovereign. Stretch out the tree frequently but never allow any of the branches to grow larger than the stem. When the branches are large and the stem is small, the tree will be unable to endure spring winds. When the tree cannot endure spring winds, the branches will damage its kernel. Likewise, when illegitimate sons are many, the heir apparent will have worries and anxieties. The only way to control them is to stretch out the tree frequently but never let its branches flourish. If the tree is stretched out often, partisans and adherents of the wicked ministers will disperse. When the roots and the stem are dug up, the tree is no longer alive.[43]

> 为人君者，数披其木，毋使木枝扶疏；木枝扶疏，将塞公间，私门将实，公庭将虚，主将壅围。数披其木，毋使木枝外拒；木枝外拒，将逼主处。数披其木，毋使枝大本小；枝大本小，将不胜春风，不胜春风，枝将害心。公子既众，宗室忧吟。止之之道，数披其木，毋使枝茂。木数披，党与乃离。掘

---

42 *Liji jijie*, 23.618 ("Li yun")

43 *Han Feizi jishi* 韩非子集释. Edited by Chen Qiyou 陈奇猷 (Gaoxiong: Fuwen Press 复文出版社, 1991), 2.124 ("Yang quan"); for another example see *Han Feizi jishi*, 7.442 (ten men planting trees that are easy to grow cannot overcome one person pulling them out; it is harder to plant them than to pull them out).

其根本，木乃不神。

Nowhere is the weeding metaphor used more famously than at the notorious banquet where Liu Zhang 刘章 (Marquis of Zhuxu朱虚侯) uses "a ploughing song" (耕田歌) to direct criticism at Empress Lü. The scene is reminiscent of encounters between snooty officials and the humble-yet-insightful peasant. The empress laughs and sneers, "Only your father knew anything about working the fields, you were born a prince, how can you know anything about fields (安知田乎)?" "I know a little," counters Liu Zhang. "Then try telling me about the fields," challenges the empress. Next Zhang leaves the empress wordless by reciting a *de facto* political song to the tune that all growth that is extraneous and not born from the crop (i.e. the Lü scions) should be weeded out:

Deep we plough and thick we sow the seed
In setting out the little plants we want them to have room to grow.
Whatever comes up that is not from our seed,
We hoe it out and throw it away![44]

深耕概种，立苗欲疏，非其种者，锄而去之。

The term "deep plowing" (*shengeng*深耕) (together with weeding thoroughly) is first attested in *Mencius* 1A.5 where it is presented as part of good government.[45] "To deepen one's plowing" (*shen qi geng*深其耕) and harrowing thoroughly are used similarly in the context of governing people in the *Zhuangzi*.[46] "Deep plowing" almost never occurs in a technical context.[47] There has been

---

44 *Hanshu*, 38.1991; *Shiji*史记 (Beijing: Zhonghua Book Company, 1959), 52.2000–2001.

45 "With a territory of no more than one hundred *li*里, one can become a true king. If the king bestows humane government on the people, reduces punishments, and lightens taxes, causing the plowing to be deep and the weeding thorough, the strong will be able to use their leisure time to cultivate filiality and brotherliness." (Cf. Bloom, p. 5).

46 *Zhuangzi jishi*, 25.897 ("Ze yang"); cf. Mair, *Wandering*, pp. 259–260.

47 In fact, aside from later references to the banquet story, it is very rare. In one *Guanzi* passage, it occurs as one of the tasks of the totally dedicated farmer. See *Guanzi jiaozhu*, 8:20.401 ("Xiao kuang"). It is not until the *Qimin yaoshu* that the term occurs outside the context of Mencius or Liu Zhang's banquet song (in the context of planting beans, but twice only).

no shortage of discussion of the term and the contested origins of the plough by historians of agriculture. However they are missing an important point: the use of the term is primarily political, hence its power in Liu Zhang's ditty. The subversive power of the agricultural metaphor works both at a linguistic level (the imagery itself) and in the social setting in which it is cast: why should royals, after all, lower themselves to the level of the peasant to communicate.

"Planting (zhong种, shu树) people" appears as a metaphor for the proper use of human talent:

> If you plant wheat, you harvest wheat, and if you plant millet, you harvest millet. There is no one who thinks that is strange. Using people also involves something like planting: not paying proper attention to "planting" and yet praying that the people will be properly used, there can be no greater delusion than this.[48]

> 夫种麦而得麦，种稷而得稷，人不怪也。用民亦有种，不审其种，而祈民之用，惑莫大焉。

The message here is that if you deploy your own kind (seed people), you will get better results. Subtle shifts in the use of vocabulary can appear intentional. In the following example from the "Quan xiu" 权修 chapter in the *Guanzi*, Master Guan emphasizes several times the need to put agriculture as a basic profession at the heart of good government. He then argues that planting people (shuren树人) delivers the best economic return:

> When planning for one year, there is nothing better than planting grain.

---

48 *Lüshi chunqiu jiaoshi*, 19.1270 ("Yong min"). For a similar statement see *Hanshi waizhuan jishi*韩诗外传集释. Attributed to Han Ying 韩婴 (fl. 150 BCE), annotated by Xu Weiyu许维遹 (Beijing: Zhonghua Book Company, 1980), 7.20; tr. James R. Hightower, *Hanshi waizhuan: Han Ying's Illustrations of the Didactic Application of the Classic of Songs* (Cambridge, Mass: Harvard University Press, 1974), p. 244, "If you plant peach and pear trees in the spring, in summer you will have shade beneath them and in autumn you will be able to eat their fruit. If you plant caltrop in the spring, in summer you will not be able to gather its leaves, and in autumn you get thorns from it. If you look at it this way, it depends on what you plant. *Now those you planted were not the right men. Truly, the superior man first makes a selection before he plants the seed.*"

When planning for ten years there is nothing better than planting trees. When planning for a lifetime, there is nothing better than planting men. Grain is something that is planted once and only produces a single harvest. Trees are things that are planted once but may produce ten harvests. Human beings are things that are planted once but may produce a hundred harvests. Having once planted them [or: 苟, if indeed I sow the seeds], spirit-like I make use of them. To undertake affairs as would the spirits, such is the gate to kingliness.[49]

一年之计莫如树谷；十年之计莫如树木；终身之计莫如树人。一树一获者谷也；一树十获者木也；一树百获者人也。我苟种之，如神用之。举事如神，唯王之门。

Two interesting issues are at work in this passage. The first six parallel phrases provide the planting analogy in terms of quasi-economic return. Then the verb shifts from *shu*树 to *zhong*种. Was the author merely chasing rhyme (*tsyowngH, yowngH*), or is there also a semantic shift implied: from planting trees to sowing the seeds of something that generates greater potential, which, in turn, leads to the "spirit-like" deployment of the people? This would also correspond to the lexical difference between *shu*树 and *zhong*种: the former is explained in the *Shuowen jiezi*说文解字 as a general term for living plants; the latter as a process of sowing something first with a view that it will ripen later.[50]

Another widely used image is that of soil as a potential facilitator of growth.[51] The following example in the *Lunheng* contains a description of procedure that is as interesting as the intellectual point it makes:

Fertility or sterility constitutes the original nature (本性) of the soil. If the soil is rich and moist, its nature is good/beautiful, and the planted

---

49 *Guanzi jiaozhu*, 1:3.55 ("Quan xiu"); cf. Rickett, vol. 1, p. 96.

50 *Shuowen jiezi zhu*说文解字注. Compiled by Xu Shen 许慎 (58—147 CE) (Shanghai: Shanghai Ancient Books Press上海古籍出版社, 1983), 6A.21 for *shu* (木生植之总名), versus 7A.39b for *zhong* (先种后熟也).

51 See e.g. *Lüshi chunqiu jiaoshi*, 6.335 ("Yin chu"); *Huainanzi*, 17.572 ("Shuilin").

crops will be exuberant. If it is barren and stony, its nature is bad. However, if one adduces human effort such as deep ploughing, thorough tilling, and a generous use of manure in order to increase the soil's power,[52] its crops will become like that of rich and well-watered fields. Such is also the case with the elevation of the land. If you fill up low ground with earth, dug out by means of hoes and spades, the low land will be on a level with the high one. If you continue adding dug up soil, not only will the low land be on a level, it will in turn become higher than the high ground. The high ground will then revert to becoming the low one. Let us suppose that human nature is partly good and partly bad just as the land may be either high or low. By making an effort to adduce the good effects of education to it, goodness can be spread and generalized. If one is good at reforming (i.e. "transforming the moisture content" 化渥) and perseveres (literally "brews" *niang*酿) with education, people will change and become still better. Goodness will increase and reach a still higher standard than it had before, just as low ground, filled up with hoes and spades, rises higher than the originally elevated ground.[53]

　　夫肥沃墝埆，土地之本性也。肥而沃者性美，树稼丰茂；而墝者性恶，深耕细锄，厚加粪壤，勉致人功，以助地力，其树稼与彼肥沃者相似类也。地之高下，亦如此焉。以镢锸凿地，以埤增下，则其下与高者齐。如复增镢锸，则夫下者不徒齐者也，反更为高，而其高者反为下。使人之性有善有恶，彼地有高有下，勉致其教令，之善则将善者同之矣。善以化渥，酿其教令，变更为善，善则且更宜反过于往善。犹下地增加镢锸，更崇于高地也。

The passage offers a discussion of human nature in an analogy with work-

---

52 A fragment attributed to Mencius (but not preserved in the transmitted text) uses the term "to fertilize the heart" (*fenxin*粪心). See *Shuoyuan jiaozheng*说苑校证. Edited by Xiang Zonglu向宗鲁 (Beijing: Zhonghua Book Company, 1987), 3.66–67 ("Jian ben").

53 *Lunheng jiaoshi*, 2.73–74 ("Shuai xing") .

ing the soil (note again the use of the term "deep ploughing"). Humans can emulate their teachers; social mobility is possible through education just as low lands can be made to be higher than their originally surrounding highlands by heaping them up. In this example the description of how to work the soil is longer than the actual analogy with human nature itself. It has information value at the surface level (terms for soil quality, moisture levels), but it also plays on ideas that are social-political. In this case, there is an inference that, like human nature, soil can be "good" (善) or "bad" (恶). Similar terms occur as descriptors for fertile or barren fields elsewhere.[54] Furthermore, the analogy exploits a theme that had become recurrent by Han times, namely, the idea that soil (i.e. biotope) shapes the character and temperament of those who inhabit or work it.[55] In the *Lunheng* example, transforming bad fields into good fields is presented as a process of moral transformation.

The Granary

The granary (*qun* 囷, *cang* 仓, *lin* 廩, *jing* 京) covers several semantic fields: it is a receptacle and storage facility for the harvest and, as such, it gathers and collects. It also functions as the engine for distribution and circulation (dispensing salaries in grain or grain as food supplies, or supplying seeds for sowing). In its function as a storage facility of seeds or seed material, it represents an entity, unit, container, vessel, or enclosure that preserves things in a state before diversification, germination, growth and development. Several granary-themed analogies make this point. Just as crops are produced in the fields and stored in granaries, sages pay attention to where things are born so that they know where

---

54 E.g. *Shangjunshu zhuizhi* 商君书锥指. Edited by Jiang Lihong 蒋礼鸿 (Beijing: Zhonghua Book Company, 1996), IV.15: 86–87 ("Lai min" 徕民), where the terms are *liang* 良 and *e* 恶; cf. Yuri Pines, *The Book of Lord Shang: Apologetics of State Power in Early China* (New York: Columbia University Press, 2017), 200 (15.1). See also Ma Zongshen 马宗申, *Shangjunshu lun nongzheng sipian zhushi* 商君书论农政四篇注释 (Beijing: China Agriculture Press, 1985), p.44.

55 See e.g. *Huainanzi*, 4.140–141 ("Di xing"); *Yanzi chunqiu*, 2.6.10 (cf. Milburn, p. 350). See also the discussion in Roel Sterckx, *The Animal and the Daemon in Early China* (Albany: State University of New York Press, 2002), pp. 101–110.

things will end up.[56] Inexhaustible granaries and treasuries are stock images for sage rule.[57] Filling a warehouse without planting or harvesting is contrary to the Way.[58] Granaries also appear in medical analogies.[59]

A striking image is that of the granary as a storage space of things in their germinal stage. In a passage in the "Guan" 观 Section of the Mawangdui *Jing*经 (the Canon) the Yellow Emperor, in what is a fragmentary sentence, speaks of things possibly amassing or grouping together (*qunqun*群群) to make a single *qun* 囷 "round granary", out of which all things (*yin* and *yang*, the seasons, etc.) are then differentiated.[60] The Mawangdui "Dao fa" 道法 section contains another occurrence of the granary. There it possibly symbolises a realm of undifferentiated stuff awaiting weights and measures to be identified and uncovered:

> Affairs are like straight trees and are as numerous as grains in a granary.
> When the *dou* and *shi* measures have been provided, and the *chi* and *cun*

---

56 *Huainanzi*, 20.694 ("Tai zu"; tr. Major, 835): "Water emerges from the mountains but flows into the sea. Crops are born in the fields but are stored in the granaries. Sages, by seeing where things are born, know where they will end up."

57 For example, the image of the granary and the treasury are invoked in a description of the methods of the sage in the *Wenzi shuyi*文子疏义, edited by Wang Liqi王利器 (Beijing: Zhonghua Book Company, 2000), 2. 104 ("Jing cheng" 精诚): 圣人之法，始于不可见，终于不可及，处于不倾之地，积于不尽之仓，载于不竭之府。

58 *Huainanzi*, 17.575 ("Shuilin"; tr. Major, 691).

59 *Huangdi neijing suwen*黄帝内经素问 (Chapter 8), notes that "the spleen and the stomach are the officials responsible for grain storage; the five flavours originate from them." The spleen and stomach are the organs that hold the five grains, as Wang Bing 王冰 (ca. 672 CE) suggests. Elsewhere ("Suwen", Chapter 17) we read that "When the granaries do not [keep what they] store, in this case the doors are not under control." Commentators note that the granaries here refer to the spleen and stomach, whereas the doors refer to the anus and tight. The stomach stores up and the spleen circulates. For the image of the stomach and spleen as storage depot of grain, see "Suwen", Chapter 9.

60 The reference to a *qun* (a round-shaped granary) here could be inspired by a phonetic pun with *qun* 群, but the sentence lacks six characters in-between. There are fewer textual references to (round) *qun*囷 type granaries in comparison with the *cang*仓 or *lin*廪 (or the square*jing*京). Yet we know that *qun* were used as the supply station for seed material at the beginning of the agricultural season. As such it appears for instance in a ritual prayer dedicated to Xian Nong先农 (First Tiller) in the recipe miscellany in tomb No. 30 at Zhoujiatai周家台 (Hubei) (ca. 210 BCE). There the *qun* is clearly the granary containing seeds for planting, and the place for a sacrifice to Xian Nong prior to and after village participants go to "set out the seeds" (*chu zhong*出种). See Hubei sheng Jingzhoushi Zhou Liangyuqiaoyizhibowuguan, *Guanju Qin Han jiandu*关沮秦汉简牍 (Beijing: Zhonghua Book Company, 2001), p. 132 (slips pp. 347–353).

rules have been arranged, then no item will escape its true spirit.[61]

事如直木，多如仓粟，斗石已具，尺寸以陈，则无所逃其神．

Again we have the image of a forest of trees and a granary full of grains, the true value or "essence" of which can only be measured by means of weights and measures. A similar use of imagery occurs in the *Heguanzi*鹖冠子, where the granary (and forest) refers to a state of indifference, the essence of which needs to be uncovered by measurement and good judgement.

> If one uses Heaven's laws of calculus, one is not few, and a myriad does not make up great quantity. Things can be as similar as trees in a forest or as packed up together as grains in a granary, but it is with the *dou* and *shi* measures that we can set them out in detail and *sheng* and *wei* measures would not lose out on any of them.[62]

> 天度数之而行，在一不少，在万不众；同如林木，积如仓粟，斗石以陈，升委无失也。

Similar to the granary as a container storing things before they reach a germinal stage is the image of the circular animal pen, or *juan*圈. In an entry in the *Shiming*释名, *qun*囷 is glossed as *quan*绻, "to be bound up."[63] The animal pen also appears as an image for containing or fencing off entities in a state of in-differentiation. An example occurs in a line from the *Huainanzi* where it is stated that "when viewed from the perspective of their similarities, the ten thousand things are in one single pen (自其同者视之，万物一圈也)."[64] Further down in the same passage a similar idea emerges:

---

61 See Robin D.S. Yates, *Five Lost Classics* (New York: Ballantine Books, 1997), p. 53.

62 *Heguanzi huijiao jizhu*鹖冠子汇校集注. Edited by Huang Huaixin黄怀信 (Beijing: Zhonghua Book Company, 2004), 9.218 ("Wang fu" 王鈇).

63 See *Shiming shuzheng bu*释名疏证补. Compiled by Liu Xi 刘熙 (d. ca. 219 CE), annotated by Wang Xianqian王先谦 (1842—1917) (Beijing: Zhonghua Book Company, 2008), 17.193 (No. 71).

64 *Huainanzi*, 2.55 ("Chu zhen"); tr. Major, p. 93: "the myriad things are a single set."

Now, alike with centipedes and worms, we (humans) mount the Heavenly Mechanism, and we receive our form as part of one set [of living things; in the same "penning"], but it is the things that fly and are light and that are tiny and minute that find [their form] sufficient to escape with their lives. How much more is this so for that which has no category![65]

夫与蚊蟯同乘天机，夫受形于一圈，飞轻微细者，犹足以
脱其命，又况未有类也！

And yet another passage uses *juan* in the sense of "encircling" or "cornering off," "therefore what exists is born from what does not exist, the full emerges out of the empty, if all under Heaven is encircled by it (the world sets up 'pens' for them), names and realities will exist at the same time (是故有生于无，实出于虚，天下为之圈，则名实同居)."[66]

Granaries and animal pens are much attested as burial goods (*mingqi*明器) in Han tombs, where they are usually explained as items that provide sustenance for the afterlife, or supplies for post-mortem sacrifices. Yet, if we think of the tomb as a dark realm of increasingly undifferentiated identity, a world slipping away from the living but containing within itself the seeds for ever-lasting life, could these granary models impart onto the death the wish to "germinate" in perpetuity in the afterlife? Might they represent a wish for continuity, or even for the renewal of life, "setting out the seeds" for the next life? Perhaps one can conceive of tomb occupants as seeds stored away in the dark interior of a granary, sheltered from light until they are exposed again to the potential for germinating life.

Transmission of Knowledge

Peasants acquire their skills through practice. Yet the world of the agronomic manual (*nongshu*农书) is mostly a tool of officialdom (and later on, the landed gentry and literati). Technical texts rarely explain how agronomic

---

65 *Huainanzi*, 2.58 ("Chu zhen"); tr. Major, p. 95.
66 *Huainanzi*, 1.29 ("Yuan dao"); tr. Major, pp. 64–65.

knowledge is passed on (except by quoting from other texts, or attributing sayings to figures such as Shennong). To get closer to what peasant life might have entailed, it is the anecdote, analogy, image or lyrical text contained in poems and songs that can be more revealing.[67] In the fields, knowledge was transmitted in a performative way. One example is a rhymed passage describing the "Grand Method of Plowing" (耕之大方) in the *Lüshi chunqiu*.[68] End rhyme and word-play (final characters repeat at the start of the next line) indicate that pieces such as this may have been didactic, possibly a song or ditty farmers knew, or a piece they could intone while working the fields:

Strong soils need weakening,	力者欲柔
Weak soils need strengthening;	柔者欲力
Fallow soils need working,	息者欲劳
Overworked soils need fallowing;	劳者欲息
Lean soils need fattening,	棘者欲肥
over-fat soils leaning;	肥者欲棘
Compacted soils need loosening,	急者欲缓
Loose soils compacting;	缓者欲急
Waterlogged soils need drying out,	湿者欲燥
Parched soils moistening.	燥者欲湿

There are other contexts in which agronomic knowledge transferred to other domains of life and vice versa. Analogies that juxtapose military weaponry with agricultural tools suggest that the battlefield may have been one. Several texts make the point that working the fields and waging battle are transferrable skills. As one passage in the *Guanzi* states: "Repair agricultural tools as though it were making war. Push and pull grubbing tools or hoes as though they

---

[67] Even Jia Sixie admits that much in his preface to the *Qimin yaoshu* 齐民要求: "Now I have collated materials from classics and commentaries all the way to songs and ditties. I have checked these with old farming hands and verified them with my own practice."(今采捃经传，爰及歌谣，询之老成，验之行事) See Miao Qiyu缪启愉, *Qimin yaoshu jiaoshi* (Beijing: China Agriculture Press, 1982), p. 18 .

[68] *Lüshichunqiu jiaoshi*，26.1731 ("Ren di"); cf. John Knoblock and Jeffrey Riegel, *The Annals of Lü Buwei. A Complete Translation and Study* (Stanford: Stanford University Press, 2000), p. 655.

were swords and halberds. Put on rain hats as though they were shields.'[69] Once familiar with agriculture, people will become skilled at war (and vice versa). In the
example from the *liutao*六韬 below, agriculture is presented as warfare with
the soil: hoes are spears; spades, axes, saws, mortars, and pestles are tools for
attacking walls; units of five people in the fields and villages create the bond that
ties men together on the battlefield. The passage contains a dozen or so technical terms for agricultural tools and techniques: some are explained through the
analogy with a weapon; some the other way round.

> The implements for offense and defence are fully found in human activity.
> Digging sticks serve as chevaux-de-frise and caltrops. Oxen and horse-
> pulled wagons can be used in the encampment and as covering shields.
> The different hoes can be used as spears and spear-tipped halberds. Rain-
> coats of straw and large umbrellas serve as armour and protective shields.
> Large hoes, spades, axes, saws, mortars, and pestles are tools for attack-
> ing walls. Oxen and horses are a means to transport provisions. Chickens
> and dogs serve as lookouts. The cloth that women weave serves as flags
> and pennants. The method that the men use for levelling the fields is the
> same for attacking walls. The skill needed in spring to cut down grass and
> thickets is the same as needed for fighting against chariots and cavalry. The
> weeding methods used in summer are the same as used in battle against foot
> soldiers. The grain harvested and the firewood cut in fall will be provisions for
> the military. In winter well-filled granaries and storehouses will ensure a solid
> defence. The units of five found in the fields and villages will provide the tal-
> lies and good faith that bind men together. The villages have officials and the
> offices have chiefs who can lead the army. The villages have walls surround-
> ing them that are not crossed; they provide the basis for the division into pla-
> toons. The transportation of grain and the cutting of hay provides for the state
> storehouses and armories. The skills used in repairing the inner and outer
> walls in spring and fall, in maintaining the moats and the channels, are used
> to build ramparts and fortifications. Thus the tools for employing the military

---

69 *Guanzi jiaozhu*, XVII.53: 1016 ("Jin cang" 禁藏); tr. Rickett, vol. 2, 220. The final "Qing zhong"
   Chapter ends with similar martial imagery. See *Guanzi jiaozhu*, XXIV.85: 1540 ("Qing zhong, ji"
   己); cf. Rickett, vol. 2, p. 516.

are completely found in ordinary human activity. One who is good at governing a state will take them from ordinary human affairs. Then they must be made to accord with the good management of the six animals; the opening up of wild lands; and the settling of people where they dwell. The husband has a number of acres that he farms, the wife a measured amount of material to weave—this is the way to enrich the state and strengthen the army.[70]

The analogy taps into two spheres of knowledge, warfare and agriculture. But this passage can also be read beyond the analogy. It may hint at ways in which military and farming knowledge were communicated. One can envisage a scene in which farmers, demobilised from war, are instructed how to handle tools and work in units based on their experience of the battle field, or a scene of soldier-recruits being told how to handle weapons and look out for each other based on what they are familiar with on the fields during peace time. Here agronomic techniques translate into military affairs.

Conclusion: Looking Beyond the Metaphor

To be sure, in selecting the examples above, I am not arguing that farmers learnt from philosophers, ritualists, and pundits. It is the masters of philosophy, the ritualists, and (in our final example) the military strategists who draw on agricultural information to make their point. Here a parallel can be drawn between the Chinese textual landscape and the general dearth of technically-intended illustrations in pre-modern China: both texts and images operate at a figurative level; they are mostly about ideology, symbolism and moral themes. As Peter Golas points out:

Paintings of farming practices…could be intended in the first instance to symbolize a well-ordered society under the benevolent rule of the emperor, or to encourage officials to carry out their responsibilities for

---

70 *Tai Gong liutao jinzhu jinyi* 太公六韬今注今译. Annotated by Xu Peigen 徐培根 (Taipei: "Commercial Press" 台湾商务印书馆, 1993), 30.138–139 ("Nong qi"); tr. Ralph Sawyer, *The Six Secret Teachings on the Way of Strategy* (Boston & London: Shambala, 1995), pp. 112–113.

the welfare of the hardworking people under their jurisdiction, or perhaps to serve as a warning that all was not well in the countryside. For the most part the viewers of these images would have little or no particular interest in the technology portrayed.[71]

Nevertheless, figurative language can be instructive as a guide on "how to do" farming, even if this is unintended. The agronomic information that makes up many of the metaphors and analogies through which early Chinese thinkers conveyed their views amounts to a sourcebook as rich as any technical manual from this period. In one way or another, figurative language intends to be didactic. The agronomic information embedded in it travels and circulates together with the (more abstract) ideas it helps convey. It is also in these analogies and metaphors that the sensory and physical engagement with land, tools, and crops comes to bear more eloquently than it does in dry and prescriptive "technical" literature. This then is perhaps where philosophy and technology meet: it does not matter whether the philosopher looks at bamboo as bamboo; what is important is how much detail he imparts in his description of bamboo to make his point. If the force of argument depends on the choice of imagery, what is described must be recognized. A more systematic inquiry might be able to chart the range and volume of agricultural metaphors out over time, and link them more closely to socio-economic and technical developments. For now I hope to have shown that figural language helps us understand how agriculture figured in Chinese thought and practice, even if that was not necessarily the intended purpose of those who devised the imagery to make their particular arguments.

---

71 Peter J. Golas, *Picturing Technology in China: From Earliest Times to the Nineteenth Century* (Hong Kong: Hong Kong University Press, 2015), xx.; cf. p.12: "The technology portrayed in the farming paintings tended to be there as a by-product, the focus of which was mainly on the people doing the work and the conditions in which they worked rather than on exactly how the work was done. And given that the paintings often represented the perspective of the elite, there were strong tendencies even in the genre paintings to idealize peasant life while at the same time regarding the peasants as curiosities, sometimes not so far different from the way barbarians were viewed."

CONFUCIUS RECONSIDERED: A SOCIO-HISTORICAL READING OF THE *LUNYU**

Kai Vogelsang 冯凯

(University of Hamburg)

The Dead Ends of *Lunyu* Scholarship

The *Lunyu* is one of the most extensively studied books in world history. Over a period of more than 2000 years, scholars have produced an enormous amount of commentaries on the book. Every one of its 16,000 characters has been glossed over and over, and every one of its 500 paragraphs has been interpreted to and fro. Onto this mountain of traditional Chinese and Japanese scholarship, Western scholars have piled further heaps of studies, commentaries, and translations.[1]

Yet despite this overwhelming amount of scholarship, our understanding of the *Lunyu* is astonishingly vague. There still is no critical edition of the text; unresolved problems concerning the dating, structure, authenticity, and transmission of the *Lunyu* are legion;[2] and many questions surrounding Confucius, his times and his connection to the *Lunyu* remain unanswered. In fact, recent scholarship has shown a tendency to *de-contextualize* the *Lunyu* in diverse ways.

---

* This is an updated and expanded version of an article first published in *Oriens Extremus* 49 (2010).

1 For works up to 1998, cf. Joel Sahleen's bibliography in Bryan W. van Norden, *Confucius and the Analects: New Essays*, pp. 303–320. For the most recent scholarship, cf. Michael Hunter and Martin Kern (eds.), *The Analects Revisited: New Perspectives on the Dating of a Classic* (Leiden: Brill, 2018 [forthcoming]) .

2 For problems of text criticism, cf. Wojciech Jan Simson, *Die Geschichte der Aussprüche des Konfuzius (Lunyu)* (Bern et al.: Peter Lang, 2006).

On the one hand, the *Lunyu* is taken as *timeless* wisdom which may be applied to present circumstances or interpreted in very personal ways.[3] On the other hand, the *Lunyu* is treated as a book, which was compiled in Han times and therefore cannot serve as a source for pre-Qin thought.[4] In addition to this historical displacement, the *Lunyu* has also been de-contextualized in a disciplinary way. *Lunyu* studies have largely become the prerogative of philologists who naturally focus on questions concerning textual details, compilation and transmission. Legitimate though these studies may be, they have sidelined sociologically or anthropologically informed approaches that may serve to interpret the *Lunyu* in a socio-historical context.

The present article will attempt to do just that. Leaving philological niceties aside for the moment, it will—naively, perhaps—take the *Lunyu* as a source for Confucius' life and teachings. In doing so, it treats Confucius not as an historical personality but as a *symbol* for social developments that took place in the 6th to 3rd centuries BC.[5] The question, then, is: What kind of society was this? What were the historical circumstances that gave rise to Confucius' teachings, and what were the social preconditions that made them plausible? Why is it that "since the beginning of mankind there had never been a Confucius,"[6] and that suddenly, 551—479 BC, there was one?

Fundamental though these questions may be, they have not been dealt with in a scholarly manner. Modern scholarship, instead of providing an answer based on academic research, has largely contented itself with a pre-scholarly narrative, which may be traced back to *Mengzi*:

---

3 For some examples, cf. Li Zehou李泽厚, *Lunyu jindu*论语今读 (Hefei: Anhui Literature and Art Publishing House安徽文艺出版社, 1998), Li Ling李零, *Sangjiagou: Wo du* Lunyu 丧家狗：我读《论语》 (Taiyuan: Shanxi People's Publishing House山西人民出版社, 2007), and Ni Peimin, *Understanding the Analects of Confucius: A New Translation of* Lunyu *with Annotations* (Albany: SUNY, 2017).

4 Cf. Michael Hunter, *Confucius Beyond the Analects* (Leiden: Brill, 2017) and Michael Hunter and Martin Kern (eds.), *The Analects Revisited: New Perspectives on the Dating of a Classic*.

5 After all, there exists no contemporary evidence for the life of Confucius, much less for the feats of administration, education and scholarship that his biography recounts. All we have are accounts that postdate his presumed life time by centuries, making Confucius no more tangible as an historical personality than, say, Laozi.

6 *Mengzi zhengyi*孟子正义 (ed. by Jiao Xun焦循, 2 vols. Beijing: Zhonghua Book Company中华书局, 1998), 2A2, p. 216: 自有生民以来，未有孔子也。

The world was in decay, and the principle was reduced to insignificance; blasphemy and violence were rife. There were cases of ministers murdering their rulers and of sons murdering their fathers. Confucius felt troubled and created the Chunqiu.[7]

The *Shiji* transmitted a very similar version of the story,[8] and Zhu Xi gave it the final seal of approval in his preface to the *Daxue*:

When the Zhou were in decay, wise and sagely rulers no longer appeared, the administration of schools was no longer provided for, the effects of teaching were obliterated, and manners and customs were spoilt—that very time saw Confucius in his sageness. Not having obtained the position of a ruler or instructor in order to carry out his politics and teachings, he simply adopted the methods of the former kings, and recited and transmitted them, thereby instructing later times.[9]

Thus the question was put to rest. Ever since, it has been understood that Confucius' efforts were a reaction to times of decay and disorder. Virtually all sinological scholarship still implicitly or explicitly follows the *Mengzi* by contextualizing Confucius in an age of "moral decadence and political unrest," "marked by the decay of the central power of the house of the Zhou kings," [10]

---

7 *Mengzi zhengyi* 3B9, p.452: 世衰道微，邪说暴行有作，臣弑其君者有之，子弑其父者有之，孔子惧，作春秋。

8 *Shiji* 史记 (By Sima Qian 司马迁, et al. Beijing: Zhonghua Book Company 中华书局, 1997), 47, p.1935: 孔子之时，周室微而礼乐废，诗书缺。追迹三代之礼，序书传，上纪唐虞之际，下至秦缪，编次其事。

9 *Sishu zhangju jizhu* 四书章句集注 (ed. By Zhu Xi 朱熹, Beijing: Zhonghua Book Company, 2003), pp. 1–2: 及周之衰，贤圣之君不作，学校之政不修，教化陵夷，风俗颓败，时则有若孔子之圣，而不得君师之位以行其政教，于是独取先王之法；诵而传之以诏后世。

10 Peter J. Opitz, "Confucius", in Silke Krieger and Rolf Trauzettel (eds.), *Konfuzianismus und die Modernisierung Chinas* (Mainz: v. Hase& Koehler, 1990), p. 518; Hans van Ess, *Der Konfuzianismus* (München: Beck, 2003), p.12. Cf. also Anne Cheng, *Histoire de la penséechinoise* (Paris: Editions du Seuil, 1997), p. 54 ; Jacques Sancery, *Confucius* (Paris: Les éditions du cerf, 2009), pp.11–12, Gu Xuewu, *Konfuzius zur Einführung* (Hamburg: Junius Verlag, 1999), pp. 22–23; Benjamin I. Schwartz, *The World of Thought in Ancient China* (Cambridge, MA: The Belknap Press, 1985), pp. 56–57, and many more.

and by "a chaos of civil and interstate wars."

Of the more than one hundred states and city-states that once had submitted to the scion of the Zhou as overlord, a mere forty had survived—each virtually independent and all at war or on the brink of war with their neighbors. Over the course of the previous two and a half centuries, thirty-six rulers had been assassinated and fifty-two domains brutally conquered. Alliances were formed only to be broken; renegotiated only to be violated. The courts of each state had become playgrounds for would-be traitors. As the fortunes of powerful households waxed or waned, factions moved quickly to betray actual and suspected enemies. To an aspiring statesman like Kongzi, such turbulent conditions represented both an opportunity and a nightmare.[11]

From this perspective, it seems all too plausible that Confucius wanted to *restore* the ideal order of the early Zhou kings which had crumbled in the preceding centuries.[12] Indeed, traditional as well as modern scholars have argued that Confucius did not teach anything fundamentally new.[13] Does not the *Lunyu* testify that Confucius "transmitted without creating," and that he "followed Zhou" in his teachings?[14] And does not the canonical *Shujing* testify to the wise institutions of the first Zhou rulers?

According to this narrative, everything falls nicely into place. For all remaining questions as to why exactly Confucius came up with his teachings, there was a simple answer: he was a sage, a *shengren*圣人. After all, Heaven used Confucius "as a bell with its wooden tongue" and "gave him free reign to approach

---

11 Michael Nylan and Thomas Wilson, *Lives of Confucius: Civilization's Greatest Sage Through the Ages* (New York: Doubleday, 2010), p. 1.

12 This is strongly emphasized by Tu Weiming, "Confucius and Confucianism", in *The New Encyclopædia Britannica*. 15th ed. Chicago. Vol. 16, 1994, p. 653, who asserts that "the story of Confucianism does not begin with Confucius." Cf. also Tu Weiming's paper in this volume.

13 Cf., for example, David Shepherd Nivison, "The Classical Philosophical Writings", in *The Cambridge History of Ancient China: From the Origins of Civilization to 221 B.C.* Anne Cheng, *Histoire de la penseechinoise* (Cambridge: Cambridge University Press, 1999), p. 754: "Did Confucius, the first philosopher, have a philosophy featuring new ideas of his own? It is not easy to find any."

14 *Lunyu zhengyi* (henceforth: *Lunyu*) 论语正义 (ed. by Liu Baonan 刘宝楠, 2 vols., Beijing: Zhonghua Book Company, 1998), 7.1, p. 251: 子曰："述而不作，信而好古，窃比于我老彭。" (Note the contradiction to the statement of the *Mengzi* [above, fn. 7] that Confucius *created* the *Chunqiu*.) 3.14, p.103: 子曰："周监于二代，郁郁乎文哉！吾从周。"

sagedom"; indeed "being humane and wise, the master is certainly a sage."[15] As such, he is "beyond good or evil, endowed with inborn intuition and cosmic-magical powers." [16] Possessed of perennial wisdom, he is beyond historical change and unmoved by social influences, his teachings are timeless. "A sage understands the Heavenly principles," states the *Wuxingpian*,[17] and the *Bohu tong* is even more explicit about the consonance between a sage and Heaven:

> What is a sage? Sageness implies penetration, principle, and resonance. There is nothing that his principle does not penetrate, nothing that his brilliance does not illuminate; upon hearing their resonance, he knows the nature (of things); he shares the virtue of heaven and earth, he shares the brilliance of sun and moon, he shares the order of the four seasons, and he shares the fortunes of ghosts and spirits. ...The reason why (sages) have such unique perception and foresight and why they join the spirits in penetrating nature is that they are all begotten by Heaven.[18]

In other words, "sage" is a God-term. An unmoved mover, a sage is the first cause of things and the last resort of reasoning.[19] The function of a God-term is to terminate a logical *regressus ad infinitum* by giving the ultimate answer

---

15 *Lunyu* 3.24, p.133: 天将以夫子为木铎。9.6, p. 329: 子贡曰："固天纵之将圣，又多能也。" *Mengzi zhengyi* 2A2, p. 213: 子贡曰："学不厌，智也。教不倦，仁也。仁且智，夫子既圣矣。" Note that these are the words of his disciples. Confucius himself modestly declined such an appellation (*Lunyu* 7.26, p. 274; 7.34, p. 282), although he did consider himself endowed with Heavenly virtue (7.23, p. 273; cf. also 9.5, p. 327).

16 Rolf. Trauzettel, "Grundsätzlicheszuraltk on fuzianischen Morallehre", in Reinhard Emmerich and Hans Stumpfeldt (eds.), *Und folge nun dem, was meinHerzbegehrt. Festschrift für Ulrich Unger zum 70. Geburtstag* (Hamburg: Hamburger Sinologische Gesellschaft, 2002), p.145.

17 *Wuxingpian* 五行篇 (in *Mawangdui hanmu boshu* 马王堆汉墓帛书, vol. 1, Beijing: Cultural Relics Press 文物出版社, 1980), line 197: 圣人知而[天]道。知而行之，圣也。

18 *Bohu tong shuzheng* 白虎通疏证 (ed. by Chen Li 陈立, Beijing: Zhonghua Book Company, 1997), 7, p. 334 and p. 341: 圣人者何？圣者，通也，道也，声也。道无所不通，明无所不照，闻声知情，与天地合德，日月合明，四时合序，鬼神合吉凶。……圣人所以能独见前睹，与神通精者，盖皆天所生也。The connection of sageness with "resonance" (*sheng*) seems to relate to the fact that the words "sage," "sound/resonance," and "hear" anciently could be written with the same character, hence thought to be related.

19 On the "sage" as a "limit-concept" in modern Confucian thought, cf. Thomas Fröhlich, *Tang Junyi: Confucian Philosophy and the Challenge of Modernity* (Leiden: Brill, 2017), esp. pp.130−137.

beyond which no more questions can be asked.[20] Questioning Confucius was out of the question.

Another factor that may have kept scholars from asking "why Confucius?" is the self-evident plausibility of his teachings. Benevolence, courteousness, truthfulness, the importance of learning: all this seems so obvious to us that there is no need to question its premises. Indeed, Confucius' teachings appear so commonplace that they have struck modern observers as banal truisms.[21]

But could Confucius have become so influential simply by teaching platitudes? Should "civilization's greatest sage" really have done no more than reinvigorate lessons of the past? And should the golden age of Chinese philosophy that began with Confucius really have coincided with altogether rotten times? Judging from the present state of scholarship, none of the above assumptions—namely, that Confucius lived in an age of decline, that he restored an old order, and that he was a sage who restored eternal truths—would seem to be acceptable without careful scrutiny.

In what follows, I will discuss the problems of these assumptions and then explore an alternative approach which rests on quite contrary premises: that Confucius lived in an age of growing social complexity, that he introduced

---

20 A moderated version of the "sage" narrative is the tendency to attribute Confucius' teachings to his *individual* characteristics. Cf. Michael Nylan's description of Confucius as "a self-absorbed, unlikable, and crabbed personality", "a sanctimonious and arrogant know-it-all" who only late in life became a "sage" (Michael Nylan and Thomas Wilson, *Lives of Confucius: Civilization's Greatest Sage Through the Ages*, pp. 2–4), or Bryan van Norden's speculation that "the early death of his father contributed to Confucius' strong traditionalism" (Bryan W. van Norden, *Confucius and the Analects: New Essays*, p.10). This "psychological" approach, too, ultimately locates the *movens* of history in the subjectivity of a great personality.

21 Cf., for example, Anne Cheng, *Histoire de la penséechinoise*, p. 55: "Au prime abord, sapensée apparaît plutô tterre a terre, son enseignement fait des truismes." Fung Yulan, *A History of Chinese Philosophy*. Trans. by Derk Bodde. 2 vols (Princeton: Princeton University Press, 1952), p. 48: "Thus looked at, Confucius would be nothing more than an old pedant." Herbert Fingarette, *Confucius: The Secular as Sacred* (Long Grove, IL: Waveland Press, 1998, 1st ed. 1972), vii: "When I began to read Confucius, I found him to be a prosaic and parochial moralizer; his collected sayings, the *Analects*, seemed to me an archaic irrelevance." For the "popular understanding of Confucius as a wise man, bearer of platitudes", cf. the Gary Larson cartoon reproduced in Lionel M. Jensen, *Manufacturing Confucianism: Chinese Traditions and Universal Civilization* (Durham, NC: Duke University, 1997), p. 6. For the historical background to these views, cf. Werner Lühmann, *Konfuzius: Aufgeklärter Philosoph oder reaktionärer Moralapostel?* (Wiesbaden: Harrassowitz, 2003).

something radically new, and that he was not a sage, but a regular member of society, a *enssociale*.[22] Subsequently, I will demonstrate how this approach could contribute to our understanding of the *Lunyu*.

A New Perspective

The view that Confucius lived in an age of decline would seem to be based on a narrowly *political* perspective of history, more specifically, on the perspective of the central government.[23] Only from this perspective does the loosening of central control—and the growth of regionalisms—appear as a deterioration of order. Viewed from a regional perspective, a wholly different picture would emerge. In fact, viewed from any other but the political perspective, the age of Confucius appears as a time of growth, progress, and upswing. The Chunqiu period saw the spread of iron technology, great advances in agriculture, rapid development of commerce and communication, the emergence of a monetary economy, the growth of cities, and a significant population increase. It marked the beginning of the classical age of Chinese philosophy. All this has little to do with decline, as Herbert Fingarette observed long ago:

> We, who look at the situation in the light of historical evidence, see that rather than a devolution from some great past civilization, an evolution toward a new and universalistic civilization was taking place. ... In short, what Confucius' idiom and imagery portray as the increasing chaos of a civilization in the course of degeneration was, in fact, the inevitable disorder attendant upon the evolution of a new, larger and greater single society out of various older, smaller, culturally separate and more primitive and provincial groups.[24]

---

22 And as such, a symbol of the society he lived in (cf. above).

23 This perspective, which implicitly underlies many sinological studies, is somewhat irritating. It seems to derive directly from official Chinese historiography which extols central order and orthodoxy to the exclusion of regional or alternative orders. Especially in view of Chinese history in the 20th century, the paradigm of the strong state appears less than comforting.

24 Herbert Fingarette, *Confucius: The Secular as Sacred*, pp. 60–61.

Confucius himself seems to have shown little concern with the political events of his age: in the *Lunyu*, there is hardly a character about wars and great states occupying small ones. Instead, Confucius' teachings were all about ordering *society*. In a telling passage,

> Duke Jing of Qi asked Confucius about government. Confucius replied, "Let the ruler be ruler, and the minister be minister; let the father be father, and the son be son." [25]

Although the duke appeared to be delighted by the answer, it is doubtful that he could have derived any political decision from it: whereas he asked about *government*, Confucius' answer was all about social order.[26] Perhaps even the translation of *zheng*政 as "government" misses the point, since for Confucius and his contemporaries there seems not to have been a clear notion of "government," "politics," or "state" as distinct from other social phenomena.[27] The less it seems apt to interpret his role with sole reference to political events.

Moreover, the idea of a golden age which Confucius aimed to restore appears less than convincing. True, the benevolent order of the early Zhou rulers is described in the *Shangshu*尚书, *Shiji*史记, and other ancient texts.[28] Modern scholarship has so far followed tradition in relying on these accounts. However, recent studies have cast doubts on this narrative. While the *Shiji* and other Zhanguo- or Han-texts could never be considered primary sources to begin

---

25 *Lunyu* 12.11, p. 499: 齐景公问政于孔子。孔子对曰："君君，臣臣，父父，子子。"

26 I owe this interpretation of *Lunyu* 12. 11 to Hans Stumpfeldt "Konfuzius und der Konfuzianismus I" (http://lecture2go.uni-hamburg.de/veranstaltungen/-/v/11598;jsessionid=456A40E4F229370AFA0 C021A8F15A293), 2010, retrieved March 2011, p.10. Cf. also Gu Xuewu, *Konfuzius zur Einführung*, p. 133, who notes that Confucius "knew no difference between state and society."

27 Certain passages of the *Lunyu* attest to a rather unsophisticated view of "government," which simply equates it with proper conduct: 政者，正也。子帅以正，孰敢不正？ (12.17, p. 505) 苟正其身矣，于从政乎何有？(13.13, p.531) The entire book does not convey political thought independent of moral precepts: politics, in the *Lunyu*, evidently has not emancipated itself from other considerations. Nor did this change in later Confucian thought: for the conflation of politics with morality and its 20th century critics, cf. Thomas Fröhlich's paper: "'Confucian Democracy' and Its Confucian Critics: Mou Zongsan and Tang Junyi on the Limits of Confucianism", in *Oriens Exremus* 49 (2010), pp. 167–200.

28 For an overview, cf. *Yishi*绎史 (ed. by Ma Su马骕, 4 vols. Beijing: Zhonghua Book Company), p.19, pp. 200–222, p. 346.

with, philological analyses have also called the value of the *Shangshu*尚书 as a primary source for early Zhou history into question.[29] With faith in these textual sources shaken, we are left with archaeological finds as the only reliable primary sources—and they do *not* seem to confirm the traditional narrative. Quite to the contrary, archaeologists relying on newly excavated material claim that the traditional view of early Zhou history "is in large part a historical fiction."[30] The archaeological record suggest that the ritual system idealized by Confucius and his followers did not come into existence at the beginning of the Zhou dynasty, as was believed until very recently. Instead, its principal features—systematic ranking of ancestors and of living lineage members and sacrifices of food in graded sets of vessels (with alcohol use conspicuously deemphasized)—took shape during a decisive reform in the mid-9th century BC ...[31]

Whatever the relationship of Confucius' teachings to the ritual system created in the 9th century "ritual reform," the view that he harked back to a putative ritual system of the early Western Zhou—11th and 10th centuriesBC, that is—seems no longer tenable. Instead, it appears that Confucius, in claiming to "follow Zhou," created the first *invented tradition* in Chinese history.[32] What he taught, was not old, but fundamentally new. Again, Fingarette pointed this out:

> We must begin by seeing Confucius as a great cultural innovator rather than as a genteel but stubbornly nostalgic apologist of the status quo ante. ... He talked in terms of restoring an ancient harmony; but the practical

29 Wolfgang Behr, "The Extent of Tonal Irregularity in Pre-Qin Inscriptional Rhyming", Unpublished paper, n.d. pp. 4–6; Vassilij M. Krjukov, *Teksti Ritual: Opyt Interpretatsii Drevnekitaiskoj Epigrafiki Epokhi In'-Chzhou*[*Text and Ritual: An Interpretive Essay on Ancient Chinese Epigraphy of the Yin-Zhou Epoch*] (Moscow: Pamiatniki Istoricheskoj Mysli, 2000); Laurent Sagart, *The Roots of Old Chinese* (Amsterdam/Philadelphia: John Benjamins, 1999), pp. 57–61; Kai Vogelsang, "Inscriptions and Proclamations: A Study of the 'gao' Chapters in the Book of Documents", in *Bulletin of the Museum of Far Eastern Antiquities* 74, 2002, pp.138–209.

30 Lothar von Falkenhausen, *Chinese* Society *in the Age of Confucius (1000—250 BC): The Archaeological Evidence* (Los Angeles: Cotsen Institute of Archaeology, 2006), p. 2.

31 Lothar von Falkenhausen, *Chinese* Society *in the Age of Confucius (1000—250 BC): The Archaeological Evidence*, pp. 154–156.

32 On the concept, cf. Eric Hobsbawm and Terence Ranger (eds.), *The Invention of Tradition* (Cambridge University Press, 1983), esp. pp.1–14. On the grand tradition invented by Zhu Xi, cf. Lionel Jensen,"Zhu Xi's World Picture and the Mythistory of 'Imperial Confucianism'", in *Oriens Exremus* 49 (2010), pp. 79–114.

import of his teaching was to lead men to look for new ways of interpreting and refashioning a local tradition in order to bring into being a new, universal order to replace the contemporary disorder. What Confucius saw were in historical fact the newly emerging similarities in social-political practices, the newly emerging, widespread sharing of values that had once been restricted to a small region which included Lu. He saw the emerging of widely shared literary forms, musical forms, legal forms and political forms.[33]

In all this, Confucius does not appear as a sage who created social order of and by himself, but as a child of his times, conditioned by the society he lived in. In fact, "sageness" should not be a category, much less a God-term in scholarly discourse. In what follows, I propose to introduce *society* as a new God-term,[34] trying to answer the question "Why Confucius?" with reference to (changes in) social structure.[35] The question is: what were the specific historical conditions that made it possible, perhaps necessary for a personality like Confucius to appear? The answer is in a nutshell: increasing social complexity.

A New Society

The societies of Shang and early Zhou, centuries before Confucius' times, were primarily structured along kinship lines. Shang society has been character-

---

33 Herbert Fingarette, *Confucius: The Secular as Sacred*, p. 60. Benjamin I. Schwartz, *The World of Thought in Ancient China*, p. 59, notes that there was "intellectual progress and creativity" in Confucius' times, but stresses "that they are not particularly germane to the concerns of the Master". Cf., in a similar vein, Heiner Roetz, *Konfuzius* (München: Beck, 1995), pp. 9–10.

34 This, of course, is the fundamental tenet of sociology. Society functions as a God-term most radically in sociological systems theory which insists that society is *autopoetic*, that is created and re-created entirely by itself (Niklas Luhmann, *Soziale Systeme: Grundri ßeinerallgemeinen Theorie*, Frankfurt/M: Suhrkamp, 1984). Biological, geographical, climatic and other external factors affect society but never determine its operations.

35 By "social structure" I do not mean demographic factors such as age, gender, or income distribution, nor hierarchical orders or kinship systems. Rather, I take the term to signify the communicative relationships within a society. Social structure determines which people get into touch with one another and who communicates with whom in what ways.

ized as a "conical clan" in which "lineages were key elements." [36] These lineages (*zu* 族) were largely autonomous units that "must have developed their own customs."

Since the *zu* lived in the same place and the members knew each other, the customs of a *zu* were very probably known to all its members, especially to the parents of the families. Furthermore, the customs of a particular *zu* might apply only to its own members, and thus there were probably few, if any, conflicts between the customs of different *zu*.[37]

This social structure may aptly be described as a *segmentary society*, comprised of numerous similarly structured groups that may be in contact, exchanging commercial and cultural goods, but that ultimately remain autonomous. They are not integrated in an overarching unity but treat each other as external.[38] This social structure certainly did not come to an abrupt end when the Zhou conquered the Shang in the middle of the 11th century BC. Quite to the contrary, archaeological evidence suggests that "for its first two centuries the Zhou essentially continued the traditions of the preceding Shang dynasty." [39] Only gradually, in a process that is not yet clearly understood, Zhou society outgrew the structure inherited from earlier times. In his book of *Chinese Society in the Age of Confucius (1000—250 BC)*,[40] Lothar von Falkenhausen identi-

---

36 David N. Keightley, "The Shang: China's First Historical dynasty", in Michael Loewe and Edward Shaugnessy (eds.), *The Cambridge History of Ancient China: From the Origins of Civilization to 221 B.C* (Cambridge: Cambridge University Press 1999), p. 290. The author suggests that in certain respects the Shang king "was still functioning like the 'big man'of a prestate chiefdom."

37 Liu Yongping, *Origins of Chinese Law: Penal and Administrative Law in Its Early Development* (Hong Kong: Oxford University Press 1998), p. 28. Liu stresses that "there existed neither a centralized state organization nor a unified law which could be applied to all the *zu*." (p. 29)

38 The concept of "segmentary society" was first introduced by Emile Durkheim; cf. Emile Durkheim, *Übersoziale Arbeitsteilung: Studieüber die Organisationhöherer Gesellschaften* (Frankfurt/M.: Suhrkamp, 1992)(1st ed.: Paris, 1930), p. 229–237. For more recent studies, cf. Hannes Wimmer, *Evolution der Politik: von der Stammesgesellschaft zur modernen Demokratie* (Wien: WUV-Universitätsverlag, 1996), pp. 163–216; Niklas Luhmann, *Die Gesellschaft der Gesellschaft*. 2 vols (Frankfurt/M.: Suhrkamp, 1997), pp. 634–662.

39 Lothar von Falkenhausen, *Chinese* Society *in the Age of Confucius (1000—250 BC): The Archaeological Evidence*, p. 2; Jessica Rawson, "Statesmen or Barbarians? The Western Zhou as Seen Through Their Bronzes", in *Proceedings of the British Academy* 75, 1989, pp. 71–95.

40 It may be noted that this "age of Confucius" refers to quite a different time frame than the present paper. In fact, the title is perhaps the only questionable point about this admirable piece of archaeological scholarship, given that there is not a shred of archaeological evidence that would testify to Confucius as an historical personality.

fies two decisive caesurae: the "ritual reform" of ca. 850 BC and the "secondary transformation" of the 6th—3rd centuries BC. Whereas this is not the place to discuss details of these transformations, two aspects deserve to be pointed out.

Firstly, the "ritual reform," which changed virtually all aspects of bronze culture,[41] introduced standardized vessel sets that were correlated to the social rank of their recipient: high court officials would be endowed with nine *ding* cauldrons and eight *gui* tureens, lower administrators with seven *ding* and six *gui*, local rulers with five and four, respectively, and so on.[42] Such imposing vessel sets, made to be viewed from a distance, suggest that "the ritual performances now took place in larger and less intimate spatial settings."[43] The ancestral sacrifices now seem to have been performed not among clan members exclusively, but in front of broader elite circles that transcended kin groups.[44] Apparently, the growing emphasis on rank differences among the elite correlated with higher visibility: with a universally accepted ranking system in place, ranks of nobility became comparable beyond the confines of kinship groups. All of this must have created a heightened sense of coherence among members of the elite. Perhaps the 9th century BC was the time when the segmentary, kinship-centered society of early Western Zhou was transformed into a stratified

---

41 Some old vessel types disappeared entirely, while new vessels were introduced; massive food vessels gained importance, and chime bells became part of the ritual display; the calligraphy of inscriptions changed, and the zoomorphic decoration of earlier vessels gave way to strictly geometric patterns; vessels became bigger, more imposing and somewhat coarser. For a detailed description, cf. Jessica Rawson, *Western Zhou Ritual Bronzes in the Arthur M. Sackler Collections*. 2 vols. (Washington, D.C.: The Arthur M. Sackler Foundation, 1990), pp. 93–125.

42 Cf. *Shang Zhou kaogu*商周考古 (ed. by Beijing daxue lishixi kaogu jiaoyanshi shangzhouzu北京大学历史系考古教研室商周组编, Beijing: Cultural Relics Press, 1979), pp. 203–215; Lothar von Falkenhausen, *Chinese Society in the Age of Confucius (1000—250 BC): The Archaeological Evidence*, p. 51, table 4.

43 Lothar von Falkenhausen, *Chinese Society in the Age of Confucius (1000—250 BC): The Archaeological Evidence*, p. 299. The author also speculates that the "demise of wine-drinking during rituals may well encapsulate this loss of 'communitas.'"

44 Cf. Martin Kern, "Bronze Inscriptions, the *Shangshu*, and the *Shijing*: The Evolution of the Ancestral Sacrifice During the Western Zhou", pp. 184–185, in John Lagerwey and Marc Kalinowski (eds.), *Early Chinese Religion*, Part One: Shang Through Han (1250 BC to 220 AD) (Leiden: Brill, 2009), pp. 143–200, who notes that in "mid- and late Western Zhou times ... the practice of the ancestral sacrifice was expanded into a much broader culture of commemoration" just like court rituals "were no longer addressed to a small group of clan members but to a much broader political elite."

elite society that transcended kinship bounds. With the appearance of this elite society, an entirely new problem presented itself "to maintain a shared culture over a distance without the possibility of all-round direct contacts."[45]

Secondly, this brings us closer to Confucius' times, "particularly from the Middle Chungiu, period onward, (when) one can trace the division of the ranked elite into two distinct social strata."[46] While the higher elite became increasingly remote, mortuary evidence suggests that the lower elite was by and by degraded to the point of merging with the commoner classes.[47] The finely graded elite that evolved in the 9th century BC split into a two-tiered society, and high culture was clearly separated from popular culture. This would seem to have been the precondition for the well-known "rise of the *shi* 士" as an intermediary class.[48] Such an intermediary class that sociology informs us, serves as the crucial stabilizing element in society that makes social order possible.[49] It is this class that shapes society.

To sum up, around the 9th centuryBC there occurred a transition from a segmentary society, in which a lineages or perhaps a few lineages provided the basic frame of social interaction, to a stratified society that transcended local and kinship borders. To be sure, this elite society was very small, the vast majority of people still living in segmentary, locally limited societies.[50] But since the 6th century BC, increasing numbers of commoners howe qualified to participate in and shape this elite society.

This was a quantum leap in complexity that changed everything. "With the

---

45 Friedrich H. Tenbruck, *Geschichte und Gesellschaft* (Berlin: Duncker und Humblot, 1986), p. 318.

46 Lothar von Falkenhausen, *Chinese* Society *in the Age of Confucius (1000—250 BC), The Archaeological Evidence*, p. 326. Whereas the tombs of rulers now reached unprecedented sizes, the largest even dwarfing those of the Shang kings, tombs of the lower elite "had nothing even remotely resembling the splendor of these funerary complexes." (p. 336)

47 Cf. Lothar von Falkenhausen, *Chinese* Society *in the Age of Confucius (1000—250 BC), The Archaeological Evidence*, pp. 370–399.

48 Cf. the classic description by Hsü Cho-yun, *Ancient China in Transition: An Analysis of Social Mobility, 722—222 B.C.* (Stanford: Stanford UP, 1965), pp. 34–51, and *passim*.

49 Cf. Bernhard Giesen, *Die Entdinglichung des Sozialen: Eineevolutions¬theoretische Perspektive auf die Postmoderne* (Frankfurt/M.: Suhrkamp, 1991), pp. 24–35, and pp. 32–37.

50 In fact, this has remained the mode of existence for the great majority of the Chinese people until well into the 20th century.

passage to stratified society man enters a completely new area of social life."[51] In segmentary societies, as described by anthropologists and sociologists, the basic frame of reference, even for elites, is the own kinship group. These people, as Edward Banfield put it, "live and die without ever achieving membership in a community larger than the family or tribe." [52] Incidentally, this is the characteristic of Laozi's ideal community:

> In a small state with few people, let them, though they possess weapons of war, not make use of them. Let the people honor the dead and not roam a far. Though they possess boats and carriages, they never mount them; though they have arms and shields, they never take them up. Let the people revert to the use of knotted cords; let them find sweetness in their food, beauty in their garments, peace in their dwellings and joy in their customs. Though there be a neighboring state in sight and the voices of its chickens and dogs heard, the people will grow old and die without having intercourse with it.[53]

Segmentary societies are largely self-sufficient, mobility is restricted and "people's horizons are limited by locale and their decisions involve only other *known* people in *known* situations." [54] Contact with strangers is rare. In fact, they are regarded as inherently dangerous, vile and contagious, not even fully

---

51 Morton H. Fried, "On the Evolution of Social Stratification and the State", in, Stanley Diamond (ed.) *Culture in History: Essays in Honor of Paul Radin* (New York: Columbia University Press, 1960), p. 721.

52 Edward C. Banfield, *The Moral Basis of a Backward Society* (Glencoe: The Free Press, 1958), p. 7. For the following description, cf. also Bernhard Giesen, *Die Entdinglichung des Sozialen: Eineevolutions theoretische Perspektive auf die Postmoderne,* pp. 25–29.

53 *Laozi jiaoshi*老子校释 (ed. by Zhu Qianzhi朱谦之, Beijing: Zhonghua Book Company, 1996), 80, pp. 307–309: 小国寡民，使有什伯之器而不用，使人重死而不远徙。虽有舟舆，无所乘之；虽有甲兵，无所陈之。使民复结绳而用之。甘其食，美其服，安其居，乐其俗。邻国相望，鸡狗之声相闻，民至老死，不相往来。

54 Daniel Lerner, *The Passing of Traditional Society: Modernizing the Middle East* (Glencoe: The Free Press, 1958), p. 50.

human: "Strangers are incomprehensible, are enemies, are eatable."[55] Linguistic, cultural and physical barriers are so high as to keep them nicely apart from the own group.[56] People stay within their group, where socialization takes place as a matter of course through everyday interaction with one's own kind. The norms of such societies are simply rules for practical behavior which are created and recreated in direct interaction. There is an unspoken consensus about these norms, needless to discuss or codify them. Members of such societies understand the rules of behavior like they understand the grammar of their language without being able to name or describe them.[57] Since specific situations define the frame for social interaction, there is no need for general and abstract normative structures. It is a world of certainties and self-evident truths.

All of this changed with the emergence of an elite that transcended regional and familial barriers. In the Chunqiu era, many city states of Western Zhou times grew to become territorial states, creating a network of cities, connected through country roads. These developments facilitated travel within and between states and led to an unprecedented degree of mobility and exchange.[58] Rather than

---

55 Niklas Luhmann, *Die Gesellschaft der Gesellschaft*, p. 645, fn. 81. Thus the human sacrifices of the Shang, who slaughtered thousands of Qiang captives and offered them to their gods, may be explained not by primitive blood-thirst, but by social structure. In a "conical clan," people beyond the confines of the extended kin-group were simply not human, hence free to be slaughtered like animals.

56 Cf. Klaus E. Müller, *Das magische Universum der Identität: Elementarformen sozialen Verhaltens. Ein ethnologischer Grundriß* (Frankfurt: Suhrkamp, 1987), pp. 86–87, 255–256, with many anthropological examples, as well as Bernhard Giesen and Kay Junge, "Vom Patriotismuszum Nationalismus: Zur Evolution der 'Deutschen Kulturnation'", in Giesen (ed.), *Nationale und kulturelle Identität: Studien zur Entwicklung des kollektiven Bewußtseins in der Neuzeit* (Frankfurt/M.: Suhrkamp,1991), p. 262.

57 Bernhard Giesen, *Die Entdinglichung des Sozialen: Eineevolutions¬theoretische Perspektive auf die Postmoderne,* pp. 28–29. On mutual understanding in kin groups, cf. Müller, *Das magische Universum der Identität: Elementarformen sozialen Verhaltens. Ein ethnologischer Grundriß,* pp. 67–68, and Tenbruck, *Geschichte und Gesellschaft,* p. 318: "The meaning of mutual action needs to be verbalized but imperfectly, since in direct togetherness the non-verbal carriers of meaning are fully present."

58 Mark Elvin, *The Pattern of the Chinese Past: A Social and Economic Interpretation* (Stanford University Press, 1973), p. 25, reckons that "the average mileage covered by the diplomatic missions sent out by the state of Lu increased from 112 miles per mission in the late 8th centuryBC to 454 miles per mission in the late 6th centuryCB." For a detailed study, concentrating on the states of Qi and Lu, cf. Hans Stumpfeldt, *Staatsverfassung und Territoriumimantiken China: Über die Ausbildung einer territorialen Staatsverfassung* (Düsseldorf: Bertelsmann Universitätsverlag, 1970).

disintegrating, China was actually growing together in these centuries, bringing the elites of regional states into ever closer contact with one another.[59]

Confucius and the New Society

Confucius' very biography seems to exemplify the new mobility of Chunqiu times. Traveling for thirteen years through the states of the North China plain, he became precisely the kind of "mobile personality" that Daniel Lerner has contrasted with members of segmentary society: a personality characterized by rationality, "a high capacity for identification with new aspects of his environment," and empathy.[60] Confucius experienced the emergence of a new interstate elite society, in particular: the emergence of *public* life. This must have been a truly new experience in Confucius' times, since "in segmentary society there is no need to name the public as such and to distinguish it from other, equally possible forms of sociality."[61]

Now, Confucius and his peers found themselves confronted with people, institutions, and situations that were *unknown* to them.[62] Whereas in segmentary societies the world is a familiar place, a stratified society is infinitely more complex. In order to live in this new society, one first had to recognize the basic fact that most of the world is unfamiliar. In the words of the master: "To realize what

---

59 The much-deplored warfare, rather than being the basic characteristic of the times, appears to have been a secondary phenomenon, attendant on the coalescence of Chinese society. Closer contacts are a precondition not only for mutual understanding, but also for conflicts.

60 Daniel Lerner, *The Passing of Traditional Society: Modernizing the Middle East*, p. 48.

61 André Kieserling, *Kommunikation unter Anwesenden: Studien über Interaktionssysteme* (Frankfurt: Suhrkamp, 1999), p. 454. Cf. Niklas Luhmann, *Systemtheorie der Gesellschaft* (Berlin: Suhrkamp, 2017), p. 426: "Segmentäre Differenzierung...benötigt und verträgt keine Differenzierung von öffentlich und privat." Confucius, however, seems to have been well aware of the difference between public and private, as seen in *Lunyu* 2.9, p. 52: 退而省其私，亦足以发, perhaps also 10.5, p. 385: 私觌，愉愉如也。

62 Cf. Liu Yongping, *Origins of Chinese Law: Penal and Administrative Law in Its Early Development* (Hong Kong: Oxford University Press, 1998), p. 90: "One may safely assume that when he stayed in these states, Confucius observed and studied the various customs and usages followed by peoples of the numerous *zu*." Liu goes even further in assuming that Confucius' ancestors, having come from Song to Lu, "must have experienced the conflicts between differing customs and usages of the Shang and Zhou" .(p. 89)

one knows and to realize what one does not know: that is knowledge."[63] This fundamental awareness of the limits and the contingency of knowledge was a sign of the times. An equally disturbing and stimulating thought, it permeates the *Lunyu* and other Zhanguo-texts.

The most concrete manifestation of the unknown was having to deal with *strangers*.[64] A stratified society includes many more people than an individual will ever meet. It is full of strangers. Thus for the elite, interaction with the Other writ large grew ever more common, finally becoming the rule. It is no mere coincidence that the problem of being unknown to others is a recurrent theme in the *Lunyu*:

> "Is he not a junzi, who feels no indignation though men may not recognize him?"
>
> "Do not worry about others not knowing you, but worry about not-knowing others."
>
> "Do not worry if nobody knows you, but seek to be worthy to be known."
>
> "Do not worry about others not knowing you, but worry about why they should not be able to." [65]

Evidently, Confucius and his disciples had to reckon with strangers (or people for whom they themselves were strangers). In dealing with strangers, problems of trust and understanding acquired an entirely new dimension. Having grown up in humble, locally restricted circumstances,[66] even the master himself had to learn how to behave toward strangers:

> "At first, I would listen to people's words and trust in their conduct; now

---

63 *Lunyu* 2.17, p. 61: 知之为知之，不知为不知，是知也。

64 Not "barbarians", be it noted. Whereas the "barbarian" is not worth dealing with at all, the stranger certainly is: he is different, but nevertheless to be taken seriously. In fact, through his otherness, the stranger draws attention to the contingency of one's own customs; the barbarian does not, since his customs are simply beyond consideration.

65 *Lunyu* 1.1, p. 4: 人不知而不愠，不亦君子乎? 1.16, p. 34: 不患人之不己知，患不知人也。4.14, p. 150: 不患莫己知，求为可知也。14.30, p.589: 不患人之不己知，患其不能也。

66 *Lunyu* 9.6, p. 329: 吾少也贱，故多能鄙事。

I will listen to their words and observe their conduct." [67]

If dealing with strangers was a delicate task for Confucius, it certainly was a challenge for his disciples, most of whom do not seem to have been raised in elite families, either. Quite a few of them, surnamed Yan, were probably maternal relatives of Confucius, and others apparently came from lowly families. Names like Ran Geng ("Plow", his style was Boniu: "Elder Ox"), Qidiao ("Lacquer-carver") Cong, or Gongye ("Ducal blacksmith") Chang suggest a peasant or craftsman background.[68] Confucius himself characterized some of his most prominent followers as outright country bumpkins: "Chai is stupid, Shen is dull, Shi is ordinary, You is crude." [69] And Yan Hui, Confucius' favorite disciple, eked out a living in a narrow lane, with a single bowl of rice and a single cup of drink. While others would not have endured this misery, Hui never changed his joyful mood.[70]

These were no cosmopolitans. Yet, it was Confucius' ambition to release his disciples from segmentary society and prepare them for the intricacies of public life which—it needs to be stressed—was *new* in their times. It is a common observation in sociology and anthropology that "traditional man" —living in a segmentary society—"has habitually regarded public matters as none of his business."[71] In the age of Confucius and his disciples, this was to change. "Wearing worn-out shirts and hemp coats, yet standing with those dressed in

---

67 *Lunyu* 5.11, p. 179 : 始吾于人也，听其言而信其行；今吾于人也，听其言而观其行。

68 For lists of Confucius' disciples, cf. *Kongzi Jiayu yizhu* 9.38, pp. 405–420, and *Shiji* 67, pp. 2185–2226; H. G. Creel, *Confucius: The Man and the Myth* (London: Routledge&Kegan Paul, 1951), pp. 72–83 characterizes the most prominent disciples.

69 *Lunyu* 11.18, p. 457: 柴也愚，参也鲁，师也辟，由也喭。In 13.3, p. 521, You is again put down as "coarse": 野哉，由也!

70 *Lunyu* 6.11, p. 226: 贤哉，回也! 一箪食，一瓢饮，在陋巷，人不堪其忧，回也不改其乐。

71 Daniel Lerner, *The Passing of Traditional Society: Modernizing the Middle East*, p. 70. Edward C. Banfield, *The Moral Basis of a Backward Society* has given a striking example for the lack of "public-spiritedness" in the Southern Italian town of "Montegrano": "No one in town is animated by a desire to do good for all of the population"; in fact, "not only is public-spiritedness lacking, but many people positively want to prevent others from getting ahead" (p.18). Banfield concludes: "In a society of amoral familists, no one will further the interest of the group or community except as it is to his private advantage to do so. In other words, the hope of material gain in the short-run will be the only motive for concern with public affairs." (p. 85)

furs without being ashamed," [72] they were expected to "comport themselves with dignity and, sent out to the four quarters, not to disgrace their ruler's mandate." [73] Confucius' disciples were meant "to manage the levies," "to be chancellor," or "to converse with visitors and guests" at court.[74] All of this must have meant a radical departure from their familiar surroundings. In fact, it was a radical departure from a society, which *was* the family.

But what about familial values? It has often been noted that Confucius modeled his ideal of society after that of the family. While this is certainly true, one may ask: why did familial values need to be emphasized at all? Apparently, they could not be taken for granted any more. It would seem that Confucius preached them precisely because the family-based segmentary society was giving way to a stratified elite society. In this society, which brought together people of widely different backgrounds, the fundamental contingency of all values became all too visible. Old certainties crumbled. Neither the newly emerging public roles nor the time-honored familial roles could claim self-evident validity, and everything had to be re-considered and re-defined. It is an "oft-repeated anthropological observation" that in segmentary societies "there is no or hardly any privacy." [75] A real private sphere, then, appeared only as a counterpart of an emerging public sphere: this means that *both* spheres were new and had to be organized. Members of the elite now had to get to grips with a multiplicity of roles, all of which had become uncertain: this was the problem Confucius and his contemporaries tried to solve. In the *Lunyu*, these roles are often mentioned side by side:

> If a man respects worth and disregards appearance, if he exerts himself
> in serving his parents and devotes himself to serving his ruler, if in inter-

---

72 *Lunyu* 9.27, p. 355: 衣敝缊袍，与衣狐貉者立，而不耻者，其由也与？

73 *Lunyu* 13.20, p. 538: 行己有耻，使于四方，不辱君命，可谓士矣。

74 *Lunyu* 5.8, pp. 172–175: 由也，千乘之国，可使治其赋也……求也，千室之邑，百乘之家，可使为之宰也……赤也，束带立于朝，可使与宾客言也，不知其仁也。

75 André Kieserling, *Kommunikation unter Anwesenden: Studien über Interaktionssysteme*, p. 454. Cf., in the same vein, Philippe Aries and Georges Duby, *Geschichte des privatenLebens*, vol. 5: *Vom Ersten Weltkriegzur Gegenwart* (Frankfurt/M:S. Fischer, 1995), p. 21: "Die erhöhte Differenzierung zwischen Privatem und Öffentlichem in der Gesellschaftinsgesamtverändertsowohl das öffentliche Lebenalsauch das private Leben. Jeneswie dieses gehorchennichtmehrdenselbenRegeln.Mit der Verschiebung und Präzisierungihrer Grenzenwandeltsichihr Wesen."

course with friends he is true to his words, then though he may be called unlearned, I will definitely call him learned.

In (serving) the state be without resentment, and in your family be without resentment.

Away from home, to serve rulers and ministers; at home, to serve father and mother; at funerals by all means to exert oneself;[76] not to be overcome by alcohol—which of these can I achieve?[77]

Indeed, one of Confucius' most famous (and most puzzling) statements, "let the ruler be ruler, and the minister be minister; let the father be father, and the son be son", (cf. fn. 25) may perhaps be adequately explained with reference to this social background. Members of the elite had now to fulfill diverse roles in public and private: they could be ruler and father, minister and son, friend and husband, teacher and relative. The more important it was to keep these roles apart and define adequate conventions for each one of them. Confucius' "role ethics" were the solution to the problem that in an elite society roles had become ambiguous and problematic.

Confucius, then, tried to order a new society—and from where else should he have derived a model for it if not from the old society? Thus, it is not surprising that he routinely refers to kinship terminology in his teachings. However, this does not mean that they were primarily aimed at organizing kinship groups, quite to the contrary. While interaction within kinship groups or small communities certainly engenders squabbles,[78] such problems appear insignifi-

---

76　Such lavish funerals, later vehemently criticized by the Mohists, would seem to reflect the culture of segmentary society. George M.Foster, "Peasant Society and the Image of Limited Good", in *American Anthropologist* 67.2, 1965, p. 305, 307, observes that there "is good reason why peasant fiestas consume so much wealth in fireworks, candles, music, and food, and why in peasant communities the rites of baptism, marriage, and death may involve relatively huge expenditures. These practices are a redistributive mechanism which permits a person or family that potentially threatens community stability gracefully to restore the status quo, thereby returning itself to a state of acceptability. ... Heavy ritual expenditures, for example, are essential to the maintenance of the equilibrium that spells safety in the minds of traditional villagers."

77　*Lunyu* 1.7, p. 19: 贤贤易色；事父母，能竭其力；事君，能致其身；与朋友交，言而有信。虽曰未学，吾必谓之学矣。12.2, p. 485: 在邦无怨，在家无怨。9.16, p. 348: 出则事公卿，入则事父母，丧事不敢不勉，不为酒困，何有与我哉？Cf. also 12.20, p. 507, and 16.1, p. 649.

78　On these, cf. George M. Foster, "Peasant Society and the Image of Limited Good", pp. 301-302.

cant compared to the complexities of public life in a stratified society. The family was not at issue, bwt *society* was.

Unlike Laozi (cf. above), Confucius certainly did not advocate a return to homely, self-sufficient kin groups. Significantly, the *Lunyu* records hardly a Charalter about Confucius' family life; and a rare passage which does mention Confucius' son is equally telling:

> Chen Kang asked Boyu: "Have you perhaps heard anything extraordinary (from your father)?" Boyu replied: "Not yet. Once, he was standing alone, when I passed by the hall in a hurry. He said to me: 'Have you learned the songs?' On my replying 'Not yet,' he said, 'If you do not learn the songs, you will have nothing to say.' So I retired and studied the songs. Another day, he was again standing alone, when I passed by the hall in a hurry. He said to me: 'Have you learned the rituals?' On my replying 'Not yet', he said, 'If you do not learn the rituals, you will have nothing through which to become established.' So I retired and studied the rituals. These two things I have heard." Chen Kang, upon having retired, happily said: "I asked about one thing and gained knowledge of three: I heard about the songs, about rituals, and about how a *junzi* stays aloof from his son." [79]

Such "aloofness" from one's family is an indicator of social stratification in which ultimately "between upper class and lower class no kinship relations, not even distant ones, are recognized."[80] Confucius' ideal, the *junzi* 君子, is cer-

---

[79] *Lunyu* 16.13, p. 668: 陈亢问于伯鱼曰：“子亦有异闻乎？”对曰：“未也。尝独立，鲤趋而过庭。曰：‘学诗乎？’对曰：‘未也。’‘不学诗，无以言！’鲤退而学诗。他日，又独立，鲤趋而过庭。曰：‘学礼乎？’对曰：‘未也。’‘不学礼，无以立！’鲤退而学礼。闻斯二者。”陈亢退而喜曰：“问一得三，闻诗，闻礼，又闻君子之远其子也。” Boyu also appears in 17.8, p. 690, which may reflect the same situation.

[80] Niklas Luhmann, *Die Gesellschaft der Gesellschaft*, vol. 2, p. 659. The consequence of this is *endogamy*, not within a clan or community, but within a social class. Sinologists have usually treated this well-documented phenomenon as *exogamy*, stressing the necessity to take a wife from another clan, sometimes even considering genetic arguments as the reason (e.g. Lü Simian 吕思勉, *Zhongguo zhidu shi* 中国制度史, Shanghai: Shanghai Educational Publishing House 上海教育出版社, 1985, pp. 321–324). It would seem that the sociological argument—namely, coherence within an elite class that transcends clans—provides a better explanation for this marriage custom. Thus, endogamy appears to be the apt term.

tainly not a family man. Quite to the contrary, the *junzi* is by definition a *man of public life*. This is crucial: he was not simply a morally "superior man," but a man who needed to acquire a certain habitus due to his role in public life. It was this habitus that distinguished him from the *xiaoren*小人 who never transcended the petty confines of his village or kin group.

> "The *junzi* is catholic and not partisan. The *xiaoren* is partisan and not catholic."
> "The *junzi* cherishes virtue; the *xiaoren* cherishes his turf. The *junzi* cherishes penal law; the *xiaoren* cherishes favors." [81]

Village life does not require particular cognitive or social skills. What Marx and Engels have called the "idiocy of rural life" is a practical, unpretentious and straightforward demeanor, unfettered by much reflection or control of emotions. For the *junzi*, this changes when kinship bonds are replaced by a much wider frame of reference. In a remarkable dialogue between Confucius' disciples Zixia and Sima Niu, the latter sighs:

> "Other men all have brothers, but only I do not have any." Zixia said, "I have heard, 'Death and life have their mandate; wealth and honor depend upon Heaven.' If the *junzi* is reverent and without fail, respectful to others and observant of rituals, then within the four seas everyone will be his brother. Why should a *junzi* worry because he has no brothers?" [82]

An elite society in which all men are brothers: this thought would have been unthinkable in a segmentary society. Now it became very real, and the *junzi* would have to be prepared for this new reality. The guiding principle of this new society is no longer local custom but the "decree of Heaven" (*tianming* 天命) which transcends families and regions.

---

81 *Lunyu* 2.14, p. 56: 君子周而不比，小人比而不周。4.11, p. 148: 君子怀德，小人怀土；君子怀刑，小人怀惠。

82 *Lunyu* 12.5, p. 488: 司马牛忧曰："人皆有兄弟，我独无。"子夏曰："商闻之矣：死生有命，富贵在天。君子敬而无失，与人恭而有礼，四海之内皆兄弟也，君子何患乎无兄弟？"

> The *junzi* has threefold respect: he respects the decree of Heaven, great men, and the words of the sages. The *xiaoren* knows not the decree of Heaven and does not pay it respect, he is obsequious towards great men, and he defiles the words of the sages.[83]

Transcending his kin group, a *junzi* is "sent out to the four quarters," his realm is the "ecumene," (*tianxia*天下) not his family turf.[84] He is "not partisan," and "proficient in righteousness," while the *xiaoren*, sticking to his peasant *egoísmo*, is "proficient in gaining benefits." [85] The difference between the *junzi* and the *xiaoren* has always been interpreted as one of moral qualities. While this is certainly true, I would argue that the moral difference is only a secondary phenomenon. The *primary* difference between the *junzi* and the *xiaoren* is one of social integration: Confucian morals, as I will argue below, were specifically designed for an elite society. Only the members of this society were moral persons, while the *xiaoren*, remaining in segmentary confinement, had no need for such abstract notions. The very last paragraph of the *Lunyu* might be understood as a summary of Confucius' program:

> "Without understanding the decree, there is no way to become a *junzi*; without understanding rituals, there is no way to become established; without understanding words, there is no way to understand men." [86]

All of these injunctions are about succeeding in a society where "men" are not familiar by birth but must actively seek mutual acquaintance, where

---

83 *Lunyu* 16.8, p. 661: 君子有三畏：畏天命，畏大人，畏圣人之言。小人不知天命而不畏也，狎大人，侮圣人之言。

84 *Lunyu* 13.5, p. 525: 使于四方，不能专对；虽多，亦奚以为？ 4.10, p. 147: 君子之于天下也，无适也，无莫也，义之与比。

85 *Lunyu* 2.14, p. 56: 君子周而不比，小人比而不周。(Cf. 7.31, p. 279: 吾闻君子不党，君子亦党乎？ 15.22, p. 630: 君子矜而不争，群而不党。) 4.16 子曰："君子喻于义，小人喻于利。" For the characteristic peasant *egoísmo*, cf. George M. Foster, "Peasant Society and the Image of Limited Good", p. 304, who plausibly explains this "as a function of an image of Limited Good". Cf. also Banfield's rule of the "amoral familist": "Maximize the Material, Short-run Advantage of the Nuclear Family; Assume That All Others Will Do Likewise" (Edward C. Banfield, *The Moral Basis of a Backward Society*, p.85).

86 *Lunyu* 20.3, p. 769: 不知命，无以为君子也。不知礼，无以立也。不知言，无以知人也。

in the absence of tacit understanding words—*logoi*—are necessary to achieve consensus,[87] where knowledge of formal rules is necessary to become established. There is no need to "become established" (*li*立) within one's own kinship group, but only in an elite society. Confucius became "established" at the age of thirty, when according to his biography in the *Shiji* he was first asked for advice by a ruler.[88] "Becoming established" meant entering into *public* life.

Whereas the *xiaoren* stuck to his home territory, the *junzi* was in a position to "travel far" and receive "friends from afar." [89] Only for the *junzi* selecting and treating "friends"—perhaps even this was a new concept—became a problem which needed to be treated with great care: "Do not befriend those who are not your equal," says the *Lunyu*, "bring friends together through culture", and

> speak to them sincerely and lead them well, but if they do not assent, then let it be, lest you disgrace yourself by them.[90]

"Disgrace" always lurked beneath the surface of public life. For the *junzi*, social intercourse was full of pitfalls, it became a delicate problem that required utmost circumspection. This, then, would seem to have been the fundamental problem that Confucius faced in his times.

---

87 In his famous letter to Gu Dongqiao顾东桥, Wang Yangming王阳明 explains the genesis of communication by the lack of mutual understanding: a pristine community, he argues, was characterized by "the wonder of tacit understanding" (不言而喻之妙). Only when this sagely learning was lost, there arose a need for "verbal explanations and rhetorical embellishments" (讲明修饰) as well as the arts of commentary (训诂), recitation (记诵), and literary composition (词章). Communication, then, is a remedy for deficient understanding and as such symptomatic of a decadent or, as I would prefer to call it: a complex society.

88 *Shiji* 47, 1910. *Lunyu* 2.4 p. 43: 吾十有五而志于学，三十而立，四十而不惑，五十而知天命，六十而耳顺，七十而从心所欲，不逾矩。For further evidence pointing to the connection of *li* and public life, cf. *Lunyu* 9.27 (fn. 72), 5.8 (fn. 74), 16.13 (fn. 79), 20.3 (fn. 86).

89 *Lunyu* 4.19, p. 157: 父母在，不远游，游必有方。1.1, p. 3: 有朋自远方来，不亦乐乎？

90 *Lunyu* 1.8, p. 22: 无友不如己者；12.24, p. 513: 君子以文会友；12.23, p. 513: 子贡问友。子曰："忠告而善道之，不可则止，毋自辱焉。" One may contrast this with peasant societies where "true friendship is a scarce commodity, and serves as insurance against being left without any of it" (George M. Foster, "Peasant Society and the Image of Limited Good", p. 298). For more instances of this widely discussed topic, cf. *Lunyu* 1.4, 1.7, 4.26, 5.25, 5.26, 9.25, 10.22, 10.23, 12.24, 15.10, 16.4, 16.5, 19.15.

Rituals

When dealing with strangers on a regular basis, it was not possible to keep one's emotional distance like in a segmentary society. Instead, new conventions for civilized and peaceful communication were required.[91] The homegrown rules were no longer self-evident, since they were different for everybody, as the *Lunyu* observes in a famous passage: "By nature, (men) are close to one another, but by their habits, they are distanced from one another."[92] This sentence, which later appeared in the opening paragraph of the *Sanzijing*三字经, has been judged "almost completely content free." [93] Indeed, its full import can only be appreciated if one considers the social background: in a segmentary society, people had certainly *not* been "distanced from one another." The exposure to different habits that came with a stratified society was new to Confucius and his contemporaries. Thus both the observation that habits differ and that people are nevertheless similar by nature were by no means trivial in their original context.

The most immediate reaction to the experience of otherness would seem to be humility and self-effacement. "Strangers are very 'obviously' unlike oneself. This natural difference is met by restraint."[94] Thus, in unfamiliar or uncertain situations the *junzi* should be cautious and reticent,[95] which is stressed time and again in the *Lunyu*:

---

91 Liu Yongping, *Origins of Chinese Law: Penal and Administrative Law in Its Early Development* , p. 54, also points out that it was "social changes which resulted in the transformation of *li*." She argues that "when the *zu* [i.e. lineages] started to dissolve and individual families appeared as the basic unit of society, people naturally needed moral principles and rules which would assimilate the customs and customary laws of different *zu* and thus be universally applied to all the individual families, despite their differing *zu* origins." (p. 88)

92 *Lunyu* 17.2, p. 676: 性相近也，习相远也。

93 Bryan W. Van Norden, *Confucius and the Analects: New Essays*, p. 23.

94 Bernhard Giesen and Kay Junge, "Vom Patriotismuszum Nationalismus: Zur Evolution der 'Deutschen Kulturnation'", p. 263.

95 In fact, the charalter that was later used for adherents of Confucius' teachings, *ru*, seems to imply just this quality of deference. Cf. the definition in *Shuowen jiezi* 8, p. 519: 儒，柔也。术士之称。从人需声。

The *junzi* aims to be slow in his words and swift in his deeds.

The *junzi* should be cautious about things he does not know.

Firm endurance and inarticulateness are close to humaneness.

The *junzi* is chagrined when his words surpass his deeds.[96]

But how to proceed from there? Obviously, in dealing with the Other writ large, it became necessary to define generalized and explicit rules of conduct, in other words: *rituals*.[97] "The ritual texture of Early China" has often been pointed out, and many studies have been devoted to aspects of ritual.[98] But what *are* rituals, and why exactly were they so important? It would be presumptuous to attempt a decisive definition of ritual, a term for which sociologists and anthropologists have suggested a bewildering array of explanations. But it will be useful to frame the concept in a way that has heuristic value.

I will follow Roy A. Rappaport in taking the term "ritual" to denote "the performance of more or less invariant sequences of formal acts and utterances not entirely encoded by their performers." [99] As such, rituals are ubiquitous: in Confucius' teachings, they range from holy rites to the rituals of everyday life and simple rules of propriety. Rituals "are requisite to the perpetuation of human social life," in a word: they are "the social act basic to humanity." [100] Rituals address the fundamental problem of social interaction that Talcott Parsons called "double contingency": the actions of ego are dependent on those

---

96 *Lunyu* 4.24, p. 159: 君子欲讷于言，而敏于行。13.3, p. 521: 君子于其所不知，盖阙如也。13.27, p. 548: 刚、毅、木、讷近仁。14.27, p. 588: 君子耻其言而过其行。

97 On the difference between "the highly variable local customs" (*fengsu*风俗) and *li* "that constitutes the resilient and enduring fabric of Chinese culture," cf. Roger Ames, "Achieving Personal Identity in Confucian Role Ethics: Tang Junyi on Human Nature as Conduct", in *Oriens Exremus* 49 (2010), pp. 143–166.

98 For recent works, cf. Joseph P. McDermott (ed.), *State and Court Ritual in China* (Cambridge University Press, 1999); Martin Kern (ed.), *Text and Ritual in Early China* (Seattle: University of Washington Press, 2005); Wei Yongkang魏永康, *Gudai lizhi wenhua*古代礼制文化 (Changchun: Jilin wenshi chubanshe吉林文史出版社, 2010).

99 Roy A. Rappaport, *Ritual and Religion in the Making of Humanity* (Cambridge: Cambridge University Press, 1999), p. 24. For an overview of definitions of "ritual," cf. Roy A. Rappaport, *Ecology, Meaning, and Religion* (Richmond, CA: North Atlantic, 1979), pp. 173–221.

100 Roy A. Rappaport, *Ritual and Religion in the Making of Humanity*, p. 31.

of alter—and vice versa.[101] How can this highly indeterminate circularity be resolved? One answer is: through *rituals*—through a handshake, a bow, a sermon, an offering. Such pre-determined "formal acts" serve to structure a social encounter. Through their performance, social order is created and—Rappaport emphasizes this point—the performers themselves accept and become part of the order created by the ritual.[102] In short, rituals serve to create order and achieve group cohesion in indeterminate situations.

It follows from the above that the more important rituals become, the less determined social settings and the less cohesive groups are. Little need for formalizing rituals among family members and intimate friends, where there is unspoken understanding and one feels the freedom to "be oneself." "If the natural emotions are not absent, what need is there for ritual and music", as *Zhuangzi* put it.[103] Indeed, the crucial function of ritual is "to create the *experience* of solidarity in the absence of consensus. It is precisely the fact that people cannot agree that makes rituals of solidarity necessary." [104]

This brings us back to the Chinese case: for the transformation from a homey segmentary society to a stratified society implies a precipitous drop in consensus. The emerging elite society is necessarily more diverse, and this seems to be the reason why formalized rituals came to achieve such overriding importance.

The *junzi*, being a man of public life, mainly interacted with people whose background was unlike his own. Whereas *xiaoren*, whose world was inhabited by their own kind, "are alike without harmonizing," the *junzi* faced the fundamental problem of "harmonizing, without being alike," [105] This is exactly what

---

101 Cf. Talcott Parsons and Edward Shils (eds.), *Toward a General Theory of Action* (Cambridge, MA: Harvard University Press, 1951), p. 16: "There is a double contingency inherent in interaction. On the one hand, ego's gratifications are contingent on his selection among available alternatives. But in turn, alter's reaction will be contingent on ego's selection and will result from a complementary selection on alter's part." Cf. Raf. Vanderstraeten, "Parsons, Luhmann and the Theorem of Double Contingency", in *Journal of Classical Sociology* 2.1, 2002, pp. 77–92.

102 Roy A. Rappaport, *Ritual and Religion in the Making of Humanity*, pp. 118–119. Rappaport calls this "ritual's first fundamental office."

103 *Zhuangzi* 9: 性情不离，安用礼乐！

104 Edward Muir, *Ritual in Early Modern Europe* (Cambridge: Cambridge University Press, 1997), p. 4, referring to David Kertzer.

105 *Lunyu* 13.23, p. 545: 君子和而不同，小人同而不和。

rituals serve to do: "In the practice of rituals, harmony is of utmost value," says Youzi.[106] Rituals were necessary to harmonize the disparate elements of a stratified society. This would seem to be the sociological explanation for the archaeological observation that "the ritual system idealized by Confucius and his followers" was not old, but actually very new.

It has often been stated that in Confucius' times the character *li* 礼 was transferred from the context of ancestral worship to the realm of social intercourse.[107] If this was so, it is highly significant. Rituals were necessary in dealing with the *unknown other*. In a segmentary society, only the spirits qualified for this designation; but as society widened its boundaries, the unknown others were no longer just spirits, but increasingly human strangers. Dealing with strangers involves considerable uncertainty: the other being largely unpredictable, theoretically anything could happen. In this highly indeterminate situation, rituals serve to reduce social complexity by *restraining* the options for action.[108] They ensure that anything *cannot* happen, but only certain highly restricted forms of behavior are acceptable. The restraining function of rituals is repeatedly pointed out in the *Lunyu*:

> The *junzi*, widely learned in cultural matters, if restrained by ritual, can manage to be without transgression.
> He broadened me through culture, and restrained me through ritual.
> However deliberately one may harmonize—if it is not restrained through ritual, it cannot be done.[109]

In an increasingly complex society, in which dealing with strangers

---

106 *Lunyu* 1.12, p. 29: 礼之用，和为贵。

107 It should be noted, however, that the evidence for the religious context of *li* is slim: apart from the form of the *character* (not the word!), only some odes of the *Shijing* testify to the religious origins of the word; cf. Yuri Pines, *Foundations of Confucian Thought: Intellectual Life in the Chunqiu Period, 722–453 B.C.E.* (Honolulu: University of Hawai'i Press, 2002), pp. 276–277, n. 8.

108 Müller, *Das magische Universum der Identität: Elementarformen sozialen Verhaltens. Ein ethnologischer Grundriß*, pp. 256–257 characterizes rituals as protective measures which serve to ward off the evil influence of strangers.

109 *Lunyu* 6.27, p. 243: 君子博学于文，约之以礼，亦可以弗畔矣夫 (repeated almost verbatim in 12.15, p. 504). 9.11, p. 338: 博我以文，约我以礼 (says Yan Yuan about his master's teaching). 1.12, p. 29: 知和而和，不以礼节之，亦不可行也。

becomes not the exception but the rule, restraint would seem to be good advice: "Those who fail, although they restrain themselves, are rare, indeed."[110] On unfamiliar ground, one has to reckon with infinitely more pitfalls than in familiar surroundings, and the *junzi*, being a man of public life, is under constant observation:

> If the *junzi* commits a mistake, it is like an eclipse of the sun or the moon. If he makes a mistake, everybody sees it; if he corrects it, everybody looks up to him.[111]

Hence, he is well advised to retain his composure, keep his own counsel and carefully inquire about social conventions that may apply. The master, "when coming to a given country, always asked about its government";[112] and upon entering the grand temple, he is said to have asked about everything.

> Someone said: "Who could say that the son of the man of Zou knows the rituals? Upon entering the grand temple, he asked about everything." The master, hearing this, retorted: "This is a ritual." [113]

In highly indeterminate situations where new rules of conduct must be explored, every detail may acquire great importance. "Everything that happens in such a situation, every action, every gesture, every expression, appears as a relevant, meaningful selection."[114] This explains Confucius' care to acquaint himself with everything in the grand temple—not a familiar ancestral shrine, be it noted, and it also explains the meticulous observations his disciples seem to have made about his own behavior:

> When Confucius was in his town and among his kind, he was gentle and

---

110 *Lunyu* 4.23, p. 158: 以约失之者，鲜矣。

111 *Lunyu* 19.21, p. 749: 君子之过也，如日月之食焉：过也，人皆见之；更也，人皆仰之。

112 *Lunyu* 1.10, p. 24: 夫子至于是邦也，必闻其政。

113 *Lunyu* 3.15, pp. 103–104: 或曰："孰谓鄹人之子知礼乎？入太庙，每事问。"子闻之，曰："是礼也。" Cf. 10.18, p. 429: 入太庙，每事问。

114 Raf. Vanderstraeten, "Parsons, Luhmann and the Theorem of Double Contingency", in *Journal of Classical Sociology* 2.1 2002, p. 87.

polite and appeared as if he could not speak. When in the ancestral temple or in court, he spoke clearly and fluently, but respectfully. At court, when speaking with lower officials, he was straightforward, and speaking with higher officials, he was succinct. In the presence of the ruler, he was anxious and reverent, but self-composed.[115]

When entering the ducal gate, he would be bent over as if it would not contain him. He would not stand in the middle of a gateway nor step on the threshold. Passing by the ruler's seat, his looks were agitated, his legs appeared hampered, and his voice seemed to fail him. When ascending the hall, holding his robe with both hands, he would be bent over and hold his breath as if he didn't breathe. Departing, he would descend one step and then relax his countenance, appearing cheerful. At the bottom of the stairs, he would advance swiftly, as if on winged feet. Back on his seat, he would appear anxious and reverent.[116]

There are many more descriptions of the master's every move in the *Lunyu*.[117] These would seem extremely pedantic unless one appreciates that all of this was previously unheard of. Publicity and the encounter of strangers were a new experience for an entire social class, the *shi*士. The more important it was to get everything right.

One thing that Confucius wanted to get right in particular was *names*. The "rectification of names" (*zhengming*正名) was a central concern reiterated several times in the *Lunyu*. It was the central task of "government." When asked what he would do first if entrusted with a government office, Confucius famously answered: "Of course, I would rectify the names!"[118]

---

115 *Lunyu* 10.1, pp. 363–367: 孔子于乡党，恂恂如也，似不能言者。其在宗庙朝廷，便便言，唯谨尔。朝，与下大夫言，侃侃如也；与上大夫言，訚訚如也。君在，踧踖如也，与与如也。

116 *Lunyu* 10.3, pp. 373–378: 入公门，鞠躬如也，如不容。立不中门，行不履阈。过位，色勃如也，足躩如也，其言似不足者。摄齐升堂，鞠躬如也，屏气似不息者。出，降一等，逞颜色，怡怡如也。没阶，趋进，翼如也。复其位，踧踖如也。

117 Especially in *Lunyu* 10. Bruce Brooks and Taeko Brooks, *The Original Analects: Sayings of Confucius and His Successors* (New York: Columbia University Press, 1998), p. 59, reckon that "it was presumably a useful guide for newcomers to official life." I would argue that this can be said of the entire *Lunyu*.

118 *Lunyu* 13.3, pp. 517–522: 子路曰：“卫君待子而为政，子将奚先?” 子曰：“必也正名乎！……名不正，则言不顺；言不顺，则事不成；事不成，则礼乐不兴；礼乐不兴，则刑罚不中；刑罚不中，则民无所措手足。故君子名之必可言也，言之必可行也。君子于其言，无所苟而已矣。”

This concern for names has been interpreted as the *restoration* of an old nomenclature which through abuse had become void of meaning.[119] From the perspective outlined above, this makes little sense. A radically changed society would be in need not of old, but of *new* terminology. Confucius' problem was that in a segmentary society every group quite literally acted on its own terms. In a stratified society, this was no longer feasible. The task at hand cannot have been to reinstate old terms (whose terms?), but to denominate new universal concepts valid for a stratified society. Indeed, many of Confucius' terms are new: *ren*仁, *yi*义, *zhong*忠, *shu*恕, *xin*信, indeed the entire semantic inventory of morality.[120] It is no accident that so many *Lunyu* entries record questions about these key words. Morals themselves were a new concept.

Morals

In a striking passage, Confucius is said to have told his disciple Sima-Niu that "humaneness means being reluctant about words." This statement may seem puzzling not only to Confucius' disciple SimaNiu: "Simply being reluctant about words, is that what you call humaneness?"[121] Indeed, this question may lead us to the core of Confucius' teachings the concept of *ren*, which is commonly translated as "benevolence," "humaneness," "compasssion" and the like. It is at the center of Confucius' moral teaching.

But why was Confucius so concerned with morals?[122] The moral discourse

119 For a magisterial treatment of the problem, cf. Robert H. Gassmann, *Cheng Ming. Richtigstellung der Bezeichnungen. Zu den Quelleneines Philosophemsimantiken China. EinBeitragzurKonfuzius-Forschung* (Bern: Peter Lang, 1988).

120 It may be noted that the earliest inscriptional occurrences of terms like *ren*, *zhong*, and other moral concepts date to the late 4th century BC (Zhongshan *wang* Cuo *ding*); cf. Gilbert H. Mattos, "Eastern Zhou Bronze Inscriptions", inEdward L. Shaughnessy ed., *New Sources of Early Chinese History: An Introduction to the Reading of Inscriptions and Manuscripts* (Berkeley: The Society for the Study of Early China, 1997), pp. 104–110.

121 *Lunyu* 12.3, p. 486: 司马牛问仁。子曰：“仁者，其言也讱。”曰：“其言也讱，斯谓之仁矣乎？”子曰：“为之难，言之得无讱乎？”

122 The answer, "that to be moral is joyful" (Huang Yong, "Confucius and Mencius on the Motivation to Be Moral", *Philosophy East and West* 66.1, 2010, pp. 65–87) does not seem sufficient from a socio-historical point of view.

is far from trivial, let alone self-righteous. Rather, it seems to have been fundamentally new in Confucius' times. Again, increasing social complexity may be detected as its underlying cause. Moral principles become necessary when "the living conditions in a differentiated society are too disparate as to be handled with recourse to examples and precedence." [123] They are intimately linked to the institution of rituals, which connection is especially conspicuous in the case of *ren*:

> "A man without humaneness, what has he to do with rituals?"
> "To overcome oneself and revert to rituals: that is humaneness. If for a single day, one overcomes oneself and reverts to rituals, then all under Heaven will thereupon turn to humaneness." [124]

Morals and ritual are related, or, to put it pointedly: morality is "intrinsic to ritual's structure." [125] As mentioned above, by performing rituals, the performers themselves accept and become part of the social order created by the ritual. Accepting a social order, the performers of rituals are then obliged to comply with this order. Rappaport emphasizes that failure to abide by the terms of an obligation is universally stigmatized as immoral. To the extent, then, that obligation is entailed by the acceptance intrinsic to the performance of a liturgical order, ritual establishes morality as it establishes convention. The establishment of a convention and the establishment of its morality are inextricable, if they are not, in fact, one and the same. [126]

This interconnection of rituals and morals would explain their co-occurrence in the teachings of Confucius. It is no coincidence that China's first teacher

---

123 Tenbruck, *Geschichte und Gesellschaft*, p. 322.

124 *Lunyu* 3.3, p. 81: 人而不仁，如礼何？ 12.1, p. 483: 克己复礼为仁。一日克己复礼，天下归仁焉。

125 Roy A. Rappaport, *Ritual and Religion in the Making of Humanity* (Cambridge: Cambridge University Press, 1999), p. 132. Significantly, morals and ritual coincide in the German term "Sittlichkeit."

126 Ibid., p. 132. This seems compatible with the definition of Niklas Luhmann, *Soziale Systeme: Grundriß einer allgemeinen Theorie*, p. 318: "All morals refer to the question of whether and under which circumstances men esteem or disesteem one another. Esteem is meant to signify a generalized recognition and appreciation which rewards the fact that someone else fulfills the expectations that are thought to be a precondition for the continuation of social elations." If such expectations are established through a ritual order, then adherence to this order is the fundamental moral act.

was also her first moralizer. Whereas in segmentary societies, moral codes "rested heavily on enculturation, internalized sanctions, and ridicule," [127] they were no longer tacitly understood in a stratified society. Now, just like rituals, they had to be made explicit. Rituals *and* morals gained importance when dealing with strangers. What I would like to suggest, then, is that *ren* became relevant not in village or family life, but in the realm "under Heaven," when "living in a given state." [128] In short, *ren* was called for in the public arena, when dealing with the Other writ large.

The palaces and temples, halls and academies in which the elites of Chunqiu and Zhanguo times converged were all located in newly emerging cities. These cities were the place were a public sphere emerged and where strangers had to get along with each other. They were the place where rituals thrived, and with them, the discourse of morals.

Confucius taught his disciples to be *civil* in a double sense: courteous and fit for city life.[129] In the context of public life, Confucius' central moral precept, far from being banal, becomes a useful rule of conduct: "Do not do to others what you do not wish for yourself."[130] This is the essence of *ren*. It consists in accepting the Other writ large as having the same qualities as oneself: this would hardly have to be emphasized in societies with a low level of differentiation, but it is crucial for social order in a stratified society. Daniel Lerner has singled out *empathy*—"the capacity to see oneself on the other fellow's situation" —as a key qualification for life in a mobile society:

---

127 Morton H. Fried, "On the Evolution of Social Stratification and the State", p. 721, with reference to legal principles that "required formal statement" only with the transition to a stratified society. Laws, of course, are functionally equivalent to rituals and morals insofar as they define rules of conduct.

128 *Lunyu* 17.5, p. 683: 能行五者于天下，为仁矣。15.10, p. 621: 子贡问为仁。子曰:"工欲善其事，必先利其器。居是邦也，事其大夫之贤者，友其士之仁者." Indeed, morals may even serve to get by in "barbarian" countries; cf. 15.6, p. 616: 言忠信，行笃敬，虽蛮貊之邦行矣。言不忠信，行不笃敬，虽州里行乎哉?

129 A similar observation could, of course, be made for the epithet "political," which is so often applied to Confucius' teachings. In fact, in 18th century Europe "political" designated any kind of behavior outside the home, equating "political" with "public" (Kieserling, *Kommunikation unter Anwesenden: Studien über Interaktionssysteme*, p. 455).

130 *Lunyu* 12.2, p. 485: 仲弓问仁。子曰: "出门如见大宾，使民如承大祭。己所不欲，勿施于人." Cf., for similar statements, 5.13, p. 182, and 15.24, p. 631.

> This is an indispensable skill for people moving out of traditional settings. Ability to empathize may make all the difference, for example, when the newly mobile persons are villagers who grew up knowing all the extant individuals, roles and relationships in their environment. Outside his village or tribe, each must meet new individuals, recognize new roles, and learn new relationships involving himself.[131]

Confucius did not simply appeal to his contemporaries to all be nice to each other again, but he first pointed out the fundamental necessity of accepting the other as an equal partner. In his times, this was a fundamentally new insight. In a society that was just making the transition to stratification, it became the central quality of the *junzi* to recognize the Other not as dangerous, vile and contagious, but as essentially the same as himself. Only thus the unknown could become known and be adequately judged: "Only the humane are capable of loving others and of hating others."[132] For those who are not humane, the Other remains incomprehensible, beyond love or hate, in short: beyond morals.

Education

The aspiring *junzi* were confronted with roles for which there were no precedents, roles they needed to *learn*. In fact, the very idea of learning, in the sense of active, conscious and more or less formal acquisition of knowledge, was very likely new in their times. It is no mere coincidence that Confucius

---

131 Daniel Lerner, *The Passing of Traditional Society: Modernizing the Middle East*, p. 50. Although Lerner's "major hypothesis" is that "high empathic capacity is the predominant personal style only in modern society, which is distinctively industrial, urban, literate and *participant*", the parallels to Confucius' times are striking: it witnessed a comparable surge in mobility, rationality, urbanity, and literacy, albeit without industrialization and other concomitants of European modernity. For a forceful discussion of empathy as the driving force of human civilization, cf. Jeremy Rifkin, *The Empathic Civilization* (New York: Tarcher/Penguin, 2009).

132 *Lunyu* 4.3, p. 141: 惟仁者能好人，能恶人。

is generally considered China's first teacher.[133] Arguably, there was no need for teachers in a segmentary society. In such kin-based societies, knowledge and norms of behavior are transmitted not through education but through *socialization*, that is through "a process which is detached from the intention of teaching and learning," in which not so much the formalized elements of culture are transmitted, but "deep-rooted, characteristic beliefs, feelings, values and norms, in short, an image of the world and of oneself which cannot be contained in the cognitive realm." [134]

Socialization is the informal, intuitive, often non-verbal transmission of social norms. Practiced *en famille* and *en passant*, it is virtually inseparable from everyday life. Education, on the other hand, is *intentional* socialization: formal, conscious and explicit transmission of cultural knowledge. As such, it claims an autonomous realm apart from everyday communication. There can be no professional "socializers" (except in a very different sense), but only professional teachers. By the same token, nobody in society can escape socialization, but one can certainly eschew education.[135] Education only becomes necessary under certain historical circumstances, namely when society significantly outgrows family life in terms of complexity. Education, as Hegel has taught us, means "elevation to universality." [136]

> Education increases the possibility to imagine what is going on in other
> people's minds ... even if one knows the other not or not good enough.
> ... Education ... makes this possible even in non–standardized situations,

---

133 On Confucius as a teacher, cf. Chen Jingpan, *Confucius as a Teacher—Philosophy of Confucius with Special Reference to Its Educational Implications* (Beijing: Foreign Languages Press, 1990); H. G. Creel, *Confucius: The Man and the Myth* (London: Routledge & Kegan Paul, 1951), pp. 84–109.

134 Tenbruck, *Geschichte und Gesellschaft*, p. 102. Cf. also Niklas Luhmann, *Das Erziehungssystem der Gesellschaft*, ed. by Dieter Lenzen (Frankfurt/M.: Suhrkamp, 2002), pp. 54–62.

135 In Confucius' view, such people were the most despicable (*Lunyu* 16.9)

136 Cf. the interpretation by Hans-Georg Gadamer, *Wahrheit und Methode: Grundzüge einer philosophischen Hermeneutik* (Tübingen: J.C.B. Mohr, 1990), p. 18: "Bildung als Erhebung zur Allgemeinheit ist also eine menschliche Aufgabe. Sie verlangt Aufopferung der Besonderheit für das Allgemeine."

whereas socialization remains very strongly tied to its original context.[137]

In all these respects, education caters to the requirements of an elite society, where dealing with strangers in heterogeneous, unfamiliar contexts is everyday business.

There is more to the story. In a society that transcends localities, it is no longer possible to stabilize social order through regular face-to-face interaction. Rather, the abstract rules of a stratified society need to be systematically de-contextualized. The solution to this problem was provided by *writing*, a medium that made the kind of abstraction possible that an elite society needed. Chinese writing, though available for centuries before, had so far remained in an epigraphic stage.[138] Now it developed its full potential. It is no coincidence that the age of Confucius saw the beginning of Chinese manuscript culture, nor is it an accident that the master is credited with the compilation of the canonical texts. Confucius certainly does not deserve the credit personally, but the society he lived in could not have developed without the medium of writing. Writing was the concomitant of a stratified society.

Confucius' life straddled the move from an oral to a literate culture,[139] and just like the transition from a segmentary to a stratified society, this is reflected in the *Lunyu*. The text itself, consisting almost entirely of dialogues and lacking traces of literary craft, clearly betrays an oral context. Notably, Confucius' much-praised way of "conveying his teachings according to the talent" of the student (*yincai shijiao*因材施教), adjusting his explanations to changing needs

---

137 Niklas Luhmann, *Das Erziehungssystem der Gesellschaft*, p. 81. Note that Luhmann (p. 69) associates an increased demand for education with the emergence not of a stratified, but of a functionally differentiated society. In any case, growing social complexity is at the root of the matter.

138 This is not to say that there were no writing materials other than bronze, stone and bones in use; there most certainly were. However, they do not seem to have exerted decisive influence on textual production. Writing still remained highly restricted in scope: virtually the only extant sources are bronze inscriptions, containing ritual or documentary texts. Writing remained lapidary in a very literal sense.

139 This, of course, refers only to elite culture. Just like the majority of the populace remained rooted in segmentary groups (fn. 50), this majority also remained illiterate.

and situations, is typical for oral, context-bound instruction.[140] Such flexibility is hardly possible when using textbooks. True, "one need not necessarily have read writings in order to be called learned," as Zilu put it, but this implies that one certainly *could* learn by writings.[141] Indeed, this seems to be implied when Confucius told his son to go and learn the "songs" and the "rituals": note that Boyu "*retired* and studied the songs" (cf. fn. 79), that is he studied them in private, which would seem to imply that he read them. And what, exactly, was to be learned from the "songs"?

> With the songs, you can stimulate, contemplate, congregate, and express resentment. Keeping them close, you may serve your father; taking them further, you may serve your ruler. And you will get acquainted with many names of birds, beasts, herbs and trees.[142]

In other words, the songs imparted knowledge necessary for partaking in an elite society: they conveyed social skills, and they contained practical information. The "many names of birds, beasts, herbs and trees" to be learned from them very likely do not refer to one's regional flora and fauna (which should be well-known, anyway) but to those of foreign states. The "Guofeng" section of the *Shijing* as we have it today would have been ideal for this purpose, arranging all the "names" in regional contexts.

This example may illustrate the connection between writing and the emergence of a trans-local society. Writing enables communication that transcends local borders. It makes it possible to convey just the kind of abstract, decontextualized information that is needed for interaction in such a society: information that cannot be obtained by direct observation or experience, but must be learned.

---

140 "This concreteness and situational dependence," writes Bernhard Giesen, *Die Entdinglichung des Sozialen: Eineevolutions theoretische Perspektive auf die Postmoderne*, p. 26, "imparts to the elements of knowledge a fragmentary character that makes sense only in practical usage."

141 *Lunyu* 11.23, p. 464: 何必读书，然后为学? Here, *shu* certainly does not mean "books" in a physical sense nor in the sense of a coherent œuvre; but it does seem to imply texts meant to be read and re-read.

142 *Lunyu* 17.8, p. 689: 诗，可以兴，可以观，可以群，可以怨。迩之事父，远之事君，多识于鸟兽草木之名。

This is, I believe, one of the most significant and important ideas in Chinese philosophy, and one that I have argued even had an impact on the western Enlightenment.[2] Even if it did not, its development in the "Wuxing" account of human moral psychology is uniquely detailed account of how dispositions develop to goodness in the body, and what environmental conditions are necessary for them to do so.

More recently, a number of works have tried to use insights from cognitive science to locate the basis of religious morality in the human mind. I will introduce several of these works in order to try to explain some of the ways in which these modern views are similar to the ancient Chinese view, and some ways in which they differ. In particular, I will pay close attention to the *external* aspects of these internalist pictures. At the end of the paper, I will ask whether the "Wuxing" text makes the same assumptions about the importance of a universal heart/mind that the *Mengzi* does.

The Roots of Morality in the Heart/Mind: The *Mengzi*

Do moral impulses come from the mind or are they learned? This is a key debate in early China, and it concerns the term *xing*性, which is often translated as "human nature." The *Mengzi* uses thought experiments to illustrate its claim that human nature includes an innate quality of certain feelings of right and wrong, for example. One of these thought experiments is designed to show that the ancients had a spontaneous moral reaction to the sight of the corpses of their deceased parents. The *Mengzi* uses a detailed description of a child seeing the exposed bodies of his or her parents, trying to excite the same spontaneous reaction in the reader. Each day when the child passed the corpses, "foxes were eating them, and flies and mole-crickets sucking at them." 狐狸食之，蝇蚋姑嘬之 The child reacts with revulsion: "forehead beaded with sweat, and eyes looked away so as not to see. It was not the case that the sweating was done for others, but it was the *heart/mind within expressing itself* upon the face."其

---

2 Mark Csikszentmihalyi, "Finding Altruism in China: The Confucian Corpus and the Quest for Universal Benevolence", A lecture in Harvard University, February 25, 2014.

The Heart/Mind（xin 心）in the *Mengzi* and "Wuxing" and | Mark Csikszentmihalyi
Modern Cognitive Science Approaches to the "Embodiment" | 齐思敏
of Goodness

颡有泚，睨而不视，夫泚也，非为人泚，中心达于面目[3] As a result, they "returned home for large baskets for dirt and covered the bodies with them." 归反藁梩而掩之 There are two important aspects of this description in the *Mengzi*. First, it argues that there is visual proof that internal dispositions produce bodily reactions.[4] Second, it goes on to argue that these dispositions must be "extended" (*tui*推) to become the consistent behavior patterns often called "virtues."[5]

The "biological" turn in the *Mengzi* is rooted in an emphasis on the heart/mind and the way that it is the seat of the four key moral virtues. An early reference to the four-chambered heart may be behind the division of that organ into four parts. The "heart/minds" of compassion (*ceyin*恻隐), shame (*xiuwu*羞恶), modesty and yielding (*cirang*辞让), and right and wrong (*shifei*是非) are the basis of these virtues. The *Mengzi* explains:

> The heart of compassion is the bud of benevolence; the heart of shame, of dutifulness. The heart of modesty and yielding is the bud of the ritual propriety. The heart of right and wrong is the bud of wisdom. All people have these four buds just as they all have four limbs.[6]

> 恻隐之心，仁之端也；羞恶之心，义之端也；辞让之心，礼之端也；是非之心，智之端也。人之有是四端也，犹其有四体也。

A closely related aspect of the *Mengzi* is its consistent position that anyone can become a sage. Assertions of human perfectibility appear in different forms

---

3 *Mengzi* 6A5, see *Mengzi zhengyi,* 11.405–407 (cf. Lau 1970, p. 105).

4 Philip J. Ivanhoe calls them "give-away actions" because their spontaneity and directness are seen as proof of their authenticity.

5 Emily McRae has argues that there are four main features of the method of extension that differentiate Mengzi's method from that of Yi Zhi. These features are: 1) extension is a rational process, making use of our beliefs, judgments, imaginations and values, but it does not rely on philosophical doctrine; 2) extension works with, not against, human (and individual) psychological tendencies; 3) extension is a gradual process that sustains itself, owing to a positive feedback loop; and 4) extension involves only certain starting emotions. See Emily McRae, "The Cultivation of Moral Emotions and Mengzi's Method of Extension", *Philosophy East and West* 61.4 (2011): 587–608.

6 *Mengzi* 2A6, *Mengzi zhengyi*, pp. 232–236.

same in listening to sounds. All eyes have the same standards of beauty in seeing hues. When it comes to the heart/mind, is it alone really without common features? What are these common features? These are pattern and righteousness. The sages first understood what my heart/mind has in common with others. Therefore, pattern and righteousness please my heart just as meat from grass and grain-fed animals pleases my mouth.[12]

> 口之于味也，有同耆焉；耳之于声也，有同听焉；目之于色也，有同美焉。至于心，独无所同然乎？心之所同然者何也？谓理也义也。圣人先得我心之所同然耳。故理义之悦我心，犹刍豢之悦我口。

Both writers, despite being more than 20 centuries apart, use a similar metaphor to convince the reader that the idea that the mind or heart/mind is structured similarly for all people should not be hard to accept, given that people have common tastes when it comes to food or music. This similarity underscores the way in which both approaches argue that there are innate dispositions that explain a shared sense of what is "good" in a society.

Cognitive science approaches have developed in several different directions since Boyer's book. Some earlier writers like David Sloan Wilson and Elliott Sober had written about the importance of cultural evolution in developing the moral behavior known as altruism.[13] More recently, Ara Norenzayan has argued for the evolutionary adaptiveness of "prosocial religious beliefs" in

---

12 *Mengzi* 6A7, see *Mengzi zhengyi* 11.410.

13 David Sloan Wilson and Elliott Sober, *Unto Others: The Evolution and Psychology of Unselfish Behavior* (Havard: Havard University Press,1999) argue for cultural evolution approach to altruism. Wilson and Sober address the question of whether people have other-directed ultimate desires. They use a model of biological and cultural evolution to argue that hedonism is maladaptive compared to a redundant system in which altruistic actions arise both from altruistic ultimate desires reinforced by egoistic ultimate desires using the example of parental care.

communities as a way of explaining monotheism.[14] These are both examples of attempts to combine psychology or cognitive science with cultural evolution. Other books have tried to use different models of the mind. Francisco J. Varela, Evan Thompson, and Eleanor Rosch have argued that Buddhist understandings of the mind mesh better with modern cognitive science.[15] It is hard to imagine that discussions of the roots of morality in the human mind will take place in the future without taking into account models of the mind developed using the insights of cognitive science.

Yet early critiques of Boyer indicate that debates are arising about the way that biology and culture interact. For example, Jeppe Sinding Jensen has criticized Boyer's approach because of its focus only on the individual mind, ignoring the social and cultural dimensions of religion. Specifically, Jensen writes:

> In order to move forward in theorizing religion in relation to cognition, we need to pay more attention to extended cognition, distributed cognition, social and cultural cognition and normative cognition, to the roles of intentionality and language, and—probably—to a greater extent than we can currently imagine.[16]

---

14 Ara Norenzayan, *Big Gods: How Religion Transformed Cooperation and Conflict* (Princeton: Princeton University Press, 2015) treats the cultural evolution of religion. Norenzayan argues for the adaptive value of prosocial religions with "Big Gods." "Prosocial religions, with their Big Gods who watch, intervene, and demand hard-to-fake loyalty displays, facilitated the rise of cooperation in large groups of anonymous strangers. In turn, these expanding groups took their prosocial religious beliefs and practices with them, further ratcheting up large-scale cooperation in a runaway process of cultural evolution." (p. 8)

15 In *The Embodied Mind: Cognitive Science and Human Experience* (Cambridge, Mass.: MIT Press,1993), the three authors argue that the models of the mind behind mindfulness/awareness meditation have important insights, such as the idea of "calming or taming the mind." "The purpose of calming the mind in Buddhism is not to become absorbed but *to render the mind able to be present with itself long enough to gain insight into its own nature and functioning*." (p. 24, emphasis added). Owen Flanagan points out the ways in which not just do models of the mind differ across cultures, but so do the ideas of what is human flourishing. See *The Bodhisattva's Brain: Buddhism Naturalized* (Cambridge, Mass: MIT Press, 2011).

16 Jeppe Sinding Jensen, "Religion as the Intended Product of Brain Functions in the 'Standard Cognitive Science of Religion Model': On Pascal Boyer, *Religion Explained* (2001) and Ilkka Pyysiäinen, *How Religion Works* (Boston: Brill, 2003)". In M. Stausberg, ed. *Contemporary Theories of Religion: A Critical Companion* (London: Routledge, 2009). pp. 129–155, p. 148.

Indeed, one of the reasons that Boyer's reductive model was taken seriously is that it is based on a simplistic phenomenological understanding of religion, one that tends to focus only on certain aspects of religion, and ignores others that are dismissed as simply local manifestations of religion.[17] Religion, considered as a complex phenomenon, is much harder to account for as simply a result of the inferential processes of the individual brain. If this is the critique of Boyer's innatist picture, was there a similar critique of the innatist picture in the *Mengzi*?

The Revised Account of the Roots of Morality in the Heart/Mind: "Wuxing"

There is an obvious choice in looking for critiques of the *Mengzi*'s innatist model. The *Xunzi*荀子, containing essays connected with the early third century BCE. scholar of that name (Xun Kuang荀况) holds that the strongest innate motivation is connected not with moral dispositions but with desires. However, the *Xunzi* argues that the rites and music that were developed by the ancient sage kings may restrict and re-channel desires so that one may eventually train oneself to desire to act morally. Like the character Gaozi 告子 in the *Mencius*, the *Xunzi* provides a largely external solution to the problem of morality in Early China.[18]

There is another choice, however, within the tradition of *Mengzi* interpre-

---

17 Many cognitive science approaches are vulnerable to basic critiques about complex societies: 1) If religions are "prosocial," is this in terms of dogma or effect? You count Christianity as prosocial because it sometimes features prosocial rhetoric, but is the effect really prosocial, and if it isn't, why is rhetoric adaptive? 2) While many institutions from fraternities to corporations have prosocial doctrine, arguably the real skill that these institutions teach is hypocrisy, and that is actually adaptive (for the same reason that parasitism is such a successful strategy in the animal kingdom?) —or at least in complex societies, it is one way a group can succeed. 3) If a meme succeeds, is it simply because due to its prosocial aspects? Could it also be due to geography, evangelizing, or affiliation with military power? How could one even rule out such confounding variables?

18 David Wong, among others, have pointed out that there are internalist aspects of the *Xunzi*. In addition, passages like *Mengzi* 4A17 make it clear that the *Mengzi*'s position also has externalist aspects: 富岁，子弟多赖；凶岁，子弟多暴。非天之降才尔殊也，其所以陷溺其心者然也。"After good harvests the children of the people are most of them good, while after bad ones most of them are violent. It is not any difference in the qualities conferred by Heaven that has made them different."

tation itself, one that I will call the "revised innatist model." The "Wuxing" text found at Mawangdui 马王堆 and Guodian 郭店 refines *Mengzi*'s internalist picture in a particular way that I think is more closely analogous to the critiques of Boyer's picture above. The "Wuxing" takes the four virtues of the *Mengzi* and adds to it a fifth, that of sagacity (*sheng* 圣). The ability to harmonize all five virtues was seen to be progressing a step beyond what is merely "goodness" and following the "human Way," to "virtue" and following "*tian*'s Way":

> When all five kinds of virtuous action are in harmony, it is called "virtue." When four kinds of action are in harmony, it is called "good." Good is the human Way. Virtue is *tian*'s Way.

> 德之行五和谓之德 , 四行和谓之善 。 善人道也 , 德天道也 。

This distinction between "virtuous" (*de* 德) action, and action that is simply "good" (*shan* 善) highlights a crucial difference between the *Mengzi* and the "Wuxing." In terms of its repair to the innatist picture of morality, it appears to be rather different to the "cultural" answer demanded in the cognitive science models, because it centers on the suprahuman notion of *tian*.

The idea that *tian* can suffuse virtue in a person is seen in other early texts, but nowhere is it worked out in the detail in which it is in the "Wuxing." One example is from a Han dynasty text, the "Taizu" 泰族 (Great Gathering), Chapter 20 of the *Huainanzi* 淮南子. This text makes the case that the ideal ruler is endowed by *tian* in such a way that it allows him to rule the world:

> Therefore the sage takes *tian*'s *qi* to his chest and embraces *tian*'s heart/ mind, grasps the center and holds to harmony. Without leaving his courts and halls is able to extend to the four expanses, transforming habits and changing customs. The people transform and move to the good, as if they were born that way. This is the means by which one can transform one-self into a spirit. The Odes says: "Once one attends to this and follows this, there may be harmony and peace." [19]

---

19 *Huainanzi jiaoshi* 淮南子校释 20.2040. The reference to the *Odes* is to *Mao* 165, "Fa mu" 伐木. See Mark Csikszentmihalyi, *Material Virtue* p. 157 n142 for more details.

故圣人怀天气，抱天心，执中含和，不下庙堂而衍四海，
变习易俗，民化而迁善，若性诸己，能以神化也。《诗》云：
神之听之，终和且平。

This notion of receiving *qi* from *tian* is seen in the "Xinshu" 心术 chapter of the *Guanzi*管子. It says that if one "can make empty one's desires, then the spirits will enter his dwelling" 虚其欲神将入舍 while "if not clean, then the spirits will not remain". 不洁则神不处 [20] The spirits and *qi* are external factors that will only affect you if you have undergone internal purification of the mind through eliminating desires.

What does *tian xin*天心 mean in the above passages? On this point, Yu Yingshi 余英时 writes that scholarly attention to the concept of "the unity of heaven and human beings" dates back to Qian Mu 钱穆. In addition, he credits Feng Youlan 冯友兰 and Jin Yuelin 金岳霖 for drawing further attention to the concept. [21] In contrast to these previous scholars, however, Yu Yingshi identifies the earliest stratum of this view with early Chinese shamans. He notes that *tian* expressed itself through the body of the shaman. Subsequently, it was not until this connection became abstracted that philosophers began to connect *dao*道 and *xin*心 and created a "new" view of *tian ren heyi*天人合一. [22] The examples that Yu uses of this latter development of the primitive concept begin with the moral psychology of the "Xinshu" chapter of the *Guanzi*. For Yu, this is but the first step or stage in the historical evolution of the concept of *tian ren heyi*.

Yu's insight is consistent the with way the "Wuxing" argues for the importance of an outside inspiration in the context of the development of virtue. An example is the influence of the gentleman. Just as the *Huainanzi* did, the "Wuxing" uses the *Shi* 诗as its authority for its discussion of the mind's need for an outside stimulus.

For people who are neither benevolent nor wise, "having not yet seen the

---

20 *Guanzi jiaozheng*管子校正13.219.

21 *Lun tian ren zhiji: Zhongguo gudai sixiang qiyuan shitan*论天人之际: 中国古代思想起源试探 (Tai-bei: Linking Publishing Co.Ltd. 联经出版事业公司, 2014), pp. 171–172. Yu cites Jin Yuelin 金岳霖, "Chinese Philosophy", in *Social Sciences in China* 1.1 (March 1980): 83–93.

22 Yu, *Lun tian ren zhiji*, p. 63.

The Heart/Mind (xin 心) in the *Mengzi* and "Wuxing" and
Modern Cognitive Science Approaches to the "Embodiment"
of Goodness
| Mark Csikszentmihalyi
齐思敏

Gentleman," their anxious mind cannot be "disturbed," and "having seen
the Gentleman," their mind cannot be "joyful."

"Once I see him, once I observe him,
My mind will then be [joyful]."
This [is what it means.][23]

不仁不智，未见君子，忧心不能惙惙。既见君子，心不能
悦。亦既见之，亦既观之，我心则［悦］，此之谓［也］。

In this way, people who are not yet virtuous can be moved by the influence
of the gentleman. This development of the *Mengzi*'s thought requires a person
to turn inward and examine his or her motives for action. The *Mengzi* counsels
misguided rulers to "take the measure of his own mind" (*duo xin*度心), while the
Guanzi invites the sage to "cleanse the mind" (*bai xin* 白心). By contrast, Gaozi
argues that "a person must not seek something in their mind that they cannot
attain as an external doctrine." 不得于言勿求于心 For Gaozi, the entire psychological picture developed by the school of the *Mengzi*, with its attention to
the innate dispositions to dispositions and *qi*, is, strictly speaking, irrelevant to
morality.

It is difficult to say precisely what the phrase *tianxin* means, but it is clear
that the "Wuxing" is making a form of the argument in the *Guanzi* that self-
cultivation involves making oneself receptive to the proper external influences.
While the *Mengzi*'s moral psychology does not explain why some people are
sages and others are not, in the "Wuxing" the presence or absence of the gentleman
is one external influence that determines whether one can gain access to the "*tian*'s
Way." Whether one wants to call this a cultural or a religious factor, the addition of
tian to the materialistic account of moral psychology is a significant revision to the
innatist picture within the discourse of the *Mengzi*'s discussion of virtue. Is this a
religious appeal to one of the "Big Gods" that Norenzayan insists are a universal
projection of the human mind? Not according to Chen Lai陈来, who has written
that the Mawangdui commentary to the "Wuxing" that it represents a mid-Warring

---

23 Quoting "Chu che" 出车 (Presenting chariots, *Mao* 168). See Mark Csikszentmihalyi, *Material Virtue*, p. 283.

States view that:

> The content of *tian*'s Way and the result of listening to it is a practice of guiding all kinds of virtuous action, and there is no mystical implication here.[24]

> 天道的内容和闻天道的结果是引向各种德行的实践，在这里已经并没有任何神秘的含义了。

Here, it is important to note that Chen is writing in an atmosphere where the phenomenological underpinnings of Norenzayan are not assumed, and so there is no need to assume that all references to suprahuman powers are references to the same epiphenomenal religious worldview. The problem with universal explanatory systems like those of Boyer is that they are reductive. This is a problem that the *Zhuangzi* points out by attacking the argument for universal moral sentiments expressed earlier by the *Mengzi*:

> Humans eat the flesh of grass-fed and grain-fed animals, deer eat grass, centipedes find snakes tasty, and hawks and falcons relish mice. Of these four animals, which one knows how food ought to taste?[25]

> 民食刍豢，麋鹿食荐，蝍且甘带，鸱鸦耆鼠，四者孰知正味？

Whether or not one accepts Chen's reading of the "Wuxing" commentary, it is important to point out that *tianxin* does not necessarily mean that an anthropomorphic *tian* has a mind like that of a human. The important aspect of the "Wuxing" is how it combines the discussion of the *Mengzi*'s virtues with another discourse that is about using ritual and meditation to prepare the heart/mind for the proper reception of external influences.Even when external influ-

---

24 Chen Lai 陈来 , *Zhushu Wuxing yu jianbo yanjiu* 竹书五行与简帛研究 (Beijing: SDX Joint Publishing Company 生活・读书・新知三联书店 , 2009), p. 171.

25 *Zhuangzi* 2, Watson's translation.

The Heart/Mind (xin 心) in the *Mengzi* and "Wuxing" and
Modern Cognitive Science Approaches to the "Embodiment"
of Goodness

Mark Csikszentmihalyi
齐思敏

ences are important, cultivating one's mind is a prerequisite for receiving those influences. Even the external influence requires an internal change.

Conclusion

From a comparative point of view, I have tried to show how there are some interesting parallels between the innatist pictures of the *Mengzi* and certain contemporary approaches to grounding religion in the mind. Among these is an emphasis on materialist approach to moral psychology, a view that mental structures are everywhere the same, and of course the central idea that goodness is rooted in the body. One strong difference is how writers have tried to combine the focus on the mind and heart/mind with external influences. Jensen's critique of Boyer faults him for failing to understand the role of culture and the fact that cognition is a process that happens on levels beyond that of the individual. This repair seeks to expand the scope of the "cognitive." The "Wuxing" amends the system of the *Mengzi* by adding a fifth comprehensive virtue that is infused by the suprahuman agency of *tian*. This repair seeks to combine the *Mengzi*'s virtue system with a view that the mind must also be made receptive to beneficial external influences. Both of these, however, retain the fundamental aspect that their models are universal, since they are grounded in the mind and the heart/mind, and in this way represent a distinctive and important approach to morality that fundamentally differs from the *Xunzi* and many major western religious understandings of the mind and the heart/mind.

广"小大之辩"

——从《庄子·逍遥游》说起

陈少明

（中山大学哲学系）

是否可以这样说，越是司空见惯的现象，越是不假思索的表达，背后蕴藏的问题就越复杂，因而对哲学家可能就越有吸引力？例如有与无或大与小这种习以为常的说法，在我们的传统中，至少从庄子开始，就构成玄思的对象。不过，自我们从西方把"哲学"的观念引入中国之后，因热衷西方玄学（metaphysics）缘故，有与无时不时会被提及，而大小或小大之说，除讨论庄子之外，则罕有被当成理论对象来对待的。[1] 其实，虽然有无是质的不同而大小只涉及量的变化，但在一个以"有"为基础的世界上，大小正是与之关系最密切的问题。尽管把精妙的情景展示转化成抽象的概念分析，是高难度的任务，但本文的论述，依然绕不开经典。我们将顺着庄子的视角向前瞭望，最终把眼光投向文本以外的世界。

一、论题

众所周知，《庄子》开篇为《逍遥游》，而《逍遥游》的第一论题，

---

[1] 当然也有例外，陈嘉映教授的《说大小》（原刊《读书》1999 年第 3 期，后收入《从感觉开始》，华夏出版社，2005 年），是近 20 年来罕见的相关专题论文。该文为用法决定意义的观点进行了精彩的演示，本文则试图探讨相关语言使用背后的观念机制。

则系"小大之辩"。它既是解读该篇的关键,也是理解庄书思想的重要环节。问题从对"大"的想象开始,开篇就用神话般的笔调,记述一个其规模在世间罕有其匹的存在物由鲲变鹏的故事:

> 北冥有鱼,其名为鲲。鲲之大,不知其几千里也。化而为鸟,其名为鹏。鹏之背,不知其几千里也;怒而飞,其翼若垂天之云。是鸟也,海运则将徙于南冥。南冥者,天池也。

这一基本情节随后用类似的文字又重复两次。作为对比的"小"者,则是常见的昆虫与小鸟。而"小大之辩"正是这几个小生命的窃议引起的:

> 蜩与学鸠笑之曰:"我决起而飞,抢榆枋,时则不至而控于地而已矣,奚以之九万里而南为?"
> 斥鴳笑之曰:"彼且奚适也?我腾跃而上,不过数仞而下,翱翔蓬蒿之间,此亦飞之至也,而彼且奚适也?"此小大之辩也。

就此而言,这个"辩"其实只是小者对大者无知且轻薄的议论,或许鲲鹏根本就不知斥鴳们的存在。作者的评论是:

> 小知不及大知,小年不及大年。奚以知其然也?朝菌不知晦朔,蟪蛄不知春秋,此小年也。楚之南有冥灵者,以五百岁为春,五百岁为秋;上古有大椿者,以八千岁为春,八千岁为秋。而彭祖乃今以久特闻,众人匹之,不亦悲乎!

因此,尽管情节独特,令人印象深刻,但如果囿于文本字面信息，这小大之辩，不过就是大小、高低、贵贱、是非这一非常世俗的二元对比的价值模式的生动展示而已。读者得到的教诲，也不过是人生要提高眼界、胸怀之类的道德说教。[2] 假若如是，庄子的思想魅力必将大打折扣。

幸好郭象提供了一种颠覆性的解读。他不认为存在对眼界狭小者的讥讽，而是强调无论大小，适性而已：

> 夫小大虽殊，而放于自得之场，则物任其性，事称其能，各当其分，逍遥一也，岂容胜负于其间哉！
>
> 夫质小者所资不待大，则质大者所用不得小矣。故理有至分，物有定极，各足称事，其济一也。
>
> 苟足于其性，则虽大鹏无以自贵于小鸟，小鸟无羡于天池，而荣愿有余矣。故小大虽殊，逍遥一也。[3]

适性即逍遥，这不仅扭转了文本的字面逻辑，更颠覆了世俗的价值理想。不愧为《庄子》第一解人，郭象的灵感也来自《庄子》，从《齐物论》甚至《秋水》中可以找到更充分的依据。《齐物论》就说："天下莫大于秋毫之末，而大山为小；莫寿乎殇子，而彭祖为夭。天地与我并生，而万物与我为一。"这种对常识的颠倒，背后的根源恰好是对社会纷争的异议："自我观之，仁义之端，是非之涂，樊然殽乱，吾恶能知其辩！"大小问题实质是价值问题，齐大小与齐贵贱、齐是非，殊途同归。《秋水》虽然出之外篇，但历来受注家重视，公认它得庄子精髓：

---

2 唐君毅先生就持有大优于小的观点，参见其《中国哲学原论·原道篇》（台北：台湾学生书局，1978 年版，卷一，页 349–350）。
3 郭象注，见郭庆藩辑《庄子集释》第一册，北京：中华书局，1961 年版，页 1，7，9。

> 以道观之，物无贵贱；以物观之，自贵而相贱；以俗观
> 之，贵贱不在己。以差观之，因其所大而大之，则万物莫不大；
> 因其所小而小之，则万物莫不小；知天地之为稊米也，知毫末
> 之为丘山也，则差数睹矣。以功观之，因其所有而有之，则万
> 物莫不有；因其所无而无之，则万物莫不无；知东西之相反，
> 而不可以相无，则功分定矣。以趣观之，因其所然而然之，则
> 万物莫不然；因其所非而非之，则万物莫不非；知尧桀之自然
> 而相非，则趣操睹矣。

这里，从贵贱、大小、有无到是非，作为可对位推演的二元结构通通列在一起，是对《逍遥游》《齐物论》论点的综合。对现代读者来说，随之而来的问题可能是，按事实与价值二分的观点，大小、有无只是认知范畴，而贵贱、是非属于评价问题，两者并不同类，逻辑上无必然联系。所谓认知，是对象与判断具有确定性，可以找到公共评判标准的问题。而在价值问题上，"自贵而相贱"，或公婆各有理，则是比比皆是的现象。为什么可以从大小入手说贵贱？到底是比喻还是论证？如果是论证，则不能在逻辑上跳跃。假如是比喻，只要特征相似即可成立。但后者是修辞，缺乏说理的力量。也许，这种独特的联系，背后有它根深蒂固的原因。要领略庄子的深邃，必须超出文本的界限。

二、常识

大小是生活中再普通不过的用语。在常识中，它是我们从空间打量事物的方式，如大江大海，或小草小花。庄子也是这样看的，所以他说："北冥有鱼，其名为鲲。鲲之大，不知其几千里也。化而为鸟，其名为鹏。鹏之背，不知其几千里也。"几千里长的鱼或鸟，的确大

得出奇。但是，比较大小有时并不限于使用大小的字眼，规模较大的事物如山河，我们会转化为高低或远近。高低与远近标示高度与距离，分别是用空间中的单一维度来表示大小。鲲鹏之大，也是通过长度几千里来标示的。珠穆朗玛峰比白云山高，或长江比珠江长，实际上也是在比较各自的大小。有时候，我们还把大小变成距离，然后通过特定的速度，折算成运动时间的长短，比如说所走路程用了一袋烟的工夫。庄子则进一步把旅程同准备粮草需要的时间联系起来："适莽苍者，三飡而反，腹犹果然；适百里者，宿舂粮；适千里者，三月聚粮。之二虫又何知！"他甚至直接把寿命短长称作小年与大年："朝菌不知晦朔，蟪蛄不知春秋，此小年也。"而"以五百岁为春，五百岁为秋"的冥灵，上古"以八千岁为春，八千岁为秋"的大椿，自然都是大年。而我们通常会简单些，说绕山或者环湖徒步，需要 3 小时或者 3 天，来表示其面积的大小。丈量宏观规模的对象如宇宙，即星际间的距离，有时我们用的尺度是光年。如离太阳系最近的恒星是4.3 光年。这样，大小可以借运动速度从空间转化到时间的计算上来。

　　除了用高低、远近或者折算为运动时间来表示事物或空间的规模外，大小有时候可以表示物体的轻重，或力量的强弱。轻重或强弱本来不是度量空间的概念，但由于同类的事物中轻者小重者大，它就被转化使用。所以我们说 200 公斤重的猪比 100 公斤的大，或者说，50克的黄金首饰比 80 克的小。同样材料的物体，体积大比体积小者冲击力要更强，因此也用大小表示力量的对比。能"力拔山兮气盖世"，自然是力量大，而"手无缚鸡之力"者，无疑属于小。虽然不同的物体，通过量的测度，我们可以比较其大小。但通常，我们只是在同类物体中比大小。我们既说大猫，也说小老虎，但并不意味着大猫会比小老虎的躯体实际尺寸更大，因为大猫是跟小猫比，小老虎是对大老虎而言的。同一物体中，总体称大，部分为小。大是小的充足或增补，而小是大的不足或缺失。子贡在齐景公面前，就用泰山与泥土为喻，表明其推崇孔子并非出于夸张："臣誉仲尼，譬犹两手捧土而附泰山，其无益亦明矣；使臣不誉仲尼，譬犹两手杷泰山，无损亦明矣。"（《韩诗外传》卷八）泰山大泥土小，同类对比很恰当。在常规的譬喻中，罕有用泰山与秋毫，或天地与稊米作大小对比的例子的。庄子故意两者并提，正是反其意而用之。《齐物论》说，"天下莫大于秋毫之末，而大山为小"。《秋水》则为之训诂："因其所大而大之，则万物莫不大；因其所小而小之，则万物莫不小。"离开特定的参照系，大小的判断是会有天渊之别的。这样做，正是为了颠覆常识比大小的套路。

生活中，我们不仅用大小表示空间或体积的差别，而且还用大小表达时间的久暂，速度的快慢，质量的轻重，甚至力量的强弱。但是，仔细想想，好像久暂、快慢、轻重、强弱等说法，就很少或者不容易这么方便地互相代替使用。这是为什么？一个可能的理由在于，大小最基本的表现，是显示在视觉中的，而视觉是人理解世界既直接又确定且探测范围较广的感觉通道。亚里士多德认为，人类求知需要借助感觉，"而在诸感觉中，尤重视觉。无论我们将有所作为，或竟无所作为，较之其他感觉，我们都特别爱观看。理由是：能使我们认识事物，并显明事物之间的许多差别，引于五官之中，以得于视觉者为多"。[4] 而佛教把现象称作"色"而不是声或臭、味，也意味着其对视觉的强调。简单分析可知，听觉虽然可以感知遥远的声音，但通过声音辨识事物（人类语言除外）的有效程度要低。说我看到的，比说我听到的，可信度要高。触觉有时可以破除视觉上的错觉，但只有近距离才起作用，故范围有限。嗅觉、味觉的局限就更不用说了。时间、速度、重量、力量等等，可能都不像体积那样直接呈现在视觉中。或者说，我们是借物体形态的变化，才推测其他特性的存在及变

---

4 亚里士多德著，吴寿彭译：《形而上学》，北京：商务印书馆，1983年，页1。

化的。例如，离开阳光（及相关阴影）的位移，离开物体位置或结构的变化，我们不会感知时间现象。这些变化呈现在视觉中，我们由此"看"到了时间甚至速度。西方人用"我看到"（I see）表示我明白，而我们用"我看到"表示对判断的确信无疑。我们还把如何理解事物叫作"看待"事物的方式，而看待事物的结果，则称之为"观点"（viewpoint）。在西方，那种特别强调观点随视角的变化而变化，着眼于解释的主观性，或者具有相对主义倾向的哲学，像尼采那样，则可冠名为"视角主义"或"透视主义"（perspectivism）。也许这就是为何同属认知范畴，大小比久暂、快慢、轻重、强弱等其他结对的词语，在生活中更具普遍性的原因。庄子正是指点我们从最普通的，看出不寻常的。

三、观念

大小本来是起源于比较三维空间中的事物的用词，但它也被扩展并广泛运用于对观念（idea）现象的评价上来。观念不存在于世界而存在于人的思想中，而思想是没法用三维空间来安置或度量的。中文中的观念与观点相关，都有一个"观"字。汉语的观字原意是观看或观察，如"孔子观于东流之水，子贡问于孔子曰：'君子之所以见大水必观焉者，是何？'"（《荀子·宥坐》）"观"字本为动词，可一旦观出可以定格的内容来，它就成为名词"观点"或"观念"，是某种主张或立场的代称，犹如今日之"三观"（人生观、世界观与价值观）。这只是意味着这些观念或思想内容与对世界的理解有关，但它本身没有"栖身之所"，就连存在于大脑中的说法也不对。但是，观念是复数，且观念与观念之间，存在不同的关系。有些关系源于其所对应的经验结构，有些关系则是观念的内生机制。换句话说，有关于事物的观念，也有关于观念的观念。于是，我们模拟经验世界给它安排秩序，由此就用思想现象、观念世界之类的语言来表示它们。这自然也就产生对观念的位置与作用进行评价的大小、先后、上下，甚至轻重、强弱、软硬之类词语的运用。当然，下文的焦点还是放在大与小上。

观念表现为概念或者理论。有一本书叫《西方大观念》，系由各种基本概念构成的大辞书。[5] 其中，关于观念的词条这样说："大观念也是我们借以考虑问题的概念。它们是我们借以阐述基本问题的术语；它们是我们在界定问题和讨论问题时所使用的概念。它们代表我们的思想的主要内容。它们是我们思考的内容，也是我们思考的对象。"[6] 翻开目录，它至少包含有两类概念类型。一类如存在、自然、动物、人、世界、国家或家庭等，一类如美、真理、快乐、命运、定义及形而上学等。前者属于指称经验事物的概念，而被描述的对象在三维空间中存在。虽然我们不能靠视觉来判断，但可以从经验出发推断或想象其规模之大小，称之为大观念比较容易理解。后者则不然，它们并非直接指涉经验现象。但这些观念细分起来，也有区别。有的属于观念的观念，如定义或形而上学。有的则指向人的精神生活，如快乐或幸福、智慧等等。中国文化中的心与性、道与理、仁与义，以及庄子《人间世》所说的"无所逃于天地之间"的"命"，还有西方传统中的上帝与理性等，自然也是大观念。那么，为什么没有经验尺度可衡量的观念也可以称之为"大"？原因可能是由于颇为抽象或者理解起来颇复杂，但最主要的原因是其意义重要。概言之，它是在理解生活或思想上处于关键地位的观念。而所谓关键，就在于它构成理解其他观念或问题的前提。诺夫乔伊（Arthur Oncken Lovejoy）写了一本《存在巨链——对一个观念的历史的研究》，其所界定的观念史

---

5 陈嘉映等译，《西方大观念》(*The Syntopicon: An Index to the Great Ideas of Western Civilization*)，北京：华夏出版社，2008年。
6 同上书，页596。

对象，就是历史上对思想文化有巨大影响力的观念，例如以存在为核心缠绕起来的观念丛结。[7]其实，就如人世间有权势的人物叫作大人物，影响深远的事件称大事件，支配其他观念的观念，自然就是大观念。这个大，中文表述为重大甚至伟大。

观念可以是以概念为中心的观点或者想法，也可以是某些系统的理论或学说。不同的理论也有大小之别，其判断方式同样分两个类型，一是从论题所涉及的经验的规模来确定，一是从理论的重要性来评价。黑格尔哲学体系，其所涉内容从宇宙、自然到精神，从人、社会到文化，从宗教、艺术到哲学，堪称包罗万象，即使从规模上看，也是大哲学，何况其重要性在西方哲学史上还是一座高峰。以色列新锐历史学家尤瓦尔·赫拉利（Yuval Harari）的《人类简史》（*Brief History of Humankind*），虽然篇幅远小于很多有关世界史的通论式著作，但其视野之开阔与思考之丰富，列为大学说也当之无愧。默顿（Robert King Merton）在社会学上提出"中层理论"的概念，他说："中层理论既非日常研究中大批涌现的微观而且必要的操作性假设，也不是一个包罗一切、用以解释所有我们可观察到的社会行为、社会组织和社会变迁的一致的自成体系的统一理论，而是指介于这两者之间的理论。"[8]这不大不小的选择，恰好表明社会学家是可以根据研究对象的规模来确定其论域的宽窄的。

问题在于，一些重要的思想学说，所分析的经验事实并非超大规模的对象，但其论证的内容却撼动人们习以为常的观点，它同样是大观念。我们可举两个有代表性的例子，一个是库恩（Thomas Sammual Kuhn）的《科学革命的结构》，一个是福柯的《癫狂与文明

---

7 诺夫乔伊著，张传有、高秉江译《存在巨链——对一个观念的历史的研究》（*The Great Chain of Being: A Study of the History of An Idea*），南昌：江西教育出版社，2002 年。

8 罗伯特·金·默顿著，何凡兴、李卫红、王丽娟译，《论理论社会学》，北京：华夏出版社，1990 年，页 54。

——理性时代的精神病史》。库恩的这本书是关于科学史的理论著作，它从哥白尼革命的案例分析出发，批判传统关于科学是不断排除错误，累积知识的进步过程的观点，提出一个以研究范式为核心的新的解释模式。其新说削弱了科学与客观性的联系，强化了科学家个性与社会文化对科学解释的影响。虽然其立场未必得到科学界甚至哲学界的有力支持，但是它影响了人文和社会科学的很多领域。福柯的《癫狂与文明》，从分析和批判法国古典时期社会对癫狂病人的偏执、非人道的态度与制度入手，揭示这态度背后的信念与理性的见解间的关联——即把精神病看成道德上的恶，同时赋予社会剥夺"非理性的"病人自由的权利，理性成为迫害者的帮凶。其意义在于批判西方文明的根本观念——理性。两者都从历史现象的分析出发，一是科学史，一是精神病史，但其反思都指向西方乃至整个人类思想的根基，是真正的大观念。

上述大观念，可分为规模巨大和意义重大两类。意义重大区别于规模巨大，一般称为伟大。当然，通常从事知识或观念研究的人，所处理的问题也有相对大小之分。这个分别，也可以规模与价值两方面衡量。很多文科教师指导学位论文的策略，提倡"开口要小，挖掘要大"。所谓开口小，指的是处理的题材范围不能太大，太大的话资料太多，且问题复杂，有限的时间内处理不好，就会空洞无物。但题材小不一定问题就小，关键在于问题意识，能否做出有意思的文章。林放向孔子问礼，孔子赞他"大哉问"，就是表扬他问题意识好，或提有意义的问题。同样的题材，所致结论对相关论域的理解有深浅之分，影响自然有大小之别。思想或学术的使命，当然是取意义大者为好。

从事物的大小转化为观念的大小，看起来有两条基本途径。一是由类比而来，面对经验的问题，把论域与对象的规模对应起来，由此而区分观念的大小。另一种是从隐喻而来，把有意义的问题称为大问题，因为它处于观念网络的关键位置上，是众多需要解决的问题的前提。关键即重要，有时也称重大。这个重也是因大的联系引申而来的。

四、价值

同样与大字相关，巨大、庞大，同重大、伟大的含义很不一样。前者描述事实，后者则赋予意义。但汉字的构词法让我们可能直观到后者从前者而来，有些语言有时没有这个方便，如 big，huge 与 great，就无法建立这种直观。小也是这样，细小、微小，同渺小、宵小，与描述大的结构相同。这就可以理解，为什么庄子会把有无、大小同贵贱、是非串联起来，因为人类（至少我们中国人）有重大轻小甚至尊大欺小的倾向，价值取向就蕴藏在认知结构中。

古文字中，无论甲骨还是小篆，大的原型都像个人。《说文解字注》："天大，地大，人亦大焉。依韵会订，象人形。老子曰：道大，天大，地大，人亦大。人法地，地法天，天法道。按天之文从一大。则先造大字也。人儿之文但象臂胫。大文则首手足皆具。而可以参天地。是为大。"可见，尊大崇大之风已是自古有之。有趣的是，这个解释认为，大是从人身上引申而来，然后才用到天与地上面的。

作为大的原字的人形，是四肢向外伸展的。不像今日许多公共场所的人形标志，手脚并拢，非常拘谨。伸展比之并拢，对空间要求自然要更大。人是一个物种，也在三维空间中生存。作为生物品种的人，身体不仅需要可以伸展活动的余地，同时需要消耗自然资源来维持其成长或生存。这些自然资源蕴藏在自然空间中，空间越大资源越丰富。同时，每个个体体型大小不一，获取资源的能力会很不一样。在狩猎或耕战的年代，身体大小显然是力量强弱的基础。但文明的发展不是靠单打独斗，也非单纯靠体力取胜，而是需要思想与组织。因此，"力拔山兮气盖世"的霸王（项羽），未必斗得过"手无缚鸡之力"

的书生（韩信）。人高马大，身强力壮只是体现自然人的力量，社会人的力量则以其在社会关系中的地位为基础。后者不是一对一的较量，单一个体体能的强大，意义并不大。说到底，能有效支配他人的人，就是控制社会资源的人，也就是在社会空间中有权位的人。世俗赞扬人建功立业，往往说他打拼出自己的天地。而自然空间的资源分配，正是由社会空间的结构决定的。这样，人之大就不是高大，而是伟大，如三代的圣人，才有力量如子贡说的"博施于民而能济众"。

这样看，社会生活中的尊大求大，其实就是一种力量崇拜。这种倾向渗透在整个人类文化之中。我们赞扬高瞻远瞩、胸怀大志的人，鄙视鼠目寸光、贪图蝇头小利的人。我们称赞建立丰功伟绩的人，轻视一事无成的人。我们用大人与小人、大器与小器来褒贬品格相反的人。或者说，"贤者识大，不贤者识小"。当然，人们也能举出不少对"小"重视的言行，例如"治大国若烹小鲜"，喜欢小巧玲珑，甚至欣赏小家碧玉。与之相应，人们也有对大的警惕，如"大有大的难处"，或者像惠施一样"拙于用大"。也对好高骛远或好大喜功有所批评。其实，这种护小同求大并不矛盾。求大是追求权力或利益最大化。而这种追求的过程，是需要相应的代价的。如果代价与回报对等，那是不合算的买卖。因此，需要讲求小的代价与大的利益。而小者便于操纵，有时是易于支配的象征，就像智能手机好过笨拙的"大哥大"。无论考虑的是减少代价还是方便控制，目的同样是利益的追求与权衡。至于对好高骛远或好大喜功的批评，则说明这种文化中对盲目求大存在一种制衡的思想倾向。它不仅来自道家，也为儒家所持守。

前面提及，整体上自然人的力量远不及社会人，就如很多野兽凶猛无比，但地球的统治者最终是人而非野兽一样。然而，在芸芸众生中，为何少数某些人比其他更多的人获取更大权力或取得更大影响的位置？可能的解释就是这些人拥有出色的思想能力，部分也有运气的成分。这种能力包括在特定的社会环境下，利用形势获取权势的能力。说服与压制都是能力的组成部分。思想是可以超越身体的，这就又涉及观念力量的问题，它包括策略与品德。在能与德之间，我们的传统更推崇后者。三代圣人一般是权力与美德的完美结合，孔子以后的圣人就以德为准。子贡论孔子，基本上是用"高大深"来形容其形象的：

> 他人之贤者，丘陵也，犹可逾也；仲尼，日月也，无得而逾焉。人虽欲自绝，其何伤于日月乎？多见其不知量也！（《论语·子张》）

> 夫子之不可及也，犹天之不可阶而升也。（《论语·子张》）

> 臣终身戴天，不知天之高也；终身践地，不知地之厚也。若臣之事仲尼，譬犹渴操壶杓，就江海而之，腹满而去，又安知江海之深乎？（《韩诗外传》卷八）

何谓伟大？宽广的胸怀，高远的眼界，就是最好的形容。宽广要容纳众生，高远能引导前程。陆九渊曾昌言，学圣人就是要"先立乎其大者，而小者不能夺也"。价值领域，精神世界更需要大格局。从身体的大，到资源的大，再到权力的大，最后是精神的大，不管是基于经验，是通过类比，还是借助隐喻，这些"大"在思想上是有深刻关联的。好大其实是文明的积习。

五、哲学

那么，辩"大小"究竟是不是在论哲学？其实，哲学本无固定的对象，就寻根问底以析理的方式探讨现象背后的机制而言，前面每一节都是在谈哲学。但本节说的哲学，是指哲学史上积累起来的哲学知识或理论。换一种问法，就是 "大小" 究竟归属于什么哲学范畴？熟悉教科书的读者，应该很快就联想到 "辩证法" 三个字。当然，它不是苏格拉底而是黑格尔的辩证法，前者是通过辩论诱导对话者深入思考的方式，后者是对事物本性的认识或者理解事物的重要方法，所谓一分为二或对立统一的立场或观点。这样，不仅大小，其他如多少、明暗、远近、高低、宽窄、长短、前后、上下、深浅，以及刚柔、硬软、张弛、起伏、冷热等等，每对词都有类似的结构关系。此即所谓相反相成。其实，它不是事物属性的刻画，而是理解事物的方式。同一事物，从不同角度着眼，可以获得相反的评价。而任何一对概念都可运用到不同的事物上面。

当然，不是任何结对的概念，都是理解事物的方式。例如男女、父子、君臣，看起来也是相对而存的关系，但是，这类词组是对某些人事关系的归类，它不能广泛运用到任何人事关系上，更不能放到物上面。然而，混淆两者区别者大有人在。另一方面，还有另一类对事物进行评价的对立范畴，如好坏、贵贱、善恶、美丑、是非等等。但它们与大小、多少，还是不一样，虽然都是理解评价的范畴，都可以运用到不同的事物上去，但是价值评价是非好恶明确，而大小多少却非有固定运用尺度，如一米长的猫是巨猫，而一米长的虎则只是小虎。在儒家传统中，面对大小多少的取舍，可以强调平衡，掌握适当的度，保持某种质的稳定性，或者叫执中的思想方式。而对是非善恶的态度，儒家没有讨价还价的余地。只是如前所述，大小的运用被倾向化，它与视觉对人类生存意义的重要性相关。由此导致这种理解与评价的趋同，成为世俗化的取向。因此，《秋水》的作者把有无、大小同贵贱、是非联系起来，基于其深刻的洞察力。

谈过辩证法之后，我们再来看形而上学。在相当长一个阶段里，我们的教科书喜欢把两者对立起来。把形而上学界定为一种静止、孤立、片面的理解事物的方式，是黑格尔影响的结果。"小大之辩"肯定不属于这种范畴。如果它与形而上学有关，那则是亚里士多德意义上的哲学问题，即研究关于存在（或存有）的学问。存在的第一个问题，自然是什么是存在（或者译为"有""是"）？但海德格尔不满足于这种提问方式，在论及形而上学的基本问题时，他就提出："究竟为什么在者在而无反倒不在？"[9]中国有没有西方意义的形而上学，是个有争议的问题，不适合这里讨论。但我们可以稳妥地说，庄子提出过有与无的关系问题。《齐物论》说：

> 有始也者，有未始有始也者，有未始有夫未始有始也者。有有也者，有无也者，有未始有无也者，有未始有夫未始有无也者。俄而有无矣，而未知有无之果孰有孰无也。今我则已有有谓矣，而未知吾所谓之其果有谓乎？其果无谓乎？

这是从宇宙（万有）开端的假设无限前推，从而导致"有""无"区分不清的论断。引文"有有也者，有无也者"这个句子中，第二个"有"字和"无"字一样，显然就是名词，动词名词化，"有"类于西方哲学中的"being"。形而上学的基本范畴直观上是有（存在），但什么是有（存在）呢？简明的回答是：有非无。这就是说，离开无的概念，我们无法理解有。所谓"有无相生"，不仅是局部现象如此，对世界的整体理解也如此。因此，有无是理解世界的第一对范畴。

然而，与"有"不同，"无"不是"东西"，它没有出现在经验世界中。它只是理解"有"的思想条件。要进一步理解"有"，必须进入现象即物的领域。而要了解物性，就必须从其基础入手，寻求其共同的构成者。自古以来，至少有两种假说，一种是元素说，一种是数论，两者都与大小的理解相关。元素是对物体无限分解的假说，即设

---

9 海德格尔著，熊伟、王太庆译，《形而上学导论》，北京：商务印书馆，1996 年，页 3。

想一种构成物质的无限小的材料。而从自然数的构成看, 其无限叠加是积少成多的过程, 同时也是小数目变大数目的过程。元素说是整体与部分的关系, 数论则是多与少的关系, 都可视作大小关系。而形而上学的对象是大, 否则就是常识与各种经验科学的任务。其实无论是西方的 metaphysics 还是中国的道, 都是以大 (或无限) 为讲究。故老子曰:"吾不知其名, 字之曰道, 强为之名曰大。""道大, 天大, 地大, 人亦大。域中有四大, 而人居其一焉。人法地, 地法天, 天法道, 道法自然。"(《道德经》二十五章) 这四大中, 道最大, 它是 "至大无外" 之大。[10] 然而, 这个大道的构成者, 却是基于对极微弱现象的猜测:"视之不见名曰夷。听之不闻名曰希。抟之不得名曰微。此三者不可致诘, 故混而为一。其上不皦, 其下不昧, 绳绳不可名, 复归于无物。"(《道德经》十四章)"至小无内" 者, 自然近于无。老子哲学中的道, 无论是对经验事物的推测, 还是对价值领域的隐喻, 都可借大小关系来理解。但假如再具体一点, 打量各色各样的存在物, 那么最能直接对之进行分辨的, 就是对规模或体积的比较, 简言之, 就是观大小。关于大小与有无的关系, 还可以从庄子《齐物论》中的另一说法窥其大意:

> 古之人, 其知有所至矣。恶乎至? 有以为未始有物者, 至矣, 尽矣, 不可以加矣! 其次以为有物矣, 而未始有封也。其次以为有封焉, 而未始有是非也。是非之彰也, 道之所以亏也。道之所以亏, 爱之所以成。

这四个等级中:最高级是 "无"("未始有物"); 次一级是 "有" 而不分, 其实等同于无; 第三级是开始有分别, 即 "以为有封焉", 封就是界线。而对物的分别, 即从观大小开始。不同品物有大小, 同

---

10 李巍,《〈道德经〉中的 "大"》,《中山大学学报》(社会科学版), 2015 年第 3 期。

类品种也有大小。大小是紧跟着有无而获得普遍性的。"至大无外"的大就是有或存在，而"至小无内"的小，则近于无。微不足道者，人们可以忽视其存在。大小之外的其他观察角度，如多少、远近、高低、宽窄、长短甚至明暗等等，只不过是服务于空间大小的区别而已。而有了这一区别，物的内部及物与物之间才有前后、上下、深浅的排序。一句话，它使我们获得关于事物的秩序感。各种抽象价值的关系，或者我们的精神空间，正是在这一基础上，通过隐喻而建立起来的。这正是人类理性的表现。

回到庄子，以道观物。大小是人理解世界的方式，不是世界本身的客观特性，而崇大尊大与人追求扩张自己有限的力量相关。但有限的人对物的支配总是有限的，不明白这一道理，总是用支配物的眼光打量世界，会有适得其反的后果。由于大与小是相对的，没有固定的尺度，因此，不可避免将导致对大的无休止的攀比、追逐与竞争。这样便导致庄子所描述的情势，人人"与物相刃相靡，其行尽如驰，而莫之能止，不亦悲乎！终身役役而不见其成功，苶然疲役而不知其所归，可不哀邪"（《齐物论》）。这种悲哀，根本上是与不明智的生命态度相关。要解决这一问题，不应一味在扩展权势、荼取财富上打主意，而应深化我们的精神空间，用美善的眼光打量世界，打量人生。尊重物，尊重同类，尊重自己。眼光从物质转到精神，就是从有到无。

小大之辩，大矣哉！

理学的"一多诡谲同一"论述

杨儒宾

（台湾清华大学）

一、前言：哲学论述与体证论述

当代学者对宋明理学的理解基本上是在当代学科建制下，依当代习用的学术表达方式，对宋明理学家的思想论述所作的后设反省，这是一种哲学论述。宋明理学家的理学论述则是理学家针对个人的亲身体验与所思所作的报道或反思，这样的报道或反思可称作体证论述。在理学研究的范围内，体证论述与哲学论述可以说是针对理学家的体证所作的直接的与间接的文字之说明，两种论述所用的语言不一样，但如果我们相信人的思辨理性有其普遍性，异文化的眼光有可能可以看出本土论述的盲点，那么，两种论述彼此之间原则上不一定会冲突，反而有可能更全面地理解理学家原初的亲身体验。我们很难否认：透过民国以来重要哲学家与哲学史家——如冯友兰、张东荪、牟宗三等人——的解释"接着讲"而非"照着讲"，我们对理学重要问题的理解有可能超出理学家的理解。

但我们观看理学家对自家工夫论的解释和当代的哲学诠释时，常不免有差距之感，问题很可能出在当代哲学史家所用的解释架构。我们当今所用的汉字的"哲学"一词，如果从日本明治时期的西周算起，才不过一百多年，但"哲学"现在却已变成我们人文科学中重要的一种知识。[1]"中国哲学"是隶属于"哲学"门下的一个分支部门，它基本上接受了传统知识分类中部分的子学与经学的知识，常用的哲学语汇则多是百年以来才创造出来的舶来品，或旧词赋予新义的字词。简言之，我们现在使用的"中国哲学"一词，从术语的使用到议题的设定再到体系的建构，不过百年的历史，其间的术语或议题虽有承接传统用法之处，但"新义"也不少。在这种重组的过程中，我们可预期，两个源流对议题设定的焦点不会一样。

在当代中国哲学史家的理学研究中，"工夫论"常被略过不提，或者被编入伦理学、道德哲学的名目下立论，这即是重建新学术体制的一例。这种整编不一定不可以，但就结果而论，两方可能对焦，也有可能失焦。早期著有现代形式的中国哲学史或理学研究者，如谢无量所著者，基本上受到刚起步的日本关于中国的哲学史之影响，比较像试验品，不得列为现代意义的学科著作。从胡适开始，有学科式的《中国哲学史》之著作出现，冯友兰继之，其著作后出转精，非胡适草昧时期的著作所能及。只是诚如论者所说，胡适的中国哲学史没有哲学，冯友兰的中国哲学史有哲学，但没有中国哲学。这样的判准虽嫌严苛，也不一定可以被普遍接受；但大致说来，1949 年之后，新儒家的唐君毅、牟宗三，以及劳思光等先生对中国哲学的重新诠释，其析论之精，体系之完整，已超越以往研究者的水平。透过他们的整理，我们对中国哲学史已有个较清晰的图像。他们的著作出现以后，我们对中国哲学（尤其理学）的理解再也不可能和以往一样了。

透过这些儒学研究者的著作，尤其是牟宗三与劳思光两先生的《心体与性体》以及《中国哲学史》，我们得到了一个较明晰的哲学史图像，但故事并不全面，因为我们拿这个图像去辨识理学文献的时

---

1 关于百年来"哲学"学门的演变过程，参见林从一，《哲学 101：开新局、展新页》，收入杨儒宾等编，《人文百年化成天下》（新竹：台湾清华大学，2011 年），页 199-227。

候，有时仍感扞格不通，对焦与失焦的问题依然同时存在。牟先生、劳先生这两位当代哲学巨匠对理学议题怎么可能不熟？但他们的解释常会与理学的工夫论述所呈现者对不了焦。笔者这种感觉并非仅是个人的感受，事实上，以唐君毅先生对理学理解之精以及与牟宗三先生相交之深，他对牟先生的《心体与性体》的判断即有相当的保留。唐先生与牟先生对理学判断之出入或许各有其成立之理由，但笔者认为如果我们从工夫论的角度进入理学的论述，或许可以对两人主张的异同另有所见。[2] 当代中国哲学史家帮我们整理了很清楚的理学系谱，澄清了传统学问无法有效处理的议题，但不是每个领域都是如此，在工夫论领域，便不见得可以帮助我们有更好的理解。有时我们再度使用传统的语汇如"顿、渐"，"先天、后天"，"精、气、神"之类的语汇，或者我们如果将理学之工夫论或境界论的语言放在宗教经验，而不是哲学论证的范围内理解，其解释效果反而更佳。[3]

哲学论述到底是百年来的产物，它与理学的体验论述两方的磨合仍有待持续改善，甚至我们应当考虑回到理学家体验的现场，省思其体验报道的语言到底属哪一种语言，对其定位才会更为恰当。理学家论及个人独特的心性体验时，常有"一"的体验，这种体验常被解释成"天人同一"或"天道性命相贯通"的报道，这种报道所涉及的工夫论及其体证境界的内涵被认为是理学体系中的核心。笔者同意"同一"哲学是个重要的论述，我们不妨称呼这种同一论述为超越论的同一哲学，理学缺不了这个板块。但本文想指出，超越论的同一哲学的"同一"是否意指此概念的内涵指向一无差异的绝对同一境界，后

2 笔者此处的论点受益于郑宗义，《本体分析与德性工夫——论宋明理学研究的两条进路》，收入林维杰、黄冠闵、李宗泽编，《跨文化哲学中的当代儒学——工夫、方法与政治》（台北：台湾"中研院"中国文哲研究所，2016 年），页 73-106。
3 此问题就牵涉当代中国哲学学科的定位这个烦人的议题，个中线索冗杂夹缠，不易一刀两断。但我们观宋明时期三教的称呼，以及宋明儒者主要的对话对象是佛教，而不是一般"方内"的知识，或许可以掌握理学知识性质的大致轮廓。

167

儒或许不必要说得如此绝对。如果儒家的形上学是体验的形上学，在体验的形上学之格局下，其超越的心性体验，也就是理学家常说的"觉"、"悟"、"一"或"豁然贯通"的体证经验，常会牵涉自然的存有论问题，心性经验的语言不免也是自然存有论的语言，此时，体证者报道的内容是否即为超越的绝对同一？或许还可斟酌。

笔者所述和宗教哲学中对冥契论的论述有相当紧密的关联，"一多"问题在宗教经验领域是个重要的议题，史泰司（W. T. Stace）论及"冥契论"的两种类型，亦即内向型冥契论与外向型冥契论的分别时，其关键的差别即在于：内向型冥契论主张一切存在彻底的同一，也就是无差别的同一，无能所、一多之分，体证者进入言语道断的绝对冥合层次；外向型的冥契论则主张冥契经验固然呈现"一"的状态，但其"一"乃是多中之"一"，亦即一多相融。[4] 史泰司内、外向型冥契论的分别相当著名，类似的分别在其他的宗教史家的著作中也可见到，此分别可视为冥契论命题中重要的一组概念。依据史泰司的分判，内、外向型冥契经验是不同的类型，且有层级高低之分，内向型冥契论是更成熟也更高级的经验，外向型冥契论则是仍处于发展中的未成熟类型。

笔者接受史泰司所说的冥契经验中有内向型的"无差别同一"与外向型的"一多并容悖论"的两种叙述的区分，也相信理学家的体悟报道中，两种"一"的语言都有，但不接受他所说的内、外向型冥契论的境界高低之判断。不但如此，笔者还认为理学的证悟境界之"一"当是"一多悖论"的类型，但用"悖论"或"矛盾"不恰当，史泰司认为冥契论述是超逻辑的，不属语言可以触及的范围，笔者对他的说法有相当的保留。笔者毋宁认为"一多诡谲同一"的称呼更为恰当，"一多诡谲同一"的冥契论更符合儒家天人相待的根源性的诡

---

4 史泰司（W. T. Stace）著，拙译，《冥契主义与哲学》（台北：正中书局，1998 年）。

谲之平等关系，也就是更贴近儒家形上学的主张。

二、理学的两种"同一"主张

"一"是数字概念，是量词，但在宗教或哲学的用法中，此字常指向超越者的属性，或指向工夫论传统中一种无分别性的质性，理学的"一"之问题的大宗也是出自独特的心性经验。如果理学的核心义是天道性命相贯通的话，那么，不管论者喜不喜欢"冥契论"一词，一种天人为一的心性经验即当属于宗教哲学中冥契论的一种。不管这种"天人为一"的"一"到底是"同一"，还是"合一"；也不管"天"是否无心，或是有神圣的意志。在理学的语言系统中，"一"的追求与体证一直占有显赫的地位。"一"的追求与体证乃是理学工夫论与各宗教中冥契论者共享的因素，这种共通性极明显，我们如果将理学的工夫论放在冥契论的传统下定位，毋宁是合理的选择。

我们的选择涉入"冥契经验与诠释"或"冥契经验与语言"之间的复杂关系，冥契经验与语言的关系源远流长，是哲学史上最古老的议题之一。放在当代语言哲学的框架内，极技术地讲，这个问题会变得很复杂。但就宗教现象学的观点看，不同宗教间的"与终极境界冥合"的论述可以彼此沟通，但也时常难以跨越教与教之间的界限，这种两歧现象乃是宗教史上的常态。无疑，理学家的体证报道常带有理学的特色，不见得可在佛教或基督教的冥契者身上看得到；反过来说，基督教的冥契者所作的与神合一的叙述，或者佛教冥契者常见的层层深入的禅悟语言，也不见得在儒门人物身上看得到。但这些出入无碍于他们分享了共同的，至少是共通的一组体验，而这样的体验在我们身处日常意识中的生活世界时，是很少碰到的。理学家的体证报道之所以异于其他宗派的冥契报道，是因为通常原是工夫论语言或心性经验的语言，经由理学家创造的转化——理学家在此"贯通"经验的基础上建构了理学重要的体系所致。在建构工夫论的过程中，诠释因素的加入是难以避免的，即使客观而公正的报道者也不免需要语言的媒介，因此，也不免带有语言背负的本质之诠释的成分。理学与佛、老的三教异同之辩论，其核心义往往即在"一"的性质的解释。关于冥契经验与诠释之间的关系是同是异，中国的三教交流史提供了极好的例证。

理学的体证经验中的"一多"问题并非儒家传统中原有的显性议题，道家与佛教在这个领域提供了更多的内容。道家、道教的"得一""守一""通于一，万事毕"之说，源远流长。佛教以人生解脱为大事，以涅槃寂静为究竟。迥脱尘根，灵光独耀，乃是行者修行之目标。在理学兴起前，佛老的修行者对于体证境界中的一多问题也多有所触及。相对之下，伦理的承担、文化的使命乃是儒家的核心价值，在有礼乐教化、孝悌伦理处，如何同时在主体处体证"一"，就不能不是个问题。后世反理学的儒者几乎都反对儒家走向"一"之道途的主张，他们的反对是有相当强的传统作支柱的。确实，相对于佛老，儒家的公共形象并不以追求"超越之一"见长。反而，对文化与伦理的奉献，儒者有很强的承诺，这是周、孔、孟、荀一贯的家法。

但理学家既然关心天道性命的问题，他就不能不涉及"一"的辖区。理学在三教论述中之特殊者，在于它既肯定文化与伦理的本质性之价值，同时又肯定一种超越的一之体证是不可少的。从宋代以后，理学兴起本体的理念，本体与功用两者相合的体用论，或者本体与工夫相连的本体工夫论，两者构成了理学主要的思考模式。前者通常见于程朱理学，后者则见于陆王心学；前者施用到万物的存有问题，后者则只限于具有意识转化作用的人的身上。"本体"与"功用"或"本体"与"工夫"结合，其后续效果会产生很大的不同。原则上，两条路线不一定会矛盾，如果从理论的圆融来看的话，我们甚至于不妨说两者是互涵的，即使陆王具有那么强的道德意识哲学色彩，他们也承认本心（良心）的工夫尽处即是万物存有的领域；即使朱子那么重视天理的价值，也就是万物的存有论意义，其工夫下手处依然是在意识的转化上面。如果我们不以"心与太极同一"作为判断心的无限义的唯一标准，比如说如果我们可以接受"心全幅呈显太极，而非同一于太极"，也是无限心的另一种形态，那么，程朱理学事实上也可视为"心学"。

我们如果再将目光放到非程朱、非陆王的北宋理学一系，笔者认为这一以道体流行为核心的儒学可视为独立的一系，也就是理学的第三系。他们的思想依然是以"一"的目标为旨归，但由于这一系可称为道体系（也不妨称为"道即理"或"先天气学"一系）的儒学以《中庸》《易经》为宗，特别着重道在世界中的展开，也可以说特别强调道在物上的展开，因此，他们思想中的"一"与"多"的关系相当显著，第三系儒学对"一多诡谲同一"说有独特的贡献。

"一""多"的诡谲同一关系在冥契论的传统中常会出现，佛、道两教的情况更是如此，老、庄的"大道泛兮""道在屎溺"，佛教的"因陀罗网境界门""一多相容不同门"，所说皆触及此义。到底佛道两教有很强的修炼传统，长期出入于天人性命之际。理学由于既肯定无限的人性论（笔者认为程朱学的人性论主张也应当放在无限心的视野下定位），在工夫论上追求"复性"的价值，又肯定天道流行，物与无妄的物之存有论的意义，这样的超越境界如果可以体证的话，"一多诡谲同一"的问题便不能不出现。

简言之，理学工夫论中的"一多诡谲同一"的议题之所以会出现，关键就在理学本身的结构，这个理论的结构之特色既有本质性的因素，也有来自不同经典所提供的不同模型。大体说来，凡带有"泛神论"思维模式（亦即最高存有者——如上帝、阿拉、道、太极云云——在世界中展现的主张，此主张可包含上帝与世界不一亦不异的万有在神论）的大学派如果有工夫论的主张，都很容易出现"一多诡谲同一"的问题，理学的情况似乎更加明显。理学工夫论传统中同时出现了"超越的同一"与"一多诡谲同一"的主张，笔者认为这两种主张仍当以"一多诡谲同一"说为究竟。这两种主张同时见于理学传统是有经典依据的，因为理学家既接受孟子学的人性论及工夫论的主张，亦接受"尽心知性以知天"的命题，但也同时接受《中庸》《易经》"天命遍与万物，凡物皆为诚明无妄"的主张。孟子学的传统与《中庸》《易经》的传统偏重不同，但两者同样被理学家视为圣经，同具圣言量的地位。朱子编的《四书》再加上《易经》，也就是笔者所说的"新五经"，在宋明时期实质上取代了"十三经"的地位，也可说更精粹地提炼了"十三经"的义理，成为理学家诠释一切学问的总依据。在"新五经"的系统中，孟子论性，重点在于人性，人性的自我完成是他的思想的旨归。他很少论及物性，更没有物性与超越者（太极、理、道）的关系的问题。但《中庸》《易经》思想的主轴之一在于承认天道与万物间本质性的关联，"天命之谓性"的"性"不只指人性，也指物性。"道与万物"实质上是"道在万物"，万物的本质（亦即物性）与道的一多、异同的问题，就不能不呈现。《易经》的构造最明显，它的太极既作为总体的原理，也展现在阴阳二气，展现在天、地、水、火、雷、风、山、泽之上，它既一且多。

《孟子》与《中庸》《易经》影响了不同的冥契论述，关键在于两者的"性"论。换言之，理学中的"性体"概念施用的范围之广狭，乃是他们的冥契论到底主张"超越的同一"还是"一多诡谲同一"的模式的主要关键。在孟子学系统中，心、性、天的关系被视为是同质的，其适用的对象只指向人，人以外的万物无关于超越的转化，孟子也不关心万物的存有论的问题。孟子的关心几乎都集中在人的道德问题上，性善论是他的核心思想。在工夫论领域，孟子学所体证的境界很容易被解为心与天乃超越的同一，孟子学可以说是后世儒家复性说的总源头。但在《中庸》《易经》的传统中，一种超越性的性体概念不只对"人"有效，它一样可施用到"物"的范围，物的本性也就是性体的问题在理学系统中遂占有重要的地位。"性"意指物之理，如果此概念指向超越义的物之本性，冥契经验则意味着一种同一的关系，那么，《中庸》《易经》传统下的冥契者所证者就不会只是"人"的范围，它很容易就带出"一多诡谲同一"的语言。不同类型的"同一"思想依不同的文本展开，理学的两种"同一"论述之所以不同，笔者认为和他们继承的是《孟子》或是《中庸》《易经》的传统有关。

中国有很强的同一哲学传统，"一"的追求相当显著，但"一"的内涵如何，其实还可斟酌。笔者相信理学系统中原本即存在"一多是否诡谲同一"的问题，而且"一多诡谲同一"应当是各派共同接受的主张，只是此问题以往未必很突显。此问题在当代之所以会变得尖锐，其说具有了更重要的理论价值，则与牟宗三先生对理学的分判有关。牟先生对理学系统的分判有三系说，分判的标准在于"心"与"理"的关系。依牟先生的理解，朱子一系主张"性即理"而不是"心即理"，陆王一系主张"心即理"而非"性即理"，至于第三系的胡五峰、刘宗周姑且不论。依牟先生的理解，真正的道德乃起于良知的自我立法，这是自律道德。朱子一系从南宋末期后，虽取得了政教体系的优越地位，但其学乃他律道德之学，偏离了儒门的正途，所以后世朱子学的兴盛只能是别子为宗。相对地，陆王学主张心性为一，良知的当下判断，即是本性的自我证成，即是天命在个体上的体现，一种彻底的同一哲学如是形成，这是彻底的自律道德，因此，可为正宗。有关陆王心学的心理同一说与程朱理学的心理合一（而不是同一）说，文献较充足，模式比较清楚，所以牟宗三先生的《心体与性体》三巨册与《从陆象山到刘蕺山》一书自从问世以来，得到了学界普遍的注意，几乎已成为研究宋明理学学者的常识。

相对于程朱理学与陆王心学，北宋理学家的思想倾向与依循经典明显不同，本文所说的北宋理学家主要指周敦颐、邵雍、张载、程

173

颢四人，他们可代表理学的另一系。此系理学家同样有天道性命的追求，其人多有体证道体之体验，而且多有工夫论的主张，因此也有"一"的思想内涵。只因此系的特色在当代的理学研究中较少受到独立看待，因此，他们思想的"一"之特色，在当代的研究著作中不免显得模糊。笔者认为他们追求"一"的精神是一样的，但北宋理学家的"一"具有更典型的"一多诡谲同一"的特色。北宋理学家几乎都以《易经》《中庸》为宗，《易经》《中庸》泛论万物存在的基础与意义，他们当然也关心人的尽心复性的问题，但他们同样关心万有的存有问题。由气化有道之名，北宋理学带有甚浓的道体流行的思想，他们的工夫论语言因而也就有更明确的"一多诡谲同一"的内涵。

理学家多有"一"的主张与体证，我们上述所说的理学三系中人无不如此，理学的性格决定了学问的性质。三系当中表现最明显的，当是陆王心学的学者，他们几乎都将学说的宗旨建立在超越性的"本心"或"良知"上，陆象山主张这种普遍性的"心同理同"，王阳明主张良知是造化精灵，若此之言在他们的高足——如杨简或王畿——处发挥得更是淋漓尽致。在"心即理"的思想架构底下，他们的"心"被视为是种宇宙心，天与人的关系透过了本心的扩充，直接联系起来。大体说来，陆王心学被认为是主张天人本质相同的同一说。

相对于陆王心学的宇宙心预设了人与天的同质同构，工夫直上直下，程朱理学因为主张心性的本体论差异，性即理，心不是理，加上程朱学派主张格物穷理的彻底渐教，学者下工夫，须从当下起程，迢迢长路，最后才可达到终点，因此，程朱学派对"一"的追求乍看之下，似乎平淡了许多。然而，程朱学的"心"虽然无法等同"性"，但是它乃是可"统性情"的气之灵的主体，性的实质内涵——也就是它的"为己"之存在——要透过心显现出来，程朱学的格物学最后也要指向一种天理流行之境。从心与性的本体论的差异着眼，程朱学的天人不可能本质的同一；但就心可统性情处着眼，心灵的自我转化，以趋近统体之一的能力还是很明显的，心性或天人之间因此虽然不能同一，但可合一。

在理学第三系中，笔者将举周敦颐、邵雍、程颢三人为例，这三人在理学兴起此大事因缘中，占有特殊的地位。程颢重视一本论，修行有道，体证至深。周、邵两人同样与道教的内丹之学有种种瓜葛，从内丹之学到北宋的周敦颐、邵雍之学，我们都可在他们的著作中见到一种混合宇宙论语言与心性论语言的表达方式。周、邵、程三人作为北宋理学的奠基者，都有意追求人与自然背后统一的原理。既从心体立基，也从道体立论，而心体乃是“本体”一词落实于心灵上所形成的理念，道体则是“本体”一词落在自然全体所形成的概念。“本体”一词是“体用论”的一环，宋代理学形成“体用论”的思考方式，“体用论”的思维虽然在程颐处奠下根基，在朱子处发扬光大，但我们若细考此语之名与实，就不能不同意邵雍、周敦颐与程颢其实都是“体用论”的支持者，都主张“全体大用”式的思考。“全体”的“体”是作为统一原理的“一”，“用”是作为本体展现的“多”。道体论的理学家对于“一”的省思特别着重“一”与“多”的诡谲同一关系，格局非常宏阔。

三、心学学者的“一多诡谲同一”的体验

同一性哲学在当代新儒家学者的理学研究中占有极重要的位置，这种现象和“无限心”论点的提出密切相关。首先，我们不能不承认：他们的理解是有文本依据的。我们在宋明理学家的著作中，确实可以看到大量支持心、性、天“一也”的文字。这种“一也”的文字带有鲜明的理学风格，我们不容易在西方的神学著作中见到。在理学的诸系中，一般认为陆王心学主张心即理，“即”是同构型的关系，本心的内涵即是理（太极），因此，他们会特别主张天人同一的构造。

换言之，一种超越的同一论构成了陆王心学的主旨。陆王这种超越的同一说又和他们的工夫论主张若合符契，陆王心学中人通常强调道德判断的直接性，当下即是，直通天理，也无非天理，他们的体验所得印证了他们学说的主张。

陆王心学充满了天人同根、良知是"造化精灵"之类的语言，这固然是事实，然而，"一也"的文字该如何理解，不是没有讨论空间的。接下来笔者将以陆王心学的三位有代表性的儒者：杨简、陈献章、王阳明为例，指出他们的"一也"之主张，不一定要往超越的同一性上去解释，它也可以是一多兼容的悖论性格。本文之所以没有举陆象山为例，乃因陆象山之学虽然特别着重本心的功能，他自己本人也有很深刻的体道经验，也有随缘指点学生证悟的事例，但他论及自己的悟道经验，或论及"悟"的内涵文字不多。身为一位伟大的教师，陆象山更着重的是本心在具体情境中的朗现，殊少触及悟觉的内涵。象山学是孟子学，表达的风格也近似。

宋代理学家中，特别喜欢报道体悟经验者，非杨简（慈湖）莫属。杨简是陆象山高弟，陆杨并称，陆杨在敌对学派中常以"阳儒阴释"、重静坐、重证悟的形象出现，但这种形象其实是杨简本人提供的，不是其他人强加上去的。我们首先要从一位明儒对他的批判开始谈起：

> 今观其（罗洪先）集，首"答蒋道林书"："不展卷三阅月，而后觉此心中虚无物，旁通无穷，如长空云气流行，大海鱼龙变化，岂非执灵明以为用者耶！"昔六祖闻师说法，悟曰："何期自性本自清净，何期自性本不生灭，何期自性能生万法。"杨慈湖效之曰："忽省此心之清明，忽省此心之无始末，忽省此心之无所不通。"可谓蹈袭旧套矣！然既曰：无物，又有鱼龙，而宇宙浑成一片，此即野狐禅所谓圆陀陀光铄铄也。

其与旧日冬游等记，更无二致。[5]

上述这段话是明中叶一位反王学的学者黄佐说的。黄佐这段话既批判了王阳明著名的学生罗洪先，也批判了杨简。罗洪先是江右学派中代表性的阳明后学，在阳明学诸学派中，江右学派一向被视为致虚守寂，操守特严的一个学派，以工夫见长，罗洪先又是江右学派人物当中特别以逆觉自持著称于世的儒者。在阳明后学当中，罗洪先常和王龙溪并称，两人都是追求良知学的同志友，但取径不同。王龙溪的先天型良知学直接承体起用，高明轩朗，是圆顿之学的取径。比起王龙溪来，罗洪先的言行则倾向摄用归体，深潜神渊。但因为他致虚守寂的工夫做久了，与佛老的分际问题不能不浮现上来，也免不了会涉入工夫究竟的玄秘之境，因而也就不免涉入有无、一多之争，其义此处不表。

杨简在宋儒中，是极富争议的一位大儒，争议不在人格，而在学问。他的操守之严，做事之敬业，连论敌朱子都很赞美。但他喜欢张扬冥契经验，不只谈自己个人的，也谈亲族的与朋友的经验，这种毫不避讳的态度在宋明理学家中极少见，甚至我们可以说在中国的体道传统中都颇为稀奇。因此，他的言论会引来儒门同道的批判之声，连绵不绝，这种现象也是可以理解的。在批判杨简的诸多文字中，杨简之学与禅学的类似性一直是被批判的重点，仿佛杨简是彻底投降了佛老，至少是阳儒阴释。上引黄佐这段话所述也是这个意思，只是黄佐此处是连着罗洪先与杨简两人一起批判，视两人为同路人。

上引的黄佐这段话虽然对罗洪先与杨简很不友善，但不是没有理路。在责骂声中，笔者注意到"既曰：无物，又有鱼龙，而宇宙浑成

---

5 黄佐，《复何宾岩镗》，收入黄宗羲，《明儒学案·诸儒学案中五》（北京：中华书局，2008 年），
   下册，卷 51，页 1209。

"一片"之说。黄佐这段话显然指责罗洪先、杨简的论述自相矛盾，不成话语。黄佐的论述不是作辨析道理用的，但因为没有美言饰语，他的判断反而更形象地触及了冥契经验中一种常见的"一多"矛盾统一的叙述。亦即冥契经验中，到底是浑然一片，更无能所一多之分，主体沉淀于黝黑的深层意识之海中？还是其体证之"一"乃是多中之"一"，学者在此冥契境界中时，反而万象毕现，其鱼龙变化，尤胜日常意识所现？黄佐批判这种既说"无物"又含"万物"的境界为"野狐禅"之境，基本上是非儒家的义理，罗洪先、杨简这两位悟道者已误入歧道矣！黄佐的批判很值得再作分析。

由于篇幅所限，笔者将仅从罗、杨两人中择一讨论。杨简是理学悟道传统中重要的人物，有可能是有史以来最喜论述悟境的儒者。由他入手，我们对理学家体证经验中的一多问题或许可以有新的理解。我们且先看底下这则夫子自道：

> 某尝读《大戴》所记孔子之言，谓忠信为大道，某不胜喜乐。不胜喜乐，乐其深切著明。某自总角承先大夫训迪，已知天下无他事，惟有此道而已矣。穷高究深，年三十有二，于富阳簿舍双明阁下侍象山先生坐。问答之间，某忽觉某心清明，澄然无畔，又有不疾而速、不行而至之神，此心乃我所自有，未始有间断。于是知舜曰道心，明心即道。孟子曰仁，人心也，其旨同孔子。又曰心之精神是谓圣，某知人人本心皆与尧舜禹汤文武周公孔子同，得圣贤之言为证，以告学子。谓吾心即道，不可更求。[6]

杨简也许不是理学传统中最早提出悟觉经验者，但至少是最早突

---

6 杨简，《学者请书》，《慈湖遗书》(台北：景印文渊阁四库全书，台湾商务印书馆，1983年)，册1156，卷3，页633。

显此种经验意义，并将悟觉（杨简称作"觉"）经验带到儒家核心价值地位的儒者。他对自己一生经历过的冥契经验，不惮一再言之，而且其表达的方式多出自他叙述性的报道，第一人称，平铺直叙，而非承载理论的诠释，所以参考价值很高。[7] 依据引文所说，他在富阳侍奉陆象山时，经历过一种可名为"觉"，也就是冥契的经验。而且考察他事后"吾心即道"云云的解释，这种冥契经验的类型应当是"内向型"的，整体存在浸润于浩荡的"无"之境界中。

杨简所提的"不疾而速，不行而至"，出自《易经》，《易经》此语是用以描述"至神"的状态，杨简的挪用到底是不是《易经》的原义，固难言也，但就理论效果来看，确实有说服力。"畔"指境界，"澄然无畔"意指同一，"不疾而速，不行而至"和周敦颐《通书》的"动而无动，静而无静"之说可相互诠释。这两则寓言都和《易经》有关，所以彼此诠释倒很恰当。杨简思想和周敦颐没有直接关联，但两人在描述最高阶段的一种心性经验时，竟同时使用了一种"非动非静、超乎动静"的述词，这种选择值得留意。杨简32岁这年的体证经验较特别者，乃在他是在对谈中当下顿悟。悟道的经验常见于孤子情境下的静坐，或无意间的独自行动，对谈中悟道的例子在佛教中可见，儒门少见。杨简之所以有此经验，很可能和他长年用心于方寸之间，而且之前早有悟觉经验有关。

上述内向型的悟道叙述并不是杨简类似经验的全部，我们不妨看他更早年岁时的一次经验，那年他28岁。这场经验是相当关键性的，后来他反复言之。杨简的现身报道如下：

> 某之行年二十有八也，居太学之循理斋。时首秋，入夜，

---

7 "叙述"和"诠释"之间的界线当然也不一定容易划清，但这两个概念有别，大体的划分总还是有道理的。

斋仆以灯至。某坐于床，思先大夫尝有训曰："时复反观"。某方反观，忽觉空洞无内外，无际畔，三才万物，万化万事，幽明有无，通为一体，略无缝罅。畴昔意谓万象森罗，一理贯通而已，有象与理之分，有一与万之异。及反观后，所见元来某心体如此广大，天地有象、有形、有际畔，乃在某无际畔之中。《易》曰"范围天地"，《中庸》曰"发育万物"，灼然！灼然！始信人人心量皆如此广大。[8]

　　杨简一生有多次证悟心体的经验，28岁在太学的循理斋所证者，可能是第一次的体验，也是最关键性的一次。这场经验在他求道的生涯中，地位非常重要，用基督教神学的语言讲，可说是"新生""新人"的转折点，在他的文集中，这场经验不断地被提及。这场体验明显是"一体"的经验，"忽觉空洞无内外，无际畔，三才万物，万化万事，幽明有无，通为一体，略无缝罅"，这样的语言是典型的冥契论的报道。但这段话语充斥着不少矛盾的语言，我们看看他所述及的一体经验，如果是纯粹同构型的"一体"，怎么还会有"三才万物，万化万事"？怎么还需要"通"？"通"应当预设了"杂多"的前提。反过来说，如果此境还有"三才万物，万化万事"，怎么还可以说是"一体，略无缝罅"？杨简也知道他的语言会带来困扰，所以他再度解释道：他本来以为觉悟的经验中，乃是"万象森罗，一理贯通而已"，但无际畔之中，应该还有一多、理象之别。等到自己亲身体证以后，才知道"心体如此广大，天地有象、有形、有际畔，乃在某无际畔之中"。

　　杨简的自我质疑与自我解答，费尽心力，这种慎思后的语言提供给我们很好的线索。他说"畴昔意谓万象森罗，一理贯通而已"，显

---

8 杨简，《炳讲师求训》，《慈湖遗书》，卷18，页898。

示出他在亲身体证心体朗彻的经验之前，已有关于悟觉的知识，很可能是他的父亲杨庭显传予他的，我们观此段经验所述他父亲开示的法门"时复反观"，可见一斑。杨庭显的法门没言及太多的细节，但有可能承《易经·复卦》的传统。[9] 等杨简亲身体证后，他才知道天下万物"乃在无际畔之中"。显然，他把自己亲证的"天地有象、有形、有际畔，乃在某无际畔之中"的经验，和他先前臆想的"万象森罗，一理贯通而已，有象与理之分，有一与万之异"作了区分，两者属于不同的类型。

　　看过杨简的说明后，笔者不能不承认：他的解释并没有解开我们的疑惑，反而加深了。我们不了解既然在心体广大的经验中，"天地有象、有形、有际畔"，并且在"无际畔之中"，这样的现象为什么还是"一体"的经验？为什么叙述中有"天地有象、有形、有际畔"这样的"一体"，实质上却不是"有象与理之分，有一与万之异"的"一体"？两者如何区隔开来？由于杨简叙述此段经验时，慎重其事，他一定要分出有两种万物一体的经验：一种是有"一与万"差异的"一体"；一种是"既有一与万之别但又不能以差别视之"的"一体"。前者的"一体"如何理解，杨简没有说明，但我们可以设想一种美感"一体"的经验，如陶渊明的"山气日夕佳，飞鸟相与还。此中有真意，欲辨已忘言"（《饮酒诗二十首之五》），或柳宗元在《始得西山宴游记》所说的"心凝形释，与万化冥合"。不管杨简的语言是否够清楚，至少从杨简个人的体验的立场出发，他不是报道美感经验中的"一体"之感，而是要呈现一种既有分别而又无分别的"万物一体"的特殊经验，他的用心是很明显的。

　　杨简在朱子学派眼中，一向被视为是脱儒入禅的异端，弥近理而

9　参见钟彩钧，《杨慈湖〈易〉学概述》，收入《张以仁先生七秩寿庆论文集》（台北：台湾学生书局，1999年），页179-216。

大乱真。罗钦顺此位朱子后劲，也可以说是朱子之后朱子学派最重要的儒者，即曾针对杨简之说展开过严厉的批判。但我们细观杨简的叙述，他并非是佛老信徒的体无者，他的语言终点并没有走向纯粹统体的一或无，相反地，他仍是主张一多兼容并立的体证者。他亲身报道的"体验亲切语"之所以难以说得明白，时有坎坎龃龉、不明不白之语，乃因一多诡谲同一的语式使然。不管要视一多诡谲同一为非逻辑的表达方式，还是要视为表达的语言工具本身即不够完善的问题，体证者的感受都是一多的诡谲同一。"诡谲同一"这种难以启齿的窘境在冥契论的文本中是常见的。

在理学的心学系统中，同样强调静坐、体悟，因而被冠上异端之名的著名者尚有陈献章。陈献章是明代心学的开创者，是陆象山、王阳明这两位大师间最重要的联结者。罗钦顺以程朱学的捍卫者现身于明代的思想舞台时，陈献章是另一位受他批判的对象。但陈献章虽然常言静坐、体悟，他一样在有无、一多之间颇费转折，其窘困情境不亚于杨简。两人受窘的原因恐怕也是相同的，笔者认为陈献章实际上仍是主张一多悖论的同一者，而不是主张内向型的超越性同一论者。

陈献章求道的过程充满了艰辛，他年轻时先跟随以朴实苦学著称于世的吴与弼学道，久而无成，乃筑室小隐，返身内证，久之得"把柄"入手，乃知圣学内蕴。他论及体道经验最著名者当是他写给林光的书信中所述：

> 终日干干，只是收拾此而已。此理干涉至大，无内外，无终始，无一处不到，无一息不运。会此则天地我立，万化我出，而宇宙在我矣。得此把柄入手，更有何事？往古来今，四方上下，都一齐穿纽，一齐收拾，随时随处，无不是这个充塞。色色信他本来，何用尔脚劳手攘？舞雩三三两两，正在勿忘勿助之间。曾点些儿活计，被孟子一口打并出来，便都是鸢

飞鱼跃。若无孟子工夫，骤而语之以曾点见趣，一似说梦。会得，虽尧舜事业，只如一点浮云过目，安事推乎？此理包罗上下，贯彻终始，滚作一片，都无分别，无尽藏故也。自兹已往，更有分殊处，合要理会。毫分缕析，义理尽无穷，工夫尽无穷。[10]

林光是陈献章重要的学生，早年相契极深，后来林光为了养家糊口，不能不出仕，陈献章不以为然，师徒之间乃产生隔阂。[11]但这无碍于林光是江门学派的健将，体道至深，所以陈献章才特别和他谈及自己个人的亲身体证，以为印证。

在此封信中，陈献章曾体验到"天地我立，万化我出"之境，此处的我已不是个体性意义的我，而是理学家所说的本体之意。本体彰显，契入存在之根，所以学者才能体验到"天人合一"的冥契境界，这种叙述的工夫论性质是很明显的。天人合一之境乃是理学家之共识，在意识深处隐藏了万化创造的源头，"天地我立，万化我出"，这种叙述也是理学家的常谈。但在陈献章的报道中，他提到"一"中仍有分殊，然而，此分殊乃是"自兹已往"才呈现的。恍若"多"是在"一"的境界以后，学者才需要做的事。然而，陈献章在此篇著名的夫子自道中，分明说道"无不是这个充塞"，如果无差异之物，何来"充塞"？又言"色色信他本来"，如果没有"色色"的存在，又何有于"色色信他本来"？回过头来，我们重看"自兹已往，更有分殊处"之语，其意应该不是说在体验之后，还要再反思"分殊"处，"一体"与"分殊"好像成了后添加的关系。事实未必如此，笔者认为关系是

10 陈献章，《与林郡博七则之七》，《陈献章集》（北京：中华书局，1987年），上册，卷2，页217。

11 参见朱鸿林，《明儒陈白沙对林光的出处问题之意见》，收入《明人著作与生平发微》（桂林：广西师范大学出版社，2005年），页220–248。

原本即在的，"自兹已往"是对体道经验的更深体会，更恰当的领略。简言之，"一体"与"分殊"是诡谲同一的关系。

本文的解释可以在陈献章另一封给林光的信中得到印证，陈献章在此信中说道："人争一个觉，才觉便我大而物小，物尽而我无尽。夫无尽者，微尘六合，瞬息千古"。微尘蕴含了六合，瞬间含摄了千古，时空的构造变形了，主体变得极大，世界则变小了，这种叙述是很典型的冥契语言。但在此封信的报道中，他又明言：

> 宇宙内更有何事，天自信天，地自信地，吾自信吾；自动自静，自阖自辟，自舒自卷；甲不问乙供，乙不待甲赐；牛自为牛，马自为马；感于此，应于彼，发乎迩，见乎远。故得之者，天地与顺，日月与明，鬼神与福。[12]

这种语言显示出一种一体平铺的本地风光，一切现成。这种"一体平铺"是物各如其物，差异而无差异相的叙述。同一封信里，他明言时空结构变形了，一切融于当下的一点；但同样明言的，乃是他主张一切现成，没有一物不是生活世界所显现者。这两种叙述显然是矛盾的，不能同时成立，但陈献章却同时肯定。陈献章虽然常被视为带有浓厚禅意的儒者，但笔者相信他的报道乃是一多兼容的体验语言。陈献章常被划归为明代心学的开创者，他却自认自己是朱子学门徒，[13] 事实上，他此处所说的"自"的"感应"，在程朱的文献中即可看到。我们不妨称呼这种类型的感应为内在的感应之理。[14] 笔者认为凡以内在的感应之理呈现的一体论述，应当都是"一多诡谲同一"的冥契论述。

---

12 陈献章，《与林时矩三则之一》，《陈献章集》，上册，卷3，页242。
13 "吾道有宗主，千秋朱紫阳"，陈宪章，《和杨龟山此日不再得韵》，《陈献章集》，上册，卷4，页279。
14 "内在的感应"是二程重要的思想，当另文讨论。

关于心学的体道经验与一多悖论的关系，笔者举两位最常被批判的心学大师为例，已足以显示他们有冥契太极的经验，但他们会将此经验视为一多并融，并力图与无差别相的超越之"一"划清界限。我们最后且再举心学的宗师王阳明为例，也可看出他的观点也是一样的。王阳明在龙场驿的"一夕忽大悟"是儒学史上极著名的例子，从那一晚之后，东亚迅速地增加了一系可和朱子学抗衡的王学。王阳明的龙场之悟极著名，他的后学以及王学学派中人大概很少人会怀疑这场悟觉是"直透先天未画前"的悟道经验。据年谱所记，王阳明在一夕大悟之前，已行静坐法门多年，静坐自然是要为悟道作准备。王阳明在山穷水尽之际，忽于蛮荒异域洞见心体，此事不可谓不是儒学史上的一大事因缘。但可惜的是王阳明就像典型的东方悟道哲人一样，对静坐之事，并不热衷于将它表述成为重要的修行法门。对于龙场一悟之内容，他更鲜少道及，这种善意的隐秘应是王阳明自己的选择。但我们由底下两则叙述，可以想象王阳明所悟者为何。

第一条数据见于年谱所记载，嘉靖六年（1527），王阳明56岁时的事。此年王阳明以抱病之身，奉命远征广西的思、田之乱，由于军务倥偬，他无法响应远道来问学的后生学子，只有诸生徐樾锲而不舍，一路追随王阳明的船只到了余干。

> 先生令登舟。樾方自白鹿洞打坐，有禅定意。先生目而得之，令举似。曰："不是。"已而稍变前语，又曰："不是。"已而更端，先生曰："近之矣。此体岂有方所，譬之此烛，光无不在，不可以烛上为光。"因指舟中曰："此亦是光，此亦是光。"直指出舟外水面曰："此亦是光。"樾领谢而别。[15]

---

15 吴光、钱明等编，"年谱三"，《王阳明全集》（杭州：浙江古籍出版社，2010年），册4，卷34，页1319。

　　这段指点话语充满了体道叙述中常见的隐喻：水与光。如果我们看过华严宗法藏大师对"不了无尽法界重重网义者"所作的开导，[16] 两者竟有几分相似。王阳明的指点不直接说破，颇具禅意。徐樾听了王阳明此段似答非答的话语后，"领谢而别"，也颇具禅意。

　　以光比喻心体或悟觉经验乃是宗教经验中常见的表达方式，无分于东、西方宗教，也无分于内向型或外向型的冥契论，王阳明的指示语同样来自修炼的传统。王阳明的答语可分两阶段看。第一阶段是遮拨语，我们不知道徐樾当时的说明为何，但我们观王阳明以"烛与光"为例，指光"无不在，不可以烛上为光"的答语，可以合理地推测徐樾是从主体的朗现原因着眼。"烛"代表人的主体，人能弘道，亦即只有人可以体道，只有人可以因主体的朗现道而同时朗现世界潜存的本体论意义。徐樾有可能只从主体义界定道，王阳明承认其说已近之矣，但这种主体义的良知说仍不是究竟。

　　究竟义是要由主体义进入道体义，道体义的良知在果地上表现得最明显，道体义的良知用王龙溪的语汇讲，即是乾知，乾知虽是王龙溪使用的语言，但由王阳明《咏良知诗》的"此是乾坤万有基"之语观之，王龙溪的用语是恰当的。当王阳明泛指不同处之光曰"此亦是光""此亦是光""此亦是光"时，我们有理由认定这种指引是有所说的，它是从果地的层次立言，也可以说是从"乾知"的观点立言。王阳明的"此"是感觉的直接性，直接指向当场当时的"某光"，它有普遍的具体性，这种普遍的具体性是道体的现成性。作为道体隐喻的光是在这些一一的个别性上透露的，直白地说，王阳明所述也是一种"千江有水千江月"，一种良知学意义的因陀罗网境界门。

　　笔者的解释可以从王阳明高徒王畿的一处记载中得到印证，王畿

---

16 赞宁，《宋高僧传》记载其事道："为学不了者设巧便，取鉴十面，八方安排，上下各一，相去一丈余，面面相对，中安一佛像，燃一炬以照之，互影交光，学者因晓刹海涉入无尽之义。"参见《高僧传合传》（上海：上海古籍出版社，1991年），卷5，页408。

在一次公开的场合中，对追求良知学的同志道：

> （王阳明）始究心于老佛之学，结洞天精庐，日夕勤修炼
> 习伏藏，洞悉机要，其于彼家所谓见性抱一之旨，非惟通其
> 义，盖已得其髓矣。自谓尝于静中，内照形躯如水晶宫，忘己
> 忘物，忘天忘地，与空虚同体，光耀神奇，恍惚变幻，似欲言
> 而忘其所以言，乃真境象也。[17]

　　理学家一般不太述及自己悟道的亲身体证，王阳明也是如此，甚至于更是如此。但以上的报道出自他最亲近的学生的大众会语，我们没有理由怀疑这段话的可靠性。王阳明此次的经验极具炫丽之能事，与一般常见的枯淡、直觉式的证悟报道大异其趣，在理学的工夫论史上是段值得注意的记录。由于此次经验出自他龙场驿之悟之前，因此，虽然王畿说此境"乃真境象也"，我们将此段报道视为他的体证经验的定论，或许可以质疑。王阳明此处的体验出自佛老，应当也是可以肯定的。[18] 但借人门径是一回事，进入门径证得的结果又是另一回事，不一定是同质的。我们从王阳明年谱所记载的晚年叙事，以及从阳明后学所作的类似之体证报道看来，王阳明的体证至少当是一多诡谲同一的悖论型经验，这点应当是可以肯定的，王畿这位有资格判断体悟境界之深浅异同的儒门龙象也说这是"真境象"。

　　本节以杨简、陈献章、王阳明为例，指出虽然他们一般不会分析个人悟觉经验的内涵，而只是直白陈述，但我们经由今日宗教学的眼光反思其文，可以认定他们的证悟应当都属"一多诡谲同一"的悖论形态。陆王心学传承孟子学，其学大抵皆以复性为宗，其工夫重视本

---

17 王畿，《王畿集·滁阳会语》（南京：凤凰出版社，2007 年），卷 2，页 33。
18 依据束景南先生的考证，王阳明此处体验的法门源自尹真人（尹从龙）的"真空炼形法"，
　　参见束景南，《王阳明年谱长编》（上海：上海古籍出版社，2017 年），册 1，页 111–122。

心的直接活动，感触兴发，当下即是，本末兼收。儒家心学基本上都是道德主体主义哲学，所以他们的证道叙述常带有浓厚的超越性同一哲学的韵味。然而，我们就他们的悟道语言分析，他们所见者仍当以"一多诡谲同一"的因素为大宗。

四、朱子的"月印万川"说

心学学者的体证语可分析出"一多诡谲同一"的内涵，他们本人却很少以理论证成之。以理论证成理学体道论述中的"一多"问题者，不能不有待于程朱学派。程朱在反对派的陆王学者眼中，不能算是体道有成的学者，陆象山以读程颐著作"若伤我者"，与朱子论学，作诗讥道："支离事业转浮沉。"王阳明曾依他认定的朱子工夫法门，格窗前竹子，最终格出一场病，因叹与圣人之学无分。这些都是理学史上著名的案例，理学后来分成程朱、陆王两派，是有道理的。然而，我们有理由认定程朱两人皆有经历类似冥契的经验，他们的理论之言也多是体验之语。而且对于如何达到"尽心知性"的目标，也都立下了工夫法门，此即"主敬涵养"与"格物穷理"并进的方式。至于体证境界中"一"的内涵为何，朱子继程颐之说，对此作了更多"一多诡谲同一"的规定。

程颐以严肃的渐教思想著称后世，然而，一种本体论式的同一的思考，恰恰是在程颐其人的体系中发挥得最为淋漓尽致。程颐著作中颇可见到"一人之心即天地之心，一物之理即万物之理，一日之运即一岁之运"，"性之本谓之命，性之自然者谓之天，性之有形者谓之心，性之有动者谓之情。凡此数者皆一也"（《河南程氏遗书》，卷25），"圣人之心与天为一，安得有二？至于不勉而中，不思而得，莫不在此。此心与天地无异，不可小了他"（《河南程氏遗书》，卷2上）此类的语言，而且此类语言在程颐的言论中占有相当的比例。如果我们只考虑理学家对"一"的追求，程颐著作中所显现的追求"一"之热情与数量，可能超出北宋其他理学家之上。而且，程颐表达这些"一"之语言时，通常是用疾词表之，表示中间诸概念更无差异，如"命""天""性""情"的本质相同，皆"一"也。由于程颐本人特别重视"格物穷理"的工夫，"格物穷理"的工夫是渐教类型，持此一理论的学者通常不喜说及超越之"一"的本地风光。后世学者面对程颐"一也"的表达方式，不能不生出极大的困惑。牟宗三在《心体与性体》中论程颐的《论心篇》章节处，即费了许多力量爬梳，证明这些说法都是不确定语。

有关程颐的"一也"之类的语言该如何解，确实存在着不同的理解方式。因为如果我们将他所说的"一也"之类的语句全解为一种承体起用的本心模式，那么，程颐的系统就会往陆王心学的方向，或是往程颢的方向靠拢。但这种本心论的训诂和更能突显程颐个人思想特质的"格物穷理"说颇有龃龉，至少表面上很难并存。然而，我们单单就"一也"之语观之，程颐的思考和北宋理学家的想法是相似的，他们都有性命之学的要求，都分享了中国"大周天"与"小周天"相关的思想传统，这个论断应该是可以成立的。至于其"一"的内容为何，恐怕要等到他最忠实的继承人朱子兴起，他们两人的论点才可清楚地显现出来。

朱子是智性性格很浓厚的儒家哲人，"格物致知"论与"主敬"论是朱子学的重要标志，前者意指学者体证的工夫不能脱离体认一种贯穿形上学、伦理学与认知性理则的"所以然"与"所当然"之理，后者则意指学者体道的工夫还要在全幅的身心行为的举止中维持警觉凝聚的"一"之状态。"格物"与"主敬"双管齐下，缺一不可。在典型的东方体证哲学当中，也就是以带有体证本体（本心、本性）为目的的东方哲学当中，"知识"一般常被认为是妨碍体道的因素，至少在过程中是要被扫除的，在佛教与道家的文献中，怀疑知识价值的论点大量出现。像朱子这般结合超越性的体证目标与认知性因素的价值之哲学极少，甚至可说是绝无仅有的一个大学派。在朱子后的八百年中，朱子学无疑地取得了大胜利，它从被打压的"伪学"变成孔孟正宗，为官方与社会所共认。但就以性命之学为范围的公共形象而言，朱子并不是以体证道体的冥契人形象著称于世的。在陆王学派学者眼中，朱子虽然俱足泰山乔岳般的人格，但他的学问就是"不见道"，这是陆象山给朱子下的定评。王阳明一生与朱子学奋斗，其学虽然就旨归而言近乎陆象山，但就问题意识而言，则朱子的影响毋宁更大。[19]他退一步承认朱子学纵然最后可证道，至少是很笨拙，"已费转手"。

然而，我们有理由认定，从年轻以至临终，超越向度的体证始终是朱子的核心关怀。朱子年轻时出入佛老，其诗文颇多禅机；后来遇见程门嫡传李延平，这是他一生重要的转机。朱子勇猛精进，求道心切，他的出现也带给李延平极大的冲击。年轻学生会给造诣甚深的师长压力，此事一方面显示李延平的谦冲自抑，与人为善，一方面也显示其时朱子的表现一定是相当特殊，跨迈流俗，才会引起李延平特别的注意。我们观朱子与李延平的通信，纵然很难确认朱子当时是否经历过典型的冥契经验，但我们如配合他 37 岁参透中和问题之前的论述来看，比如说"中和旧说"时期的文献，我们可以合理地推定：这时期的文献所述不仅是理论建构之言，也是体证之言，朱子应该有很深层的证道体验。

朱子 37 岁立中和新说之前，我们看到他对心体的理解，大体持心性同一的态度，性是未发，心是已发。他的工夫论也是建立在这种心性连续体的基础上，学者平素处在良心日用不知的状态中，与世同在，此时无自觉的工夫可言。等良心不安，道德意识从意识一般中迸

---

19 参见唐君毅，《朱陆之学圣之道及王阳明之致良知之道（下）》，《中国哲学原论原教篇》，收入《唐君毅全集》（台北：台湾学生书局，1984），卷 19，页 289—348。

裂而起，此种不安意味着人的真实本性的呼唤，这是东方版的苦恼意识。学者借此苦恼，反观自照，直证本心。朱子论及此工夫次第时，有云：“因其良心发见之微，猛省提撕，使心不昧，则是作工夫底本领。”这种工夫的本领可说直接在心体的朗现上作工夫，一种直接性的意识之自我转化。及乎工夫有成，学者在独特的转化意识状态中，可体证到玄妙的终极境界，也就是未发的层次。如果借用牟宗三先生的语言讲，青年朱子的工夫模式乃是不折不扣的“逆觉反证”，他可达到未发层次。

在提出中和新说之前，朱子求道心切，勇猛精进，其方式与一般东方哲学中常见的体证工夫，差异并不大。在青年朱子处，作为超越性的大本是可以被体证的，而且体证这个事件只能经由人的意识转化这条途径，无与于万物与主体之间的复杂关系。由于学者此时对道体、性体可以有积极的知识，可以无中介项地直接证成，所以他论工夫，即可承体起用、承用证体般地就意识的流行，全程以观。由纯净的未发层直接而发，性行乎心，即有大用流行；但暗默自证，不妨常有未行乎用之性存于缄默之纯一之中。“若无此物，则天命有已时，生物有尽处，气化断绝，有古无今，久矣，此所谓天下之大本。”笼统观来，他早年的体证与理学大宗的从心上立根基，返证超越之性体，并无两样。朱子在“已发”“未发”问题上费尽心思，这种体验该如何描述，或者说该如何在儒学整体的思想结构中找到恰当的位置，他不时调整其相关论证，过程颇为缴绕。但可以确定，“格物致知”此一关键性的工夫论在他前期思想体系中，并没有特殊的位置，体证论述中的“一多”难题也没有出现。

这种不确定性一直要到朱子提出“中和新说”后，他的整个学术的规模才就此定了下来，冥契经验或终极境界中的“一多”问题也才跟着出现。朱子苦参中和，就工夫论的观点看，前后两阶段的关键差异当在前期的工夫乃是直证本心，后者则切断了直通的管道，而改采"主敬涵养"与"格物穷理"双轨并行、相互涵化的渐教模式。朱子著名的"涵养""察识"先后之辨,其"察识"实乃"直证本心或本体"之意,早年主张"察识先于涵养",参透中和新说后,则力主"涵养先于察识",这样的转变乃是题中应有之论。朱子的工夫论转型当然不是孤立的事件,而是一连串理论重组过程中重要的一环,这种理论的改造工程包含了理气的二分,"心统性情"的主体模式,以及"以气释心"的本质性界定。在整体理论的重组过程中,朱子对于"心"的理解极特别,影响也极大,简言之,在"心统性情"的主体范式下,学者可以经由"格物穷理"与"主敬涵养"双管齐下,最后证成"天理流行"的境界。他的"格物穷理"的工夫过程与"天理流行"的境界之间,不但前者乃是后者朗现的前提,而且前者的内涵会构成后者的境界内涵。

朱子的格物论最后要达成"物格知至",他的"物格知至"该如何解释,学界有不同的解读。笔者认为从朱子使用"豁然贯通"的用语习惯,从朱子门人对朱子生命的描述,从历代体证有得的朱子学学者对"格致补传"的理解,朱子所说的"物格知至"只能是冥契论的一种,而且朱子所说不是造论,而是为学必达而且可达的层次,笔者曾在不同的文章中表达过类似的意思。[20] 朱子学之特殊在于他的证悟体验思想与主智穷理思想的高度结合,这种以"思量分别"始,再与"非思量分别"的解脱思想竞争,最终达成"思量分别"与"非思量分别"统一的思想,在冥契论的体系中,是个异数,其他学派少见。但诚如朱子训告高弟辅广所说的:"圣人教人如一条大路,平平正正,自此直去,可以到圣贤地位。只是要人做得彻,做得彻时,也不大惊小怪,只是私意剥落净尽,纯是天理融明尔。"圣人境界预设人与天

---

20 参见拙作,《格物与豁然贯通——朱子〈格物补传〉的诠释问题》,收入钟彩钧编,《朱子学的开展·学术篇》(台北:汉学研究中心,2002 年),页 219–246。

的位阶之等同,这种位阶必须经历一种"豁然贯通"的撕裂经验,尔后才有种种的果地风光。但朱子认为这是天理融明之本然,不值得大惊小怪。

朱子不是以建构理论见长的西方式哲学家,而是体证导向的东方哲人,他的思想如果没有体证太极此义,是很难想象的。依他成熟期的思想,朱子称呼类似冥契经验的经验为"物格""知至""豁然贯通",这三个概念可以说同时而至,"物格"意指"物"的内涵的全体朗现,"知至"指心灵功用的全幅展开,"豁然贯通"则是一种独特心性经验的描述,其语指向一种贯通一切、全幅朗现的意识突破层次。朱子《答黄商伯四》云:

> 经文"物格",犹可以一事言;"知至",则指吾心所可知处,不容更有未尽矣。程子"一日一件"者,格物工夫次第也;"脱然贯通"者,知至效验极致也。不循其序而遽责其全,则为自困;但求粗晓而不期贯通,则为自画。[21]

"贯通"是朱子喜欢用的词语,他借此词语和佛老的"顿悟"等概念区分开来,但其内涵仍是一种超越层次的"一"之朗现。《格致补传》中说的"物格""知至"同样指向冥契的经验。学者在工夫途中时,"格物致知"不能不运用理智辨析的方法,"物格知至"则是超越理智析辨的果地境界,这种以分析始,以飞跃终的工夫途径颇为特别。但朱子对向上一机的豁然贯通始终怀有戒心,但也始终视为学者为学之目的,这是确切无疑的。不要说朱子后学中多有此认定,朱子本人主张此冥契境界的语言也并非罕见。

朱子此封信对"格物致知"的工夫论法门需要同时照顾学习的程

---

21 朱熹著,陈俊明校编,《答黄商伯四》,《朱子文集》(台北:德富文教基金会出版,2000年),册5,卷46,页2074。

序以及超越的向上一机，表露得相当清楚。但他说"'物格'犹可以一事言"，其语恐怕需要斟酌。依据朱子理气论的世界观，"物格"意指"物"的本质的真正完成。但朱子对物的本质有特殊的规定，物的本质即物性，物性不只有经验科学的内涵，也有形而上的存有论意义。就学者求道的立场而言，这种物格的层次乃是物的"表里精粗"同时完成。而物的"表里精粗"的揭露是和吾心"全体大用"的完成一并进行的，没有主体的"全体大用"之彰显，也就没有物的"表里精粗"之全幅朗现。就超越的理的观点而言，"物"的本来面目乃是一物一太极，每一物都含摄全体世界的结构。所以"知至"如果是本心的全体朗现的话，"物格"也就不可能只就一事一物而言。

但朱子之所以强调"物格"以一事言，也有道理，这就牵涉理学甚至儒学的"性"或"性体"的概念。在理学的系统中，性在对应着物——包含个体物与个别性事件而论时，有物即有物之性，而物之性一方面可以指向事物的形构之理，一方面也可以指向它的所以然之理，也可以说是存在之理，至于这两种理的取舍偏重之不同，依学派而立。当代学者或许会强调形构之理与存在之理的隔绝性，不能并立，朱子学却力主两种理的性质是连续的。在《中庸》与《易经》的系统中，道是要落实于每一个别事件上的，每一个别事件也都通向了道。物的特性即是其理，也可以说是其性，物之性或物之理都是兼具超越面与经验面两者。性体一方面不能不是普遍的，但一方面也不能不是个别的。

和佛老学派或后来的陆王学派相比，朱子的工夫论特别重视知识与太极的关系，也可以说强调两者的连续性，他甚至认为知识之理乃是太极落于现实的存在之中所致。因此，在体道的过程中，他也特别强调认知活动与一体经验间的兼容。他认为凡是没有经历过认知活动，只以直证本心所达到的一体境界都是不可靠的，其虚静境界只能称作"黑的虚静"。相反地，建立在长期认知活动基础上的虚静则是

"白的虚静"。朱子此处所说"白的虚静"的"白"和庄子"虚室生白"或冥契论述中常见的"白"意象之意义不同,它意指经由理智活动呈现的理性之光。"虚静"原本来自先秦道家的体证语言,朱子此处所用仍是性命之学的用语。我们如果想要求朱子直接说出他的格物论所述即是他的体证语,恐怕不容易,朱子向来不喜说及境界语,但我们有理由认定朱子对此境界的体证就是种"白的虚静"。

"白的虚静"一词的"虚静"指向心性主体的虚一而静,"白"字则恰好不是道家用法中的心体之白,而是带有荀子学传统的理智之光的白。朱子使用此词语时,乃用以表达体证的正当境界乃是"一中有多""全体之中有秩序"之意,这样的语言颇诡谲,因"一"与"多","全体之一"与"秩序之理",语义是矛盾的。朱子之所以使用这样的语句,乃因豁然贯通的心境呈现出来的正是"一多诡谲同一"的景象。

朱子所领会的人生实相或宇宙实相为"天理流行"之境,这是确定的;他理解的"天理流行"乃是一多诡谲同一的模式,这也是确定的。他的"一多诡谲同一"的"多"可视为全体世界所有个体的总和,凡有个体义即有区别的特征处,凡可区别处即有个体义,朱子的"多"是计量词,却是本质上无法量化的计量词。但个体之中不能排斥总体之一,"物物一太极"不能排斥"总体一太极"。朱子特别喜欢用的隐喻乃是"月印万川",万川隐喻世界万物,月隐喻本体:月亮唯一,却可下印万川;万川虽殊,却上映了同一个月亮。恰如本体唯一,却可下注为物的性体,每一物原则上又都可反映整体性的太极,物物相等,不多不少。朱子认为学者体证的终极境界与物的性体的内涵皆像因陀罗网上的吊珠,每一珠皆反映了整体法界。

当程朱强调"主敬"的工夫,强调"大本"(亦即"一")的目标,而又主张"格物穷理"并行的工夫论路线,并依"理一分殊"(亦即"月印万川")的隐喻表现出来时,他们的工夫所证成的境界只能是

"一多诡谲为一"的类型。但程朱由于在心与性之间画下一道本质上无法跨越的红线，因此，他们体证所得的"一多诡谲为一"的"一"不能是陆王心学中那种"同一"的类型，而只能是"显微无间"却又有间的那种合一的类型。就此而言，程朱冥契论的类型反而接近犹太教、基督教、伊斯兰教的冥契论类型，在西方一神论的上帝绝对超越性的格局下，"人与上帝同一"的论述是很难论的。基督教的冥契者一不小心即会踏入禁区，冒犯了上帝的尊严，布鲁诺（G. Bruno）的悲惨命运即是一例。

朱子是八百年来，影响东亚最深的一位儒家哲人，但他的公共形象常与现实上的真人真事大有差距。在工夫论领域，也是如此。朱子无疑是知识性很浓的哲人，但他的每一种知识都是通向太极的管道，没有一种理是纯粹经验性的。朱子学也是以追求"大本"作为导向的，它所体证的境界仍是一种冥契型的"一"之法境，而且是"一多诡谲为一"之境。由朱子的一多昭融、物物相摄的理境着眼，我们看到朱子学在本体论上具有一种宽容、多元的因素。笔者认为朱子这种思想形态在当代仍有极高的价值，也需要重组后作更好的解释。

五、水中何故却生金：第三系理学的见证

"与上帝为一"是西方宗教冥契者危险的禁区，儒家的冥契者自然不会冒类似的风险。程朱那种蓄意在心与太极之间画下红线的学派在中国文化史上较少见，但他们使用的"月印万川"的隐喻应当具有更普遍的适用性，"月印万川"是体用论思维下容易出现的隐喻。然而，由于程朱"然"与"所以然"异质相对的思考模式，"月印万川"的隐喻不免会出现较浓厚的静止因素，动力不足。在理学的各学派中，笔者认为以道体论（笔者称为先天型气论，或牟宗三先生说的本

体宇宙论）为思想核心的理学家最能畅尽"一多诡谲同一"的内涵，他们可以称作理学第三系的儒者。他们私人性的体证报道和他们的思想体系之间的关系，也最为一致。此节，笔者将以周敦颐、邵雍、程颢为例，突显道体论型的哲人"一多诡谲同一"的悖论语言的内涵。

　　论及道体论理学，我们首先即以周敦颐为例，以兹说明。周敦颐为理学的开山祖，在工夫论这个领域，他开山祖的地位也是确定的。周敦颐的"主静说"与二程的"主敬说"是北宋理学最重要的工夫论主张，进入南宋后，二程的"主敬说"经由朱子的发扬，俨然成为理学的主流工夫论法门。然而，进入明代心学的时代，周敦颐的"主静说"又获得极大的重视，在江门学派、江右学派与东林学派处，"主静说"更隐然成为工夫论的主轴。有关后世"主静""主敬"的内涵，其真实义往往超出文字的表述之外，如："主静"之"静"常被解释成超乎动静之"静"；"主敬"之"敬"，则常被解释成贯乎意识与行动的"一"之不二法门。然不管是"主静"或"主敬"，其目的皆是以成圣为期，其证验标准大概都要有体证心体这种独特的心性事件，"静""敬"这两个字都从现实经验的语言提升到体现超越层次的语言，中间经过异质性的跳跃。若此种种，两种法门应该都是相似的。

　　周敦颐在理学传统中被视为"默契道妙"的一代宗师，他的"主静立人极"之说不但被视为是工夫论的大本正宗，周敦颐本人也被视为体证有得的开创者。然而，周敦颐"默契道妙"的觉悟状态如何，他自己本人的文字很少说明，但是，由他与陈抟及内丹道教的关系，由他"始观丹诀信希夷，盖得阴阳造化机。子自母生能致主，精神合后更知微"[22]这些文字所示，周敦颐的体道甚深，直造精微，已"得阴阳造化机"，应该是可以确定的。他的《太极图说》所说的"无极而太极"，被视为对宇宙真相的描述，但也被性命之学中人认定为心性

---

22 周敦颐，《读英真君丹诀》，《周敦颐集》（北京：中华书局，1990 年），卷 3，页 66。

体证至微的一种境界语言。《通书·圣学》中"一者，无欲也"，很明确是工夫论的语言，也是造道有得之言。这两种文献所显示的内容都是周敦颐思想的核心义，两组文字有互文性的关系，是有决定义的文字。它们同时涉入人与自然的实相层面，这样的理解应当是可以接受的。

周敦颐本人与道佛的关系甚深，这层关系本来未必直接影响到他的工夫论语言，但如果他的工夫论语言与道家语言颇有交涉，我们对周敦颐何以会追求一种超越性的一之境界，或许可以得到一些启发。周敦颐的宇宙论句式"无极而太极"以及心性论语言"一者，无欲也"，都牵涉到"一"与"无"，此"一"带有道家形上学的色泽。"一者，无欲也"的"无欲"既可指向具体下手工夫的去除私欲之主张，也可指向私欲净尽的"无"的境界。"一"与"无"在超越境界中的异同关系如何理解，可能是普遍的问题，凡有冥契合一的理念处，即不免有此玄妙的表达方式。在中国文化传统中，我们知道这个问题乃是在《老子》处被明显表述出来。事实上，《太极图说》"无极而太极"的渊源问题，乃是理学史上的一大争辩，朱陆双方争辩的焦点之一即在《太极图说》与《老子》的关系。但不管持肯定说还是否定说者，大概都不会否认周敦颐针对这两本代表作所处理的代表性议题，都指向了作为宇宙与人终极境界的玄秘之境，此境乃是处于"一"或"无"的状态。"一""无"乍看相去甚远，但纯粹统体的"一"毫无内容，其实也就是"无"，"无"的整体性原理也就是"一"。

有关周敦颐思想中"一""无"的关系，本文无能再涉入，也不宜再涉入。我们之所以在此提出周敦颐带来的问题，乃因在当代的理学研究中，周敦颐常被视为宇宙论中心的哲人，他对世界有种前科学的关心，这种关心是广义的自然科学的论述。然而，不管就周敦颐的内部思想还是就他发挥的影响（如对晚明江右学派），他都是不折不扣的性命之学的体现者，他对"一"的追求相当强烈，明代以"致虚归寂"为宗的学派多受到他的影响。周敦颐不是自然秘密的探险者，而是生命秘密的体证者，这是确切无疑的。他之所以有宇宙论的倾向，我们与其从原始科学的宇宙论方向上去理解，不如从他所继承的《易经》传统上探寻，可能更为接近。理学第三系的"一多诡谲同一"的秘密在于它们继承的经典。

周敦颐的思想以《易经》为核心，他的工夫论模式也要放在他的《易经》学模式下定位，"太极图说"即是他重要的《易经》学代表著作之一。作为带有玄门修炼之风的《太极图说》，所述既有宇宙论的文章形式，也有性命之学的内涵，这两种叙述的关系，我们可以简洁地说乃是一体的两面。而不同性质的两套语言之所以可以视为一体的两面，乃因周敦颐继承了《易经》道在万物，超越在经验中的思想，这是东方版的泛神论思想模型。在广义的泛神论表述中，天（上帝、神、太极等）与世界（万物）的关系常会出现两种完全不同方向的解释，两者原本该不异但也不一。当重点落在不异处时，泛神论容易变成唯物论；当落在不一处时，世界会被提升为天之载体，因而成了泛神论。《易经》或斯宾诺莎哲学何以常会有两种极端不同的解释，可以说事出有因。

道体论面对的问题和泛神论类似，在一多关系上的问题也类似。《太极图说》云，"一实万分，万一各正，小大有定"，其说已涉及一多兼容的论点。周敦颐这种论述其实也是"理一分殊"的另类讲法，原始科学的宇宙论句子不会是这种表现方式。朱子解释其义云："只是此一个理，万物分之以为体，万物之中又各具一理，所谓'乾道变化，各正性命也'。然总又只是一个理。"文字颇缠绕，义理却一清二楚。"太极图"那么繁复的图式，朱子总论其义道："太极非是别为一物，只是一个理而已。"朱子显然以"总体一太极，物物一太极"的格式解之，但这种解释是恰当的。北宋理学的开山祖体证至深，但可想见，其所体证者乃是"一多诡谲同一"的类型。至于他的工夫论的影响为何在明代心学中特别张扬，这是另外一个值得探索的议题。

北宋理学家当中，同样以《易经》为圣言量旨归，而且受陈抟影响者，除了周敦颐外，还有邵雍其人，邵雍同样以性命之学的学问著称于世。就工夫论的法门而言，邵雍对后世的影响不如周敦颐；但就实际的工夫操作而言，邵雍的文献则显现了更丰富的内容。事实上，我们如果不从冥契论（类似传统所说的性命之学）的角度入手，恐怕无法进入邵雍的思想世界。邵雍的思想往往透过诗歌表现出来，他的诗歌中颇多个人的修证之语，《伊川击壤集》诗风在诗史上自成一格，其诗于诗体虽是别裁，其兴感的诗趣之醇却非后世仿效其诗的内丹学者所能及。邵雍描述他自己个人的体证之诗有言："恍惚阴阳初变化，氤氲天地乍回旋。中间些子好光景，安得工夫入语言。"[23]"恍惚"一词令我们联想到《老子》的"恍兮惚兮，其中有物；窈兮冥兮，其中有精，其精甚真"（《老子·第二十一章》）。老子这段话指涉的是道的内涵，但也是体道的内涵，其语成为后世丹道人士常用以证成的口诀。邵雍与丹道本来即有特殊的渊源，他的《恍惚吟》很有资格视作《老子·第二十一章》的谛解。此诗的语言显示了日常的人格结构开始动摇，主体的变化带动了生活世界的变化，氤氲回旋。此处所说的变化，应该是种异质性的跳跃，观最后两句诗可知。在中国修炼传统中，"光景"意指意识转换后的独特心境，[24]常是不可言说的。邵雍的用语令人想起屈原在《远游》篇中所说的："因气变而遂曾举兮，忽神奔而鬼怪。"我们有理由认定"气变曾举"的景象即是《老子》所说的"恍兮惚兮，其中有物"的"物"，也就是邵雍与内丹学中的"物"之意义，意指"精""气"等原初之物被转化了，终至于超越层

---

23 邵雍，《恍惚吟》，《伊川击壤集》，收入《邵雍集》（北京：中华书局，2010 年），卷 12，页 366。以下邵雍引文，同此版本。

24 正因为"光景"指向玄妙的体证境界，此境界常带有非日常经验所能及的常乐或无乐之乐的性质，令人容易流连忘返，所以理学工夫论中有"破除光景"一义。

的"神""虚"之境。

在邵雍的诗歌中，我们常看到一些玄妙之境的叙述，如："虚室清泠都是白，灵台莹静别生光。观风御寇心方醉，对景颜渊坐正忘。赤水有珠涵造化，泥丸无物隔青苍。生为男子仍身健，时遇昌辰更岁穰。"此诗的诗题描绘坐香的情景，坐香固是修行人的生活常景。由诗的内容看来，应当是坐香有得，进入超越层的叙述。邵雍此诗运用了大量来自《庄子》的典故，我们从中看到清泠莹静的白光的内涵，看到"泥丸无物"的判语，亦即是"体一"的境界。邵雍对超越境界的追寻与体证非常热衷，我们观其诗集中的《先天吟》皆前后出现过六首，即可略见一斑。[25] 但最明确的文句当是他的《得一吟》："天自得一天无既，我一自天而后至。唯天与一无两般，我亦何尝与天异。""得一"是《老子》的语汇，邵雍不以为忌，他借以表述天一同体的"一"之理念。上述这些语言都是在歌咏心灵转化境界，我们如果知道邵雍在百泉山中刻苦的静坐生涯，即可了解这些诗句所说的，不会是知识论的命题，而是体道者的语言。和周敦颐一样，邵雍也是"一"的追寻者，"唯天与一无两般，我亦何尝与天异"是他的工夫论宣言。

邵雍对"一"的追求是很显著的，但是他所追求或所体证的"一"之内涵为何，可再细辨。朱子在《答袁机仲三》此一书信中，曾发挥邵雍的先天易学道："忽然夜半一声雷，万户千门次第开。若识无中含有象，许君亲见伏羲来。"[26] 朱子此诗是解《易》之作，但我们如果从隐喻的角度入手，不难理解朱子此诗所说也是对悟觉经验的叙述，"忽然夜半一声雷"，以雷声比悟觉时的听觉感受，此义在理学史上并非罕见。理学家中，邵雍是此隐喻的创立者，邵雍将"雷声"

---

25 其中卷 16 的《先天吟—示邢和叔》及卷 19 的《先天吟》皆有两首，实得六首。
26 《朱子文集》，卷 4，页 1548。

比喻成一个完整而长期隐蔽的生命被唤醒了，这可以模拟西方宗教哲学中述及的整体生命重生的冥契经验，我们很容易想到《易经·无妄》有名的"天下雷行，物与无妄"之说。至于此诗句言及"忽然"一语，看来也不是偶然的，因为悟觉经验的突如其来，乃是冥契传统共有的特色，柏克（R. M. Bucke）与铃木大拙皆曾一再言及。

邵雍的体悟经验就像朱子所诠释的那般，当往"无中含有"的方向理解，亦即不可放在"绝对无"的层次，而当放在"一多诡谲同一"的理境下理解。关于"无中含有"的意义，我们不妨再观看他《伊川击壤集》中的一首诗："天心复处是无心，心到无时无处寻。若谓无心便无事，水中何故却生金。"[27] 此诗有可能是内丹的修炼语，前面两句指的当是意识修行到非有非无，难以言说的玄妙之境，所以由"天心"转到"无心"。"天心"云云，来自《易经·复卦》的意象："复，其见天地之心乎！"后两句的内涵颇似禅宗的著名词句："万法归一，一归何处？"两者同样以问代答，差别只在邵雍开启了不同的发展方向，理学家不会无事地安于"无心"的绝对冥合状态。他质问道：如果心境体无至极，无即无矣，何以生有？就像水即水矣，水中何以生金？杂多的意象何以从代表无之意识的"水"中生起？

"天心复处""水中生金""夜半声雷""无中含有"此类的语言都不是日常的生活世界中的语言，而是一种非常性的冥契论述，关键问题接着来了，这样的冥契语言该如何理解？如果"忽然夜半一声雷"指向悟觉经验，冥契意义的悟觉经验总是"顿"的，刹那呈显。"万户千门次第开。若识无中含有象"则指向了另一个层次的问题，亦即此一悟觉经验的类型，到底该如何解。在一体的经验中统摄万有，此义自孟子"万物皆备于我矣"，陆象山"万物森然于方寸之中，满心而发，充摄宇宙，无非斯理"以来，早已成了理学家熟悉的义理。但

---

27 邵雍，《寄亳州秦伯镇兵部》，《伊川击壤集》，收入《邵雍集》，卷8，页290。

整个孟子学传统沿着道德意识主体的方向展延，物性不彰，所以无法畅论"万物皆备于我"之说的人性、物性之异同之内涵。此义反而要到程朱将理气论发挥到极致，人性、物性的异同以及体证境界的一多问题反而才显现出来。在道体论的北宋哲人身上，这个问题一样存在，虽然不见得更突显，但应该更重要。

第三句"若识无中含有象"，此句在文字上并没有提到"有象"是一或是多。我们虽然可以将"无中含有"这样的语式解成黑格尔逻辑的零与一的关系，纯粹的一即是无，因为没有内容差别的绝对同一性的"有"可以说即是"无"。但回溯《易经·系辞》"易有太极，是生两仪，两仪生四象，四象生八卦"，我们可以合理地说：太极以下的物象即是"无中含有"的"有"，"有"中之大者乃作为"《易》之门户"的乾坤此两仪，"两仪"以下的"有"即"有象"或"万有"。朱子以"门户"比喻道，或体道的经验，乃承自《易经》传承。至于悟道经验中，千门万户是否"次第开"，或有争议，原则上，如作"同时开"，或许更符合冥契论的语言。然而，此千门万户的光景如果在实践上有意义，它当落实到具体的世界来，它要有节奏。具体化意味着分殊化，所以"同时具足"不能不是因应时节的"次第展现"，所以"次第开"之说也不算错误。

邵雍的体道之言是和他的先天易学联结在一起的，邵雍的先天易学在晚明的两位易学大家方以智与王夫之处，受到极不相同的评价，但不管先天易学的具体内涵为何，邵雍的先天易学和周敦颐的《太极图说》的象数之学不能从术数或宇宙论的角度定位，而当高看，这点都是确定的。而所谓高看，窃以为其义之大者在于存在本源的"太极"与存在总称的"世界"并不是自然系列事件的创生与被生成的关系，而是没有时间历程的同时具足的关系，是存有论的语言，而不是自然科学的语言。邵伯温所谓"夫太极者，在天地之先而不为先，在天地之后而不为后，终天地而未尝终，始天地而未尝始。与天地万物圆融和会，而未尝有先后始终者也"。他又言：太极"自古及今，无时不存，无时不在，万物无所不禀，则谓之命。万物无所不本，则谓之性。万物无所不主，则谓之天"。[28] 邵伯温之言极痛快淋漓，不愧名父之子。朱子解"无极之前"曰"本无先后"，[29] 亦是此意。他论周敦颐"太极动而生阳"、《易传》"易有太极，是生两仪"曰："其生则俱生，太极依旧在阴阳里。"[30] 也是此义。王夫之论太极与万物的关系，指出太极之生，并不是母生子的类型，而是"同有之则俱生"，[31] 所说仍是此义。理学家凡是从道体论立论而又受《易经》影响者，其解《易》之"生"大概都是没有生与被生的"同时俱生"之意。

周敦颐、张载的"一多诡谲同一"的体道论与"太极—万物"的关系乃是"本无先后，同时俱生"的道体论之论述，两者互为表里，相互诠释。然而，论及从体证观点进入，而又能畅尽道体论的诡谲同一之说者，其公共形象最突显的，我们不能不首推程颢。程颢追求"一"的精神不但在北宋理学家中戛戛独造，即使在整体儒学史上，这种思想特色也是很明显的。程颢充养有道，体证自得，他的体证之深在理学传统中是相当著名的。程颢的"一"之精神见于著名的"一本论"，诚如他所说的："天人本无二，不必言二。""一本论"的语言默认了没有历程，没有差别，当下就超越了时间与杂多的阻隔，进入"一"之境界。如他所说："诚便合内外之道，今看得不一，只是心生。除了身只是理，便说合天人。合天人，已是为不知者引而致之。天人无闲。夫不充塞则不能化育，言赞化育，已是离天而言之。"此处言及儒家经典所说"合内外之道"的"合"，"赞天地化育"的"赞"这种统合意义的词汇该如何解释。程颢认为这种词句都是多余的语言，

---

28 引自黄宗羲等编，《宋元学案·百源学案》（台北：河洛图书公司，1975），卷10，页90。
29 黎靖德编，《朱子语类》（北京：中华书局，1994），卷65，页1615。
30《朱子语类》，卷75，页1929。
31 王夫之，《周易外传》（台北：广文书局，1981），卷5，页23。

都是尚未到家的"生语"。他不只批判了"合""赞"两字，在其他的语录里，我们看到他对"充塞于天地间"的"充塞"，"体天地之化"的"体"，都视作赘语。换言之，凡还有待意识的努力以达成目标的工夫语词，程颢皆视为权法，不足以当成如实的圣谛。

程颢个性坦易，天资聪敏，他几乎成了后世理学家终身追求的人格原型。程颢的"一本论"原则上是境界语言，不是工夫论语言，他的语言当中没有断句的空间，"穷理尽性，以至于命，三事一时并了，元无次序"。"穷理""尽性""至于命"三个语词并列，纵使三者可以指向同一种境界，但既然并列，则三者的内涵即不会一致，《易经》的原义或许如此。但在程颢的语言使用习惯里，这些语词的差异，不管是语义的，或是语词所指涉的语词对象，都是透明的，构不成独立的单位，都要"一时并了，元无次序"。程颢的语言最后只会剩下一种圆融心性的当下性，往古来今、八纮一宇、草木鸟兽、天龙八部皆聚于言说的当下，"只此便是天地之化，不可对此个别有天地"，"只在京师，便是到长安，更不可别求长安。只心便是天，尽之便知性，知性便知天。当处便认取，更不可外求"。就现实世界而论，京师汴京（开封）不是长安，心不是天，但程颢认为体道者转化了现实认知的构造，知道"在京师便是到长安，只心便是天"。类似这种抹杀现实的差异相，一切如现成，在程颢的言论中处处可见。理学家当中，程颢特别以"一本"之说著名，此说支持了一种当下圆顿，但物物平等的理念。

程颢喜欢使用圆顿的语言，这种语言很容易让我们想起陆王心学的用语，程颢确实也颇能为心学中人所接受，陆、王两人可以说都是程颢的私淑弟子。但程颢的思想类型与其说是近乎道德意识哲学，还不如说近乎道体论的即体即用哲学，他思想的客观面之强不下于主观面。我们不妨观看此一面向的体道语，程颢言：

如此则亦无始，亦无终，亦无因甚有，亦无因甚无，亦无有处有，亦无无处无。[32]

悟则句句皆是这个道理，道理已明后，无不是此事也。[33]

形而上为道，形而下为器，须看如此说，器亦道，道亦器。但得道在不系今与后，己与人。[34]

心学、理学或以道论为主的理学家言及悟觉处的风光，皆趋于"一多诡谲同一"的类型，但论及论说之圆融，似乎无人超过程颢。他说的道无始无终，不能以生成灭空解之；他的道在世间，贯穿世间，但又不等于世间。这种论述和周敦颐、邵雍并无出入，但程颢的表述特别圆融自在。

在各种道亦器、器亦道，只此即是长安、只此即是天地之化的思想图式中，任何个体都通向了绝对，"这个道理"也在任何叙述句所指的事项上显现。这是广义的泛神论的提法，而凡泛神论类型而又有工夫论成分的论述，都不能不是"一多诡谲同一"的类型，程颢的思想立下了最明赫的地标。

六、结语

冥契经验的语言带有矛盾的性质，体证者叙述自己的巅峰体验时，常有既动又静（如周敦颐所说的"动而无动，静而无静"），既有又无（如老子所说的"常无欲以观其妙，常有欲以观其徼，两者同出而异名"），既黑又白（如苏索所说的"炫丽之幽玄"[35]）或既一且多的

---

32 程颢、程颐，《戌冬见伯淳先生洛中所闻》，《河南程氏遗书》，《二程集》（北京：中华书局，1985年），册1，卷12，页135。

33 程颢、程颐，《传闻杂记》，《河南程氏外书》，《二程集》，册2，卷12，页438。

34 程颢、程颐，《端伯传师说》，《河南程氏遗书》，《二程集》，册1，卷1，页4。

35 引自史泰司著，拙译，《冥契主义与哲学》，页113。

语句（如林光所说的"都滚作一块，又个个饱满"[36]），理学的冥契论情况亦然。关于这种带着矛盾语式的悖论论述是如何产生的？到底是经验本身即提供了这种玄妙的内容，还是体证者报道其经验时，即不免将不自觉的诠释带入其中？由于所有的冥契叙述都脱离不了语言，也就是都需经由语言的信道，体证者的"内在"体验才可因语言化以公共化。哲学性的悖论叙述有可能是冥契论语言的产物，冥契论语言则是语言介入冥契经验的成果。冥契语言的悖论性质到底是经验本身的客观叙述，还是因语言干扰所产生的扭曲性质？冥契论语言的矛盾性质是否也是一种语言之病？

　　史泰司在其名著《冥契主义与哲学》中，即宣称悖论乃语言介入的结果。如论纯粹冥契经验本身，所谓的纯粹也就是他力主的内向型冥契经验，它是超言语的，也是超越逻辑法则的，逻辑法则只有在我们生活世界中才有效。因此，我们用生活世界里才可运作的规则施加到超逻辑领域的冥契经验上去，才会造成矛盾现象，这种运用根本是犯了错置范畴的谬误。冥契经验的性质既不是矛盾的，也不是非矛盾的，它与矛盾律完全不相干。依史泰司的话语推衍，真正的冥契经验是不可言说，超越叙述的，他称这种超乎言语、逻辑的冥契经验为内向型冥契经验，他的内向冥契经验之说颇有禅师"说是一物即不中"之风。按照史泰司的冥契经验的分法，冥契经验有内向型与外向型之分，内向型才是成熟的，代表冥契经验更高级的发展。相对于无从表述的内向型冥契经验，那些带着矛盾语句的冥契论述如果不是将语言误用到它不该运用的领域上去，这种非纯粹同一的悖论语言就该是外向型的冥契经验。

　　不可言说性常被视为冥契经验的核心特性，这个因素如推论至极，冥契经验将如同康德的"物自身"一样，永难表述，成为永恒的

---

36 林光，《南川冰蘖全集》（北京：中国文史出版社，2004年），卷4，页77。

黑洞。史泰司将冥契论述中常见的矛盾语句现象和冥契经验的非逻辑性质联结在一起，他这种联结引发的问题一样地严重。因为如果冥契经验真是超逻辑的，我们对这个经验就不可能有表达的可能性，因为一有表述，即须遵守语法的法则，其知识性质也须遵守逻辑的律则，说即不中。冥契经验的"一多诡谲同一"特性其实也是无一可表述，它如果被表述出来了，其语句如要成立，或许可解作诗的语言，语言的暧昧通常被视为诗的特权，"花落春犹在""鸟鸣山更幽"，语义矛盾则矛盾矣，固是诗中警句。但冥契论者却又力主他们的论述不能视作感性的诗歌语言，它有知悟性的性质。一种具有知悟性性质的悖论语句如何成立，确实是很难想象的，说到底是一种具有更高级知识的内涵但又超越矛盾律性质的叙述，我们不容易在生活世界里找到类似的案例。依据史泰司的超矛盾律之说，冥契经验将会是永远打不开的黑盒子，内容永难知悉。

　　回到理学家的冥契论述上来，笔者认为史泰司的冥契经验的超逻辑性之说，以及他的内外型冥契经验的价值位阶之说，都有相当强的争议空间。冥契经验之难以言说以及矛盾性是那么明显，笔者认为其难以言说或不可言说，很可能正是矛盾性产生的主要原因。[37]"一多悖论的同一"确实是难以言说的，但我们不能不指出一个明显的现象，即它还是被言说了，而且此言说的模式还见于许多不同文化的冥契者的语言中，它具有相当的普遍性，此种悖论的性质很可能就是冥契经验的内涵。我们或许该换另一种角度思考：冥契经验的体证者是在如实地报道他们的经验所得，矛盾的语言就是矛盾的语言，矛盾的语言也可以解释，并没有超逻辑法则那般的玄秘。

　　如果"一多悖论的同一"是外向型的冥契论述，而"纯粹的同

---

37 另外一个同样重要的原因当是此经验强烈的感受，而且此感受还带有特殊的知识性质，因此，体验者遂感无从言说。可以模拟的经验如美的经验或爱情的经验——虽然冥契经验的知悟性（noetic quality）是非美感、非情缘的。

一"是内向型冥契经验的特征，我们关于史泰司所作的对两种经验的价值高低的判断，也可以提出另类的价值判断的看法。事实上，在理学的传统内，虽然有少数像邓豁渠那般，以走进绝对同一、言语道断为目标的理学家，试图走向所谓"不属有无，不属真妄，不属生灭，不属言语，常住真心，与后天事不相联属"[38]的境界。但邓豁渠久假而不归，实质上已完全脱离了儒学的范围。理学不管何宗何派，他们所追求的"一"都不会是绝对冥契无分的内向型的一。纵使他们有此体验，他们后来都会从此体验的框架中走出来，走向外向型的冥契经验，其一不离多，其静不离动，理学家的套语如"理一分殊""全体大用"，其说如可成立，所述大概都会走上"一多诡谲同一"的理境。我们在阳明后学罗洪先及朱子学后劲罗整庵身上，都可看出这种上下回向的过程。

理学家不管是陆王还是程朱一系，或者以道体论为核心的第三系儒者，都有"一"的追求，但追根究底，他们的"一"几乎都是"一多诡谲同一"的类型的"一"。这种强烈的对"超越的同一"的不安，就像他们同样对不能用任何述词强加其上的"纯粹的无"的经验的不安一样，都显示了儒家对任何隔绝于此世的理念总是有戒心的。我们这样的解释，显然认为体验和诠释是难以完全切割的。但如果"一多诡谲的同一"现象不只见于理学传统，它也见于许多宗教的冥契报道，那么，我们还是可以说"一多诡谲同一"的叙述应该有普遍的意义，它虽然不能不扎根于各文化的传统，但仍是种理性的宗教知识。

如果"一多诡谲同一"的类型是理学家自觉选择的类型，也是亲身体验中所证及的恰当的叙述，我们对理学的判教或者儒家经典的价值位阶的安排，或许也可以有不同的解读。无疑，在儒家的经典中，既能突显道德主体性的意义，又能彰显物的存有论意义者，莫如《中

---

38 引自黄宗羲，《明儒学案·泰州学案一》，下册，卷32，页706。

庸》《易经》；理学诸系中，同样能兼顾人的道德生命的完成以及物的存有论意义的肯定者，当是以《中庸》《易经》为宗，以气化之道为本的北宋理学家（如周、张、邵、程颢）与晚明儒者（如王夫之、方以智、黄宗羲），也就是笔者所说的第三系。至于本文论理学工夫论中的"一多诡谲同一"问题，没有探讨此系的核心儒者如张载、王夫之，乃因此系的问题需要重作，张载、王夫之思想的解释尤为复杂，不是本文所能承担的。但笔者相信他们的论点不会修正本文的主要论点，只会有强化的作用，这是另一个阶段该探讨的议题。

THE HEWAI REGION AND THE FOUNDING OF THE NORTHERN SONG (960—1127)

Chang Woei Ong 王昌伟

(The National University of Singapore)

The set phrase "cherishing the civil, ignoring the military" (*zhongwen qingwu*重文轻武) has been used by scholars and laymen alike to explain why the Song was not the powerful Han or Tang. According to this conventional wisdom, the Song founders, after witnessing how the loss of control over the military had cost the rulers of the late Tang and the Five Dynasties their empires, became wary of the possibility of themselves falling prey to the recurring problem. Immediately after he ascended to the throne, Emperor Taizu 太祖 (r. 960—975) "disarmed" his generals during the dramatic episode of "removing military command over a cup of wine." (*beijiu shi bingquan*杯酒释兵权)[1] Following this, Emperor Taizu and his successor Emperor Taizong 太宗 (r. 976—997), put together a series of measures aimed at minimizing the threat of the military, including 1) "strengthening the stem, weakening the branches," (*qianggan ruozhi*强干弱枝) another popular set phrase, which is to strengthen the forces at the center while weakening those at the periphery; 2) splitting the command, administration, recruitment, etc., of the armies and designating them to different institutions; and 3) favoring the civilian over the military by letting civilian officials handle military affairs. These measures were then enshrined as the "law of our founders" (*zuzong zhi fa*祖宗之法) and persistently followed by later Song rulers. As a consequence, the Song army was weakened to the point where it

---

1 This incident is most vividly depicted in Li Tao (李焘, 1115—1181), *Xu zizhi tongjian changbian*续资治通鉴长编 (hereafter XCB), (Taipei: Taiwan World Jowrnal Bookstore 台湾世界书局, 1983), 2.10b-11b. Li's narrative is based on a shorter account of the same event in Sima Guang (司马光, 1019—1086), *Sushui jiwen*涑水纪闻 (Beijing: Zhonghua Book Company, 1989), 1.11-13.

could not defend against foreign invasions. It is therefore not surprising that the Song would eventually collapse, first under the Jurchen invasion in 1126 and later under the Mongol invasion in 1279.

Despite several attempts over the past few decades to rectify this perception,[2] it has remained prevalent. The implications of this narrative about the founding of the Song state and its consequences are multifold. For the purpose of this paper, suffice it to note that the narrative is based on the assumption about how the growing regional power of the military governors since the 8th century resulted in the disintegration of the Tang. From then onwards, the story revolves around the two poles of centralization and decentralization. It has been demonstrated that, faced with the perpetual separatist threats coming from the military governors who established their de facto kingdoms and challenged the authority of the central government, emperors of the late Tang and the Five Dynasties sought and devised measures (and often failed) to curb the power of these governors and regain control of the empire. Although it was not until the reign of Emperor Zhenzong (r. 998—1022) that the court finally succeeded in putting the governors under control and eventually removing them, the process had begun as early as the early 10th century. In his classic study of the political transition during the Five Dynasties written more than half a century ago, Wang Gungwu delineated the complex process through which the court of the various regimes gradually consolidated power at the expense of the independent military governors. Toward the end of the process, new military and civil institutions were formed not by rejecting the old system of military governorship

---

2 As early as in the late 1940s, Nie Chongqi聶崇岐 had already demonstrated that regional military power persisted at least into the Zhenzong reign (真宗, r. 998—1022). See Nie Chongqi, "Lun Song Taizu shou bingquan"论宋太祖收兵权, *Yanjing xuebao*燕京学报, 6 (1948), pp. 85–106. In an important dissertation, Edward Worthy argues that the military was the most crucial and preponderant among the various integrative factors that shaped the course of the early Song. See Worthy, *The Founding of Sung China*, (Ph.D. dissertation, Princeton University, 1976). John Labadie, in another dissertation, has also tried to contend the perception that the Song was militarily weak. To the contrary, according to Labadie, the Song army had proved its strength many times on the battlefield. Furthermore, the incorporation of the military establishment into a distinct and identifiable part of the government bureaucracy had produced a new set of relationship between the government and the armed forces that could be characterized as "modern." See Labadie, *Rulers and Soldiers: Perception and Management of the Military in Northern Song China (960—ca.1060)* (Ph.D. dissertation, University of Washington, 1981).

but by incorporating it. In other words, the ability of the new imperial government of the Song to finally dissolve independent and potentially hostile military establishments was the result of a lengthy strategy beginning with Song's predecessors to turn the imperial government into an expanded version of the military governorship system.[3] In her recent book on Song political geography, Ruth Mostern traces the ways through which the Five Dynasties rulers dealt with regional centrifugal forces. She argues that the Military Commissions were significantly weaken over the course of the first half of the 10th century when the rulers divided Commissions into smaller units while establishing new court-controlled administrative entities such as prefectures, counties and garrisons within the Commissions. The success of the Song was the result of this reassertion of state power.[4]

The question, then, is that if the processes had started long before the Song, how was it that it was only the Song rulers who were able to accomplish what their predecessors wanted to do but failed? For instance, pertaining to Mostern's observation, why were the commissioners so passive when the central government was clearly trying to undermine their power? And why had not the newly appointed prefects, like some commissioners during the 8th and 9th centuries who were also appointed by the court, become a threat to the central government themselves? Answers to these questions are absent from Mostern's study. Similarly, while Dieter Kuhn acknowledges that the Song founders' investment in the military actually increased when they were trying to transit to a civil order, he did not, other than recounting the "removing military command over a cup of wine" episode, attempt at providing a convincing explanation about why the military did not turn against the throne. Peter Lorge postulates that the Song's success in finally establishing a civil-bureaucratic state could be attributed to two factors: 1) the personal traits of the rulers and the decisions that they made (rather than the differences in capabilities); and 2) more important, a watershed event as in the 954 Battle of Gaoping高平, when the then emperor of the Later Zhou dynasty Chai Rong柴荣 (r. 954—959) personally led the central govern-

---

3 Wang, *The Structure of Power in North China During the Five Dynasties* (Stanford: Stanford University Press, 1963).

4 Mostern, *Dividing the Realm in Order to Govern: The Spatial Organization of the Song State* (Cambridge, MA: Harvard University Asia Center, 2011).

ment armies into the battle with Northern Han and khitan forces. Chai had to resort to this because, according to historical accounts, many of his commanders either betrayed him or escaped from the battlefield. After executing these commanders, Chai was able to impose firm control over the armies. This gave him and the central government an edge over centrifugal forces, a fruit that his trusted commander and the founder of the Song Zhao Kuangyin赵匡胤 (r. 960—976) continued to enjoy. According to Lorge, the transition from loyalty to the ruler as a person to loyalty to the ruler as the emperor as the head of a civil-bureaucratic institution was possible only after the rulers had gained better control of the central government armies, thus allowing them to keep regional powers at bay.[5] Yet it is clear that Chai's control over the armies and his commanders ceased after his death, as Zhao was able to declare himself as the emperor without much resistance. Lorge's explanation also stops short at revealing the changes in regional powers that led to their eventual decline.

Therefore, while not diminishing the merits of the propositions, I would suggest that they could not adequately explain the historical developments that led to Song's success. A book-length study is needed for proposing previously less discussed ways of understanding how the Song reversed the fate of its predecessors. The objective of this paper is more limited. I will only focus on the border regions and try to show that, apart from delineating how regional separatist powers were gradually defeated—or incorporated if we accept Wang Gungwu's thesis—by the central government over the course of the 10th century, it may also be useful to examine how power relations at the border regions were gradually reconfigured at the local level over the course of the 9th and 10th centuries. Consequently, the new power arrangements set the stage for the development of a new set of central-regional relations that formed the foundation of the Song's ascendancy.

To illustrate this point, we need to go beyond the political entity that we retrospectively call "China" today and recognize that north China was an integral part of a cross-border political, military, social and economic system that bound the various societies in that part of the world together. This paper will use the Hewai 河外 (*lit.* beyond the Yellow River) region as a case to examine how changing

---

5 Lorge, "The End of the Five Dynasties and Ten Kingdoms". In Peter Lorge ed., *Five Dynasties and Ten Kingdoms* (Hong Kong: The Chinese University Press, 2011), pp. 221–242.

regional dynamics had contributed to shaping the strategies that the Song government pursued for strengthening their control over newly acquired territories
in the north. It will further suggest fresh perspectives for understanding the historical transformations that took place in the 9th to 11th centuries which led to
the emergence of new kinds of political arrangement that were adopted by the
Song state.

The Rise of "Local Strongmen" in Hewai

Hewai was used informally in the Northern Song to name the territory that fell under the three prefectures of Linzhou麟州, Fuzhou府州
and Fengzhou丰州, located at the northwestern tip of the Hedong河东 circuit, whose territory covers most part of present-day Shanxi 山西 and a small
part of present-day Shaanxi 陕西.[6] As the name suggests, this region was
separated from the rest of Hedong by the Yellow River. The territories immediately to the north and to the west were controlled by the Khitan Liao and
the Tangut Xi Xia respectively and the region formed the first line of defense
against these two foreign regimes. Reflecting military needs, walled settlements
(cheng城), forts (bao堡) or stockades (zhai寨) formed the majority of the basic
administrative units. Also, quite to be expected, wasteland was abundant and
troops often outnumbered civilian residents in this region. Ouyang Xiu 欧
阳修 (1007—1072) mentioned in a memorial submitted to the court around 1044
when he was sent to Hedong to inspect border defense that the number of troops
stationed at Fuzhou and Linzhou amounted to about 20,000, but there were only
a few hundred households of border dwellers in these two prefectures (Fengzhou had fell to the Xi Xia in 1041).[7]

Since the Tang, Hewai had been the battleground for the various groups
active in that region. In particular, the significant presence of non-Han groups

---

6 Part of the military prefecture Jinning晋宁 was also "beyond the Yellow River" but this area was
often excluded from the more precise definition of "the three prefectures beyond the Yellow River."
(hewai sanzhou河外三州)

7 Ouyang Xiu, "Lun Lunzhou Shiyi Zhazi"论麟州事宜札子, in Ouyang Xiu, Ouyang Xiu quanji 欧阳
修全集 (Shanghai: World Bookstvre 世界书局, 1936), pp. 919–921.

was a major concern for the regimes controlling China proper from the eighth century onwards. In 721, the Tang's army defeated a combined force of "barbarians," comprised mainly of Turks and Tanguts, near Hewai and Linzhou , which was specifically set up three years later to provide settlement for the Tanguts who accepted the Tang's rule after the conflict.[8] Although Linzhou was established as a "regular prefecture" (*zhengzhou*正州) and while it may not be the intention of the Tang's government, the significant presence of resettled population made up mostly of Tanguts and Turks propelled it to gradually move closer to a system resembling a "loosely rein" (*jimi*羈縻) prefecture where the Tang's government only imposed indirect rules while allowing the local chiefs to govern the communities.[9] By the late Tang, traces of local Tangut leaders started to appear in historical sources, indicating that their leadership role had become increasingly important. The famous She折 family was one of the most prominent examples.[10] Linzhou in this period also witnessed the rise of a family surnamed Yang杨 who were probably of Han origins. But many believed that they were related to the Tangut Shes by marriage. Whether this was really the case requires further research.

The Yangs was one of the most well-known families in Chinese history thanks to popular culture. Stories about how its members, both male and female, defended the Song against foreign invasions for generations are abundant in traditional and modern dramas and fictions and the family stands tall in the Chinese tradition as a symbol of loyalty and perseverance. In reality, the history of this family is extremely obscure but apparently it was sufficiently powerful by the early 950s that Yang Hongxin杨弘信 (n.d.) could self-appoint as the prefect (*cishi*刺史) of Linzhou. He was succeeded by his son Yang Chongxun杨重勋 (n.d.). Over the course of the 10th century, the Yangs had to negotiate and battle for survival among regimes controlling the territories of north China and beyond either successively or concurrently, including Later Jin 后晋(936—947), Later

---

8 Liu Xu刘昫, *Jiu Tang shu*旧唐书 (Beijing: Zhonghua Book Company, 1975), 97.3052–3053.

9 For a succinct discussion of the *jimi* system in the Tang, See Yihong Pan, *Son of Heaven and Heavenly Qaghan: Sui-Tang China and Its Neighbors* (Bellingham, Washington: Western Washington University, 1997), pp.197–202. Pan translates *jimi fuzhou*羈縻府州 as "subordinated area commands and prefectures." For a detained Chinese-language study, see Liu Tong刘统, *Tangdai jimi Fuzhou yanjiu* 唐代羈縻府州研究 (Xi'an: Northwest University Press, 1998).

10 Zhou Weizhou周伟洲, *Tangdai Dangxiang*唐代党项 (Guilin: Guangxi Normal University Press, 2006), pp. 133–140.

Han 后汉 (947—950), Later Zhou 后周(951—960), Northern Han 北汉(951—
979), the Khitan Liao 辽(907—1125), Song, and a powerful Tangut group controlling Xiazhou夏州 (administrative seat in present-day Jingbian靖边 county,
Shaanxi), which later established the Xi Xia dynasty in 1038. Key members
of the Yangs were highly regarded by the Song court for their military talents
but their political connection with Linzhou seemed to have diminished not long
after the founding of the Song, although it is unclear from historical sources
how much of a presence the family still maintained in Linzhou.[11]

In contrast, the She family followed a different path. It was probably during the 720s that they migrated to Hewai. In the early 10th century they were
recruited by Li Keyong 李克用 (856—908), who was then battling the Later Liang
regime, to deal with the Khitans and other Tanguts. For their services, the
Shes were granted hereditary rights to Fugu府谷 Township, the place where they
resided, in Linzhou in exchange for their service. Fugu was later upgraded to
county and then to prefecture and renamed Fuzhou in 921. The trend continued
into the Song and the Shes became a force that the Song court relied heavily
upon for defending against the Liao in the early years of the dynasty.

Besides the Shes, another non-Han family that the Song court managed to
recruit was the Wangs王 of Fengzhou. The Wangs had been identified as eth-
nically belonging to Zangcai藏才, probably a sub-group within the Tangut. In
969, Wang Jia 王甲 (n.d.), originally serving under the Liao, surrendered and
submitted Fengzhou to the Song. In return, the Wangs received hereditary rights
to the post of prefect until 1041 when Fengzhou fell to Xi Xia. A new Fengzhou
was later established in 1062 by carving up part of the Fuzhou territory, but the
Wangs were unable to reclaim the hereditary rights.[12]

The Hewai administrative arrangements, as could be discerned from

---

11 Nie Chongqi聂崇岐, "Linzhou Yangshi yiwen liuji"麟州杨氏遗闻六记, in Nie Chongqi, *Songshi
congkao*宋史丛考 (Beijing: Zhonghua Book Company, 1980), pp. 376–387. Wang Dong王东, Yang
Fuxue杨富学, "Wudai Songchu xibei zhengzhi geju zhi zaisikao: yi Bei Han yu Dangxiang guanxi
wei zhongxin de kaocha"五代宋初西北政治格局之再思考：以北汉与党项关系为中心的考察,
*Lan Zhou Xue Kan*兰州学刊, 1(2014): 1–7.

12 Li Ziliang李子亮, "BeiSong Lin Fu Feng sanzhou shouchen suoyin" 北宋麟府丰三州守臣索隐
[*Journal of Yan'an University* (*Social Science Edition*) 延安大学学报（社会科学版）, 1 (2001):
89–92; Zhou Qunhua周群华, "Song Lin Fu Feng sanzhou jianzhi ji qi zhanlue diwei" 宋麟府丰三
州建置及其战略地位], *Sichuan Cultural Relics*四川文物, 6 (1995): 59–64.

the above, were bore out of the need to achieve two closely related goals: co-option and defence. Families like the Yangs, the Shes and the Wangs were central to the endeavours. Who were these people? Historical sources identify them as "local strongmen" (*tuhao*土豪). For instance, in Ouyang Xiu's 1044 memorial, among the various recommendations that he presented to the court for defending against Xi Xia was appointing a *tuhao* as the prefect:

> My fourth point pertains to enlisting the help of *tuhao*. We face a dilemma in Linzhou present. If we choose to keep it, it will deplete Hedong's resources; if we abandon it, Hewai will be lost. If we wish to preserve both, there is no better way than enlisting a *tuhao* and task him with the responsibility of defending his own hometown. Linzhou is strategically located and hard to access, and can be guarded with a troop of two thousand men. Moreover, *tuhao* are those who have earned a reputation of being talented and brave, and are feared by the enemies. They are also familiar with the enemies' conditions and schemes, so when it comes to battles, the strategies that they devised will not be far off. If we entrust them with defending the prefecture, they would naturally treat the prefecture as their own house and realize that their fortune is tied to the survival of the prefecture. As such, they will be brave going into battles and the defense will naturally be solid. And since they are natives, they are close to the conditions on the ground. Because the people, having to rely on the strength of these *tuhao*, will tend to gather around them, therefore we should entrust them with recruiting both Han and non-Han people. In this way, we could wage wars against external invaders and internally, we could assemble the people to strengthen the border regions. All these could be done effortlessly and with reduced expenditures and armies. This strategy is one hundred times better than appointing a government official to the post and he in turns has to rely on the court for providing everything. If using *tuhao* is necessary, there is no better person for the job other than Wang Ji. Wang Ji is currently at the Jianning stockage and there are about three hundred households of both Han and non-Han people living and farming at the periphery of the stokage under Wang's protection. Wang's talent and bravery is well-known and based on his official rank, he is eligible for the post of prefect. We could then appraise

his accomplishment after one to two years, and if he is indeed capable of
defending Linzhou, we should make the post hereditary and entrust the
family to help guard the border.[13]

四曰委土豪者，今议麟州者，存之则困河东，弃之则失河
外。若欲两全而不失，莫若择一土豪，委之自守。麟州坚险，
与兵二千，其守足矣。况所谓土豪者，乃其材勇独出一方，威
名既著，敌所畏服，又能谍敌情伪，凡于战守，不至乖谋。若
委以一州，则其觉当自视州如家，系己休戚，其战自勇，其守
自坚。又其既是土人，与其风俗情接，人赖其勇，亦喜附之，
则蕃、汉之民可使渐自招集。是外能捍贼而战守，内可辑民以
实边，省费减兵，无所不便，比于命吏而往，凡事仰给于朝廷，
利害百倍也。必用土豪，非王吉不可。吉见在建宁寨，蕃、汉
依吉而耕于寨侧者已三百家，其材勇则素已知名，况其官序，
自可知州。一二年间，视其后效，苟能善守，则可世任之，使
长为捍边之守。

The value of *tuhao*, as Ouyang posited, lay both in their personal traits (talent, bravery) and in their being local. The term first appeared in the Six Dynasties texts. According to Osawa Masaaki, the earliest usage of the term points to
an image of powerful but lawless figures以behaving like local bullies or worse,
bandits and rebels. Over time, the negative connotation became less prominent,
with the discourse gradually shifted to underscoring *tuhao*'s political influences
at the local level, especially their abilities to mobilize manpower and resources
for organizing local militia. Osawa further argues that the changing discourse
signalled the rise of *tuhao* as a new group of local elites who gradually consolidated their political power over the course of the late Tang-Five Dynasties peri-

---

13 Ouyang Xiu, "Lun Lunzhou Shiyi Zhazi", pp. 919–921.

od.[14]

The "newness" of *tuhao* lies not so much in the fact that local strongmen of this sort did not exist in the past. Rather, as Osawa has shown, *tuhao* had by this historical juncture grown in their strength to challenge the old social structures and therefore been given the recognition by the state to act as middlemen to assist in governing the local societies. It is in this respect that *tuhao* could be considered a new political force that gained traction after the breakdown of the old system.[15] The rise of *tuhao* occurred in many places across China, but regional variations are apparent. In Hewai and the larger northwestern frontier zones, the composition of *tuhao* was closely related to the activities of the various ethnic groups and regimes controlling the region. In order to understand the historical implications of the *tuhao* phenomenon in Hewai, we need to briefly examine the power structure underlying the old system, which was also a product of massive contacts and conflicts of peoples across fuzzy borders.

Locating Hewai in the Politics of Tang Provinces

The region known as Hewai in the Song fell under the jurisdiction of Guannei关内 (*lit.* "within the passes") Circuit in the Tang. Yet the Tang circuits (*dao*道) were nothing more than administrative arrangements established for surveillance purposes. Theoretically the central government should have direct control over the prefectures and counties, but often it was the military commissioners (*jiedushi*节度使) who were the real source of authority. The relationship between the central government and the provinces known as *fanzhen*藩镇 headed by the military commissioners is one of the most well-studied aspects of the Tang's history and need not be repeated here. Suffice it to note that the provinces exhibited great regional variations. Zhang Guogang classifies the provinces into four types in his comprehensive study of the Tang's *fanzhen*: 1) Hebei where separatist power was at its strongest; 2) Henan and Shanxi which helped defended

---

14 Osawa Masaaki大泽正昭, "Tomatsu Godai 'dogo' ron" 唐末五代 "土豪" 论 (On the 'local magnates' at the end of the Tang and in the Five Dynasties",in *Jochi shigaku*上智史学, 37 (1992): 139–161.

15 Osawa Masaaki "Tomatsu Godai 'dogo' ron", pp. 142–145.

the Tang's court against the Hebei separatists; 3) the southeastern provinces where the Tang relied upon for revenue, and 4) provinces in the northwest and southwest whose main function was to provide border defence against non-Han peoples.[16] In fact, the need for border defence in the north was what created the *jiedushi* system in the first place.

Some scholars working from a Marxist perspective have argued that evidences from the early years of the system suggest that the *jiedushi's* power base was formed not through aligning their interest with big landowners. They further posit that the military base of the provinces was mainly comprised of professional armies recruited from displaced farmers, refugees, non-Han groups and so on. [17] In this respect, the military composition of the provinces was a significant departure from the old *fub-ing* 府兵 (farmers-soldiers) system based on conscription. With this change came the need to explore new revenues for financing the armies. Since their establishment, these military provinces had been relying on state mechanism to generate revenues, including but not limited to direct support from the central government, standard taxes, military and agricultural colonies (*tuntian*屯田 and *yingtian*营田), miscellaneous taxes and income from salt and iron monopoly, commerce and trade, and so on. The only difference lay in how much autonomy they had in collecting and handling the revenues, which varied greatly over time and across space.[18]

The northwest saw the earliest formalization of the system in 711.[19] The region that we are concerned with in this paper was first put under the charge of *Shuofang jiedushi*朔方节度使, established in 721 and then under *Zhenwujun jiedushi*振武军节度使 in 758. *Zhenwujun* was abolished in 764 but reinstated

---

16 Zhang Guogang张国刚, *Tangdai Fanzhen Yanjiu*唐代藩镇研究 (Changsha: Hunan Education Publishing House, 1987), pp. 77–103. In his study of the Lulong卢龙 army, David Graff convincingly shows that the need to defend against the steppe peoples created common ground for the central government and the supposedly separatist Hebei Province to work together. See Graff, "Provincial Autonomy and Frontier Defense in Late Tang: The Case of the Lulong Army," in Don J. Wyatt ed., *Battlefronts Real and Imagined: War, Border, and Identity in the Chinese Middle Period* (New York: Palgracw Macmillan, 2008), pp. 43–58.

17 Yang Zhijiu杨志玖, Zhang Guogang张国刚, "Fanzhen Geju Yu Tangdai De Fengjian Datudi SuoyouZhi: zailun Tangdai Fanzhen Geju De Shehui Jichu"藩镇割据与唐代的封建大土地所有制：再论唐代藩镇割据的社会基础, *Academic Monthly*学术月刊, 6 (1982): 45–50.

18 Zhang, *Tangdai Fanzhen Yanjiu*, pp. 200–221.

19 Ouyang Xiu, *Xin Tang Shu*新唐书 (*New History of the Tang*) (Beijing: Zhonghua Book Company, 1975), 50.1329.

in 779.[20] It has been established that as compared to the other provinces, the northwestern ones were more dependent on the central government for financial support and less likely to develop a separatist inclination. Conversely, the central government needed these provinces to defend against military aggressions from non-Han peoples active along the borders at different times, including the Turks, the Uighurs, the Tibetans and also the Tanguts.[21]

But large scale military confrontations were only part of the picture. In fact, since the beginning, the Tang had shown great flexibility and deployed a variety of strategies in engaging with its neighbours and these strategies varied according to the changing circumstances in the greater Inner Asian region.[22] In terms of geographic administration, the imposition of the *jiedushi* provinces on top of the *jimi* prefectures (see above) and the protectorate (*duhufu*都护府) was indicative of the Tang's plans to respond to or even incorporate new emerging trends in the Inner Asian world. Emperor Taizong's (r. 627—649) primary goal in establishing the *jimi* and *duhufu* system in 630 was to accommodate the Turks who migrated and sought to resettle in the Tang's territories after the collapse of the Eastern Turk empire. Chinese sources have generally credited Tang's military campaign in 629 for bringing about the downfall of the once powerful Turk empire, but in reality, the situation was much more complex. At the very least, the Tang's forces were not alone; they were joined by other subjects of the Turkish qaghan (many of whom were Turkic people) who revolted because of harsh taxes imposed by the qaghan, who employed the sogdians to do the collection even when famine struck. Moreover, the Turk empire was already weakened by internal rifts within the royal house. In other words, while the Tang played a

20 Ibid., 64.1761–1771.

21 Wang Shounan王寿南, *Tangdai Fanzhen Yu Zhongyang Guanxi Zhi Yanjiu*唐代藩镇与中央关系之研究 (Taipei: Jiaxin shuini gongsi wenhua jijinhui嘉新水泥公司文化基金会, 1969), pp. 299–302. Wang Fengxiang王凤翔, "Tangdai Xibei Fanzhen Yu Diyu Shehui"唐代西北藩镇与地域社会, in *Tang Du Journal*唐都学刊, 26.5(2010): 29–31. Of course, it doesn't follow that the northwest witnessed absolutely no rebellion. The famous rebellion led by Pugu Huai'en仆固怀恩 (d. 765) was one such case. But Pugu's turning against the Tang seemed to be instigated by an ambiguous episode where he was accused of treason and which was therefore rather incidental. See Charles Peterson, "P'u-ku Huai-en and the T'ang Court: The Limits of Loyalty", in *Monumenta Serica*, 29 (1970—1971): 423–455.

22 Wang Zhenping, *Tang China in Multi-Polar Asia: A History of Diplomacy and War* (Honolulu: University of Hawaii Press, 2013).

prominent role in taking down the Turk empire, it was but one of the players in a changing Inner Asian landscape where environmental, political, economic and migration issues were intertwined.[23]

After defeating the Turks, Emperor Taizong made a decision to assume the title and role of "Heavenly Qaghan," previously held by the Turkish rulers, and the political arrangements that came with it. The relationship between the government and some faraway *jimi* prefectures was nominal at best, but the system allowed the Tang to expand its territory and preside over Inner Asia as an overlord.[24] Apparently, the "loose rein" system worked at that moment because no equally powerful challenger existed on the horizon.

But the system's effectiveness diminished when new powers emerged. The rise of the Tibetans in the middle of the seventh century shook the foundation of the Tang's domination of Inner Asia. Seizing the opportunity, the Turks rebuilt their empire and pushed into the Tang's territories. At the same time, other non-Han peoples, including the Tanguts who are our main concern here, were drawn into process of mass migration when the big powers forced them into abandoning their lands. By the early 8th century, it had become clear to the Tang's rulers that the previous "loose rein" arrangement that was designed primarily for co-option and expansion was ill-fitted to tackle the new challenges. A new approach was required to upgrade the defensive capacity of frontier administration, and hence the establishment of the *jiedushi* system, whose core mission was to coordinate large-scale military operations across multiple administrative units for effective border defence.[25] While many have viewed the *jiedushi* as a tumour of Tang politics, overall the system had help the Tang to fend off aggression beyond the frontier. This was especially true for the northwestern provinces which, as stated earlier, had a better "working relationship" with the central government.

---

23 Mark Edward Lewis, *China's Cosmopolitan Empire: The Tang dynasty* (Cambridge, MA: Harvard University Press, 2009), pp. 147–153. Michael R. Drompp, "Imperial State Formation in Inner Asia: The Early Turkic Empires (6th to 9th Centuries)", in *Acta Orientalia Academiae Scientiarum Hungaricae*, 1 (2005): 101–111.

24 Liu Tong, *Tangdai Jimi Fuzhou Yanjiu* pp. 109–110.

25 Li Hongbin李鸿宾, *Tangchao Zhongyang Jiquan Yu Minzu Guanxi: Yi Beifang Quyu Wei Xiansuo*唐朝中央集权与民族关系：以北方区域为线索, (Beijing: The Ethnic Publishing House, 2003), pp. 114–119.

Moreover, these northern provinces, especially the one led by the *Shuofang jiedushi*, played an important role in supressing the An Lushan rebellion of 755 and some of the derivative rebellions. But various factors—prolonged warfare, lack of financial support from the central government, its territory split and parcelled out to form smaller *jiedushi* units, among others—contributed to the decline of the power of the province and crippled its ability to defend the Tang and itself against both internal and external threats.[26] By the early 9th century, the court started to appoint civil officials to govern *Zhenwujun*, who now controlled the Hewai region originally under *Shuofang*. For instance, in 814, Hu Zheng胡证, a civil official with no known military background was appointed as such. The official reason given was that the previous commissioners were military men with little knowledge of frontier administration and therefore civil officials were brought in to "pacify" the region.[27]

It was unlikely that military men lacked the knowledge of frontier administration. Rather, the appointment seemed to be consistent with the court's decades' long effort to regain centralized control of the empire in the aftermath of the An Lushan rebellion. As Nicolas Tackett has shown, apart from Hebei province, the effort was by and large successful. But when the Huang Chao rebellion shook the empire again in the 870s—880s, the Tang finally lost control of the provinces and collapsed.[28] But the trend toward recentralization did not end with the fall of the Tang in 907. After several decades of political chaos, social transformation and frequent warfare, powers were reconfigured at the local level that significantly weakened the foundation of the provinces. Among the various factors, the rise of *tuhao* deserves special attention. To illustrate this point, the following section will focus on the extraordinary story of the She family of Fuzhou.

---

26 Fan Wenli樊文礼, "Tang Shuofang Jiedushi Lunlue"唐朔方节度使论略, in *Journal of Inner Mongolia University (Philosophy and Social Science)* 内蒙古大学学报（哲学社会科学版）, 3,(1988): 110–118.

27 Wang Qinruo王钦若et al., *Cefu Yuangui*册府元龟 (N.p.: 17th century), 120.2b.

28 Tackett, *The Deconstruction of Medieval Chinese Aristocracy* (Cambridge, MA: Harvard University Asia Center, 2014), pp. 146–186.

From "Local Strongmen" to Loyal Song Subjects

In his study of 10th-century garrison commanders (zhenjiang镇将), Hino
Kaisaburo observes that in the Tang, the garrison commanders were mostly
staffed by key personnel of the *jiedushi*'s personal armies who had very little connections with the local communities. The trend continued into the late
Tang and Five Dynasties period. But during this period another group emerged
and began to challenge the monopoly of the former. These were the *tuhao*. An
important development during the 10th century was that the various regimes
had tried to limit the power of the first group. Moreover, most Five Dynasties'
garrison commanders reported to the prefect, who in turns reported directly to
the court, by passing the provinces. This was one of the most important factors
contributing to the decline of the power of the provinces and the rise of the prefectures over the course of the 10th century.[29]

But there were exceptions, albeit rare, and one such case cited by Hino
Kaisaburo relates to the She family. The Shes first appeared in historical sources
as *tuhao* like many others all over China during the same period, but the family was also a product of peculiar Inner Asian geopolitics. Scholars have long
speculated about the Shes' ethnic origins but no conclusive evidence could be
offered. What is clear is that they had been already intimately integrated into the
Tangut communities by the 9th century and became politically prominent in the
last days of the Tang. The first She whose life we have a substantial account of
life was She Silun嗣伦 (n.d.), a contemporary of the Later Tang ruler Li Keyong.[30]
Silun's father She Zongben宗本 (n.d.) was appointed the Supreme Military Com-

---

29 Hino Kaisaburō 日野开三郎, "Godai chishō ko" 五代镇将考, *Tōyō gakuhō*, 2 (1938): 54–85. Hino
    Kaisaburō, "Hanchin taisei to chokuzoku shu 藩镇体制と直属州, *Tōyō gakuhō*, 4(1961): 485–520.
    For the relative strength of the provinces and the prefectures, see also Zhang Dazhi张达志,
    *Tangdai Houqi Fanzhen Yu Zhou Zhi Guanxi yanjiu*唐代后期藩镇与州之关系研究 (Beijing: China
    Social Sciences Press中国社会科学出版社, 2011), p. 229.
30 "Cishi She Sizuo bei"刺史折嗣祚碑, in Wang Chang（王昶, 1725—1806), *Jinshi Cuibian*金石
    萃编 (N.p.: 1805), 119: 7ab. According to the findings of Dai Yingxin戴应新, the name should be
    Silun instead of Sizuo, and this stele was erected around 905. See Dai Yingxin, *Sheshi Jiazu Shilue*
    折氏家族史略 (hereafter SSJASL), (Xi'an: Sanqin Press三秦出版社, 1989), pp. 53–55. This is a
    book-length study devoted to the She family, which includes several valuable tomb inscriptions from
    archeological excavation at the site of the family graveyard of the Shes.

mander (*du bingma shi*都兵马使) of five towns along the Yellow River in the Zhenwu province, while Silun himself was appointed the prefect of Linzhou, the place where the hometown of the She, the Fugu Township, was located.[31]

Fugu's status was raised from township to county in 910. It was then separated from Linzhou and became a prefecture (named Fuzhou) in the following year. But it was Zhu Wen朱温 (885—926), the reigning emperor of the Later Liang dynasty, who granted the rise in status. Fugu at that time was in fact under the control of Li Cunxu 李存勖 (886—925), the future emperor of the Later Tang dynasty. She Silun's son, Congruan从阮 (n.d.), helped Li recruited a group of Uighurs (*huihe*回纥), and the latter repaid his service by making him the prefect of Fuzhou. This marked the beginning of the Shes' domination of Fuzhou.[32] Hatachi Masanori argues that the Shes were useful to Li in two ways: 1) the Shes, who were familiar with the local ethnic situation, could help him pacify and recruit the various tribes that were active in the region; and 2) the Shes could help in Li's war against the Tanguts of Xiazhou夏州 also surnamed Li李, the future founders of the Xi Xia empire, who were then trying to push eastwards at a time when Li Cunxu was also waging war against the Later Liang regime.[33]

No doubt the official appointments greatly enhanced the status of the Shes, but office-holding was a consequence of, rather than a cause for their initial success. For instance, Shi Jingtang 石敬瑭 (892—942, r. 936—942), the emperor of the Later Jin (936—947) regime, presented the Liao with the territories south of the Great Wall. Apart from the sixteen prefectures surrounding the present-

---

31 Xu Song ed., *Song Huiyao Jigao*宋会要辑稿 (hereafter SHY), fangyu方域21. SSJZSL, 13-14. Hatachi Masanori畑地正宪, "Godai: Hoku-So ni okeru Fushu Setsushi ni tzuite"五代：北宋における府州折氏について, *Shien*史渊, 110 (1973): 137-173. A discussion of She Zongben's and She Silun's careers could be found in pp. 144-145. Hatachi's article is translated into Chinese by Zheng Liangsheng郑梁生, "Wudai: Beisong De Fuzhou Zheshi"五代：北宋的府州折氏, *Shihuo yuekan (fukan)* 食货月刊（复刊）, 5 (1975): 29-49.

32 Yue Shi 乐史, *Taiping Huanyu Ji*太平寰宇记, Yingyin Wenyuange Siku Quanshu影印文渊阁四库全书 (Taipei: Taiwan Commercial Press 台湾商务印书馆, 1983), 38: 18b-19a. The *Old History of the Five Dynasties* has a slightly different version of She Congruan's promotion. It is recorded that Congruan was first promoted to be a Military Specialist (*yajiang*牙将) of Hedong and concurrently held the appointment of Vice Prefect of Fuzhou. He was again promoted to prefect during the Tongguang同光 (923—926) era. Li Cunxu promoted him because of frequent "border turbulences" (*bianhuan*边患) and there is no reference to the Huihe. See Xue Juzheng薛居正 (912—981), *Jiu Wudai Shi*旧五代史 (hereafter JWDS) (Beijing: Zhonghua Book Company, 1976), 125: 1647.

33 Hatachi Masanori, "Godai: Hoku-So ni okeru Fushu Setsushi ni tzuite", pp. 144-146.

day Beijing, the Hewai region was also initially part of the gift, but when the Liao ordered a forced resettlement, moving the Hewai population to Liaodong 辽东, the Shes refused to submit and remained independent. When the second emperor of the Later Jin, Shi Chonggui石重贵 (914—964, r. 942—947), severed ties with the Liao and ordered the Shes to attack the Liao, She Congruan immediately led an army into the Liao's territory and captured several stockades. Because of this, Congruan was handsomely rewarded with a series of official titles, including the *Zhenwujun jiedushi*.[34] This episode clearly demonstrates that maintaining firm control over their Fuzhou home base was crucial for the Shes' survival. In this respect, She Congruan was a very different kind of *jiedushi* as compared to those in the heyday of the Tang who were mostly leaders of professional armies with little connections to the local communities.

The localness of the Shes could also be discerned from their marriage networks. They had been consciously trying to form alliances with strongmen controlling Linzhou and Fengzhou since the 10th century. For instance, She Deyi's 德扆 (n.d.) daughter was married to Yang Ye (杨业, d. 986), whose father Yang Hongxin (see above), identified as a "local strongman of Linzhou" in the *Comprehensive Mirror for Aid in Government*.[35] But unlike the Shes, the Yangs did not receive hereditary rights to Linzhou. In fact, the Yangs' "official" ties to Linzhou seemed to have ended in the generation of Hongxin's grandchildren.[36] Nevertheless, it is beyond doubt that Linzhou provided the base for the Yangs' eventual ascendancy. The marriage between the Yangs and the Shes was therefore an alliance forged by two powerful families, both trying to tighten their grips on a highly volatile region.

Besides the Yangs, the Shes also forged marriage ties with the Wangs of Fengzhou, also discussed above. Wang Chengmei 承美 (d. 1012), Wang Jia's son, was married to a female member of the Shes. Although we have no other information about this woman or any other marriages between the two families, it

34　JWDS, 125: 1647–1648.
35　Sima Guang司马光, *Zizhi Tongjian*资治通鉴, (Beijing : Zhonghua Book Company, 1956), 291:9487. The official history of the Song, however, identifies Yang Ye as a native of Taiyuan. Tuo tuo et al., *Song Shi*宋史（Hereafter SS）(Bejing: Zhonghua Book Company, 1974) 272: 9303. Nie Chongqi believed that this was because Yang first served the Later Han regime, the capital of which was at Taiyuan. See Nie Chongqi, "Linzhou Yangshi Yiwen Liuji", pp. 376–377.
36　Nie Chongqi, "Linzhou Yangshi Yiwen Liuji," pp. 384–387.

is clear that the Shes maintained profound influence on the affairs of Feng-zhou until it was captured by Xi Xia in 1041. For instance, When Chengmei died in 1012, the court ordered She Weichang 惟昌 (978—1014), the prefect of Fuzhou, to assess his descendants to determine who could be his successor. Eventually, Wang Wenyu 文玉 (d. 1024), Chengmei's grandson and adopted son,[37] was chosen under Weichang's recommendation. Again, in 1024, When Wenyu died, a dispute occurred within the Wang family as several members fought over the hereditary position. Wenyu actually recommended his eldest son Yuqing 徐庆 (d. 1041) to be his successor, but one of his younger brothers Huaixin 怀信 (n.d.) was displeased and showed an intent to overthrow Yuqing. The court thus sent She Weizhong 惟忠 (n.d.), Weichang's younger brother who succeeded Weichang to be the prefect of Fuzhou, to investigate the matter and suggest a replacement. She Weizhong recommended another younger brother of Wenyu named Huaijun 怀钧 (n.d.) and the court went with his recommendation. Angered by Weizhong's interference, Huaixin submitted a memorial to the court, claiming that Huaijun was incompetent: not only had Huaijun driven away seven households of residents, both Chinese and non-Chinese, within eight months, the Zangcai tribe also refused to come to pay tribute as a consequence. Moreover, he (Huaixin) was the one who had the support of the tribal leaders, but Weizhong suppressed and threatened those leaders into submission.[38] Huaixin's appeal failed, as it was Yuqing, not him, who was named the next prefect and killed in 1041 when Fengzhou fell to Xi Xia.[39] The Shes thus seemed to command respect in Feng-zhou, and the marriage ties between the Shes and the Wangs ensured the Shes the means to intervene with the affairs of Fengzhou when they needed. Through marriages with these local strongmen, the Shes thus extended their reach to the entire Hewai region.[40]

---

37 Wenyu's original name was Huaiyu怀玉, and he was actually the son of Chengmei's eldest son Wen-gong（文恭, n.d.), but because Wengong had been away for many years while serving his official duty, Chengmei thus adopted Wenyu as his son.

38 SHY, Fanyu 21; XCB, 79: 1808; 102: 2365.

39 XCB, 133: 3168–3169.

40 The Shes' marriage networks were not entirely local. For instance, in the early 12th century, She Yan-wen折彦文 (n.d.) was married to a woman surnamed Cao曹, who was from one of the most presti-gious military families. See She Yanwen, "Song Gu Shuiguo Caoshi Muzhiming Bing Xu"宋故谁国曹氏墓志铭并序, SSJZSL, p. 113; SS, 242: 8620–8622. But it is apparent that local marriage ties were more essential for the Shes' early success.

Apart from securing official appointments and forging marriage networks with other local strongmen, what were the other means by which the Shes produced and reproduced their success? From the limited sources that we have, we know that farming was a source of income for the Shes.[41] But as Hatachi has argued, while the climate of Fuzhou was suitable for farming, the main form of economic activity undertaken by the nomadic tribes was pasturing. The animals, however, were of no value as an exchange commodity among the tribal people, so they were eager to trade with the Chinese, both officially and privately (even after the Chinese court repeatedly prohibited such trade), exchanging the animals for tea, silk and other commodities. The rise of the Shes owed much to such border trades, especially horse trading. In fact, the Shes were conferred hereditary rights to Fuzhou partly because they were able to ensure the Five Dynasties and the Northern Song regimes a regular supply of good horses. The conferment was also to acknowledge the Shes' rights to monopolize horse trading and this might be one of the reasons that eventually drove the Lis of Xiazhou, who were also competing for such rights, to turn against the Northern Song.[42]

The Xiazhou Li was definitely the greatest enemy of the She. Already in 955, when both families were still dependent on the Later Zhou regime, Li Yixing李彝兴 (n.d.), the leader of the Xiazhou Li who was then appointed the *jiedushi* of Dingnan定难, had expressed displeasure over the fact that Emperor Shizong世宗also appointed She Deyi as a *jiedushi*. He threatened to severe his ties with the Later Zhou, causing some officials at the court to urge Emperor Shizong to abandon the Shes in order to pacify Li Yixing, who were much stronger at that time. But Shizong was confident that because the Lis had to rely upon the Later Zhou for the supply of all kinds of goods, they would not dare to

---

41 In 1060, for example, She Jizu (折继祖, n.d.) requested to resign from the post of prefect because he was forced to come out with his own money to perform official duties. It was said that the She had only about three hundred members at that time, but there were many non-Chinese inhabitants (*fanzu* 蕃族) under their command. Whenever these people were to be rewarded, She Jizu would have to pay for the expenses using his official salary. He even had to borrow oxen from the non-Chinese to cultivate previously uncultivated land (*xiantian*闲田) and use the income to contribute to the payment. The court, after learning about his dilemma, issued an edict to pacify him. See SHY, fangyu 21. While we could only guess the true intent of She Jizu, it is apparent that farming was among the various means by which the Shes accumulated wealth.

42 Hatachi Masanori, "Godai: Hoku-Sō ni okeru Fushu Setsushi ni tzuite", pp. 158–169.

revolt. He thus delivered an edict admonishing Li Yixing, who quickly apologized to the emperor.[43]

Both the Shes and the Lis continued to submit themselves to the Song, which replaced the Later Zhou.[44] But while the Lis were far more unpredictable and eventually revolted in the 1030s, the Shes had remained loyal to the Song and helped the latter in its defense against the Lis who later founded the Xi Xia dynasty. The Song's government was well aware of the value of the Shes' ability to help reduce the cost of having to deploy a large army at the border. Fan Zhongyan 范仲淹 (989—1052), for example, noted in 1044 (a few months before Ouyang Xiu submitted the aforementioned memorial) that in the early days of the Song when the Shes were still powerful, the court only needed to deploy about two thousand Chinese soldiers to Fuzhou. But now Fuzhou was already in a state of ruin, yet the court often needed to deploy more than ten thousand troops to defend the area. The significant military presence had caused serious problems in providing provisions for the army and Fan thought this was Xi Xia's way to wear the Song down. He thus suggested to build forts and walled settlements and to assemble border dwellers, both Han and non-Han, who were forced to abandon their land because of Xi Xia's invasions.[45] Quite contrary to our conventional impression about the Song's policy of "strengthening the forces at the center while weakening that of the periphery," Fan saw the decline of the Shes as a matter of regret.

This, however, does not mean that the Shes could completely ignore the court in dealing with local affairs. In fact, if we accept Hatachi's argument, then the weakening of the Shes was the consequence of an increased centralization of power, as the court tried to strengthen the power of the circuit level institutions at the expense of the Shes and also to appoint prefectural level officials to Fuzhou to take over some administrative powers from the Shes.[46] Yet the Shes could be seen resisting the court's interference, and sometimes successfully. In

---

43 Sima Guang, *Zizhi Tongjian*, 292: 9522–9523.

44 Some scholars argue that changes in climate in the mid-10th century which resulted in the frequent occurrence of natural disasters in Xiazhou and its precincts had forced the Lis to maintain an amiable relationship with the Song. See Wang Dong王东, "Ziran Zaihai Yingxiang Xia Song Xia Guanxi Shulun: Yi Songchu Wei Zhongxin"自然灾害影响下宋夏关系述论：以宋初为中心, in *Tangut Research* 西夏研究, 2 (2012): 117.

45 XCB, 152: 3709–3710.

46 Hatachi Masanori, "Godai: Hoku-Sō ni okeru Fushu Setsushi ni tzuite", p. 157.

1031, She Weizhong惟忠 (n.d.), the then prefect of Fuzhou, submitted a memorial to the court, requesting the court to grant him more power:

> The custom of this prefecture (i.d. Fuzhou) was mixed with that of the non-Han and Han (*fanhan*蕃汉), and in the past, [we used to] entrust judicial affairs to my personal military staff (*yaxiao*牙校). Recently, the court issued an edict ordering Wang Ding王定, Administrator of Prefectural Law Section (*sifa*司法), to be the Administrator of Public Order (*sili canjun*司理参军). [However, Wang] is not familiar with the affairs of the non-Chinese (*fanqing*蕃情), [I hereby] request to revert to the old system.[47]

According to She Weizhong, the new administrator, unlike his personal staff, did not have the knowledge for dealing with border administration effectively. The underlying message was that the court should not interfere directly with the affairs that could be better managed by a She. This was therefore a rather bold request, and could be seen as an attempt to undercut the authority of the court. But, again contrary to what we would expect from a court thought to have devoted itself, from beginning to end, to "strengthen the center and weaken the periphery", the request was approved.

There were other instances throughout the Northern Song when the relationship between the Shes and the central government was put to test. The concern here is the nature of the institutional arrangements that the central government set up to manage the Shes and their impacts on the relationship. In particular, the establishment of a Lin-Fu Circuit Military Bureau (*Lin-Fu lu junma si*麟府路军马司) in the 990s (or early 1000s, the date is not entirely clear) officially recognized Hewai as a special region that required trans-prefectural coordination. Historical sources and modern scholars have opined that the bureau was set up to undermine the power of the *tuhao* prefects of Linzhou, Fuzhou and Fengzhou, especially the Shes.[48] However, it is important to note that the main mission of the bureau was to coordinate large-scale military operations involving the imperial armies stationed at Hewai and not to weaken

---

47 XCB, 110: 2558.
48 SHY, fangyu 21. Li Yumin李裕民, "Sheshi Jiazu Yanjiu"折氏家族研究, in *Journal of Shaanxi Normal University* (Philosophy and Social Sciences Edition) 陕西师范大学学报（哲学社会科学版）, 2 (1998): 55–68.

the Shes and take over their control over the local society. Moreover, as time went by, the state began to staff the head of the bureau with local strongmen with background similar to the Shes, and even members from the family, by the late 11th century.[49] This clearly indicates that the relationship between the Song's central government and the Shes was not one of zero-sum game. Rather, it was built upon an acknowledgement of the fact that the best way to govern Hewai was to incorporate the Shes and the cross-border political, social and economic networks that the family inherited into the state system.

Hence, rather than focusing exclusively on how the Song state devised institutions to dilute the power of the Shes at the local level, it may also be useful to examine how these institutions helped absorb existing local arrangements into the state apparatus, thereby creating a sophisticated regional system in which the *tuhao* who thrived under an Inner Asian landscape became loyal subjects of the Song.

Conclusion

The success of the She family was part of a larger 9th to 11th centuries phenomenon characterized by the rise of *tuhao*. Although this new class of militarized local strongmen could be found in many places, *tuhao* in Hewai and the greater northwestern frontier zone of Tang-Song China took on some distinctive attributes peculiar to the region, home to constant, massive inter-state warfare, and complex networks of cross-border trades and mass migration and resettlement of Han and non-Han people.[50] As a consequence of this change in local power configuration, the state adapted and revised its regional administration to encompass the new elite. Herein lies the social dimension of the marginalization of the old Tang *jiedushu* system and the growing importance of pre-

---

49 Gao Jianguo高建国, *Xianbei Zuyi Fuzhou Sheshi Yanjiu* 鲜卑族裔府州折氏研究, (PH.D. Dissertation, Inner Mongolia University, 2014), pp. 31–46.

50 Hatachi Masanori畑地正宪, "Sōdai ni okeru RinFu ro ni tzuite" 宋代における麟府路について について, *Tōyōshi kenkyu* 东洋史研究, 3 (1992): 413–443. See also Hatachi Masanori, "Sōdai ni okeru seihoku enbō to docyaku shugōsei ryoku ni tsuite" 宋代における西北边防と土着酋豪势力について, *Hagi gakugei daigaku ronshu*萩国际大学论集, 1 (2006): 57–81.

fectures as a regional administrative unit alluded to by Mostern. It was not simply a matter of the central government trumping over the provinces but rather
a reconstruction of regional state apparatus based on existing local conditions.
A deeper investigation may shed some light on the question that I raised in the
introductory section: how was the Song able to finally overcome the two-
century problem of provincial separatism? But this would be a topic reserved
for future studies.

More importantly, what can all these tell us about the nature of the Song
state? In his introduction to a recently published conference volume on imperial China and its relationship with its southern neighbors, Wang Gungwu out-
lines four perspectives that scholars have adopted for studying the interactions
between the regions we now call "China" and "Southeast Asia": 1) the sinocen-
tric perspective that tells the story from the perspective of the regimes that controlled "China" in history; 2) the northward perspective that pieces together
information about how the southern regimes viewed their relationship with the
more powerful north; 3) the universal history perspective that presents a picture
of universal and linear development of all nations that also frames the narratives
about Southeast Asian regimes' interactions with China; and 4) the new history
perspective that goes beyond political history and applies theories and methods of social sciences to give accounts of ongoing movements of people, capitals and cultures not confined by the imaginations of the nation-state. With the
exception of the last one, the other perspectives are all strongly influenced by a
national narrative that is more interested in explaining how a nation is destined
to become the way it is by evoking a sense of timeless past. The fourth perspective, on the other hand, traces the development of regional networks that transcend the physical and cultural boundaries of modern nation-states.[51]

Using Wang Gungwu's classification as the point of department, the current study hopes to make a case for adopting a theoretical approach akin to the
fourth perspective. It argues that we could not truly appreciate the historical
development of Hewai if we see it simply as a border region of the Song without considering the larger geopolitical environment within which it was situ-
ated. For instance, it has been established that the Song state had adopted differ-

---

51 Wang, "Introduction", in Victor H. Mair and Liam Kelley eds., *Imperial China and Its Southern
    Neighbors* (Singapore: Institute of Southeast Asian Studies, 2015).

ent strategies in dealing with non-Han people in different regions. In the southern frontier regions generally, the Song inherited the *jimi* system from the Tang, allowing the non-Han communities to operate in a discrete realm with only minimal oversight from the state. The separation of the state and these communities was maintained. In the northwestern regions, as we have seen in the Shes' case, local leaders and their modes of dominances derived from political, social and economic capitals, made available from cross-border networks, were absorbed into the regular state system, thus altering the basic features of local administration.[52] Also in his creative take on the popular novel *The Water Margin*, Paul Smith argues that the kind of civil rule that we so often attributed to the Song was only fully manifested in the Ming times (1368—1644). During the Song, military culture was prevalent both in politics and in society, at least in the north. This was because the Song operated in the multi-state system populated by powerful steppe polities and therefore had to sustain, even nurture, a military subculture for very practical reasons.[53]

What these studies reminded us is the flexibility of the Song state in securing and managing its territories. I am not simply implying that there were regional variations; that is already a well-known fact. My contention is that these regional disparities were contributed as much by factors that went beyond the confines of the Song. In the case of Hewai, we could even argue that what it shows us is the "Inner Asian-ness" of the Song state, at least in terms of how it incorporated the northwestern regions.

52 An Guolou安国楼, "Lun Songchao Dui Xibei Bianqu Minzu De Tongzhi Tizhi" 论宋朝对西北边区民族的统治体制, in *Ethno–National Studies*民族研究, 1 (1996): 57–66.

53 Paul Jakov Smith, "'Shui Hu Zhuan' and the Military Subculture of the Northern Song, 960—1127" , in *Harvard Journal of Asiatic Studies*, 2 (2006): 363–422.

重访钱穆的《中国近三百年学术史》[1]

王汎森

（台湾"中研院"史语所）

"中国近三百年学术史"是一个非常光辉的学术领域，梁启超、胡适、钱穆都曾围绕这个主题，做了各式各样引人入胜的研究。这使我想起班雅明（即本雅明，Walter Benjamin）在《历史哲学论纲》一文中，借用了保罗·克利（Paul Klee）的一幅画《新天使》（Angelus Novus）阐释他对历史的看法："历史天使的脸望向过去，身体前进到未来。"[2] 历史的研究即带有这个特色，故每一代人"身体前进到未来"时，他们对所讲的过去选材叙述并不一定相同。如清代嘉庆年间形成的《儒林传稿》，其中所选的人物与近百年学者所关注的就有许多不同，在当时的标准中被认为最精彩、最有代表性的人物是：高愈、谢文洊、应撝谦、严衍、潘天成、曹本荣、薛凤祚、陈厚耀、沈彤、朱鹤龄、刘源渌、范镐鼎、徐文靖、李光坡、孔兴燊。[3] 但这些学者大多不再出现在后来的学术史中，或是不再被当成那么重要的学术人物。

晚清思潮动荡甚大，外国思想资源涌入、内在社会政治环境的大

---

1 本文是为台湾商务印书馆新版钱穆《中国近三百年学术史》一书所撰写的《导论》。

2 Walter Benjamin, Hannah Arendt ed., *Illuminations* (New York :Schocken Books, 2007), p.257. 中译参考本雅明，《历史哲学论纲》，收入汉娜·阿伦特编，张旭东、王斑译，《启迪：本雅明文选》（北京：生活·读书·新知三联书店，2008 年），页 270。

3 阮元，《儒林传稿》，收入《续修四库全书》（上海：上海古籍出版社，1997 年），第 537 册，页 620–621。

变等，都使得"新天使"的脸所看到的近三百年思想有所变化。特别是经过晚清的变法、革命思潮洗礼之后，学者所关注的重点及人物，每每与先前有所不同，而这一波又一波的冲击与"近三百年学术史"这个学域的形成是有密切关系的。以《国粹学报》《国粹丛书》为例，当时至少有几种现实关怀深刻地影响到"国粹运动"的参与者对近三百年思想学术的取舍。他们重视的是：一、与"君学"相反的"民学"，重视"细民""下"的思想。二、批判专制制度，以及与它关系密切的"利禄之学"。三、强调比较接近现代科学精神的"客观征实"之学。四、重视任何能与近代西方民主思想合拍的传统思想质素，其中有些是带有创新性、异端性、解放性的。五、带有西方近代功利主义意味的思想家。六、关注经世致用议题者。

在这些新标准之下，被突出的人物是李贽、顾炎武、黄宗羲、王夫之、颜元、李塨、戴震、章学诚、汪中、包世臣等。即使在刊刻书籍时，背后也每每有上面提到的关怀。譬如邓实在戴震《孟子字义疏证》《原善》合刻本的跋语中说："其解理字也，以为理出于欲，情得其平，是为循理，与西国民主之制公好恶于民，而倡人类平等之说相合。"[4]刘师培跋包世臣《说储》云："其说多出于昆山顾氏，行之于今，颇与泰西宪政之制相合。"[5]邓实也认为《湖隐外史》一书实可称为"民史"，"世每谓中国无民史，此非其一邪"。[6]又认为宋代邓牧的《伯牙琴》："黄梨洲著《明夷待访录》，其'原君'、'原臣'二篇，斥君权，排专制，为千古之创议，然其说原出于先生'君道'、'吏道'二篇。"[7]都是这方面的例子。

---

4 邓实，《〈孟子字义疏证〉〈原善〉合刻引》，转引自王波编，《邓实集》（出版中）。

5 刘师培，《〈说储〉跋》，收入《小倦游阁集说储》（合肥：黄山书社，1991年），页199。

6 邓实，"《〈湖隐外史〉跋"，转引自叶绍袁原编，冀勤辑校，《午梦堂集》（北京：中华书局，1998年），下册，页1080。

7 邓实，《邓牧心〈伯牙琴集〉跋》，载《国粹学报》第3年第11号（总第36期），1907年12月24日，页6。

我们可以说，在形成"近三百年学术史"的系谱时，晚清以来的时局与思潮起了重要的作用，人们做了很多筛选，使得他们笔下清代儒者"全神堂"的人物与地位大幅改变了。

一、"中国近三百年学术史"领域的形成

对"近三百年学术史"这个领域有过影响的人物很多，章太炎、刘师培等都是，但就钱穆的《中国近三百年学术史》而论，起比较直接影响作用的是梁启超的《论中国学术思想变迁之大势》以及《中国近三百年学术史》。梁启超的《论中国学术思想变迁之大势》曾分期刊于《新民丛报》，他认为清儒饶有科学的精神。在这个阶段，胡适显然受到梁启超启发，故跟着主张清儒体现科学精神。[8] 但是即使在这个阶段，梁启超对清代学术的看法也有多面性。梁启超一方面说清儒"饶有科学精神"，同时也说"本朝考据学之支离破碎，汩殁性灵，此吾侪十年来所排斥不遗余力者也"。[9]

这与梁氏的学术倾向有关。梁启超早年对学术的态度比较倾向其师康有为，强调今文经学和宋明理学，尤其是王阳明这一脉。所以，他一方面肯定清儒的治学方法，但同时也痛骂清代二百年来之学问"皆牛鬼蛇神"。[10] 可是在新文化运动后，因胡适提倡以科学精神"整理国故"，并得到四方景从，梁氏也随即跟上。胡适在 1921 年 5 月的日记评论《清代学术概论》说："此次付印，另加惠栋一章，戴氏后学一章，章炳麟一章，此原稿所无。此外，如毛西河一节，略有褒辞，袁枚一节全删，姚际恒与崔适的加入，皆是我的意见。"[11]1922 年

---

8 胡适在《四十自述》中反复强调自己早年受到梁启超很大的影响。见胡适，《四十自述》（台北：远东图书公司，1959 年），页 50–54。

9 梁启超，《论中国学术思想变迁之大势》（台北：台湾中华书局，1977 年），页 87。

10 梁启超，《新民说》（台北：台湾中华书局，1978 年），页 126。

11 曹伯言整理，《胡适日记全集》（台北：联经出版事业公司，2004 年），第三册，页 18。

12 月，胡适在日记中又认为梁启超在 1920 年出版《清代学术概论》是受其影响，他说："其实任公对于清代学术的见解，本没有定见。他在'论私德'篇中，痛诋汉学，有云：'夫宋明之学，曷尝无缺点之可指摘？顾吾独不许卤莽灭裂之汉学家容其喙也。彼汉学则何所谓学？……吾见夫本朝二百年来学者之所学，皆牛鬼蛇神类耳！'……任公编集时，不删此文，而独删去《中国学术思想变迁之大势》之第八章。近来因为我们把汉学抬出来，他就也引他那已删之文来自夸了。"[12] 也就是说胡适先受到梁启超的启发，后来梁启超这一个本来视清代考证学为"牛鬼蛇神"的人，反过来受胡适的影响，写成《清代学术概论》，并开课讲授"中国近三百年学术史"。[13]

在五四运动之后，"以科学整理国故"之风大畅，"历史的天使"身体到了五四，但他面向过去的脸，所看到的是不大一样的场景。此时一批不同的学术人物登上舞台，从胡适与梁启超的书中便能看出这一点。梁启超强调经世致用，现实的、实践的，所以颜元、李塨出现在他的视野之内；他强调与西方民主自由比较相近的价值，所以黄宗羲等人也在内。又因为强调科学精神，故讲王锡阐、梅文鼎，以及比较重视以客观精神考证文献的胡渭、阎若璩等人，尤其是在《中国近三百年学术史》中用了四章的篇幅讲"清代学整理旧学之总成绩"。

二、梁启超与钱穆

民国二十年，钱穆先生在北大历史系任教，是其在大学讲授历史课程之开始。依钱先生回忆，他所开授的课，一为中国上古史，一为

---

12 曹伯言整理，《胡适日记全集》，第三册，页 433–434。
13 吴稚晖便观察到梁启超反过来受到胡适影响，他在《箴洋八股化之理学》中讲梁启超："受了胡适之《中国哲学史大纲》的影响，忽发整理国故的兴会。先做什么《清代学术概论》，什么《中国历史研究法》，都还要得。"见吴敬恒，《吴敬恒选集（哲学）》（台北：文星书店，1967 年），页 133。

秦汉史，皆是由学校所指定的必修课，另一门选修课由他自定，决定开"近三百年学术史"。他说："此一课程，梁任公曾在清华研究所已开过，其讲义余曾在杂志上读之，任公卒后，某书肆印此书，梁家以此书乃任公未定稿，版权所属，不准书肆发行。"后来他终于在北京东安市场的非正式管道中买到一部，"余因与任公意见相异，故新开此课程，自编讲义"。[14] 钱穆对梁启超书中反复强调的两个重点并不同意：第一，清学是对宋明理学的反动；第二，清学是客观征实之学，近于科学。[15] 钱穆说："余本好宋明理学家言，而不喜清代乾嘉诸儒之为学。及余在大学任教，专谈学术，少涉人事，几乎绝无宋明书院精神。人又疑余喜治乾嘉学，则又一无可奈何之事矣。"[16] 所以，钱穆的这本书虽然承继了梁启超"中国近三百年学术史"的题目，但它的宗旨其实与梁启超是有出入的。借用余英时先生的话说，钱穆在动手撰写《中国近三百年学术史》时便已将"体"或"框架"确立下来。[17] 在"体"确认下来之后，钱穆所选取的人物与思想潮流便与梁启超有所不同。

梁启超《中国近三百年学术史》一书的第一部分是对明末清初大儒的阐发：黄宗羲、顾炎武、阎若璩、王船山、朱舜水。接下来是史学：万斯同、全祖望。程朱学派：张履祥、陆世仪、陆陇其、王懋竑。实践主义：颜元、李塨。科学之曙光：王锡阐、梅文鼎。这些安

---

14 钱穆，《八十忆双亲师友杂忆合刊》（台北：东大图书公司，1986 年），页 141。按：钱先生此处回忆有所出入。梁任公于 1923 年 9 月间于清华学校讲授"中国近三百年学术史"课程，其时清华尚未设立大学部与研究院；1926 年 7 月上海民志书局出版《中国近三百年学术史》一书，尚在任公生前。参看赵灿鹏，《梁启超〈中国近三百年学术史〉成书问题辨析》，《社会科学研究》2015 年 4 期，页 188-191。

15 梁启超在《清代学术概论》（台北：台湾中华书局，1987 年）中揭"反动说"："'清代思潮'果为何物耶，简单言之，则对于宋明理学之一大反动，而以'复古'为其职志者也。其动机及其内容，皆与'文艺复兴'绝相类。"（页 3）又说："一言以蔽之，曰用科学的研究法而已，试细读王氏父子之著述，最表现此等精神。"（页 33）

16 钱穆，《师友杂忆》，页 137。

17 余英时先生为《国史大纲》写的导论，见《〈国史大纲〉发微——从内在结构到外在影响》，《古今论衡》第 29 期（2016 年 12 月），页 4-16。

排有两个重点，即清学"厌倦主观的冥想而倾向于客观的考察"，"排斥理论提倡实践"。梁任公书的第二个主体是"清代学者整理旧学之总成绩"（13—16章），这个部分应该是受到"整理国故运动"的影响，故以科学的客观精神为主体，一方面说清代学术中为科学的，一方面突出清代学者整理旧学的成绩。从目前梁书的样子看，钱穆云"梁家以此书乃任公未定稿"，恐怕是事实。[18]比之于《清代学术概论》，后者主旨明确，线索贯串、一气呵成，则《中国近三百年学术史》显然并未完全定稿。

与梁书相比，钱书有一些不同的安排。书中的安排、取材、所选人物虽与梁启超有所重叠，但是重点却有不同。钱穆的整个主脉是：清学与宋明理学的发展是不可切断的，它对宋明理学有修正、有反动，但更有抹不掉的底色。如钱穆自己说："余本好宋明理学家言，而不喜清代干嘉诸儒之为学。"[19]故钱穆反对梁任公近三百年学术史一开始的标题"反动与先驱"。用余英时先生在《清代思想史的一个新解释》中所说的，"反动论"好像认为"反"即可以"反"出一部清代学术史来。[20]另外，钱穆对梁氏所说的清儒"厌倦主观的冥想而倾向于客观的观察"，也并不完全同意。这里的"主观冥想"显然是指宋明理学，而他认为如果说"厌倦"宋明理学是启动清学最主要的动力，显然不合乎史实。梁启超认为，清学与宋学不大有关系，钱穆则注意到，即使在考证学最盛时，清代理学仍有其活力，应当正面陈

---

18 钱穆，《师友杂忆》，页141。杨树达日记中也提到1930年，他接受林志钧之托检校此书，似可说明其为未定之稿。见杨树达，《积微翁回忆录》（上海：上海古籍出版社，1986年），页53—54。

19 钱穆，《师友杂忆》，页137。钱穆在《宋明理学概述》之《序》中有一段话扼要讲述其对宋学、清学态度之发展："宋明之语录、清代之考据，为姚、曾古文者率加鄙薄，余初亦鄙薄之，久乃深好之。所读书益多，遂知治史学"，"其得力最深者莫如宋明儒"。钱穆，《宋明理学概述》（台北：台湾学生书局，1977年），页2。

20 余英时，《清代思想史的一个新解释》，《历史与思想》（台北：联经出版事业公司，1976年），页125—126。

述。尤其在晚清，宋代理学的流衍及复兴发挥了很大的现实作用。

钱穆在《中国近三百年学术史》的《引论》是这样说的："治近代学术者当何自始？曰：必始于宋。何以当始于宋？曰：近世揭橥汉学之名以与宋学敌，不知宋学，则无以平汉宋之是非。且言汉学渊源者，必溯诸晚明诸遗老，然其时如夏峯、梨洲、二曲、船山、桴亭、亭林、蒿庵、习斋，一世魁儒耆硕，靡不寝馈于宋学。继此而降，如恕谷、望溪、穆堂、谢山乃至慎修诸人，皆于宋学有甚深契诣。而时已及乾隆。汉学之名，始稍稍起。"[21] 接着他从唐宋一路讲下来，讲清学开山三大儒——黄宗羲、顾炎武、王夫之，此后在讲清代中晚期思想时，也指理学在当时像是泡在水中的咖啡，虽然看不到咖啡粉，但时时可见其色彩。此外，在处理清代的朴学时，钱穆认为他们不只是在"整理"旧学，还有思想的面向。

可能因为上述的倾向，所以钱穆撰写《中国近三百年学术史》时，在有意无意之间也产生了一个有趣的现象，即他的书虽以"学术史"为名，但多讲思想，且对若干清代考据学大家像王念孙之流竟而完全未加着墨。

三、仿佛寻宝之历程

我个人在阅读《师友杂忆》中与《中国近三百年学术史》的撰写过程有关的段落时，常常有一种兴奋感，即这是一个观点不断翻新与史料不断扩充的过程，每每受其牵引，仿佛参与寻宝的过程。钱穆回忆说，当时的北平一如书海，在以科学整理国故的运动之后，于新学术观点的烛照之下，若干历史人物受到人们前所未有的重视，搜罗罕见文本的风气很盛。《师友杂忆》中所提到的，举凡陈确的《大学

---

21 钱穆，《中国近三百年学术史》（台北：台湾商务印书馆，1966 年），页 1。

辨》、潘平格的《求仁录》、章实斋遗书之家传本及戴震的《孟子私淑录》，顾祖禹《读史方舆纪要》的嘉庆刊本、雷学淇《竹书纪年义证》、《三朝北盟会编》的半部抄本等，[22] 其得书经过莫不动人心弦，后人读来宛如阅读侦探小说。所以钱穆的《中国近三百年学术史》虽不特别提倡新得史料，但史料的扩充却是此书的一个重要特质。以潘平格的《求仁录》一书为例，梁启超只能从唐鉴《清学案小识》的引文中转引，而钱穆已能读到原书，两者之间便有莫大的差异。正因为材料获得的难易程度不同，故梁启超书中对《求仁录》只是一笔带过，而钱穆就认为《求仁录》跟理学、心学的发展以及清初的思想界有很重要的关系。

在铺陈内容时，钱穆似乎比较少用外部评断的视角，而多是平心静气地涵泳原典，并将其中最重要的部分做一番钩玄提要的功夫作为引文，使得读者披览之后，可以把握到一家思想之要旨。同时，他也把可进一步发掘的问题放入双行夹注中。在多次披览之后，我感觉到书中涉及了许多曲折的学术问题，对于这些问题，钱穆都曾仔细思考过才行诸文字，故用语特别简当，而指涉却相当深远。所以我觉得凡阅读这一部书的读者，应该采取"循环往复"的态度，也就是先通读一遍—从事某种专题的研究—再回去仔细玩味《中国近三百年学术史》中相关的章节或段落。

在这里随举一例：《中国近三百年学术史》第十二章"曾涤生"中有一段话说："清儒考证之学，盛起于吴、皖，而流衍于全国，独湖、湘之间被其风最稀。"[23] 大多数人在读《中国近三百年学术史》中这一章时，对这几句话很可能会一阅而过，可是如果比较集中地研究清代湖湘地区的思想、学术之后，便会发现在清代考证学势力如日中天之时，各大区域之间有一个"重心转移"的进程。如果将当时考

---

22 钱穆，《师友杂忆》，页 142，160–165。

23 钱穆，《中国近三百年学术史》，页 575。

证学的圈子分成三级，则第一级地区以江苏、浙江、安徽为主，第二级以山东、河南、河北、山西为主，第三级则是后来的福建、广西等地。而湖南、湖北在考证学盛时，几乎没有什么代表性人物。如果翻查《皇清经解》与参考《皇清经解提要》等书，可以发现清代经学名人中，就很少或几乎找不到湖南、湖北的学者。[24] 再看梁启超的《中国近三百年学术史》中第六章"清代经学之建设"中所列的几张表——"附亭林学友表""附初期经学家表"，亦无一湖北人，且几乎没有湖南人。经此一番探究，则知"清儒考证之学，盛起于吴、皖，而流衍于全国，独湖、湘之间被其风最稀"一段所指为何了。但道咸之后，学风大变，湖、湘成为新思想的发源地，湖南唐鉴等人在北京所形成的理学团体，在后来历史的发展中占有关键性的地位。

此外，我觉得钱穆对重要思想家言论的把握，它们如何影响时人，及这些思想家与论敌之间观点的出入，也是书中讨论的核心。这是受传统学案的影响，所以他的书也是采学案式、纲目体的写法。因为钱穆对传统古籍掌握深入，且非常用心体会，所以在上述几方面都写得非常好。但作为一个后代读者，我比较注意的是：受他人影响的人，在被影响的同时，其实对他自己而言，也是一次扩充与创造。所以，我觉得钱穆在讲影响时，忽略了被影响的人本身其实也在主动扩充、创造自己。

四、清代学术史的"史料革命"

前面提到，在读《中国近三百年学术史》时，读者处处感到一种史料"出土"的兴奋与趣味，但近年以来，随着清代文献大出，尤其是几部大型材料书的出现，如《四库存目丛书》《四库禁毁丛书》《四

---

24 沈豫撰，赵灿鹏校注，《皇清经解题要》（北京：华夏出版社，2014年）。

库未收书辑刊》《清代诗文集汇编》《稀见清代四部丛刊》《晚清四部丛刊》《民国学术丛刊》等，乃至于各种电子文献数据库，使许多原先只能在图书馆抄录的罕见书以及大量稿抄本，都不难寓目，造成了另一种形式的明清"史料革命"。

以潘平格《求仁录》为例，前面提到，当梁启超写《中国近三百年学术史》时，尚未能见到《求仁录》原书，故只能从唐鉴的《清学案小识》中转引，而钱穆写《中国近三百年学术史》时，则因偶然机缘得以直接读到《求仁录》。但是在《四库存目丛书》中，则有卷帙更富的本子。《四库存目丛书》中的《求仁录辑要》共有十卷，而钱书中摘述的只有第一、二卷。钱先生可能因为只见《求仁录》第一、二卷，故书中的阐发仍然有限，在辨清学脉方面，所重视的多在"破"的一面，忽略其"立"的一面，故对于潘氏如何建立一套积极救世哲学，使得原来有关个人修养的材料，多变成治国平天下的概念，且突然具有新的意义这些方面显然未多加注意。[25]

关于史料限制这一点，此处再以清初的汪绂与江永为例。汪、江二人是同一时代、同一地域的朱子学代表人物。《中国近三百年学术史》中提到清代徽歙间讲学渊源，远自无锡之东林有汪知默、陈二典、汪佑、吴曰慎、施璜讲朱子之学于紫阳书院，又因汪学圣问学于东林之高世泰，实为徽州朱学正流，江永、汪绂皆为其余波。"故江浙之间学者多从姚江出，而皖南则一遵旧统，以述朱为正。惟汪（绂）尚义解，其后少传人，江（永）尚考核，而其学遂大。"[26]钱穆在这一段的双行夹注中说："汪双池年谱有与江慎修书三通，及江覆书两首，可证两家治学之歧趋。"[27]钱先生非常敏感地点出，汪、江论学

---

25 钱穆，《中国近三百年学术史》，页204。
26 钱穆，《中国近三百年学术史》，页309-310。
27 钱穆，《中国近三百年学术史》，页300。

不合。他们两人往复争论的这几封书信，即收在《善余堂文集》中。[28]
我直觉以为江、汪这件公案，钱先生把握非常真切，不过钱先生似未
读过卷帙浩繁的《汪双池遗书》，故讲到汪氏的部分比较简略。这部
遗书收藏的地方不多，但史语所傅斯年图书馆即有一部二十八种本，
可供进一步考索。[29]

　　以上两个例子是为了说明，这个"史料革命"对于重估钱穆的
《中国近三百年学术史》可以产生莫大的作用。我曾与学生一起将
《清代诗文集汇编》等丛书中的稀见之书标出，其数目达到一个难以
想象的比例，这一情形几乎出现在前述的每一部大型丛刊中，值得我
们注意。

五、余论

　　《中国近三百年学术史》是一部九十多年的书了，在这么长的时
间内，思想史的写法已有相当大的变化。

　　至今为止思想史的写作方式中有比较明显的两派，一是个人派，
一是思潮派。前者着重个人及授受源流，认为个别思想家可以产生重
大的思想或现实影响，后者则比较重视整体思潮的变化。钱穆似乎比
较属于前者，而这也是从两部《学案》，或《儒林宗派》等方面以来
的传统。后来的学术史或思想史，则偏向写一片又一片的思想场景，
一次又一次的思潮变化，个别人物在其中有地位，但不单只是孤独地
站立在舞台上，这也使得思想史或学术史的解释变得更为复杂。

　　此外，我个人认为钱穆《中国近三百年学术史》的解释是复调
的，是两种以上色彩的学术史发展，而梁启超受到科学整理国故运动
之风潮的影响，比较倾向从单一方向去综理清代学术。最近一二十

---

28 林胜彩点校，钟彩钧校订，《善余堂文集》（台北：台湾"中研院"中国文哲研究所，2013 年）。
29 另有浙刻《双池遗书》八种，光绪 21—22 年（1895—1896）刊，较多见收藏。

年来，人们不那么坚持认为晚清以来思想殿堂只有一个基调，而那个基调是科学的、客观的、革命的，所以学术界回过头去重看近三百年学术思想时，可以有一些新的方向与解释。在这个时候重新阅读钱穆《中国近三百年学术史》，相信读者们可能产生不同的领会。

钱穆对"中国近三百年学术史"这个题目，是在不断思考发展的。抗战期间，他受托重编《清儒学案》，其书虽已遗失，但有《序目》留存，或可略窥钱穆对清代理学发展之看法。此外，贺麟在《当代中国哲学》中批评钱穆的《中国近三百年学术史》未有章太炎一章，当时章太炎虽仍在世，但其学问却已可盖棺论定。后来《中国学术思想史论丛》第八册便收录多篇有关清代学术思想的论述，即包括《章太炎学述》。

最后，我要再度以"新天使"来说明读者与钱穆《中国近三百年学术史》的关系。不同时期的学者从各种不同角度阅读钱书时，仿佛是新天使移动的脚步。譬如杨树达日记里说："阅钱宾四（穆）《近三百年学术史》。'注重实践'，'严夷夏之防'，所见甚正。文亦足达其所见。佳书也。"[30] 钱书在抗战前夕写成，当时日本入侵之势已在眼前。杨树达读此书时在1943年，此时"历史天使"的身体前进到了对日战争，但他的脸望向过去、望向钱穆的《中国近三百年学术史》时，所看到的重点是"注重实践""严夷夏之防"，与之前之后的读者有所不同。我个人相信未来不同时代的读者，也都将在这本书中看出不同的重点与意义来。

---

30 杨树达，《积微翁回忆录》，页82. 余英时先生引此条并评论说："杨树达特别指出'文亦足达其所见'这一点，是有眼光的，因为钱先生在此书中每写一家必尽量揣摩其文体、文气而仿效之，所以引文与行文之间往往如一气呵成，不着剪接之迹，但读者若不留意或对文字缺乏敏感，则往往不易看得出来。《中国近三百年学术史》特'严夷夏之防'，正是因为这部书是在抗战前写成的。这时中国又面临另一次'亡国'的危机。"见余英时，《一生为故国招魂》，《犹记风吹水上麟》（台北：三民书局，1991年），页26. 此外，也有学者认为钱穆的《中国近三百年学术史》远远不如梁启超的《中国近三百年学术史》，见汪荣祖，《钱穆论清学史评述》，《台大历史学报》第26期（2000年2月），页99–119.

恶的起源：熊十力与朱熹的比较

John Makeham 梅约翰

(La Trobe University)

恶的起源是熊十力（1885—1968）晚年著作《明心篇》焦点问题之一。[1]熊先生认为释迦牟尼佛和他的后学从来没有提出"痴惑"的起源问题："人生诚有黑暗的方面，孰是有智而堪否认？但痴惑何处起此一问题，释迦氏与其后学始终不曾提出。"[2]无明和愚痴两个烦恼是痛苦和罪恶的肇因。他的意思是，尽管佛教徒把无明作为十二因缘的开始，但他们没有进一步追查无明等烦恼的本体来源。《明心篇》的目的之一就是要做到佛教徒所没有做到的。

本文试图论证熊十力和南宋理学魁首朱熹（1130—1200）在各自的核心理论的架构上具有一定的同构性。[3]这就意味着，或者熊十力有意地参照、吸取了朱熹本人的理论架构，或者（抑或而且）熊十力有意地参照、吸取了朱熹所吸取的理论架构。[4]

---

1 郭齐勇，"题记"《明心篇》，《熊十力全集》卷3（武汉：湖北教育出版社，2001年）页146："《明心篇》曾于一九五九年四月由龙门书局印行。作者原作《体用论》（1958年），末章'明心'因病未能完成。《体用论》出版之后，本论即以篇行世。"

2 熊十力《明心篇》，《熊十力全集》卷7，页182。

3 同构性就是事物相同的或者相类似的系统结构。举个例子，九大行星围绕太阳转动，电子围绕质子转动是这两个事物的同构性。

4 当然，熊十力对"心"以及有关概念的阐释也大量参照、吸取了王阳明（1472—1529）的思想，但那不是本文所关心的焦点。

1. 好人为什么做坏事？缘和因

依熊十力的观点，人生的境况 (the human condition) 是由行善、为恶的抉择能力所塑造的："人生而含灵秉气，以成独立体。[5] 便能以自力造作一切善行与不善行。"[6] 那么，既然人有这个抉择的能力，为什么还会有人做坏事呢？熊十力再三强调，人的本性没有任何坏根：

> 人的本性元无一切坏根。（言本性中不曾含有一切坏的根也。坏，谓痴惑诸杂染。）[7]

> 人性本善，而良知即是本性，如何又作罪恶以致失良知、丧本性？据此而论，则人生罪恶断不可谓其出于良知或本性。然人之作恶犯罪者确尔不为少数，此亦无可否认。善恶矛盾之故，将于何处寻求？[8]

至于"善恶矛盾之故，将于何处寻求？"这个问题，熊十力和朱熹所作出的一致答复涉及两个因素，一为缘，一为因。这共同的因素表明，熊、朱各自的形上学系统的架构上具有显著的同构性。这同构性的第一个例证跟"性"有关系，第二个例证跟"心"有关系。

---

5 "独立体，谓身体。"《明心篇》，页 264。
6 《明心篇》，页 148-149。
7 《明心篇》，页 183。括号内为熊氏自注。
8 《明心篇》，页 269-270。

1.1 形气为缘（条件）

道德行为根基于本性或真性，[9] 即便性与气相结合而构成人体，道德行为依然要赖于本性才能实现：

> 人之德行根于性……然人既禀性而生，则成为形气的独立体，便有权能。可以率性而为善，亦可以违背本性而顺从躯体的盲动，用纵其恶。[10]

熊十力对于"人为什么做坏事"一问题，首先指出尽管人的心应该控制人的身体，但是有的时候人的身体反而控制人的心。[11]接着就说明身体也能遮蔽本性的自觉：

> 我生自有真性。然而自有生以后，则为形气的躯体所锢蔽，乃冥然莫能自识其本性。[12]

在此段，熊十力区分了真性与人生下来后具备真性的具体状况。生下来后，此真性或者本性才开始受到形气的障蔽。

朱熹也有类似的论述。与程颐（1033—1107）和张载（1020—1077）一样，朱熹也区分了"气质之性"与"天地之性"。但是，在程、张那里这个区分是用来划分两种不同的性，而朱熹用这个区分来辨别同一

9　熊十力将真性也当作实体，见《明心篇》页 230："实体即是我生真性。"熊氏在 1944 年语体文本《新唯识论》写道："本体乃真性之异语。以其为吾与万物所以生之实理则曰真性。即此真性，是吾与万物本然的实相，亦曰本体。此中实相犹言实体。"《熊十力全集》卷 3，页 20（武汉：湖北教育出版社，2001 年）。

10《明心篇》，页 229。

11《明心篇》，页 207-208。

12《明心篇》，页 230。

个性的两种状态。[13] 对朱熹而言，天地之性纯是理，而气质之性是理寄托于气质状态下的性。这个区分就代表着本体状态的性（亦称为太极、理）与发用状态的性：

> 人有此形气，则是此理始具于形气之中，而谓之性。才是说性，便已涉乎有生，而兼乎气质不得为性之本体也。然性之本体，亦未尝杂。[14]

天地之性（天命之性）纯然是理，而气质之性则兼容理与气。然而，尽管天地之性纯是理，少了气就没有理可寄托的场所：

> 天命之性，若无气质，却无安顿处。且如一勺水，非有物盛之，则水无归着。[15]

而恰恰是这个理气和合的人性本身，提供造恶作孽的条件：

> 石氏《集解》引"'生之谓性。'性即气，气即性"[16] 一章，窃谓此章先明理与气不相离，遂言气质之性虽有善恶，然性中

---

13 举程颐为例。他将理和气的关系当成一种二元论来处理恶的起源问题。人性本善、纯是理，恶的起源只能与人的气禀有关系：见程颢、程颐，《河南程氏遗书》,《二程集》（北京：中华书局，1981 年），页 18，313。

　　问："人性本明，因何有蔽？"曰："……性无不善，而有不善者才也。性即是理，理则自尧、舜至于涂人，一也。才禀于气，气有清浊。禀其清者为贤，禀其浊者为愚。"
　　"'生之谓性'与'天命之谓性'，同乎？""性字不可一概论。'生之谓性'止训所禀受也。'天命之谓性'，此言性之理也。今人言天性柔缓，天性刚急，俗言天成，皆生来如此，此训所禀受也。若性之理也则无不善，曰天者，自然之理也。"
14《朱子语类》，黎靖德（约 1263 年）编，（北京：中华书局，1986 年）卷 95，页 2430。
15《朱子语类》卷 4，页 66。
16 石子重（约 1165—1173）《中庸集解》引程颐文，参《河南程氏遗书》，页 10。

> 元无此两物相对而生，其初只是善而已。由气禀有昏浊，又私
> 欲污染，其善者遂变而为恶。当为恶时，非别有一善性也。故
> 有恶不可不谓之性，浊不可不谓之水之说。[17]

由上可见，熊十力"真性（本性）"/"人生下来后具备真性（本性）的具体状况"的区分与朱熹"天地之性"/"气质之性"的区分具有同构性。熊、朱各自区分了本性的两种状态，即作为普遍本体形态的本性（亦称为实体、太极、理）与人生下来后所具备的真性（本性）。正是人生下来后具备真性（本性）的状况构成了人之所以能造恶作孽的必要条件。

1.2 私欲为因

另外，熊十力和朱熹也都同意，罪恶的正因是私欲。不过在进入这个主题之前，首先需要描绘出熊十力将"本心"/"习心"区分开来的轮廓。[18]本心是先天的："本心者，非后起故，遂名曰本。"[19]"夫人之生也，莫不有本心；生而成为独立体，亦莫不有习心。"[20]习心是后天的，经验的：

> 独立体利用天明为工具以交于事物，则有习染发生。习染

17《朱子语类》，卷4，页58。

18《明心篇》里，本心亦称为诸如良知、良能、良心、仁心、觉、明几、天明等。参阅页155，227，239，240，259等。1947年发行的《十力语要》，已采用了本心／习心的区分。可参阅《熊十力全集》卷4，页420–421。《十力语要》汇集了熊十力1936年至1940年的书札、短论。《十力语要》页396载牟宗三致函熊十力，也采用了本心／习心的区分。其实，刘宗周（1578—1645）《人谱》中也采用了本心和习心来进行区分："颜子之知，本心之知，即知即行，是谓真知。常人之知，习心之知，先知后行，是谓常知。"

19《明心篇》，页152。

20《明心篇》，页149。

并不是无有势能的东西，其潜伏吾人内部深，处便名为种子。习种又得出现于意识界。易言之，意识的活动即是习种的活动。是故独立体利用天明作工具易治理事物，乃不期而创生一种新势能，所谓习心是也。[21]

熊十力把习染分成两类："知见习染"与"情意习染"。知见习染"须慎于防治而不可去"，[22]这是因为在本心的主导下，知见习染还能发挥积极的作用：[23]

本心运行于独立体中，而独立体便可利用本心天然之明，以主动治理当前的事物。易言之，独立体即以天明为其治理事物之工具。（本心天然之明，简称天明。）在此种情况之下，本心亦未变易其天然的明性，但不得自己作主而已。[24]

人生而成为有形气的独立体，有实际生活，即此独立体亦自有权能，故本心运行于独立体中，而独立体便可利用本心天然之明，以主动治理当前的事物。[25]

但独立体也可以有不好的影响：

吾人从有生来，学语、发知而后，习于实用，浸于尘俗，故本心天然之明不能避免后起的习染之杂乘。思维作用起时，虽是天明之动，而习染的余势潜伏习藏中跃起，便与天明之

21《明心篇》，页262。
22《明心篇》，页242。
23《明心篇》，页149："善习依本心而生。"
24《明心篇》，页262。
25《明心篇》，页264。

动混杂而行。故曰思维作用不纯是本心天然之明，不纯是良知
也。凡过去的一切经验都是习染。一切习染的余势都潜伏在习
藏中为种子，其从习藏中出现则为记忆。[26]

因此，"影响最为恶劣"的情意习染"必克去务尽"，不然"杂染
之习缘小己而起……易逞其势"。[27]

本心／习心的区分对熊十力所谓的"尽心之学"至关重要："尽心
之学（尽心，见孟子。发展本心之德用，曰尽心）其要旨，在究本心、
习心之大别。"[28] 因为本心微妙又很容易受到习心恶习的侵犯，所以熊
氏特别强调要充分发展本心，才能发生应有的作用：

> 明几发于灵性，此乃本心。（明者，照然灵明之谓。几者，
> 动之微。灵明之动，曰明几。良知发动，即此明几，可返己体
> 验也。）[29]

> 本心只是天然一点明几。（一点，是吾乡俗话，言其微细
> 之极也。今用之以形容本心的明几隐微至极，然虽隐微而发
> 展则广大无量。）吾人须以自力利用此明几，而努力去逐物、
> 辨物，治理物，才有精确的知识。……我的意思，人当利用
> 本心之明，向事物上发展，不可信赖心的神灵，以为物来即
> 通。[30]

26《明心篇》，页 240。
27《明心篇》，页 242，149。
28《明心篇》，页 152。
29《明心篇》，页 148。
30《明心篇》，页 264–265。如陈来指出："熊十力习染论与传统儒学的气质论或习气论的一个很
　　大的不同，是他的习染论不仅是一个伦理学的讨论，而且明确包含着认识论的部分。"《熊十
　　力哲学的明心论》，收入《当代新儒家论文集——内生篇》（台北：文津出版社，1991 年），页
　　173。

> 良知乃是吾人本心天然之明。(……然本心亦只是灵明而已，却要学习而后显发其灵明之用。)[31]

易言之，在本心的潜力尚未得到充足的发展之前，本心的呈现只能是"隐微至极"，而且易受习心恶习的遮蔽。

接下来，我将表明熊十力"习心"/"本心"的区分与朱熹"人心"/"道心"的区分也具有同构性。朱熹把心当作认知活动和道德判准能力的主体，能体会和辨别本性所具备的理以及弥漫生活世界以及宇宙的理。这个心有两个状态：

> 心一也。操而存，则义理明而谓之道心；舍而亡，则物欲肆而谓之人心。自人心而收回，便是道心；自道心而放出，便是人心。顷刻之间，恍惚万状，所谓出入无时，莫知其乡也。[32]

> 存亡出入固人心也，而惟微之本体，亦未尝加益；虽舍而亡，然未尝少损；虽曰出入无时，未尝不卓然乎日用之间而不可掩也。若于此识得，则道心之微初不外此。不识，则人心而已矣。盖人心固异道心，又不可做两物看，不可于两处求也。[33]

在朱熹看来，心是单一的但具有两个状态，即体会理抑或不体会理。道心可以直接体会万理，因为人的本性无非是理。少了这个知觉就是人心。

如果人心与道心分不清，就会导致道心的亡失：

31《明心篇》，页 239。
32《朱熹集》，郭齐、尹波点校（成都：四川教育出版社，1996 年）卷 39，页 1786。
33《朱熹集》卷 32，页 1377。

> 心之虚灵知觉，一而已矣，而以为有人心、道心之异者，
> 则以其或生于形气之私，或原于性命之正，而所以为知觉者不
> 同，是以或危殆而不安，或微妙而难见耳。然人莫不有是形，
> 故虽上智不能无人心，亦莫不有是性，故虽下愚不能无道心。
> 二者[34] 杂于方寸之间，而不知所以治之，则危者愈危，微者愈
> 微，而天理之公卒无以胜夫人欲之私矣。精则察夫二者之间而
> 不杂也，一则守其本心之正而不离也。[35]

"微"指的就是道心，而"危"指的就是人心。朱熹也把本心等同于
道心。而且，正如熊十力描述本心为"隐微至极"，朱熹也描述道心
为"微妙"。

对熊十力本心／习心区分的解析到此告一段落，接下来转而考察
罪恶行为与私欲的关系。在熊十力看来，人生境况总的情势使得人类
难免私欲与私意的诱惑。放纵私欲就是造恶：

> 小己之私欲便成乎恶，欲而无私即是善。……小己之私
> 欲，纯是发于躯体的妄动，此与禽兽同焉者也。仁心即生命力
> 之发现。生命者，大生广生，无穷竭也。[36]

> 吾人良心（良心即是生命[37]之德用显露，亦是仁心之别称。
> 不曰仁心而曰良心者，随俗故。）初一刹那倾乍动，是仁心之
> 发，纯是天机，[38] 未挽杂人事。后一刹那倾，吾人便自起意思，
> 即挽以人事。此际意思如仍继续良心而不放失，此即刚决，于

---

34 道心和人心。
35 朱熹，《中庸章句序》，《四书章句集注》，（北京：中华书局，1983 年），页 14。
36 《明心篇》，页 219。
37 生命就是实体、本体的异称。
38 《明心篇》，页 248："天机是一点明几骤然开发。"

时发为善事，成其德行，是乃以人事继天而不丧天机也。假若此际意思是私意私欲之动，即违背良心，吾人将为私意私欲所驱使，造作罪恶。[39]

这就是熊十力之所以特别强调要扩充本心（良心、仁心），才能成就人的德行：

人生要在保任本心之明几，（保者，保持而勿丧失也。任者，任本心流行，勿以恶习障蔽之也。）而常创起新的善习，以转化旧的杂染恶习。乃得扩充本心之善端而日益弘大。此人道之所由成，人极之所由立也。[40]

人的德行出于性，德修矣，而性适赖人之德以弘。……然生命之德用，必须吾人返在自家内部生活中，亲自体认良心，而不敢且不忍失之，确然自动乎中，直发之为行事，始成吾人之德行。[41]

实体（本体、性）与心的关系是体用关系。[42] 本心（良心）具有

39《明心篇》，页 227。

40《明心篇》，页 149。

41《明心篇》，页 227。

42《明心篇》，页 274。熊十力批评程颐（此处有 "见《识仁篇》"，说明是程颐）和王阳明都没有区分实体的体和用：

宋儒之于天理，王阳明之于良知，皆视为实体，固已不辨体用。（良知与天理之心，皆用也。）程子言天理，则以为只是诚敬存之。（见《识仁篇》）阳明言良知，则以为良知无所不知，而改变大学格物之本义。

此处，熊十力认为天理之心（即仁心）与良知都是用而不是体。他批评程颐忽略了实践的作用。而王阳明一方，熊十力指的是王阳明说 "圣人无所不知" 一段。熊十力好像担（转下页）

体和用两个模态。（在这点上，朱熹的理和熊十力的本心都是类似的。）
从体的模态来看，本心非异于实体或性；从用的模态来看，本心在生
活世界中发用。[43] 为了能够体会本心作为实体的发用，人不能只维持
本心"天然一点明几"的状态，而必须"扩充本心之善端而日益弘大
……直发之为行事"。在这个过程中，自然而然就会克制私欲。

　　对朱熹而言，认知和道德抉择是否受到私欲的浸染，是仁心 / 道
心区分的关节所在：

　　　　盖心一也，自其天理备具随处发现而言，则谓之道心；
　　自其有所营为谋虑而言，则谓之人心。夫营为谋虑非皆不善
　　也。便谓之私欲者，盖只一毫发不从天理上自然发出，便是私
　　欲。[44]

（接上页）心王阳明那段也可能导致消极反知识的心理。王阳明写道：

　　　　圣人无所不知，只是知个天理；无所不能，只是能个天理。圣人本体明白，故
　　事事知个天理所在，便去尽个天理；不是本体明后，却在天下事物都便知得，便成
　　得来也。天下事物，如名物度数，草木鸟兽之类，不胜其烦，圣人须是本体明了，
　　亦何缘能尽知得。（《传习录》，陈荣捷编《阳明传习录详注集评》，台北：台湾学生
　　书局，1992 年，页 303）

正如英冠球解读："圣人本体明白，对天理作为心性感应的本然理序当然是无所不知。外物的
经验知识（包括礼仪节目名物制度数）不是由本心良知而来，圣人未必知道。"（《王阳明伦理
学思想的哲学重构》，刘国英、张灿辉编《求索之迹：香港中文大学哲学系六十周年系庆论文
集·校友卷》；香港：香港中文大学出版社，2009 年，页 361）熊十力的此批评与他 1948 年
致函牟宗三的评论可谓南辕北辙。请参阅《致牟宗三转唐君毅》（1948 年 12 月 31 日），《熊十
力全集》卷 8，页 522–523。

[43]《明心篇》页 269："良知即是本性。"《十力语要》页 390 也写道："本心者，生生不息的实体
　　也，是人之所以生之理也，是人之一身之主也。"
[44]《朱熹集》卷 32，页 1376。

一言一行都可以用是非的标准来判定。关键是：合乎天理还是放纵私欲？"天理、人欲，只要认得分明。便吃一盏茶时，亦要知其孰为天理，孰为人欲。"[45] 如果喝茶的目的是为了满足私欲，那就不是在喝茶。

本节表明，比较熊、朱各自的形上学系统，可以发现两个重要同构性的实例。第一个同构性的例子是熊十力"本性"/"人生下来后具备本性的具体状况"的区分与朱熹"天地之性"/"气质之性"的区分。第二个同构性的例子是熊十力"习心"/"本心"的区分与朱熹"人心"/"道心"的区分。这两个例子也显示，围绕着缘和因的不同作用，熊、朱对于恶的起源问题实际上提出相同的双层解释。第一个例子显示，熊和朱都肯定，正是人生下来后具备本性的具体状况本身构成了人之所以能够造恶的必要条件。第二个例子则显示，熊和朱都肯定私欲是罪恶的正因。

2. 熊十力的理论创新

从 6 世纪到 11 世纪，中国佛教思想家构造了一系列论证来调和恶的起源和本体一元论之间的张力。这一类话语往往采用"理—事"范畴进行论证。到 11 世纪"理—气"范畴开始取代"理—事"范畴。例如，为了处理恶的起源问题，北宋理学家像程颐采用二元论的框架来解释理、气的关系，认为人性无不善，不善者的肇因专归于气。

朱熹的重要创新之一是针对恶的起源问题提出了一个崭新的理论进路，避免了五百年以来佛学理论者以极端的理论体系来处理这个问题的尝试。[46] 朱熹的解决办法是根基于本体一元论，设定罪恶能够发

45《朱子语类》卷 3，页 963。
46 天台宗"魔外无佛，佛外无魔"之"性具善恶"说就是典型的例子。

生的条件仅仅涉及气，毫不涉及理，而更为关键的是，还进一步规定少了气就没有理。一方面，理是气（物）之所以然的本体；而另一方面，气（物）是理的承载体。没有现象界作为承载体，理就无法实现。理气相待；少了气，理就没有意义。

这个"理—气极性"(li-qi polarity) 架构是朱熹一元形上学的核心，可以说是一种"极性一元论"(polar monism)。[47] 尽管针对恶的起源问题朱熹能够提出一个崭新的理论进路与解决办法，但是他一直没有解释，罪恶能够发生的条件何以只涉及气而并不涉及理（太极）。极性一元论可以解释罪恶为什么能够发生在现象界，但是不能解释为什么作为本体的理（太极）在恶的起源中没有扮演角色。这就成为理论上的美中不足之处。

熊十力实体（本体）一概念扮演着类似于朱熹形上学中的"太极"或"理一"[48] 概念的角色。然而，因为实体自身本来具有极性的特点，熊十力能够弥补朱熹那种理论中美中不足之处：

> 善恶矛盾之所在本不难寻。本体不能只有阳明的性质，而无阴暗的性质。（……阳明者，心灵也。[49]阴暗者，物质也。）故本体法亦有内在的矛盾，否则无可变动成用。[50]

其实，1932 年的《新唯识论》文言文本里已开始描述翕辟作为相

---

47 详可参拙文 "Monism and the Problem of the Ignorance and Badness in Chinese Buddhism and Zhu Xi's Neo-Confucianism"（《中国佛学、朱熹理学中一元本体论以及无明、恶的起源问题》），载 John Makeham 编，*The Buddhist Roots of Zhu Xi's Philosophical Thought*（《朱熹哲学思想的佛学根荄》，纽约：牛津大学出版社，2018 年）。

48 《朱熹集》，郭齐、尹波编（成都：四川教育出版社，1996 年），卷 46，页 2243："所谓理与气，此决是二物。但在物上看，则二物浑沦不可分开各在一处。然不害二物之各为一物也。若在理一看，则未有物而已有物之理，然亦但有其理而已，未尝实有是物也。"

49 《明心篇》，页 54："以其为道德、智慧或知能等作用之原，则号心灵。"

50 《明心篇》，页 279。

反相成的法则。

1934 年书信中熊氏就开始用"矛盾"一词来概括翕和本体的关系：

> 夫翕既即是本体之流行，易言之，即是本体所显现底一种
> 作用，而且是自为矛盾的一种作用。[51]

---

[51]《十力论学语辑略》，《熊十力全集》卷 2（武汉：湖北教育出版社，2001 年），页 257，258。
他接着说：

> 昔朱子亦尝谓造化合有一个翕聚的道理，不然便是空洞无物。(此说似见《语
> 类》。兹不及检。) 吾所参验，质之彼说，适足印证。夫翕既即是本体之流行，易
> 言之，即是本体所显现底一种作用，而且是自为矛盾的一种作用。……本体固不
> 是物质性，但其作用显现，不能不有所谓翕。翕即幻似成物。是则翕之用 (翕
> 即是用)。疑与体不相顺。易言之，即此翕者，乃本体上显现自相矛盾之一种作
> 用。《新论》云："翕则疑于动而乖其本也。"(二十六叶左，"转变"章) 又曰"翕
> 而幻成乎物，此所以现似物质宇宙，二疑于不守自性也。"(五十七叶右，"明心
> 上") 曰"翕则若将不守自性，而至于物化，此退义也。"(二十七叶左，"附识"
> 语) 凡此皆明其作用之自为矛盾，即以其将至物化而不守自性故也。……《新论》
> 云："恒转毕竟常如其性故。(恒转者，本体之代语。) 唯然，故有似主宰用，乃
> 以运乎翕之中而显其至健，有战胜之象焉。即此运乎翕之中而显其至健者，名之
> 为辟。"(第二十六叶左) 据此。则所谓翕者，乃以显辟。

我认为这段所表现的思想极可能就是牟宗三"良知自我坎陷"说的前身。在 1947 年
发表的《王阳明致良知教》一书中，牟宗三最早使用了"良知自我坎陷"一语：

> 此种转化是良知自己决定坎陷其自己，此亦是其天理中之一环。坎陷其自己
> 而为了别以从物。从物始能知物，知物始能宰物。及其可以宰也，它复自坎陷中
> 涌出其自己而复会物以归己，成为自己之所统与所摄。如是它无不自足，它自足
> 而欣悦其自己。此入虎穴得虎子之本领也。此方是融摄知识之真实义。在行为宇
> 宙中成就了知识宇宙，而复统摄了知识宇宙。在知识宇宙中，物暂为外，而心因
> 其是识心，是良知自己决定之坎陷，故亦暂时与物而为二。然及其会归于行为宇
> 宙而为行为宇宙之一员，则即随行为宇宙之统摄于良知之天心天理而亦带进来。

见牟宗三，《致知疑难》，收入《从陆象山到刘蕺山》(上海：上海古籍出版社，2001
年)，页 177。《致知疑难》原为《王阳明致良知教》中的一章，现在附在《从陆象山到刘
蕺山》一书中。

1944 年的语体文本里再解释说：

> 我们应知，翕辟是相反相成，毕竟是浑一而不可分的整体。……万变的宇宙底内容，是涵有内在的矛盾而发展的。……一切事物，均不能逃出相反相成的法则。[52]

到 1958 年发表《体用论》，在解答本体何以能够"成变"一问题时，熊氏也进一步说明实体内在矛盾及其作用：

> 当于万变无穷中寻出其最普遍的法则，余以为不外相反相成的一大法则，因为说到变化，必是有对。易言之，即宇宙实体内部含有两端相反之几，乃得以成变而遂其发展。变化决不是单纯的事情。（单者，单独而无对。纯者，纯一而无矛盾。）[53]

> 实体本有物质、心灵等复杂性。是其内部有两性相反，所以其变动而成功用。（物质性是凝结、沈坠，心灵性是建动、升进、照明，两相反也。相反，故其变动。）功用有心灵、物质两方面，因实体有此两性故也。[54]

熊十力也常用乾和坤来象征实体的内在矛盾。乾和坤并不即是实体本身，而是象征实体以及实体"变动而成功用"所共有的内在张力。为了说明这点，熊十力区分了乾元和乾坤：

52《新唯识论》，《熊十力全集》卷 3，页 105。
53《体用论》，《熊十力全集》卷 7，页 15。
54《明心篇》，页 166。

《易》明乾元分化为乾坤。（明者，阐明之也。乾元者，乾之元，非乾即是元。坤之元即是乾元，非坤别有元。乾元亦名太极，是乾坤之实体也。）[55]

虽然实体是一元，但是这一元实体本来也具有极性的特征："一元本具乾坤二者之性质。"[56] 这个特征表现为相互抵触的状态，而这种状态使得辟和翕、乾和坤（即性和形气、心和物、本心和习心等）的互动成为善与恶能够发生在生活世界——功用层面而不是本体层面——的基本引发条件：

善恶互相违，本于乾之阳明与坤之阴暗两相反也。[57]

《大易》以乾元为乾坤之实体，乾坤为乾元之大用。[58]

大化之流，不有反对，无由成变。不极复杂，何有发展？（大化，犹云大用。流者，流行。乾阳，坤阴，以相反对而成变化。）[59]

有问："本心无恶，而人类多造罪恶，此何故欤？"答曰："……上穷宇宙根源，不有复杂之端，何从发展？不有相反之几，何由成变？是故有坤之阴暗，万物禀之以成形；有乾之阳明，万物禀之以成性。性以帅形，是理之大正；形而累性，则

55《明心篇》，页110。
56《明心篇》，页266。
57《明心篇》，页285。
58《明心篇》，页182。
59《明心篇》，页110。

事有反常。事与理违，而万物于是乎多患矣。"[60]

熊十力不仅避免了朱熹的理论缺陷，而且凭借将乾、坤相反的性质直接设置于形而上的一元实体本身，避免实体受任何杂染、罪恶的浸染，因而强化了极性一元论的理论基础。

60《明心篇》，页265，267。

牟宗三的情感世界及其"觉情"说

彭国翔

（浙江大学哲学系）

内容提要：无论是牟宗三的情感世界还是其"觉情"说，都是以往学界未尝措意的课题。本文充分利用牟宗三的未刊书信，结合《全集》中的相关文献，全面展示牟宗三情感世界的各个方面，包括爱情、亲情、师友之情以及自然之情，特别是他爱情与晚年亲情的方面。同时，还将检讨牟宗三的思想中"觉情"这一核心观念深刻与细腻的内涵，并力求在世界哲学的整体脉络中，尤其是在晚近中西方哲学重视和强调"情感"的动态中，指出牟宗三"觉情"说的价值和意义。

关键词：牟宗三　情感世界　觉情说　当代中西方哲学

一、引言

如果认为牟宗三只是一个驰骋观念的思辨哲学家，没有政治与社会的现世关怀，不过是"盲人摸象"之见。同样，如果认为牟宗三只有冷静的理智而"太上忘情"，也只能是不知其人遑论其世的一种"错觉"。只要阅读牟宗三的相关文字，就足以感受到其人情感之强烈与真挚。而他对于自己各种情感的表达、反省和剖析，本身也正是其真情实感的表现。可惜的是，在以往关于牟宗三的各种研究中，对其情感世界的探究基本上是阙如的。因此，对牟宗三的全面了解，就不能仅限于其"理智",同时也要触及其"情感"。

本文首先根据各种原始文献,尤其是学界之前尚未使用的牟宗三的未刊书信,呈现并展示其情感世界的各个方面,包括爱情、亲情、师友之情以及自然之情,特别是他爱情与晚年亲情的方面。早期的亲情、师友之情以及对于大自然所流露之情,虽然以往也极少受到研究者的关注,但在《牟宗三先生全集》(以下简称《全集》)所收的文献中或多或少都有记载。至于牟宗三的爱情世界,除了他自己在《五十自述》中提到少年时代的萌动之外,目前《全集》所收的文字中几乎完全无迹可寻。但是,这绝不意味着牟宗三的情感世界中没有爱情的位置。事实上,在牟宗三与亲密友人的书信中,有很多爱情方面的坦诚相告与自我剖析。由于这些书信没有收入全集公开发表,为绝大部分人所不知,本文对于这一方面就特别加以留意,以期尽可能一探其爱情的世界。同样,牟宗三晚年的亲情,在《全集》所收的文字中也没有多少反映,而是在他给亲人的家信中得到了充分的流露。本文也利用这些以往并未公开发表也没有收入《全集》的家信,结合《全集》中相关的文字,来呈现其亲情的世界。

此外,牟宗三的情感世界与其哲学思想又是紧密关联的。在他的哲学思想中,"觉情"正是一个十分重要甚至具有核心地位的概念。而牟宗三其人重"情"的一面,与其哲学思想中对"觉情"的强调,可以说是互为因果而彼此一贯的。遗憾的是,在以往有关牟宗三哲学思想的研究中,"觉情"这个概念也基本上是受到忽略的。因此,在通过历史文献重建其情感世界的基础上,本文还将检讨其"觉情"观念深刻与细腻的内涵,并力求在世界哲学的整体脉络中,尤其是在晚近西方哲学中重视和强调"情感"的动态中,指出牟宗三"觉情"说的价值和意义。

总之,牟宗三自己曾说:"这邪恶的时代,实须要有'大的情感'与'大的理解'。'大的情感'恢弘开拓吾人之生命,展露价值之源与生命之源。'大的理解'则疏导问题之何所是与其解答之道路。"[1] 如果说牟宗三的"大的理解"主要反映在他一系列哲学与哲学史的著作，那么，牟宗三的"大的情感"这一面，正是本文所要尝试予以全面呈现与展示的。而对于本文的主要构成来说，牟宗三"情感世界"的部分主要在于"历史的重建"，其"觉情"说的部分则主要是"观念的澄清"。

二、大自然之情

在牟宗三已刊的所有文字中，《五十自述》应该是流露其个人情感最为充分的著作。其中，首先表达的就是他少年时期即怀有的对于家乡大自然的情感。当他回忆家乡的自然环境时，笔下的文字不只是描述，同时也是深深的情感。他说：

> 我生长在山东胶东半岛的栖霞，那是一个多山的小县，四季气候分明。邱长春当年说："走遍天下，不如小小栖霞。大乱不乱，大俭不俭。"我的村庄是处在环山的一块平原里。村后是我们牟氏的祖茔，周围砌以砖墙，范围相当大，在乡间，也算是一个有名的风景区。白杨萧萧，松柏长青。丰碑华表，绿草如茵。苔痕点点，寒鸦长鸣。我对这地方常有神秘之感，儿时即已如此，一到那里，便觉清爽舒适，那气氛好像与自己的生命有自然的契合。我那时自不知其所以然，亦不知其何种感觉。这暗示着我生命中的指向是什么呢？夏天炎热郁闷，那里却清凉寂静，幽深邃远，那不是苍茫寥廓的荒漠，也不是森林的浓密，所以那幽深邃远也不是自然宇宙的，而是另一种意味。[2]

1《五十自述》，《全集》（台北：联经出版事业公司，2003 年），册32，页118。
2《五十自述》，《全集》，册32，页1。

这种情感，在他紧接着描写清明寒食季节自己作为一个"混沌的男孩"融化于大自然的文字中，得到了更为生动活泼的流露。

> 清明寒食的春光是那么清美。村前是一道宽阔的干河，夏天暑雨连绵，山洪暴发，河水涨满，不几日也就清浅了。在春天，只是溪水清流。两岸平沙细软，杨柳依依，绿桑成行，布谷声催。养蚕时节我常伴着兄弟姊妹去采桑。也在沙滩上翻筋斗，或横卧着。阳光普照，万里无云，仰视天空飞鸟，喜不自胜。那是生命最畅亮最开放的时节。无任何拘束，无任何礼法。那时也不感觉到拘束不拘束，礼法不礼法，只是一个混沌的畅亮，混沌畅亮中一个混沌的男孩。这混沌是自然的，那风光也是自然的，呼吸天地之气，舒展混沌的生命。鸟之鸣，沙之软，桑之绿，水之流，白云飘来飘去，这一切都成了催眠的天籁。不知不觉睡着了，复返于寂静的混沌。这畅亮，这开放，这自然的混沌，动荡的或寂静的，能保持到什么时候呢？发展到某时候，也可令人有这种感觉：其去放纵瘫软堕落又有几何呢？这当然不是我那时之所知。我那时只感觉到配置于那种境况里是最舒畅的，而且有一种说不出的荒漠寥廓，落寞而不落寞的浑处之感。我是最欣赏那"落寞而不落寞"的境况的，因为那是混沌。[3]

就这一段文字来看，对牟宗三而言，那种"说不出的荒漠寥廓，落寞而不落寞的浑处之感"，可以说是一种与大自然融合无间的"舒畅"之情。而另一方面，除了"舒畅"之外，对于春光与春色，牟宗

3《五十自述》，《全集》，册32，页1。

三同时生起的，还有一种无端的伤感，他称之为"伤春"之情：

> 暮春初夏是不容易清醒的。一方面诗人说："春色恼人眠
> 不得"，一方面又说"春日迟迟正好眠"。正好眠，眠不得，这
> 正是所谓"春情"。说到春情，再没有比中国的香艳文学体会
> 得更深入的了。那春夏秋冬四季分明的气候，那江南的风光，
> 在在都使中国的才子文学家们对于春情感觉得特别深入而又蕴
> 藉。《牡丹亭·游园惊梦》中那些清秀美丽的句子，如："原来
> 姹紫嫣红开遍，似这般都付与断井颓垣。良辰美景奈何天，赏
> 心乐事谁家院？如花美眷，似水流年，烟波画船，雨丝风片，
> 锦屏人忒看得这韶光贱。"正是对于这春情着意地写，加工地
> 写，正是写得登峰造极，恰如春情之为春情了。而《红楼梦》
> 复以连续好几回的笔墨，藉大观园的春光，小儿女的诟谇，把
> 这意境烘托得更缠绵、更细腻、更具体、更美丽。"凤尾森森，
> 龙吟细细，正是潇湘馆"，这是春情中的春光。"尽日价情思睡
> 昏昏"，这是春光中的春情，只这一句便道尽了春情的全幅义
> 蕴，说不尽的风流，说不尽的蕴藉。这是生命之"在其自己"
> 之感受。由感而伤，只一"伤"字便道尽了春情的全幅义蕴，
> 故曰"伤春"。[4]

　　这种伤春之情，似乎很容易与因"爱"而生的伤感之情相混淆。
不过，牟宗三在撰写《五十自述》时早已观念清晰。因此，虽然情感
细腻，但他也很明确，这种因大自然的春光和春色而生起的无端的伤
感之情，与"爱情"之情毕竟不同。牟宗三特别指出：

> 伤春的"春情"不是"爱情"。"爱情"是有对象的，是

---

[4]《五十自述》,《全集》, 册 32, 页 7。

生命之越离其自己而投身于另一生命，是向着一定方向而歧出，因此一定有所扑着，有其着处，各献身于对方，而在对方中找得其自己，止息其自己；但是"春情"却正是"无着处"。"闺中女儿惜春暮，愁绪满怀无着处"[5]，这"无着处"正是春情。爱情是春情之亨而利，有着处；结婚是利而贞，有止处。春情则是生命之洄漩，欲歧而不歧，欲着而无着，是内在其自己的"亨"，是个混沌洄漩的"元"。中国的才子文学家最敏感于这混沌洄漩的元，向这最原初处表示这伤感的美。这里的伤感是无端的，愁绪满怀而不知伤在何处。无任何指向，这伤感不是悲哀的，我们说悲秋，却不能说悲春，而只能说"伤春"。秋之可悲是因万物之渐趋向于衰杀与凄凉，这已是有了过程中的指向了。但是春情却只是个混沌洄漩的元，所以春情之伤无何指向，伤春之伤他不是悲伤。欧阳修"秋声赋"云："夷，戮也，物过盛而当杀；商，伤也，人既老而悲伤。"[6]这悲伤也是有历程中之指向的。但是春情之伤却只是混沌无着处之寂寞，是生命内在于其自己之洋溢洄漩而不得通，千头万绪放射不出，即不成其为直线条，每一头绪欲钻出来而又钻不出，乃蜷伏回去而成一圆圈的曲线。重重迭迭，无穷的圆曲，盘错于一起，乃形成生命内在于其自己之洋溢与洄漩，这混沌的洄漩。所以这伤的背景是生命之内在的喜悦，是生命之活跃之内在的郁结，故曰春情。春光是万物发育生长的时候，是生之最活跃最柔嫩的时候。它的生长不是直线的，而是洄漩绸缪的，这就是春情。若是直线的，便一泄无余了，便无所谓情。洄漩绸缪，郁而不发，便是春情之伤，春生如此，小儿女的生命也

---

5 该句出自《红楼梦》中黛玉的《葬花吟》。

6 按：欧阳修原文两句是倒过来的，即"商，伤也，人既老而悲伤；夷，戮也，物过盛而当杀"。

正在生长发育之时，故适逢春光而有春情，敏感者乃有春情之伤。春情之为春是恰如其字，只象征着混沌的洄漩，并无其他意义，而这也就是最丰富的意义。[7]

显然，牟宗三这里对于"春情"与"爱情"的区别，尤其是以文学性而非哲学性的文字进行的区分，既是他自己情感世界这一方面的自然流露，也是他对自己情感世界这一方面的自觉描绘。

以上引用的牟宗三的这些文字，完全不同于其辨名析理的哲学话语，而是细腻鲜活，其情感的强度与厚度扑面而来，读之不免令人产生强烈的同情（empathy）与共鸣（resonance）。

《五十自述》是 1956 年开始撰写，1957 年完稿的。牟宗三在书写这些文字时，正值盛年。而在 1968 年，即差不多十一二年之后，年近六旬的牟宗三在给香港中文大学艺术系作"美的感受"演讲时，再次回忆起少年时期那种"落寞而不落寞"的情感。他说："我记得幼年在我们家乡，当春末夏初的时候，我常常仰卧在河边的沙滩上，仰望辽阔的天空，旁边是小溪流，有桑树两行，有杨柳几株，上面有布谷鸟鸣之声。在这一种清明辽阔的境况里，我一藐然之身，横卧在沙滩上，一种落寞而不落寞之感便在心中浮现。"[8] 由此可见，这种"对于大自然"或者"因大自然而起"的情感，可以说是牟宗三情感世界中的一个始终不可化约的方面和向度。

三、亲情

关于牟宗三的"亲情"，根据他自己的各种文献，我们目前可以看到三个方面的表现，一是父母之情，二是兄弟姐妹之情，三是对于

7《五十自述》,《全集》, 册 32, 页 7–8。
8《牟宗三先生晚期文集》,《全集》, 册 27, 页 203–204。

儿子和孙女的情感。

在牟宗三已刊的《全集》中，反映其亲情的文字主要是父母之情和兄弟姐妹之情。首先，让我们看看他对于父母的情感。

1941年12月至1942年2月之间，在大理接到父亲亡故消息时撰写的《亲丧志哀》中，牟宗三记载了丧母时的情感流露。母亲去世时，牟宗三正在寿张师范学校任教。他得到消息抵家时，其母已经去世，所谓"抵村头，即遥见灵柩发祖茔"。[9] 牟宗三记述当时的心情是"心如刀绞。大哭不能已"。[10] 不过，相比于关于母亲的记载，牟宗三记载更详的，是他对于父亲的情感。

牟宗三对于父亲情感的直接流露至少有三次。一次同样是在《亲丧志哀》中，牟宗三回忆了他印象中的父亲。所谓：

> 我在前常提到先父之严肃。他是白手起家的人。刚毅严整，守正不阿；有本有根，终始条理。祖父弃世时，薄田不过七八亩，安葬时只是土圹，并无砖砌。伯父含混，不理家业。叔父年幼，体弱多病。他一手承担起家庭的重担。十八岁即辍学，应世谋生。祖父留下来的骡马店，他继续经营了若干年。神强体壮，目光四射。指挥酬对，丝毫不爽。每当傍晚，骡马成群归来，他都要帮着扛抬。那是很紧张的时候，很繁重的工作。无论人或马都是急着要安息，他安排照应，宾至如归。当时二掌柜之名是远近皆知的。后来他常对我们说：开始原也是糊涂的，后不久忽然眼睛亮了，事理也明白了。人总须亲身在承当艰苦中磨练，这话给我的印象非常深。他看人教子弟，总说要扑下身弯下腰，手脚都要落实，不要轻飘飘，像个浪荡者。他最厌那些浮华乖巧，从外面学来的时髦玩艺。他是典型

---

9 《牟宗三先生未刊遗稿》，《全集》，册26，页1。
10 《牟宗三先生未刊遗稿》，《全集》，册26，页1。

的中国文化陶养者。他常看《曾文正公家书》，晚上也常讽诵古文，声音韵节稳练从容。我常在旁边听，心中随之极为清净纯洁。写字整齐不苟，墨润而笔秀。常教我们不要了草，不要有荒笔败笔，墨要润泽，不要干黄，因为这关乎一个人的福泽。他是有坚定的义理信念的人。我觉得中国文化中的那些义理教训，在他身上是生了根的，由他在治家谋生的事业中生了根，在与乡村、农业、自然地理、风俗习惯那谐和的一套融而为一中生了根。"安土敦乎仁"是不错。那些义理教训都在这"安土敦乎仁"中生根，一起随之为真实的，存在的。因此他的生命是生命之在其自己的生命。那些义理教训也随他的生命之在其自己而亦内在化于他的生命中。所以他的信念贞常、坚定，而不摇动。在他的生命中，你可以见到宇宙间有定理、有纲维。这是建构的、积极的，同时也是创造的、保聚的生命。他从不方便讨巧，随和那些一阵一阵的邪风。[11]

　　这里，所谓"刚毅严整，守正不阿；有本有根，终始条理"，"信念贞常、坚定，而不摇动"，"在他的生命中，你可以见到宇宙间有定理、有纲维"，"他从不方便讨巧，随和那些一阵一阵的邪风"等等，显然并不只是一种描述和记录。在这样的文字中，深深渗透着牟宗三对于父亲无比的敬重。在牟宗三看来，他的父亲完全是一位中国传统文化价值的身体力行者，所谓"中国文化中的那些义理教训，在他身上是生了根的"。牟宗三说他小时候经常听父亲晚上"声音韵节稳练从容"地"讽诵古文"，而自己"心中随之极为清净纯洁"，可见父亲对于牟宗三的影响，自幼扎根，极其深远。牟宗三也曾经记述自己在去北平读北大预科时，一度受当时的"左"倾风潮影响，但自始即自

11《五十自述》，《全集》，册32，页31-32。

觉"异样",很快就意识到那一风潮与中国传统文化尤其伦理风尚根本不合,从而摆脱了其影响,这不能不说正是他从小深受其父价值观的影响使然。

不仅如此,牟宗三在《亲丧志哀》这篇文字中,更是记录了当他接到家信获悉父亲病危时伤痛不已的心情,所谓"余见此信,泪夺眶出。时与友人下棋,当时即不能自持。然力事镇静。草草终局。晚餐,食未半,一念酸鼻。吃不下嗓,急离座,人不之知也"。[12]

除了《亲丧志哀》一文之外,牟宗三另外两次表达对于父亲的怀念之情,一次是1943年10月在成都撰写的《父丧二周年忌辰感恩》,另一次是1944年8月在大理撰写的《父丧三年述怀》。前一篇记述父亲的若干生平事迹:早年如何创业持家,中流砥柱;晚年如何儿女情长。尤其回忆1926年家中遭遇土匪的经历,栩栩如生。后一篇更是回忆当初父亲临终之际,自己的生活却一度陷于荒唐,由此而产生极度愧疚之情。他说:

> 尤使吾深痛者,当吾昏聩之日,正先公呻吟之时。每一念及,痛悔无地。无以对父母,无以对兄弟,无以对妻子。家庭骨肉,俱在水深火热,而吾则酒色缠绵,夜以继日。及接大兄家报,告知父亲卧病,一念不泯,五衷如焚。拔刀斩乱丝,掉头不一顾。然神明内疚,常无已时。此当为吾有生以来最大之罪恶,亦为吾今日最大之忏悔。梦寐之中,犹不觉泪洗双颊。自此以后,吾渐觉有敬畏之感。与人生真理常怀严肃心,非是前此之一任兴趣奔驰矣。[13]

这段文字,足见父亲病逝对于牟宗三的震动。正是这种情感的震

12《牟宗三先生未刊遗稿》,《全集》,册26,页2。
13《牟宗三先生未刊遗稿》,《全集》,册26,页9。

动，将牟宗三从一度不检点的颓废生活中振拔出来，令其道德意识得以真正树立。将这段话与奥古斯丁的《忏悔录》相对照，或许不无异曲同工之处。

除了对父母的感情之外，对自己的兄弟姐妹，牟宗三也是一往情深。他在《五十自述》中感叹自己"聋哑的叔弟在廿岁左右即亡故"，感叹自己"兄弟姊妹子侄个个皆散离失所而受苦"，感叹"那些不得享受其位育以完成其各人自己的兄弟姐妹与子侄"。在1954年1月28日致唐君毅的信中，牟宗三更是直言自己的悲苦以及对自己长兄的担忧，所谓："弟前天忽然心绪暗淡，悲从中来，不觉哭起来，此为从来所未有。我很担心大家兄有问题，论年龄他才五十八岁，但时代太摧残人，生活太坏，金刚也磨损。现在也无法打听。"

总之，对于父母兄弟姐妹的亲情，牟宗三是极其深厚的，关于这一点，在《五十自述》中有一段感人至深的文字：

> 但是睡着睡着，我常下意识地不自觉地似睡非睡似梦非梦地想到了父亲，想到了兄弟姊妹，觉得支解破裂，一无所有，全星散而撤离了，我犹如横陈于无人烟的旷野，只是一具偶然飘萍的躯壳。如一块瓦石，如一茎枯草，寂寞荒凉而怆痛，觉着觉着，忽然惊醒，犹泪洗双颊，哀感宛转，不由地发出深深一叹。这一叹的悲哀苦痛是难以形容的，无法用言语说出的。彻里彻外，整个大地人间，全部气氛，是浸在那一叹的悲哀中。[14]

晚年的牟宗三，其情感更多地在儿子和孙女那里得到了流露。这一方面的内容，在已刊《全集》的文字中无法获知，但在牟宗三未刊的书信中，尤其是晚年的家信中，却有着充分的反映。

14《五十自述》，《全集》，册32，页135。

　　改革开放之后，牟宗三晚年居香港时曾经和前来探亲的两个儿子（伯璇、伯琏）见过面。他不仅常有书信寄往栖霞老家，更常常汇款帮助家人，不仅是他的原配夫人和两个儿子，还有他的孙子、孙女以及侄孙等等家族成员 。在牟宗三给两个常年在栖霞老家生活、几乎没有什么文化的儿子的信中，一位老父的亲情，跃然纸上。而尤其能反映牟宗三亲情这一面的，是他为两位孙女（鸿贞、鸿卿）能够从栖霞老家到香港所付出的心力。其间的种种曲折以及牟宗三所投注的心力，限于篇幅，此处不能详述。这里我仅略举一例，足见其情。

　　一般认为，牟宗三 1949 年夏秋之间离开大陆之后终其一生没有再回来过。甚至改革开放之后，在大陆学界已经开始研究他的思想并邀请他至大陆参加以其思想为主题的学术研讨会的情况下，牟宗三仍没有回来。但是，为了看到自己一直未能谋面的孙女，牟宗三不惜以八十以上的高龄，两次专程前往深圳。如果我们曾有罗湖桥排队过海关的经历，就知道这两次出行对一位八十以上高龄的老人来说，即便不是在酷暑天，也是一件多么不容易的事。并且，我相信体力上的耗损尚在其次，对牟宗三来说，违反自己的初衷驻足大陆，恐怕更不是一个轻易的决定。而促成他终于如此的，正是作为爷爷对于孙女的一片爱心。这一款款深情，在牟宗三给鸿贞的另一封书信中，直接表露无遗，所谓"想到有一个小孙女在身边叫爷爷，多么愉快"。这里，让我们看到的，显然不是一个冷峻理智的哲人，而是一位饱含亲切情感的慈祥老人。

牟宗三致孙女鸿贞的信

四、师友之情

古云"师友夹持"，对于一个人的成长，尤其是注重精神思想方面成长的人物，师友之情的作用尤其不能忽视。而师友之间的情感，也往往成为一个人生命历程与情感世界中的重要方面。在这一方面，牟宗三也不例外。不过，与那些遍地友朋的人物不同，牟宗三一生以之为师并终生认同的，除了《五十自述》里提到的启蒙老师之外，大概只有熊十力了。尽管牟宗三在思想方面与熊十力并不完全一致，尤其在如何从事中国哲学的研究与建构方面，两人之间还有过激烈的争执。比如在其亲笔记载的《湖上一席谈》中，牟宗三就表现出了"吾爱吾师，吾尤爱真理"的精神。但是，在情感上，牟宗三与熊十力始终极为亲近。对熊十力也始终表现出高度的敬重和认同。

1941年12月，牟宗三离开大理，赴重庆北碚金刚碑勉仁书院投靠熊十力。牟宗三抵达时，熊十力已经由于和梁漱溟不睦而离开。那个时候，可以说是师生二人处境最为艰难萧瑟的一幕，对此，牟宗三用这样的文字记录了当时师生二人的情状：

> 吾即由重庆往拜，薄暮始达。至则见师母补缀衣裳，并告以先生在里屋，余即趋入，时先生正呻吟榻上，一灯如豆，状至凄凉。问安毕，相对而泣。并言人情之险。时同门韩裕文兄随侍，与先生共进退。（裕文兄抗战胜利后去美，在美逝世，可伤。）晚间告以离嘉之故甚详。[15]

这里"呻吟榻上，一灯如豆，状至凄凉"的文字，固然是对熊十力当时情形的写照，更是牟宗三自己的情感流露。并且，这种情感，可以说不仅是当初与熊十力相见时所具有的，恐怕也是牟宗三在回忆起当初情境而写下这段文字时再次涌上心头的。

至于牟宗三对熊十力的高度肯定，《五十自述》中也有清楚的交代。

> 熊师那原始生命之光辉与风姿，家国天下族类之感之强烈，实开吾生命之源而永有所向往而不至退堕之重大缘由。吾于此实体会了慧命之相续。熊师之生命实即一有光辉之慧命。当今之世，唯彼一人能直通黄帝尧舜以来之大生命而不隔。此大生命是民族生命与文化生命之合一。他是直顶着华族文化生命之观念方向所开辟的人生宇宙之本源而抒发其义理与情感。他的学问直下是人生的，同时也是宇宙的。这两者原是一下子冲破而不分。只有他那大才与生命之原始，始能如此透顶。

15《五十自述》，《全集》，册32，页89。

……这只是有"原始生命"、"原始灵感"的人，才能如此。这不是知解摸索的事，而是直下证悟感受的事。若说证悟感受是主观的，但在这里，主观的，亦是客观的。这是创造之源，价值之源，人生根柢的事，不是知识的事，熊师学问最原始的意义还是在这一点。这是打开天窗，直透九霄的灵感。……我所感受于熊师者唯此为亲切，故我说他是一个有光辉的慧命。这是最足以提撕人而使人昂首天外的，此之谓大开大合。惟大开大合者，能通华族慧命而不隔。在以往孔孟能之，王船山能之，在今日，则熊师能之。[16]

由这段话可见，牟宗三认为，正是熊十力的生命所显发的"光辉"与"风姿"，提撕了自己的生命而使其不至于堕落。并且，在牟宗三看来，当时只有熊十力足以称得上是"能通华族慧命"的人。正如牟宗三认为："这不是知解摸索的事，而是直下证悟感受的事。若说证悟感受是主观的，但在这里，主观的，亦是客观的。这是创造之源，价值之源，人生根柢的事，不是知识的事，熊师学问最原始的意义还是在这一点。"这种评价，并不只是一种理智的判断，而是饱含了自己个人的情感认同。

牟宗三与熊十力之间，体现的是师生之情。而牟宗三情感世界中平辈之间的友情，则体现在牟宗三与为数不多的几位友人之间。在牟宗三自己的记述文字中，有两例可以让人充分感受到。一是抗战时避居昆明期间慷慨接济他的张遵骝；另一个则是他终生的挚友唐君毅。

与张遵骝之间的友情，《五十自述》中有详细的记录。以下三段文字，最能说明牟宗三当时的境况，尤其是他的心情。

16《五十自述》,《全集》, 册 32, 页 91–93。

　　抗战初期，生活艰困。我在广西教中学一年。应友人张遵骝之邀，至昆明。无职业。租一小屋居住，生活费全由遵骝担负。遵骝，张文襄公（之洞）之曾孙，广交游，美风仪，慷慨好义，彬彬有礼。[17]

　　吾信赖遵骝之友情，如兄如弟，毫无距离之感。彼解衣衣之，吾即衣之。彼推食食之，吾即食之。彼以诚相待，我以诚相受。我自念，我生于天地之间，我有生存之权利。而何况遵骝以诚相待，吾焉得再有矜持以撑门面？吾坦然受之而无愧：彼无望报之心，吾亦无酬报之念。盖吾与彼之心境已超过施与报之对待，而进入一无人无我绝对法体之相契。遵骝诚有其不可及之性情与肝胆，吾亦诚有其不可及之开朗与洒脱。[18]

　　我虽对遵骝之友情坦然受之而无愧，然吾带累朋友，吾心中不能无隐痛。彼之经济并不充裕，彼为吾奔走着急，而不露声色，吾虽不露声色而受之，吾心中尤不能无隐痛。……暑过秋至，遵骝须返沪一行。吾送之车站。彼即留下七八十元，并谓若有所需，可向其姑丈相借，吾即领而受之。吾并非一感伤型的人，然当时直觉天昏地暗，一切黯然无光。淡然无语而别。当时之惨淡直难以形容。我事后每一想及或叙及，辄不觉泣下。鲁智深在野猪林救下林冲，临起程时，林冲问曰："兄长将何往？"鲁智深曰："杀人须见血，救人须救彻，愚兄放心不下，直送兄弟到沧州。"我每读此，不觉废书而叹。这是人生，这是肝胆。我何不幸而遇之，我又何幸而遇之。[19]

　　由此可知，张遵骝是张之洞的曾孙。抗战期间，牟宗三衣食无

17《五十自述》，《全集》，册32，页81。
18《五十自述》，《全集》，册32，页86。
19《五十自述》，《全集》，册32，页87。

着，一度流落到广西在中学任教为生。张遵骝知晓后，即邀请牟宗三至昆明。张遵骝视牟宗三如兄弟，牟宗三的衣食起居等一应费用，完全由张遵骝负担。两人之间，一个是"以诚相待"，一个是"以诚相受"，彼此之间毫无距离感。张遵骝为牟宗三奔走着急，却不露声色；牟宗三不露声色而接受，心中却不能无隐痛。后来，张遵骝因故离开昆明，牟宗三至车站送行。行前张遵骝仍不忘赠送牟宗三生活费，并嘱咐牟宗三紧急时可向张遵骝的姑丈相借。这一幕分别，令牟宗三极为感伤，正如上引文中所谓"当时直觉天昏地暗，一切黯然无光。淡然无语而别。当时之惨淡直难以形容。我事后每一想及或叙及，辄不觉泣下"。在那种心情之下，牟宗三不由联想到《水浒传》中鲁智深搭救林冲并护送其到沧州这兄弟之间仗义而感人的一段，并极为动情地写道："我每读此，不觉废书而叹。这是人生，这是肝胆。我何不幸而遇之，我又何幸而遇之。"如今我们读到这样的文字，设想当时的情景，也不免会感同身受，唏嘘不已。可惜的是，1949年牟宗三渡海赴台之后，两岸隔绝，张遵骝留在大陆，两人不得再见。只有到了改革开放之后，张遵骝一度得以赴香港，两位老友才再次得以相见。我曾经看过两人在香港相聚的照片，为之感动不已。

至于牟宗三与唐君毅之间的友情，包括牟宗三对于唐君毅的高度肯定，我们不妨也从《五十自述》中选取三条记载：

> 整个时代在破裂，吾之个体生命亦破裂。此是时代之悲剧，亦是吾之悲剧。世人憧憧不能知也。惟友人君毅兄能知之。吾当时有云："生我者父母，教我者熊师，知我者君毅兄也。"当时与熊师与君毅兄有许多论学之信件，亦有许多至情流露之信件。惟此为足慰。[20]

20《五十自述》，《全集》，册32，页90。

在那困阨的五年间（民国廿六年至卅一年），除与熊师常相聚外，还有一个最大的缘会，便是遇见了唐君毅先生。他是谈学问与性情最相契的一位朋友。……我那时对于西方形上学亦无所得，而君毅兄却对于形上学有强烈的兴趣。又是黑格尔式的，而我那时亦不懂黑格尔，而且有强烈的反感。因此，我意识中并不甚注意君毅兄。熊师常称赞他，常对我说："你不要看不起他，他是你的知己。《唯物辩证法论战》中的文字，他认为你的为最有力量。"……我自昆明返重庆，编《再生》杂志。他因李长之之介来访，我觉得他有一股霭然温和，纯乎学人之象。我自北大那散漫无度的环境出来，又处于一政治团体中，所接友朋，流品混杂。我自己亦多放荡胡闹处，言行多不循礼。我见了他，我觉得他干净多了，纯正多了，我因而亦起自惭形秽之感。……第一次相见，没有谈什么。第二次相见，提到布拉得赖，[21] 我说："我不懂他，亦不懂辩证法的真实意义究竟在那里，若唯物辩证法实不可通，请你给我讲一讲，简别一下。"他即约略讲了几句，虽然不多，但我感觉到他讲时颇费吞吐之力，我知道这须要有强度的内在心力往外喷。我马上感到他是一个哲学的气质，有玄思的心力。这是我从来所未遇到的。我在北平所接触的那些师友，谈到哲学都是广度的、外在的、不费力的、随便说说的，从未像他这样有思辨上的认真的。……他确有理路，亦有理论的思辨力。我并且因着他，始懂得了辩证法的真实意义以及其使用的层面。这在我的思想发展上有飞跃性的开辟。我的《逻辑典范》那时已写成，我已接近了康德。但对于形上学，我并无积极的认识，只是根据"知性"有一个形式的划分。但自此以后，我感觉到只此形式的划

---

21 按：即英国哲学家 Francis Herbert Bradley（1846—1924），新黑格尔主义的代表。

分并不够。对于彼岸，我还差得远。我知道里面有丰富的内容，须要从只是形式的划分，还要进到具体的精察。这就是黑格尔所开辟的领域，我因此对黑格尔也有了好感。这都是由君毅兄所给我的提撕而得的。我得感谢他，归功于他。[22]

吾对于精神哲学之契入，君毅兄启我最多，因为他自始即是黑氏的。熊师所给我的是向上开辟的文化生命之源。关于这一骨干，光宋明儒亦不够，佛学亦不够。惟康德、黑格尔之建树，足以接上东方"心性之学"，亦足以补其不足。而环观海内，无有真能了解黑氏学者。惟君毅兄能之。此其对于中国学术文化之所以有大功也。[23]

牟宗三与唐君毅之间的友情，在于一生的相知，即牟宗三所谓"生我者父母，教我者熊师，知我者君毅兄也"。在牟宗三看来，1937—1942 是他最为"困阨的五年"。就是在那期间，除与熊十力常相聚之外，牟宗三认为自己"还有一个最大的缘会，便是遇见了唐君毅先生"。并且，牟宗三将唐君毅视为"谈学问与性情最相契的一位朋友"。

而除了上引三段以及已刊《全集》中其他相关的文字之外，对于牟宗三和唐君毅之间的友情，最能让人感受至深的，在我看来，恐怕得是牟宗三写给唐君毅的那些书信了。可惜的是，这些书信没有收入《全集》之中。正是在那些书信中，牟宗三向唐君毅坦陈自己的各种心迹，尤其是毫无保留地剖析自己个人的情感。只有对完全信赖和志同道合的莫逆之交，如西塞罗（Cicero）意义上的 *alter ego*，才能如此。事实上，唐君毅也的确可以说是牟宗三的不二知己。他不仅很早就看到牟宗三在哲学思考上堪称不世出的天才，而报之以英雄惜

22《五十自述》，《全集》，册 32，页 97–99。
23《五十自述》，《全集》，册 32，页 101。

英雄的殷殷之情，更是为了牟宗三的个人感情生活，竭尽全力予以帮助。这一点，在下面考察牟宗三的爱情世界部分，我们尤其可以看到。

在师友之情中，牟宗三不仅有在与熊十力的关系中作为学生的一面，还有在与他自己的学生中作为老师的一面。在此，我仅以50年代台北的人文友会为例，略加说明。

1954年8月，在台湾师大任教的牟宗三发起成立人文友会，若干学生在课程之外，每两周聚会一次，由牟宗三主讲，大家讨论。后来很多重要的弟子，都是当时讲会的参与者，如蔡仁厚、刘述先等。人文友会持续了两年，共聚会51次，是牟宗三与其弟子们师生之情的一个见证。后来的《人文讲习录》，就是讲会记录的汇编。对于讲会所体现的师生之情以及对于参会学生成长的意义，负责编订《人文讲习录》的蔡仁厚有这样的回忆：

> 当时，先生（按：牟宗三）在台北主持"人文友会"，每两周有一次聚会讲习。那里当然有师友之夹持，有道义之相勉，有精神之提撕，有心志之凝聚，而且亦有宽容、慰藉、提携、增上。……与会诸友的感受与开悟，容有强弱深浅之差异，但两年的亲炙，则是这二十年来无时或忘，而一直感念于心的。……在台北最后一次聚会，是讲师友之义与友道精神。亲切眄恳，语语由衷而出，叮嘱期勉，句句动人心弦。平常想象昔贤讲学的风范，在这里获得了最真切的验证。[24]

而这一方面的师友之情，牟宗三不同年龄段的学生门人也都各有感受。这一类文字中所流露的浓厚的师友之情，显然不仅是单方面作

24《牟宗三先生学思年谱》，《全集》，册32，页134。

为学生的情感表达，也反映了作为师长的牟宗三的情感状态。

五、家国天下之情

除了对于大自然的情感、亲情、师友之情以外，牟宗三的情感世界中还有着与时代密切相关的"家国天下之情"。

牟宗三的"家国天下之情"，主要与中国的政治、社会变迁密切相关。关于牟宗三的政治社会思想，我已有专论，[25] 这里不赘。但是，如果政治思想主要是理性的结晶与反映，那么，由于政治和社会变迁所致牟宗三在情感方面的激荡与表露，我恰好在此做些补充。牟宗三这一方面的情感流露，集中反映在抗战后期到 1949 年这几年之间，所谓"就吾个人言，从成都到共产党渡江，这五六年间，是我的'情感'（客观的悲情）时期"。有三个时间段以及相关事件，足以反映他的"家国天下之情"。

首先，是抗战后期在成都期间，那时一方面是国民党的腐败，一方面是大部分知识人的"左"倾，所谓"人们不是左倒，就是右倒"。在这种局面之下，牟宗三痛感中国文化正在遭遇前所未有的挑战，而他必须肩负坚持原则、护持文化命脉的使命，所谓："我的依据不是现实的任何一面，而是自己的国家，华族的文化生命。一切都有不是，而这个不能有不是，一切都可放弃、反对，而这个不能放弃、反对，我能拨开一切现实的牵连而直顶着这个文化生命之大流。"在这种强烈的文化使命感与时局的激发之下，牟宗三斗志昂扬，以极大的情感投入与他认为的"左右颠倒""塌散崩解"的社会风潮的斗争之中。用他自己的话来说，即是："我那时的道德感特别强，正气特别高扬，纯然是客观的，不是个人的。意识完全注在家国天下、历史文

---

25 彭国翔：《智者的现世关怀——牟宗三的政治与社会思想》（台北：联经出版事业公司，2016年）。

化上。"[26] "国家、华族生命、文化生命、夷夏、人禽、义利之辨，是我那时的宗教。我那时也确有宗教的热诚。凡违反这些而歧出的，凡否定这些而乖离的，凡不能就此尽其责以建国以尽民族自己之性的，我必断然予以反对。"[27]

到了内战临近尾声的阶段，国民党大势已去。那个时候，牟宗三对时局极为关注。1947年年末，他曾经作《自立铭》赠给自己的侄子牟北辰。

> 体念民生，常感骨肉流离之痛。收敛精神，常发精诚恻坦之仁。
> 敬慎其事，宜思勿忝厥职。勿悖祖训，宜念完成孝思。
> 理以养心，培刚大正直之气。学以生慧，聚古今成败之识。
> 闲邪存诚，勿落好行小慧言不及义之讥。
> 常有所思，庶免饱食终日无所用心之陋。
> 忠以律己，于穆不已凭实践引生天趣。
> 恕以待人，团聚友朋以共业引发公心。
> 须自己立人，心本历史文化。
> 任凭邪说横行，不背民族国家。[28]

牟宗三念兹在兹的是民族文化，其家国天下之情，溢于言表。正如他自己紧随《观生悲歌》其后所写："举时大乱，无可用力。慷慨伤怀，悲歌抒情，使来者有以知我与斯世之痛苦也。"

1949年夏秋之间，牟宗三从浙江大学离开大陆前夕，其心情

26《五十自述》，《全集》，册32，页105。
27《五十自述》，《全集》，册32，页105–106。
28《牟宗三先生未刊遗稿》，《全集》，册26，页11。

近乎决绝。当有人担心他离开后恐无法返回时，牟宗三的回答是这样的："得返不得返，亦非吾所注意。从此以后，浪迹天涯，皆无不可。反正地球是圆的，只有前进，决无后退之理。只要有自由生存空间，吾即有立足地。吾之生命依据不在现实。现实一无所有矣。试看国在那里，家在那里？吾所依据者华族之文化生命，孔孟之文化理想耳。"[29] 这一方面再次表露了他的家国天下之情，另一方面也再次表明，他在"出处"问题上的取舍标准，并不是现实的政治，而始终是文化的立场和原则。

六、爱情

上述牟宗三情感世界的几个部分，包括对于大自然之情、亲情、师友之情以及家国天下之情，在刊行的《全集》中，或多或少都有文字记载。但是，作为人类情感世界中另一个极为重要的方面——爱情，在目前已刊的《全集》中，却几乎是无迹可寻的。

当然，在收入《全集》的《五十自述》这部最能反映牟宗三情感世界的著作中，牟宗三曾经记录了自己少年时代近乎爱情的一种纯情的萌动。那是他对于一个马戏团的少女所莫名而生的一种爱恋。请看如下这段文字：

> 有一次，来了一个马戏团，正在天气严冷，风雪飘零之时，他们圈了一个广场，先是鸣锣开场，继之一个十三四岁的小女孩骑在马上，绕场一周。矫健的身段，风吹雪冻得红红的皮色，清秀朴健的面孔，正合着上面所说的清新俊逸的风姿，但是可怜楚楚的，是女性的，不是男性的，我直如醉如痴地对

29《五十自述》，《全集》，册32，页117。

> 她有着莫名其妙的感觉。先父严肃，不准小孩常去看这类江湖
> 卖艺的把戏，我不知不觉地偷去了好几次，我一看见了她，就
> 有着异样的感觉，既喜悦又怜惜。事后我每想起，这大概就是
> 我那时的恋情。一霎就过去了，这是我一生唯一的一次爱情之
> 流露，此后再也没有那种干净无邪而又是恋情的爱怜心境了。[30]

在这段细腻而颇具文采的表述中，牟宗三毫不掩饰地将当时的
那种情感称为"我那时的恋情"。这里记录的，自然还只是一个青
春少年的单相思。然而，这里的文字所流露的，又何尝不正是一种
最为单纯和美好的爱情呢？事实上，牟宗三虽然在回忆中指出那是
其一生唯一的一次爱情流露，但并不意味着后来他不再有对于爱情
的追寻，尽管他大概不幸终究没有得到他心目中的爱情。不然，在
《五十自述》中，他也不会写下"这是我一生唯一的一次爱情之流
露，此后再也没有那种干净无邪而又是恋情的爱怜心境了"这段感
伤甚至沉痛的话了。

不过，虽然《全集》中的文字无法让人得见牟宗三的爱情世界，
但值得庆幸的是，在牟宗三给唐君毅、徐复观尤其是唐君毅的私人书
信中，保存了不少有关牟宗三爱情世界的素材。由于这些内容以往不
为人所知，如本文开篇所述，在这一部分，我就根据这些未刊的资料，
来特别呈现牟宗三的爱情世界，或至少是其爱情世界的一些空间与光
影。以便尽可能让读者对于牟宗三的感情世界，能有较为充分的了解。

首先需要说明的是，牟宗三早在 1932 年前后即在山东老家成婚。
但除了 1933—1936 年这三年间曾数次短暂回乡小住之外，其余时间
都不在老家，1936 年之后则基本没有再回过老家。由于牟宗三父亲
的缘故，牟宗三至少在早年对这个妻子并不满意。对此，他在《亲丧

30《五十自述》，《全集》，册 32，页 13。

志哀》中有明确的交代：

> 吾岳家至鄙俗，订婚时，父亲即嫌弃。至吾结婚十余年，从无好感。过门后，言谈举止，无一能当。尤嫌弃之。从不允其侍奉。[31]

因此，他早年的这段婚姻几乎是名存实亡的。至于 1949 年牟宗三渡海赴台之后，两岸隔绝，这段婚姻也就实际上终结了。

当然，也不能说牟宗三对原配毫无感情。例如，他在晚年给山东老家两个儿子（伯璇、伯琏）的信中，就曾嘱咐要安慰其母：

> 说我也很惦念，我不能忘记她的劳苦。（某年 12 月 22 日）

> 望你们好好奉养你母亲，使其晚年略得一点安慰，我在远方亦可以略得心安也。（某年 3 月 12 日）

在给孙子（红成）的信中，牟宗三也表达了对于原配的情感：

> 她苦了一辈子，我没有忘掉她。（某年 3 月 29 日）

不过，这种感情应该主要是一种复杂的包含歉疚的恩义之情，与爱情无关了。

牟宗三赴台湾时年方 40 岁，有其爱情与婚姻的追求是完全可以理解的。而目前我所看到的这些反映牟宗三爱情世界的书信，恰好也都是 1949 年之后的。

31《牟宗三先生未刊遗稿》，《全集》，册 26，页 4。

1950 年 10 月前后，牟宗三曾遇到一位沈姓小姐，一度为之倾倒。他在 10 月 13 日给唐君毅的信中写道：

> 弟现在无心过问此事，又为那位沈小姐吸住了。蓦然间遇见了五百年冤孽，不然，何以如此倾倒？

这里，牟宗三直言自己被那位沈小姐"吸住了"、为之"倾倒"，甚至认为自己遇见了"五百年冤孽"。不过，这位沈小姐大概与他无缘，很快便从他的生活中消失了。因为在 10 月 23 日牟宗三写给唐君毅的信中，末尾已经这样写道：

> 弟现在作无出息想，身体坏，日常生活亦无办法。四十而后，感觉需要女人，须有家庭。如有机缘，则弟必解决此问题也。

从这一段话，可以推测十天前信中的那位沈小姐，应该已经是无缘而散了。否则，以他上封信中所言对这位沈小姐的迷恋程度，怎会丝毫不再提及而语气如此呢？事实上，从他差不多一个月后再次写给唐君毅的信中可知，那位令其倾倒的沈小姐的确已经不知所之，而已有人为他另外介绍对象了。

在 11 月 27 日给唐君毅的信中，牟宗三这样写道：

> 近来李定一为弟谋婚事。此人虽不学，颇富世智。彼介一女，甚好，然未必能成。弟有一念，若年内能有一满意之对象，必有一谈爱之书，写给普天下有情的儿女。若没有，则此书不能出现。天地间亦缺一典。

更为关键的是，由这里牟宗三的自述可见，他当时可以说正沉浸在"爱情的追寻"之中。同时，对于爱情本身，牟宗三一定有着相当的反省与思考。不然，他不会有写一部关于爱情的著作的打算。并且，对于这部书，他还颇为自许。用他自己的话来说，如果写不出来，则"天地间亦缺一典"。可惜的是，由于牟宗三对爱情的追寻大概一直未果，始终未能获得一位"满意之对象"，这样一部他认为"写给普天下有情的儿女"的可以成"典"的书，终究没有像他那些在中国哲学史上成为经典的著作一样写出来。

1951 年间，牟宗三继续追寻爱情，谋求婚事，但仍然挫折不遇。这一情况，从他 7 月 11 日给唐君毅的信中可以看到：

> 弟所认识之小姐，花木瓜，空好看，极不易感发，也是努力志趣不足，相距甚远，很难接得上。弟初识时，即决定作但丁式的恋，但对方不能有反应，此或已不能久。……前些时，佛观自日来信，谓如不能成，便望主万小姐玉成其事（今春他曾写一信介绍过）。他说万小姐比弟所识者好，其实他也是瞎闹，他何能坚主耶？看书无用，佛观早说过，她决看不懂。不过是一中学生，其程度甚低。总须见面才能说。女性重具体，就是表现她的智力与志趣，也须在直接谈天生活中。经过文字总不行，具体的，若能接得上，抽象的书籍理论便能增加她的向往崇拜；否则，与她不相干。了解我们这类人，总得有相当程度才行。否则，如兄说简单素朴的最好。

这一段交往显然没有结果，因为到了 9 月 13 日，在牟宗三同样是给唐君毅的信中，已经流露出对于婚姻和家庭极为悲观的情绪。所谓："年来生活泛滥，心思不能凝聚，为女人所困，此亦无出息之甚耳。男子生而愿有其家，弟恐终不能有家也。……弟个人生活无着落，但愿向广大人群，与广漠宇宙传达其呼声。某小姐照片寄上。"这里

"弟恐终不能有家也",真是非常沉痛的一句话。如今读来,其感伤之情仍不免跃然纸上。不过,尽管如此,牟宗三仍然没有放弃成婚成家的打算和尝试。因为即使在这样一封充满感伤与沉痛之情的信中,他还是附上了一位小姐的照片。自然,这位小姐应是他当时正在交往的一位女性,但彼此之间显然没有多少感应。否则,这封信中表露的就不会是"弟恐终不能有家也"的失落之情了。

牟宗三于 1951 年 7 月 11 日致唐君毅的信

不过,到了 1952 年,牟宗三的婚事似乎一度有了转机。他自己似乎已经觉得有可能成婚了。在 1952 年 2 月 28 日写给唐君毅的信中,牟宗三说:

> 吾兄年来悱恻通施,故精进警策。弟则泛滥而思成家,实
> 则乱世不要亦好。现在这一段因缘很可能成。小姐所疑虑者,

对于弟之性情不甚能摸着边，对于弟之生活情调不甚能欣赏，哲学家一词尤使一般人头疼。当然她的了解程度差。弟对此有长函解说，使她拨云雾，再进一步看，颇有效力。

由这封信来看，此时的牟宗三对于婚事似乎很有信心，所谓"现在这一段姻缘很可能成"。他自己也曾努力增进双方的了解，所谓"有长函解说，使她拨云雾，再进一步看"。但是，到了 4 月份，牟宗三的恋爱又有波折。这令他再次产生了挫折之感。

在 4 月 17 日写给唐君毅的信中，牟宗三写道：

> 弟婚事最近无可成。若成，当在八九月间。此小姐与遵骝家一支不同，完全是时代风气中的女性：断灭的思想，虚无主义的情调，感受的现实主义，自私的个人主义，矜持的虚面子，没落的世家女性的形式主义，嗜尚以现实的美国为标准。这些都是她不自觉。其实，若能引起了她的感触的舒适感，亦无所谓。她的老太太及兄妹等都赞成，唯独她如兄所说有许多考虑，但亦不拒绝。弟处此，亦拖之而已，不成就算了，看来十之八九要成。关键当在秋天也。

这里"遵骝"即"张遵骝"，张之洞的曾孙。由此可知牟宗三当时谈婚论嫁的这位小姐应是一位张姓的小姐。而由信中语气来看，这位张小姐似乎已经不是 2 月份谈的那位小姐了。这里牟宗三虽然有"不成就算了"的话，笔下对这位张小姐的气质也有不少负面的评价，但似乎还是自以为能成，所以最后仍说"看来十之八九要成"。牟宗三在 5 月 27 日给徐复观的信中，也提到了这位张小姐，可以与他 17 日给唐君毅的书信彼此印证。所谓"张小姐处颇有进展。如无意外，秋冬可成婚也。弟明天到她那里去过节"。不过，这桩婚事终究还是没有成功。

1952 年 10 月前后，牟宗三还曾和一位刘姓小姐有过谈婚论嫁之事。这在 10 月 16 日和 21 日给徐复观的信中有清楚的记载。例如，在 10 月 21 日的信中，牟宗三写道：

> 刘小姐前天（星期日）始过台中，此次实是错怪了陶某。那几天，不知以何因缘，很不愉快。虽有刘小姐来台北之讯，亦未能鼓起关切与之与会。又因种种心理原因（不便写在纸上），很起反感。……等了两天，未有消息。莫老亦惊讶，说是不通（这是照常情论。这却不是怨万老头子）。这才动了火气。原想刘小姐必早回了台中，不想她竟在这里呆了一个礼拜。过去算了。对于此事，弟心中总不十分慰藉，不意其能成。昨天占了一卦，说是能成。但不知如何，总不十分与会积极。《新生报》介绍，并无岁数，她们自是乱想，不过说弟老，刘小姐亦亲自说过。

当然，从这里的文字来看，这或许只是一般意义上的谈婚论嫁。但如果没有对于爱情的向往，牟宗三显然也不会如此费心，以至于还专门"占了一卦"。不过，这一次同样是没有结果。

到了 1954 年，牟宗三在爱情生活方面依然毫无进展，在他 1 月份给唐君毅的信中，再次表示了他对爱情和婚姻失望与希望并存的复杂与无奈的心境。

> 婚事早停了，据说乙未年（后年，不久即可说明年）尚有一个好机会。过此，大概无望。能找一个人照顾生活就算了。庐毅庵先生相法甚精。彼所言当甚准也。

相信卜筮、命理之学，对于中国传统文化熏陶之下的学者来说，即便到了现代，也还是所在多有，不足为异。但是，牟宗三这里将自己的婚姻之事诉诸相士之说，也不能不说无形中透露出了其无奈的心情。至于"能找一个人照顾生活就算了"的话，则已是在爱情上近乎绝望的表示了。

作为牟宗三最为知心的友人，唐君毅一直希望自己能够和徐复观一起，帮助牟宗三尽早解决爱情与婚姻的问题。在唐君毅的相关文献尤其是书信之中，足以为证。而这也成为透露或反映牟宗三在爱情与婚姻方面的情状的证据来源。例如，在 1951 年 10 月 21 日与徐复观的信中，唐君毅最后特别提到了牟宗三的婚事，所谓"宗三兄婚事，兄可令为力否？弟看原来之人恐无一定成功之希望"，[32] 既显示了唐君毅对牟宗三的关心，无形中也透露了后者的失落。唐君毅在 1956 年 10 月与程兆熊的信中，也曾言及牟宗三感情生活上的孤寂，并嘱托程兆熊代为物色太太。他在信中写道：

> 宗兄事，有一日深夜，彼曾至旅馆谈至二时而去，其心情所感，皆所谓事在性情之际，非言语所能尽。弟亦只能体会得之。后彼来言，亦所言所谈未能尽其感伤。人之精神生活不能只孤怀长往，日常生活亦不能在寂天寂地中，此必须要有人相共，此要在有一家庭。望兄多为之留意也。[33]

显然，牟宗三一直为爱情和婚姻的问题苦恼，曾经专门到唐君毅那里诉说心事。但始终没有结果的情况一直到 1956 年都没有改变。可

32《致徐复观》，《唐君毅全集》（台北：学生书局，1991 年），卷 26，《书简》，页 70。
33《书简》，《唐君毅全集》，卷 26，页 190。

惜的是，牟宗三在爱情和婚姻方面，远不如唐君毅幸运，[34]他一直未能遇到一位足以令其情感得到安顿并在生活上能够精心照料他的女性。

不过，在1955年年底之前，牟宗三曾经与一女子交往，并一度想与该女子成婚。但是，该女子曾已婚并育有一子，也经历过不少生活的磨难。这件事想必牟宗三也一如既往地对唐君毅诉说过。然而唐君毅并不赞成，劝说牟宗三终止这一关系。最终牟宗三听从了唐君毅的建议，结束了与那位女子的交往。这件事情，在1955年12月25日唐君毅致牟宗三的信中有所记载。

> 宗三兄：十二月二十日示昨日奉到。知兄已决定遣归某女，己为之欣慰，亦殊深慨叹。在某女方面，自不免受一创伤，因彼亦人子也。唯彼有一小孩，其所历风尘中之甘苦已多，当可淡然过之。兄以拔之于风尘之心，此在古人纳之为婢妾，亦未妨不可，然终不足当君子之配，因其以往生活已使其心思散乱，芸芸众生皆旧习难除，终成家庭之祸。此处只能运慧剑断葛藤。人与人之间既有一段关系，恻怛之情亦必与一般人情相裹挟而俱动，遣之以诚并为其前途祝福斯可矣！[35]

从这封信的内容来看，是唐君毅给牟宗三的回信。之前牟宗三来信，就是告诉唐君毅他已经决定终止与那位女子的关系，所谓"遣归某女"。既然牟宗三的信在1955年12月22日，说明这段关系在此之前发生而至此已经结束。在我目前看到的牟宗三给唐君毅的书信中，没有1955年12月22日的这一封。但由唐君毅的书信可见，这位女

---

34 唐君毅也是一位极重情感的人，但唐君毅在爱情和婚姻的问题上，比牟宗三幸运得多。他与妻子谢廷光女士的爱情与婚姻故事，仅由《致廷光书》(《全集》，卷25)即可见一斑，此处不赘。
35《书简》，《唐君毅全集》，卷26，页166。

子似乎有过风尘的经历。在唐君毅看来是不配与牟宗三成婚的，所谓"不足当君子之配"。但是，从唐君毅的叙述来看，牟宗三显然是对那位女子动了真情。而牟宗三能够一度不顾那位女子的出身和经历，或许只能从爱情的角度予以解释了。可是，这一段大概令牟宗三萌生了爱情并一度打算以婚姻相成全的经历，最终也没有结果。

总之，从 1950 到 1956 年这几年之间，牟宗三有过数次感情甚至婚姻的尝试，但都未成功。从他给唐君毅和徐复观的相关书信来看，牟宗三自己常常满怀希望，以为能够成功。这一点，说明他一直怀有对爱情和婚姻的追求。无论如何，牟宗三在爱情问题上遭遇的挫折与失落，特别是他自己的情感因此而生的种种起伏跌宕，在他的这些书信中，得到了无比生动与清晰的呈现。

正是由于在希望与失望之间的多次跌落，不能不使牟宗三心灰意冷，以至于一度落入"醇酒妇人"的放任与颓废生活之中。这一点，从牟宗三分别在 1953 年年初和年尾给唐君毅的两封信中，可以很清楚地看到：

> 弟在此孤寂苦闷，只说抽象的话，又所谓醇酒妇人，已不光是婚姻问题，客观方面亦有使然之势。
>
> 弟在此太孤，所以才想婚事。这本是孤寂中的反动，所以是消极的，消极的本不易成也。弟现在生活上常有破裂之感，不是圆盈饱满的。即躯壳生活方面常有宁愿醇酒妇人之感，而心灵亦只凝缩而为著书事，书写出来就算了，这就是破裂。不能进德修业，日进无疆，此可哀也。然顺世俯仰，荒腔走调，玩弄小聪明以艺大道，则不肯为。

这两封信，前者在 1953 年 1 月 9 日，后者在 1953 年 12 月 11 日。两封信中都提到"醇酒妇人"，后一封中甚至对"常有宁愿醇酒妇人之感"

直言不讳，足见牟宗三的恋爱与婚事在这一整年中已经毫无进展，完全搁置。根据这两封信中牟宗三的自我陈述，我们可以想象，在他一整年的生活中，除了读书、写作、讲学，其余恐怕多是与酒色相伴度过的。

这种情况，在唐君毅的书信中可以得到印证。1952年12月19日，唐君毅在与徐复观的信中，恰好也提到牟宗三"宁醇酒妇人"的自我陈述，并表达了自己的挂念之情，希望能和徐复观一道，帮助牟宗三尽快解决婚姻的问题。唐君毅的信是这样写的：

> 宗三兄来函，言及其近来心境，精神只凝聚于著书，现实生活上太孤寂，有宁醇酒妇人之感。弟甚为挂念。其婚事亟须想一办法，使其精神趋乎顺，否则将更趋高亢，社会亦更接不上。彼乃天才型人，不易为人所了解也。[36]

但是，"醇酒妇人"显然不过是一种外在的虚无，丝毫不能解决牟宗三情感上的问题。他在这两封信中反复自陈的"孤寂""孤"，正是其心情的写照。此外，"醇酒妇人"只是牟宗三在爱情和婚事无望情况下的一度消沉，可以说是"孤寂"中的一度荒唐，他自己对于这种消沉与荒唐，其实是一直反观自照，知其为"破裂"生活的。第二封信的最后两段话，正说明了牟宗三不仅对自己的行为十分自觉，更能够向唐君毅坦陈这种"破裂"的生活，并直接自我反省和批评，所谓"不能进德修业，日进无疆，此可哀也"。并且，在这种破裂的生活中，牟宗三也始终没有放弃自己在社会生活中立身处世的基本原则，不肯去"顺世俯仰，荒腔走调，玩弄小聪明以艺大道"。由此可见，爱情与婚姻的极度挫折，虽然使得牟宗三一度在现实生活中陷入"醇酒妇人"的"破裂"之相，但其内心的灵明，却时刻未有丝毫的

36《致徐复观》,《书简》,《唐君毅全集》,卷26,页79。

熄灭。他能在给唐君毅的信中剖析自己的心绪，足可见这一点。

牟宗三极为强调和注重所谓"存在的感受"。这一点，在其《五十自述》等作品中有着极为生动因而感人甚深的描写和流露。而这些年间在爱情方面的挫折，一定令他"存在的感受"获得了极大地激发。他曾经有一次致函唐君毅，细致地向唐君毅描述了他在现实生活中"时有如躯体横陈旷野"的心境。对此，唐君毅有一封长信回复，详细描述了自己存在的感受，可谓"同情的共鸣"。在"将心比心"的基础上，唐君毅劝牟宗三在现实的伦理家庭生活上有所安顿。由唐君毅的回信，也足以印证牟宗三因爱情问题的刺激而在个人情感世界里的挣扎以及缺乏家庭伦理生活的孤寂。唐君毅 1955 年 11 月 10 日致牟宗三的这封信是这样写的：

> 兄来函所述兄现实生活上之心境，时有如躯体横陈旷野之感，颇令弟生感动。唯弟于此不尽完全体会。弟在大学读书及大学毕业后之数年中，其时尚未与兄相遇，亦常有种种荒凉空虚之感。有时从此中升起许多向上之感情，有时亦生起向下沉堕之意，并曾著文赞美自杀。一次于夜间，曾觉此身横陈于床上，如一大蠕动之虫，甚觉可怖；此心如与此身不相属而隔离，但旋即相合。又有两次见日月蚀时，闻民间敲椠鼓驱天狗，心中觉有无限感动。此感动中有宇宙性悲戚，亦有对自己生命之感伤。此等等感觉，近来亦不全断，但较少。此亦不必与兄感相类。但弟只能凭此等经验体会兄所感。弟意吾人之生理的有机体与自然的原始生命，对人之纯精神生活与外在之自然世界间，实有二面之原始的生疏与深渊之间隔。此在常人生活中，或因两边之山谷皆倾圮，或因由他人之心灵代为搭桥，故似两面过去皆无困难，亦不觉此中有何问题。此可算为较健康之生活型。唯因其不感此中之问题，亦即有一无明。但人在

孤独寂寞中生活过久，而其用心又素向抽象遥远之境地或慕超越世俗之理想者，[37] 则其精神先已向旷野而远驰，于是其再回来，即将感此原始的生疏与深渊之间隔，如觉不能再回到其原始生命。而此时即可生一种如 Kierkegaard 所谓存在之怖栗感。此怖栗感在交叉之深渊之上，说不出属于那面，亦非传统之神魔人禽交界之谓，而只当为一存在之实感。而此感中本当有一无限之空虚与荒凉。但人于此深渊前，亦可由纵跳而回至其自然的原始生命与生理之有机体中。而此纵跳之力，则可使吾人落于此后者之黑暗中。此黑暗及后者中之本能欲望与诸般之业力，此由于人之前生或源远流长之人类生命之往史，与其往史之通于原始人类生命、生物生命处，皆可说。到此方成魔障，而见精神之危机。而人再由此跳出时，则上述之无限之荒凉与空虚，即成为自觉的而如自四方八面迫胁而来。弟想兄近来之所感，当属于此最后阶段一类。此是由兄之精神生活之振幅较他人为大，故此感特别明朗。而其来源，亦在兄二十年来之缺乏直接之伦理生活。因此中只有直接之伦理生活可自然弥缝人之自然生命与外在世界及精神生活世界之原始之深渊，即上所谓搭桥是也。而舍此，则只能求之于宗教。但在此之宗教生活，太艰苦，不同世俗人信宗教之安稳。Kierkegaard 于此亦是在挣扎中。故弟意兄之生活仍须有直接之伦理生活，夫妇父子师生等是伦理的，此可搭上述之桥。但非伦理的生活则不然。在和尚虽不婚，但其共同之生活亦可去孤独。而在家人缺伦理生活，其精神上之担负，则至少倍之。熊先生晚年养女，亦为伦理生活。要见此事之不可少。况兄之精神生活振幅尤大耶？

---

37 此处“在孤独寂寞中生活过久，而其用心又素向抽象遥远之境地或慕超越世俗之理想者”，直接所指的自然是牟宗三，而古今中外很多思想家和学者，恐怕也都在不同程度上适用于这种描述。

相距千里，弟亦不知将何以告慰，亦不知天意之何所在。然兄之为大根器，则请兄更不复疑。[38]

牟宗三在个人情感方面的挣扎与孤寂，一直持续到 1958 年他和赵惠元女士成婚才方告结束。不过，这个时候，对牟宗三来说，婚姻或许多半已经成了他所谓"能找一个人照顾生活就算了"的事，爱情的因素恐怕也已经所剩无几。当然，这并不意味他后来的婚姻没有感情，只是那种感情，也许更多地已经体现为亲情而非爱情了。晚年的牟宗三在给孙女鸿贞的信中，有这样一段沉痛的话：

我这个家并不是很健全的。你叔叔是个废人，你奶奶也不是很谐和的。而我也老了。

如此来看的话，他在《五十自述》中回忆那个马戏团的少女时，之所以会写下"这是我一生唯一的一次爱情之流露，此后再也没有那种干净无邪而又是恋情的爱怜心境了"这样的话，或许就不难理解了。

七、"觉情"说

与牟宗三丰沛的情感世界相匹配的，正是其哲学思想中"觉情"这一观念。根据前文的考察，我们可以说，恰恰是由于牟宗三对"情感"的几乎各个方面都有丰富而深刻的体验，"情"在其哲学思想中扮演一个中心的角色，恐怕就是理所当然的了。当然，牟宗三对"觉情"观念的强调，不仅可以视为其情感世界的理性表达，更是中国哲学传统内在

38《书简》，《唐君毅全集》，卷 26，页 162–163。

理路的必然结果。他在道德情感问题上与康德的异趣以及对于康德的批评，正是后一特点的自然反映。不过，"觉情"这一观念在以往的牟宗三思想研究中几乎是缺席的。什么是"觉情"？"觉情"在牟宗三的思想中居于什么样的位置？"觉情"与牟宗三哲学思想中其他的核心观念又是怎样的关系？本文这一部分所要专门探讨的，正是这些既有研究未曾措意的问题。

如果说《五十自述》是最能够展现牟宗三情感世界的一部著作，那么，"觉情"一词出现频率最高的，也正是在《五十自述》。前文提到，该书开始的部分描述了"伤春之情"。就在那段文字之后，牟宗三紧接着就提到了"觉情"一词。所谓"满盈无着是春情，虚无怖栗是'觉情'"。而在"觉情"之后，牟宗三自己在括号内注明"觉悟向道之情"。如此看来，"虚无怖栗"作为一种情感本身，还并不就是"觉情"。严格而论，现实世界和人生的"一无所有"和"生命无挂搭"之感，令人超越"虚无怖栗"而"觉悟向道"的情感，才是"觉情"的内容。这一层意思，在"虚无怖栗是'觉情'（觉悟向道之情）"这一句中还并不十分清楚。在《五十自述》全书倒数第三段话中，这个意思就表达得十分明确了。牟宗三说：

> 我已说过，真正虚无之感来临时，甚至良知、天命之性，亦成不相干的。何况上帝？因此，这函着的对于有之要求真成无着处的绝境。内外全空，所以怖栗，但是不要紧。你就让其"内外全空而痛苦怖栗"之感无萦绊地浮现着，你就让他惶惑无着吧！你就让他含泪深叹吧！一无所有，只有此苦，只有此怖，只有此叹。此之谓苦、怖、叹之解放，亦得曰苦怖叹三昧。你让这苦怖叹浮现着荡漾着，你在这里，可慢慢滋生一种"悲情"：无所悲而自悲的悲情。此时一无所有，只有此悲，此谓悲情三昧。这悲情三昧之浮现也还是消极的，但仍表示一种

> 内心之战斗：这函着对于我这可悲的情境之否定之要求。我如何能消除这可悲的情境？这悲情三昧是可贵的，它就是消除这情境的根芽。由这悲情三昧，你将慢慢转生那满腔子是悱恻恻隐的慧根觉情。到此方真是积极的，你所要求的"真有"即在这里。这是你的真主体，也是你的真生命。由苦怖叹之解放而成为"苦怖叹三昧"必然函着"悲情三昧"，由悲情三昧必然函着"觉情三昧"，这本是一体三相。[39]

如果说这段话澄清了"觉情"一词的含义，表明"觉情"并不是"虚无怖栗"所"滋生"的消极否定的"悲情"，而是由此"悲情"进一步所"转生"的积极肯定的"悱恻恻隐"之情，那么，《五十自述》全书的最后一段话，尤其所谓"一切从此觉情流，一切还归此觉情"，则充分显示了"觉情"一词在牟宗三思想中的核心位置。

> 凡我所述，皆由实感而来。我已证苦证悲，未敢言证觉。然我以上所述，皆由存在的实感确然见到是如此。一切归"证"，无要歧出。一切归"实"，不要虚戏。一切平平，无有精奇。证如窒悲，彰所泯能，皆幻奇彩，不脱习气（习气有奇彩，天理无奇彩）。千佛菩萨，大乘小乘，一切圣贤，俯就垂听，各归寂默，当下自证。证苦证悲证觉，无佛无耶无儒。消融一切，成就一切。一切从此觉情流，一切还归此觉情。[40]

"觉情"一词，在《心体与性体》中还曾经被牟宗三表述为"本体论的觉情"（ontological feeling）。而当"觉情"之前被冠以"本体

39《五十自述》，《全集》，册32，页174-175。
40《五十自述》，《全集》，册32，页176。这里"一切从此觉情流，一切还归此觉情"应当是借自《华严经》"无不从此法界流，无不还归此法界"的句式。

论的"这个形容词时，就进一步触及"觉情"一词的含义问题了。"觉情"固然不是消极、否定性的悲情，更是积极、肯定的"怵惕恻隐"之情，但一般意义上的"情"，总属于感性经验的领域和层面，并不能成为一种"本体的"东西。从西方思想传统的主流尤其是康德批判哲学建立之后的立场来看，显然如此。但是，牟宗三使用"本体论的觉情"，显然是针对这一传统，而特意强调"觉情"与一般作为感性经验的情感有着根本的不同。那么，这种具有"本体论"地位的"觉情"究竟具有怎样的特点呢？这一点，在牟宗三批评康德关于"道德情感"的理解时，得到了进一步的说明。

牟宗三对康德"道德情感"的批评，以及在此基础上对"觉情"的进一步说明，主要反映在他翻译康德的《实践理性批判》和《道德形而上学原理》并将两书的中译合为一册出版的《康德的道德哲学》一书之中。牟宗三撰写《五十自述》时尚在中年，而他翻译康德的《实践理性批判》与《道德形而上学原理》时已在晚年。因此，这个时候牟宗三的"觉情"观念，可以视为其晚年定论了。

严格而论，牟宗三的《康德的道德哲学》并不只是一部译作，同时也是反映牟宗三自己哲学思想的文本。他曾经花了很长的篇幅以注释的方式表达了他对"道德情感"的看法，"觉情"如何具有"本体论"的意义？它与中国哲学尤其儒家哲学传统中其他一些核心的观念如"理""心"之间具有怎样的关系？这些都在牟宗三对康德"道德情感"的注释和批评中得到了进一步澄清与说明。

康德如此说道德情感，以及不允许假定有一种道德的感取，恰如朱子说心以及其反对以觉训仁。朱子视知觉为智之事，即是视之为"指向一对象的一种知解的（理论的）知觉之力量"。但"以觉训仁"中的那个"觉"（明道与上蔡所意谓者）却只是道德情感，而不指向对象，亦不是一知解的知觉力

303

量，此可名曰"觉情"，此亦可说"觉"，即"恻然有所觉"之觉。康德在此只说情（情感之情），我们可加一"觉"字而直说"觉情"。但此觉情却又不只是一种感受，只是主观的；它是心是情亦是理，所以它是实体性的仁体，亦可说是觉体，此则比康德进一步。纵使就"是非之心智也"而言，智亦不是如朱子所理解，为"一种指向对象的知解的知觉力量"（借用康德语），为一认知字，而乃是本心仁体底一种决断力，实践的知觉力量（觉情之知觉力量），非知解的（知识的）知觉力量，故阳明由之而言良知以代表本心仁体也。故此"是非之心智也"之智亦同时是心是情是理者。此则既驳朱子亦驳康德。[41]

若康德所说的道德情感上提而为觉情，即以之指目本心仁体或良知之知体，则此即是吾人之性体，心性是一，心理是一，则此性体亦不能被获得，亦不能说"去有此性体"为一义务。因为既是性体，焉能再说被获得？义务乃是性体之所发以赋诸吾人者。[42]

在这两段文字中，牟宗三对"觉情"这一观念的含义讲得再清楚不过了。"觉情"是什么？它"是心是情亦是理"，"是实体性的仁体，亦可说是觉体"。显然，在这两段文字的表述中，儒家哲学最为核心的观念，"心"或"本心"、"性"或"性体"、"理"、"良知"以及"仁体"，可以说都被统合到了"觉情"这一概念之中。对牟宗三来说，这些概念究极而言都可以说是异名同实的关系。换言之，在本体的意义上，对于"心""性""情""理""仁"或者说"心体""性体""觉情""天理""仁体"这些不同的概念来说，各自的所指其实为一。

41《康德的道德哲学》，《全集》，册15，页504。
42《康德的道德哲学》，《全集》，册15，页504–505。

牟宗三的这一思想，早在他撰写《五十自述》时其实已经有所流露，只不过当时他的用语是"慧根觉情"、"心觉"和"常性"。

> "天生蒸民，有物有则，民之秉夷〔同彝〕，好是懿德。"这是不错的，这是点出"心觉"。孔子说："为此诗者，其知道乎？"蒸民即众民。物，事也。有此事必有成此事之则。朱子注云："如有耳目，则有聪明之德，有父子，则有慈孝之心。"夷，常也。言常性。秉夷言所秉受之"常性"。民所秉受之常性即好此善德，言民有好此善德之常性。有此事即有此"则"，此则亦由常性发，故顺其常性而好之。此孟子所谓"理义之悦心"。故此"常性"即心之"慧根觉情"也。[43]

牟宗三如此重视"觉情"，将其视为一个高度统合性的终极观念，绝不只是出于抽象的理智思辨，而有其深刻的实感与体证。对于那种实感和体证或者说身心经验，牟宗三自己多次有过具体而生动的说明。例如，在《五十自述》中，他特别提到曾有一晚自己在旅店里忽闻邻舍传来梵音时而产生的"悲情三昧"。对牟宗三来说，那种情感是如此的强烈而深刻，如他所谓："我直定在这声音、这哀怨中而直证'悲情三昧'。那一夜，我所体悟的，其深微哀怜是难以形容的。"

> 我在这将近十年的长时期里，因为时代是瓦解，是虚无，我个人亦是瓦解，是虚无，我不断的感受，不断的默识，亦不断地在这悲情三昧的痛苦哀怜中。我让我的心思、生命，乃至生命中的一尘一介一毛一发，彻底暴露，彻底翻腾，彻底虚无，而浮露清澄出这"悲情三昧"。一夕，我住在旅店里，半

---

43 《五十自述》，《全集》，册32，页144。

夜三更，忽梵音起自邻舍。那样的寂静，那样的抑扬低徊，那样的低徊而摇荡，直将遍宇宙彻里彻外最深最深的抑郁哀怨一起摇拽而出，全宇宙的形形色色一切表面"自持其有"的存在，全浑化而为低徊哀叹无端无着是以无言之大悲。这勾引起我全幅的悲情三昧。此时只有这声音。遍宇宙是否有哀怨有抑郁藏于其中，这无人能知。但这声音却摇荡出全幅的哀怨。也许就是这抑扬低徊，低徊摇荡的声音本身哀怨化了这宇宙。不是深藏定向的哀怨，乃是在低徊摇荡中彻里彻外，无里无外，全浑化而为一个哀怨。此即为"悲情三昧"。这悲情三昧的梵音将一切吵闹寂静下来，将一切骚动平静下来，将一切存在浑化而为无有，只有这声音，这哀怨。也不管它是件佛事的梵音，或是寄雅兴者所奏的梵音，或是由其他什么发出的梵音，反正就是这声音，这哀怨。我直定在这声音、这哀怨中而直证"悲情三昧"。那一夜，我所体悟的，其深微哀怜是难以形容的。[44]

这种对于外人来说甚至近乎神秘体验的经历，应该发生在 1956 年 12 月初，因为 1956 年 12 月 9 日牟宗三在给唐君毅信中，曾经特别提到这一令他在身心两个方面都产生极大感动的"最具体""最真实"经历。他说：

> 上星期夜宿旅舍，隔壁梵音忽起，哀感低徊，穷于赞叹，深悟佛之悲情。此是最具体、最真实的，事后亦写不出也。

既然此信写于 12 月 9 日，而事在"上星期"，所以当在 12 月初

---

[44]《五十自述》，《全集》，册 32，页 152–153。

的某一天。无疑，对牟宗三来说，这一"最真实""最具体"的身心经验其意义显然非同寻常，以至于1968年他在给香港中文大学艺术系的学生演讲《美的感受》时，再次提到，可见他对当时那种心情感受得是多么深刻。他说：

> 又有一次，我夜宿在一家旅客里，半夜三更正在睡觉迷离之际，忽有乐声起于邻舍，那声音的低回悠扬大类梵音。在它的抑扬回旋之中，直可把那天地的哀怨给全部摇拽出来。我们常说天地也含悲。我想这天地的哀荣就是天地之美、神明之容了。我常有这苍凉之悲感的。[45]

显而易见，这样一种具体而真实的身心经验，也可以说恰恰正是牟宗三自己"觉情"的流露和作用。对此，牟宗三也很清楚，所以他紧接着上面那段话不久就说："我之体证'悲情三昧'本是由一切崩解撒离而起，由虚无之痛苦感受而证。这原是我们的'清净本心'，也就是这本心的'慧根觉情'。"[46]并且，牟宗三1988年12月在为《五十自述》撰写的自序最后就曾直接指出，他后来思想的展开，其根源就在于这样一种"实感"。所谓"吾今忽忽不觉已八十矣。近三十年来之发展即是此自述中实感之发皇"。[47]

通过以上基于原始文献的分析，可见"觉情"一说在牟宗三成熟的思想中贯穿始终，完全可以说是牟宗三哲学的一个"核心观念"。不过，我在以往也曾经指出，牟宗三哲学的"核心概念"是"自由无限心"。[48]这一判断主要是基于牟宗三哲学最主要的著作《现象与物自

45《牟宗三先生晚期文集》，《全集》，册27，页204。
46《五十自述》，《全集》，册32，页153。
47《五十自述》，《全集》，册32，页4。
48 彭国翔：《牟宗三哲学的基本架构与核心概念》，收入《儒家传统与中国哲学：新世纪的回顾与前瞻》（石家庄：河北人民出版社，2009年），页203-218。

身》和《圆善论》。那么，这一判断是否与我如今将"觉情"视为牟宗三思想的核心观念有所冲突呢？显然，根据前文对于"觉情"观念含义的考察，在牟宗三自己看来，"觉情"和"自由无限心"也不过是"异名同实"的关系，在本体的意义上，二者本来是一。

事实上，意识到各种不同的观念在本体的意义上具备"异名同实"的关系，在儒家的哲学传统中原本也是渊源有自。比如，宋明理学的传统中就有不少人意识到，《中庸》"言性不言心"，《大学》"言心不言性"，但其实"心"与"性"的本体为一。牟宗三《中国哲学的特质》中的一个核心论点，所谓"主观性原则"与"客观性原则"为一；《心体与性体》中讨论宋明理学时强调的一个核心论点，所谓"天道性命相贯通"，其实都是在指出"心"与"性"在本体意义上的是一非二。

不过，虽然儒家思想中的这些核心观念在本体上是一非二，牟宗三提出并强调的"觉情"一说，不但在中国哲学传统自身的发展脉络之中，即便在当今世界哲学整体的发展脉络之中，仍有其特别的意义。在本文的最后部分，就让我对此稍加提示，以结束这篇专题性的研究。

在20世纪以来当代中国哲学的发展脉络中，除了牟宗三的"觉情"说之外，也有其他几位对"情"这一观念极为重视的学者。例如，蒙培元曾经专门对中国哲学中的"情感"问题予以考察，通过分析情感与理性、欲望、意志和知识等方面的关系，指出了中国哲学重"情"以及作为一种"情感哲学"的特征。[49] 对于"情"是否具有本体的意义，尽管蒙培元似乎仍有语焉未详之处，但他将"情感"视为与"理性"同样重要的方面，则距离牟宗三"本体论的觉情"，似乎也相距不远了。至于李泽厚的"情本体"一说，学界更是广为人知，不

---

49 蒙培元:《情感与理性》（北京：中国人民大学出版社，2009年）。

仅同样强调了中国哲学传统重"情"的一面，更是将"情"作为一个哲学观念特别加以发挥并赋予其"本体"的地位。他以"理本体"和"情本体"分判中西哲学传统主流在基本取向上的差异，也可以说能够得中西哲学传统之大者。

不过，除了认为牟宗三"纯以西方模式的'理'说中国哲学"这一评判有失公允之外，[50]李泽厚的"本体"一词，已经不是形而上学意义上的"本体"概念，如他自己所谓："这个'情本体'即无本体，它已不再是传统意上的'本体'。……情本体之所以仍名之为'本体'，不过是指它即人生的真谛、存在的真实、最后的意义，如此而已。"[51]而这个意义上的"情本体"，正如陈来所指出的，"终究难免于中国传统哲学对'作用是性'的批评，情之意义在感性生活和感性形式，还是在用中讨生活，不能真正立体。"[52]事实上，李泽厚所谓"传统意义上的'本体'"，正是形而上学意义上的本体。而无论我们对"形而上学"采取如何的看法，是西方以柏拉图主义为主流的形而上学，视本体超绝于现象世界或经验世界之外，还是以儒学为代表的中国哲学"体用不二"的形而上学，视本体内在于现象世界或经验世界之中，本体自身都不是世间诸相之一，或者说不能化约为现象或经验之一。[53]牟宗三的"本体"，则恰恰坚持了这一层意义。因此，也正是在这个意义上，根据以上的考察，牟宗三的"觉情"才可以说是真正的"情本体"。

此外，正如牟宗三自己所说，具有本体地位的"觉情"同时也就是"心体"、"性体"、"天理"和"仁体"。而就这一点来说，对于陈

---

50 李泽厚:《该中国哲学登场了》(上海:上海译文出版社，2011 年)，页 55。

51 李泽厚:《该中国哲学登场了》(上海:上海译文出版社，2011 年)，页 75。

52 陈来:《论李泽厚的情本体哲学》,《复旦学报》(社会科学版)，2014 年第 3 期，页 3。

53 彭国翔:《重思"形而上学"——中国哲学的视角》,《中国社会科学》，2015 年第 11 期，页 60–75。

来所建构的"仁本体"而言,[54] 如果"情"不能不构成"仁"的一个重要内容,那么,"仁学本体论"与"觉情"说之间,应当也是所异不胜其同的。[55] 事实上,陈来在其仁学本体论的论述中,也正有"情感本体"的专章讨论。这一点,恐怕只能说是反映了 20 世纪以来中国哲学传统自身的现代发展在"情"这一观念上的"理有固然"与"势所必至"。

现在,再让我们看看西方哲学。虽然"情"的问题自始即不能说没有在西方哲学中受到讨论,如亚里士多德以及希腊化时期的斯多亚(Stoics)和伊壁鸠鲁(Epicureans)学者在其伦理学中关于"emotion"的论说,但将理性主义作为西方哲学传统的主流,应当是大体不错的观察。不过,20 世纪晚期以来,"情"的问题日益引起西方不少一流哲学家的关注与反省。像努斯鲍姆(Martha C. Nussbaum)这样出身希腊哲学研究而涉猎极为广泛的哲学家固然不论,[56] 即便在素重分析哲学传统(analytical tradition)中的若干哲学家中,"情"的问题也同样引发了深入的思考。正如所罗门(Robert C. Solomon)在其《真实面对我们的情感》一书导论开头所说:"我们不像亚里士多德所界定的那样仅仅是理性的动物,我们也拥有情感。我们通过我们的情感来生活,是我们的情感给予了我们生命的意义。我们对什么感兴趣,我们为什么而着迷,我们爱什么人,什么东西让我们生气,什么东西令我们厌倦,所有这些东西定义了我们,赋予我们品格,构成了我们之

---

54 陈来:《仁学本体论》(北京:生活·读书·新知三联书店,2014 年)。

55 当然,如果就"仁体"或"仁本体"作为一个确定的哲学概念而言,牟宗三只是点到为止,并未有详细的解说。而陈来则专门对此进行了阐释,其"仁学本体论",就是以"仁体"或"仁本体"为"拱心石"而进行的哲学建构。也正是在其多方位、多层次的诠释与建构中,"仁体"或"仁本体"丰富与深邃的含义获得了更为具体而清晰的展示。

56 努斯鲍姆的许多著作都涉及对"情"深入细致的探讨,包括 *The Therapy of Desire: Theory and Practice in Hellenistic Ethics*, Princeton University Press, 1996; *Upheavals of Thought: The Intelligence of Emotions*, Cambridge University Press, 2001; *Hiding from Humanity: Disgust, Shame, and the Law*, Princeton University Press, 2004; 等等。

所以为我们。"[57]无论是所罗门自己所著的《真实面对我们的情感》,还是之前他邀请分析哲学传统中若干卓有建树的哲学家分头撰写而编成的《情的思考:当代哲学家论情感》,[58]都是对"情"极为深入细致的哲学探索。

当然,无论这些西方哲学家对"情"的探讨如何穷深研几,"情"是否可以具有"本体"的地位?即如牟宗三所谓的存在着一种"本体论的觉情",恐怕仍是需要大部分西方哲学家殚精竭虑的。例如,因继承休谟而非亚里士多德的传统而在晚近"德行伦理学"(virtue ethics)领域独树一帜的斯洛特(Michael Slote),也属于分析哲学的阵营,这些年同样注重对于"情"的哲学思考。并且,他虽然不通中文,近年来却对中国哲学传统表现出了格外的兴趣。[59]但是,对于"情"的理解,斯洛特仍然只能在后期康德或主流西方哲学的意义上将其仅仅限于经验现象和心理学的领域,而无法设想一种不为经验所限、不仅仅是一种心理构造而具有"本体"地位的"情"。不过,斯洛特等人虽然无法设想"本体论的觉情",但就前引所罗门所说的话而言,如果"情"是某种界定人之所以为人的东西,那么,"情"的本体地位,也许已经是呼之欲出了。此外,晚近有些西方学者有所谓"情感本体论"(emotion ontology 或 the ontology of emotion)一说,往往还结合神经科学(neurosciences)加以研究。[60]虽然这基本上还只是从"本体论"的角度来思考"情"的问题,与将"情"本身视为

57 Robert C. Solomon, *True to Our Feelings: What Our Emotions Are Really Telling Us*, Oxford University Press, 2007.

58 Robert C. Solomon, *Thinking About Feeling: Contemporary Philosophers on Emotions*, Oxford University Press, 2004.

59 斯洛特著、刘建芳、刘梁剑译:《重启世界哲学的宣言:中国哲学的意义》,《学术月刊》,2015年第5期。

60 例如Richard J. Davidson, Klaus R. Scherer, and H. Hill Goldsmith, *Handbook of Affective Sciences*, Oxford University Press, 2003. Katrina Triezenberg, "The Ontology of Emotion," Ph.D. thesis, Purdue University, 2005.

具有本体论的地位仍有根本的不同，但毕竟已经有向本体论而趋的态势。就此而言，牟宗三的"觉情"说，也许未尝不可以说已经着了西方哲学传统对"情"的反省的先鞭。

清人张潮（1650—1707）曾在其《幽梦影》中说："情之一字，所以维持世界。"的确，情感与理性是任何人都具备且彼此不可化约的两个方面，不会"此消彼长"。即便被认为是最为理性的哲学家，情感的方面不仅不会减弱，反而与其理性一样，较之常人往往更强。"大智之人，必有深情"，应该是一个不错的判断。并且，情感的力量在决定人的行为时，常常比理性更为强大。在儒家看来，人的终极实在如"仁""恻隐之心"，历来也恰恰不仅是道德理性，同时也是道德情感。对此，牟宗三的情感世界及其"觉情"说，可以说恰恰提供了一个绝佳的案例。

二、书评论文

柯文的镜子

——评《向史而言：勾践故事在 20 世纪中国的传播》

董铁柱

（北京师范大学—香港浸会大学联合国际学院）

美国汉学家柯文（Paul Cohen）的《向史而言》一书像一面镜子，不同的读者在其中会发现不同的影像。或者也可以说，柯文的《向史而言》至少可以被看成三面不同的镜子。

一

第一面镜子是送给他自己，或者说是以他为代表的研究中国历史的西方汉学家的。正如柯文自己所言，他一开始并不想研究勾践，当时他甚至都没听说过勾践这个名字，更不了解勾践是谁。他想研究的是在饱受磨难的 20 世纪里，中国人面对国耻的态度。这当然本身就是一个很有趣的话题。然而在搜集材料的过程中，柯文注意到"勾践"这个名字在各种情况下反复出现，于是转而对勾践产生了兴趣。他所思考的第一个问题是：为何在中国几乎家喻户晓的勾践，对很多研究中国史的美国汉学家来说却是一个陌生的名字？

对柯文来说，似乎这个问题才是他想真正探讨的，描述勾践故事在 20 世纪各个时间段具体如何在中国传播的过程，不过是为了寻找这一核心问题的答案。如果从这个角度来看，勾践也好，中国的国耻也罢，都是柯文寻求广义历史规律的切入点。也就是说，他寻求的不仅是中国某一历史现象、历史事件或是历史阶段的发展脉络，而是通过考察中国的某一历史现象或事件来揭橥同样存在于其他国家或民族历史中的规律。

在这个意义上，柯文彻底完成了从"中国历史学"家到"历史学"家的转变。其完成于 20 世纪 70 年代的早年著作《在传统与现代性之间：王韬与晚清改革》[1]有着深深的"汉学家"烙印，"传统和现代"正是费正清、史华慈等早期哈佛的中国研究专家们专门用来剖析中国近现代发展的一个重要理论利器。出身于哈佛学派的柯文自然也继承了这一理论。他在书中探究了王韬于晚清参与改革的经历，为理解中国晚清思潮、政局和社会变迁之间的关系提供了新的思路，然而其出发点在于诠释"中国"。

柯文关于义和团的著作《历史三调》就已经不再满足于把中国历史局限于"中国"了，[2]当他在阐述三种不同的"历史"时，义和团更多的只不过是这一理论的一个例子。无论是讲述作为事件的义和团，作为经历的义和团，还是作为神话的义和团，他并不是要找出义和团之所以出现或失败的原因，而是想通过考察义和团这一历史事件中不同种类的历史叙述，来证明这"三种历史"理论的正确。这样的理论，当然也同样适用于其他国家或是其他文化的其他历史事件。

《向史而言》可以说是《历史三调》的继续。柯文认为各个文化都有着自己特殊的"共同记忆"。对于该文化圈中的每一个人来说，这些记忆不需要从书本中学习得到，而是在每一个人的成长过程中耳濡目染不知不觉就了解的。而这种记忆对于该文化圈外的人来说，则可能是完全陌生的，甚至是没有地方可以学习或了解到的——因为圈内人觉得这些记忆并不需要专门写成书或是从书本上学习。在柯文看来，勾践的故事对于中国人来说就是这样的一种记忆。

---

1 柯文：《在传统与现代性之间：王韬与晚清改革》；南京：江苏人民出版社，2006 年。

2 柯文：《历史三调：作为事件、经历和神话的义和团》；南京：江苏人民出版社，2000 年。

当然，"共同记忆"理论并不是柯文的专利。在著作《告诉我一个故事》（*Tell Me A Story*）中，认知心理学家罗杰·申克（Roger C. Schank）罗列了五种不同类型的故事：官方的、创造的、第一手经验的、二手的和文化共同的。柯文采用了申克的理论，认为"尽管这几种类型之间并没有明确的界限，有一个故事可以归为不止一个类型，但是勾践故事明显属于最后一个类型：文化共同的。这意味着它是一个被无数人所分享的故事，而这些人生活在中国文化的世界里"。[3]

根据申克的理论，像勾践这样的故事常常是"被提到而不是讲到"的。这意味着人们在交流时会用极为省略的方式提到它们。在《向史而言》的第二章中，柯文考察了清朝末年和民国时期勾践故事是如何在各种场合被提及的，他列举了大量的例子，表明尽管勾践故事被提到的方式都很简略，但是却会起到足够的效果，让人直接将勾践与当下的国耻相联系。1904 年，刚创立不久的《东方杂志》上连续发表了多篇讨论中国人应该怎样面对国耻的文章，其中不少都提到了勾践，不过它们并没有详细讲述勾践的故事以号召和激励国人，而都只是简单提及勾践，默认读者应该对勾践故事很熟悉。例如一篇由笔名为"可轩"的作者所作的文章中只是说到"勾践保会稽而霸"，以此表明中国所受的耻辱是暂时的。

更为有趣的例子来自当时的香烟广告。由于 1915 年 5 月日本强迫中国签订"二十一条"，在随后每年的五月，大家都会纪念国耻日。1925 年和 1926 年的 5 月间，上海的一些报纸上出现了金龙牌香烟的广告，广告明确指出吸金龙牌香烟是爱国之举。广告最左端的小插图里，一群人正站在树下，树枝上挂着一根根写着"国耻"的纸条。在广告的底部中间偏左处，是一个坐在一堆木柴之上的勾践，手里举着一个苦胆悬在嘴上，双眼正好注视着树上的纸条。柯文觉得有趣的

3　Paul Cohen, *Speaking to History: The Story of King Goujian in Twentieth-Century China*, University of California Press, 2010, p.230.

是："尽管这个广告的目的在于推销金龙牌香烟的同时，在勾践和警告国人勿忘国耻之间建立明确的联系，然而广告的设计者显然觉得没有必要暗示读者那个坐着的人是谁，或是他手里举着的是什么东西。"[4]

和不需要任何暗示的中国人相反，柯文坦白地承认自己虽然专研中国历史几十年，但是当第一次看到这样的图片时，对图中的人物完全一头雾水，更不知道那颗东西是苦胆。他咨询了不少同样致力于中国近现代史研究的西方汉学家，他们也对此一无所知。正是这种勇于承认自己知识面局限的勇气让柯文发现了一个非常有趣的研究切入点：在特定的历史环境下，中国人熟悉而西方人不了解的中国典故对中国社会所起到的影响。

在第三、第四章里，柯文分别探讨了 1949 年后蒋介石如何在台湾利用宣传勾践故事鼓舞士气，以及大陆的作家和戏剧家们如何通过勾践故事阐发政治主张。毫无疑问，作为几乎每个中国人都熟悉的故事，勾践的"卧薪尝胆"在台湾和大陆的特定历史阶段都起到了潜移默化的作用。通过勾践故事这个切入点，西方汉学家的的确确可以更好地了解中国人在某些历史环境下的言行举止，可以更深入地分析中国文化。更重要的是，他们可以以勾践的故事为起点，去找寻更多的类似故事，从而扩大西方人对于中国历史和文化的视阈。

而最重要的是，在将勾践故事定位为文化的共同记忆之后，勾践故事就不再仅仅是一个中国的故事，它和世界上其他国家的文化共同记忆一样，成了可以证明中国文化与世界文化相似性的载体。于是，柯文的勾践研究就不仅是"中国"研究，而是世界性的"历史"研究。

这样的区分并不是在玩文字游戏。众所周知，中国研究在美国长期以来在很大程度上属于地区研究。柯文毕业于哈佛大学，在哈佛，

---

4 同上，p. 59。

中国历史的研究隶属于东亚语言文明系，而不是历史系。这微妙地反映了一个事实：二战后以哈佛大学为代表的美国汉学研究就初衷而言，是将中国视为对手，试图通过了解中国的方方面面，以期找到制衡中国的最佳手段，这与本尼迪克特的《菊与刀》的目的相仿佛，后者也是通过研究日本文化的特点来找到处理战后日本的途径。这样做的一个理论前提，是认为中国文化和西方文化有着本质的差异，因此才需要专门的研究。其研究的侧重点也是为了找到差异，而不是找到共同点。

当柯文在《向史而言》中将勾践故事在中国的影响与马萨达事件对犹太人的影响相比较，[5] 并进而认为两者有着共通性时，他的研究目的显然从发掘中国历史的特性转移到了发现中国文化与西方文化的共性。这是否意味着美国汉学家的中国历史研究中的政治色彩开始淡化，是否意味着中国历史研究对美国学者来说开始成为"历史"研究，而不仅是"中国"研究？当然，这并没有简单的答案。

二

对于研究中国历史的中国学者来说，柯文的《向史而言》也提供了一面很好的镜子。

将勾践故事这样在中国家喻户晓的典故作为研究的切入点，这本身也会给中国的中国史学者以启发。21 世纪以来，越来越多的中国历史学者也不再局限于政治史、经济史或是社会史的研究，开始开辟新的研究点。不过对中国的学者来说，《向史而言》最大的借鉴之处可能并不在于提供了新的研究切入点，而是在于柯文在研究中所做的

---

5 公元 73 年，在马萨达山顶要塞的一群奋锐党守卫者集体自杀，这是犹太人反对罗马起义行动中的最后一部分，这一事件标志着犹太人从他们的故土被放逐长达数个世纪的开始。而现代犹太人觉得这一事件和他们有着紧密的关联。

跨学科努力。

也许有不少中国的中国史学者会觉得柯文的研究流于琐碎。诚然，柯文在第六章探讨改革开放以来勾践故事在大陆的影响时，在材料的选择上有一些值得商榷之处。这一时期柯文所使用的主要文献材料都来自网络搜索，他个人也非常赞赏网络搜索引擎给研究带来的便利。然而搜索引擎的弊端同样明显，在众多的材料中柯文所找到的一些材料可能并不具有足够的代表性或权威性。

柯文试图表明尽管在改革开放后勾践故事的传播不再具有强烈的政治色彩，然而在爱国主义教育、党员教育、个人和集体奋斗等方面，勾践故事依然有着广泛的生命力。遗憾的是，他所引用的一些中小学教师所撰写的关于加强爱国主义教育的文章出自中国较为低端的报刊，以此来说明勾践故事在新时代爱国主义教育中的影响，似乎缺乏足够的说服力，和前几章所采用的材料相比存在着明显的不足。

可是瑕不掩瑜，柯文在材料选择上存在的问题，恰恰反映了他在材料运用上的广度，而这正是可以给中国学者提供借鉴之处。作为一个历史学家，柯文对于材料的选择可谓种类繁多。之所以说是材料而不是文献，是因为他所使用的材料绝不局限于文献。如前所述，香烟广告都可以成为分析的对象，这让人看到了罗兰·巴特的风格，尽管后者是在文化批评领域这么做的。除了香烟广告外，柯文所使用的材料还包括歌词、连环画、戏曲、话剧、电视剧、宣传海报和中小学课本等通常历史学家会忽视的元素。

因此基于种类繁多的材料，柯文在一定程度上在《向史而言》中展示了跨学科研究的趋向。在第五章中，柯文着重分析了两位中国当代作家关于勾践故事的作品，分别是萧军的长篇历史小说《吴越春秋史话》和白桦的话剧《吴王金戈越王剑》。他不但介绍了两位作家的创作历程和特色，而且在对两位作家的作品进行研究时，做了非常细致的文本分析，让人觉得这是一位文学领域教授所做的工作。例如在讨论《吴越春秋史话》时，柯文指出伯嚭这个吴国的大奸臣"在吴国战败后，几乎所有的版本中勾践都会将其处死，以作为其背叛君王和国家的惩罚。但是在萧军的小说中，这个腐败的吴国大臣有着非常不同的命运。也许是为了衬托勾践对那些忠心耿耿为他和越国服务的人的忘恩负义，大奸臣伯嚭并没有被处死，而是在越国朝廷内获得了一个高官要职"。[6]

　　文学批评和历史研究的结合当然不是新鲜事物，然而却是很多大陆的历史学者所忽视的。这关系到如何看待文学作品在历史研究中的地位问题。卢卡奇在《小说理论》中指出小说是一个时代的史诗，通过文学作品可以反窥一个时代的精神。柯文能够选择萧军和白桦的作品作为研究对象，并令人信服地探讨了两者作品中的政治暗示，尤其是明确指出了白桦剧本中所包含的政治寓言，这一切充分表明柯文对于如何在历史研究中选择和分析文学作品有着自己的判断。当代文学史的一部分也就自然地成为广义历史研究的一部分。

　　应该说，柯文将文学批评与研究融入历史研究的做法并不是仅仅表现在第五章。在第三章柯文就详细地分析了在当时台湾地区出现的关于勾践的剧本，比如陈文泉所作的《勾践与西施》。在第四章讨论 20 世纪 60 年代大陆的勾践热时，柯文也对曹禺的《胆剑篇》做了详尽分析。柯文敏锐地注意到勾践形象在台湾和大陆的不同，指出：在台湾的文学作品中，勾践的形象一般都是正面的，几乎不会提到勾践在复仇成功后的种种负面行为；而在大陆，勾践的形象大多充满了各种问题。他进一步指出了这种差异背后的原因，在台湾勾践的形象代指的是蒋介石，而在大陆由于历史唯物主义理论和阶级论的流行，很

---

6 Paul Cohen, *Speaking to History:The Story of King Goujian in Twentieth-Century China*, University of California Press, 2010，p. 185。

多作家认为勾践作为一个封建时代的帝王，是不可能完美无缺的。当柯文做这样的分析时，很难将其狭义地归类为"历史学"家，似乎也完全可以被视为一位文学评论家。就这一点而言，柯文超越了他的两位老师：费正清和史华慈。他们对中国历史的研究基本上停留在传统的历史领域，还没有包含文学评论。

在第二章讲述民国时期的勾践故事传播时，柯文也指出这些传播于 20 世纪 20 年代、30 年代和 40 年代的勾践故事有着一些明显特性。首先，勾践一直被描述成为了一雪前耻而甘愿遭受生活的贫困和个人的羞辱的形象，与此同时，他耐心准备，等待越国可以复仇成功的日子到来。其次，勾践和夫差两人的所作所为表明，如果想要通过自身努力获得成功的话，纳谏对于君王来说是极其重要的。最后，在所有的例子中，勾践故事都以越国灭吴和勾践圆满复仇为结局。在越国胜利之后，勾践和其重要大臣之间日益紧张的关系则被完全忽略，尽管在古代的流传过程中，这一关系是该传奇的重要部分。柯文解释说从文学角度来看，勾践故事以这样的方式结尾并不令人意外。

当然，将文学作品作为研究材料并不应该是历史研究的专利。美国加州大学伯克利分校的罗伯特·阿什莫尔（Robert Ashmore）就曾通过分析陶渊明的诗歌，指出陶渊明的诗歌可以被视为中国哲学研究的史料。他认为陶渊明的很多诗歌是对《论语》的诠释。这种跨学科的材料运用和对某种思想与某位文学家之间关系的简单探究相比，有着本质的不同。后者如谢思炜的《禅宗与中国文学》，依然将传统的文学材料视为"文学"研究的对象；而柯文和罗伯特则彻底消除了所谓文学材料和历史或思想材料之间的界限。

如前所述，中国历史研究在美国的很多高校属于地区研究的一部分。以哈佛大学为例，中国的文学、历史、思想和文化研究隶属于同一部门，学科间的界限自然就会比较模糊。这样的学科分类方式和中国高校的学科分类有着很大的不同——对于中国学者来说，中国文学、中国历史和中国哲学分属于中文系、历史系和哲学系。长期以来的学科分野早已成为了不少学者研究过程中潜移默化的习惯，要真正自觉地进行跨学科研究尚有不少的路要走。而柯文的《向史而言》正是在这一点上给中国的学者提供了很好的借鉴。

三

对中国的普通读者来说，《向史而言》也是一面闪亮的镜子。柯文认为对中国人来说，勾践故事是耳熟能详的，这样的看法既对又不对。也许每个中国人都知道勾践，都知道他卧薪尝胆，但是他卧薪尝胆的过程究竟如何，并不是每个人都了解；而至于在过去的一百多年里勾践故事是如何被宣传的，绝大多数人可以说一无所知。

在《向史而言》的第一章里，柯文详细地讲述了吴越争霸的整个过程。他所依据的史料主要是《吴越春秋》《史记》《国语》《左传》和《吕氏春秋》等典籍，也参考了不少英文的译本，因此他的描述可以说是全面而翔实的。在描述的基础上，柯文指出勾践故事的核心是"复仇"，是关于面对耻辱应该怎么做的思考。在柯文看来，中国人之所以把勾践的卧薪尝胆视为后人的榜样，是因为中国人认为面对耻辱时不能鲁莽，而是要通过长期的耐心和周密的准备，以期最终复仇，而在准备的过程中，中国人愿意接受各种羞辱或难堪。这种强调忍耐和自制的精神，是中国人的传统。

柯文的这一论断无疑是准确的，而且也是大多数中国人承认并引以为豪的。然而在随后讲述晚清和民国时期的第二章里，柯文指出，在清朝末年，最初革命者们喜欢用郑成功或是岳飞来号召大家进行革命，并不会宣传勾践的故事。到民国初期，随着"二十一条"等国耻一次又一次地被强加在中国人身上后，大家却似乎变得越来越麻木了。一开始，每年的 5 月大家还会纪念接受"二十一条"的国耻日，而随后国耻日就完全流于形式了。正是为了让大家真正铭记国耻，勾践的故事才开始受到越来越多的重视，因为勾践的最大特点就是永远都不会忘记自己所遭受的耻辱。

因此，勾践故事被广泛宣传恰恰是因为中国人对国耻的健忘。那么，愿意卧薪尝胆的中国人和容易忘记耻辱的中国人之中，到底谁才是真正的中国文化的代表？柯文并没有探讨这个问题，也许他认为这个问题并不属于这本书的研究范畴。然而这却是第一个值得中国读者思考的问题。

值得中国读者思考的第二个问题和抗战有关。从 20 世纪 20 年代以来，国民政府在平民教育读本、戏剧和其他宣传方面都大力介绍勾践故事。在日本入侵东北后，蒋介石甚至明确要求在军队中宣传勾践，并处处以勾践自比。在九一八事变两天后，蒋介石在日记中写道："卧薪尝胆，生聚教训，勾践因之霸越，此正我今日之时也。"[7] 一周后，因东北沦陷而压力巨大的蒋介石希望所有中国人能在国民党的领导下团结一致，这样他们就会"生聚教训，严守秩序，服从纪律，期于十年之内，湔雪今日无上之耻辱，完成国民革命之大业"。[8]

至此，第二个问题也就呼之欲出了：通过了解勾践对蒋介石的影响，我们是否应该重新认识和理解蒋介石在九一八事变之后的种种决策？

柯文在第三章"蒋介石在台湾的困境"中的描述让我们有了第三个值得思考的问题。一方面，台湾地区的作家、导演和历史学家们不遗余力地向中小学生、退伍军人和社会大众宣传勾践的故事；另一方面，由于勾践和蒋介石形象的相似性，在台湾勾践的宣传和蒋介石的宣传口径是高度一致的：只做正面宣传。柯文提到了台湾当时中小学

---

7 *Speaking to History*, p. 73.
8 同上，p. 74。

语文课本中的一些内容，上了年纪的读者都会对它们报以会心一笑。从某些方面来说，50、60 年代大陆和台湾在宣传的手法上是极其相似的。

第四个问题和文学有关。在第四章中，柯文详细讲述了大陆在 20 世纪 60 年代的"卧薪尝胆"热。仅从 1960 年到 1961 年，全国出现有关勾践的地方戏剧剧本就超过 70 种。在这样的情况下，历史剧显然不再只是与历史有关，而是与当时的形势有着紧密的联系。以茅盾为代表的一些作家对应该如何创作历史剧，如何用马克思主义理论来刻画历史人物做了广泛而深入的讨论，最终产生了曹禺的《胆剑篇》，尽管后者也遭到了一定的批评。在那个时代，历史剧是一个危险的领域。吴晗的《海瑞罢官》就是一个典型的例子。如果当时历史剧和历史小说中对现实的影射是普遍事实的话，那么我们应该怎么看待吴晗的遭遇，在今天又应该怎么来诠释《胆剑篇》《蔡文姬》等一系列这一时期出现的历史剧？

柯文还向我们提供了至少两个值得注意的问题。在第五章讲述了萧军和白桦的作品后，柯文在第六章——也就是最后一章——里谈到了在改革开放后的今天，勾践故事在社会上所具有的影响。事实上，柯文自己也提出了这个疑问，那就是在经济越来越发达的今日中国，勾践故事还会有这么大的影响力吗？它是否依然能给人以精神力量，还是在很大程度上变成了一种商业的炒作——绍兴当地把勾践和西施作为发展旅游的招牌？这种疑问在第三章也提到了。第三章最后提到 20 世纪 80 年代以后，台湾对于勾践故事没有那么重视了，而且引进了一些大陆作家所写的关于勾践的历史小说。两岸的一些历史学家甚至一起合作研究，指出台湾早期居民的根源在大陆。在这样的政治环境下，我们还会怎样宣传勾践故事呢？我们又需要怎么宣传勾践故事呢？这是作为一个普通的中国读者，在阅读《向史而言》后所需要思考的第五个问题。

　　在我看来，第六个——也许并不是最后一个——值得思考的问题正是柯文《向史而言》的盲点所在。既然《向史而言》讲述的是勾践故事在 20 世纪中国的传播，那么传播至少包括两方：传播的主体和受众。很显然，柯文主要论及了前者，无论是政府、媒体还是作家或是导演，都希望通过用不同的方式传播勾践故事以达到自身的宣传目的。那么，他们的目的达到了吗？当中小学生、普通大众或是其他目标群体在读到课文、看到小说或是听到戏曲时，他们中有多少人从中体会到了国家所遭受的耻辱，并渴望卧薪尝胆为国报仇呢？作为一个普通的读者，我们本来就是宣传的对象，那么我们在这个时代，重新审视这些不同版本、不同形式的勾践故事时，又会有什么样的反应？柯文的确在第六章提到了在当代，有年轻人在遭受挫折的时候会用卧薪尝胆来激励自己，不过在民国时期尤其是抗战时期，勾践故事对当时的大众所造成的影响，却并没有提及。也许，这本来就无从考证，而是要读者自己在镜子面前思考的罢。

三、书评

《中国传统思想中的死亡问题》

王　硕

（清华大学哲学系）

艾米·奥伯丁（Amy Olberding）与艾文贺（Philip J. Ivanhoe）主编的论文集《中国传统思想中的死亡问题》（*Mortality in Traditional Chinese Thought*）是纽约州立大学出版社（SUNY）"中国哲学与文化"系列丛书中的一本，2011年出版。该书对中国古代的死亡观进行了广泛的探讨。一般认为，死亡这一概念对于中国文化而言，不如其在西方思想中那般重要。但作为任何人都无法逃避的命运，死亡同样引发了中国古人的思考兴趣。而在具体的态度和回应方式上，则有别于其他传统。对个中差异与独特之处进行考察，不仅有助于揭示中国文化之特质，还可以帮助我们了解人类精神的复杂性与创造力。全书由11篇高质量的学术论文组成，分别从历史、艺术、哲学、宗教的研究视角，对墓葬的物理空间与艺术装饰、战争与军事文件、丧葬礼仪、儒释道思想等各个层面所反映出的多个历史时期的死亡观展开讨论。鉴于研究主题、媒介、方法与表述的多样性，编者未对论文集设定任何单一的理论框架。本文也将避开整合性的总结，而将重点放在对各篇论文核心内容的提炼与呈现上。

第一至三章的讨论都与墓葬有关。首先是蒲慕州教授的文章《中国古人对来世生活的筹备》。作者发现，最早的时候，死后世界的意义在于保存和延续现实中的社会等级与政治秩序。因此，贵族的墓穴规模、随葬器物都与他们生前的身份地位相一致。但在春秋战国时期，旧有的等级秩序遭到破坏，这种象征意义也随之消逝。自西汉起，无论是墓内环境还是随葬品，都变得越来越像死者生前的居所。对此，作者提出了一个视角极为独特的问题：按理说，生前与身后生活之间最为明显的一致性关联是家宅空间而非身份等级，却为何前者相对较晚才发展出来？在他看来，这种墓葬上的变化，与商代到东汉社会意识结构的改变密切相关。这也充分说明，对墓葬文化与死亡观念进行考查，有助于我们把握古人对生命本质的理解以及现实生活经验的变迁。第二篇文章《升天抑或停留在墓中——马王堆一号墓中的绘画与公元前 2 世纪中国有关身体空间的虚拟仪式》的作者是汪悦进（Eugene Wang）教授。近年来从物质文化层面对古代墓葬所作的研究与诠释，与早期中国礼仪实践的文字记载保持了较高的一致性。但这种研究取径也存在诸多盲点。作者选择从视觉文化的视角切入，并以此揭示中国古代死亡观所具有的一些尚未引起广泛关注的特征。文章以一项调查开篇，表明长久以来，礼仪被看作是理解墓葬视觉空间的关键。而文中最精彩的部分，当属对马王堆一号墓彩绘棺与帛画所作的颇具新意的分析。作者认为，棺椁与帛画的视觉意象表明：在汉代人眼中，身体的转化乃是更为广阔的宇宙转化过程的一部分。而这一过程又暗含着对内在（个人形体）与外在（宇宙空间）界限的否定。第三篇文章题为《新发现汉墓中的器物与文献所反映出的死亡观与来世思想》。有些学者倾向于认为，中国来世思想的形成时间，应在印度佛教传入之后。郭珏教授这篇文章却对这种判断提出了挑战。虽然中国人的来世观念在佛教的影响下发生了明显的改变，但新近发现的汉墓所提供的证据充分表明，在更早的时候，中国就已经形成了一系列与亡者的继续存在相关的身体信仰与实践。并且，这些信仰与实践无法被整合成单一的来世观。恰恰相反，它们是一种很难为任何现存的学术体系把握的复合体。作者通过对汉代墓葬，尤其是马王堆一号墓中的绘画以及多处发现的《告地书》的研究指出，关于死者居住在墓穴中抑或去往另一个世界的问题，古人并不特别固执于某一种回答。这表明，在佛教传入以前，汉代人尚未赋予来世以道德意义，也不分辨死亡的好与坏。他们对各种不同的可能性持明显的开放态度，从而包容并满足于对来世生活的多元化理解。

第四篇是安乐哲（Roger T. Ames）教授的文章《战争、死亡与古代中国的宇宙论》。此文专门探讨暴力与战争对中国古代世界观的形塑作用。作者认为，人们在战斗中对待死亡的态度可以帮助我们更好地理解古人的生死观。此前，李泽厚与何炳棣曾做过相关的研究。安乐哲在总结既有成果的基础上提出，对古代军事家而言，军事行动中最重要也是最不理论化的一种二元关系，乃是生与死之间的平衡。例如，《孙子》一书未对战争作任何美化，也拒绝使用占筮，而是强调军事指挥官必须首先对生死存亡问题给予高度关注。在战场上，将领必须能够很好地把握住生死之间的张力，并学会利用这种全局观念，集中最大力量去赢取胜利。安乐哲主张，通过这项考察，可以发现古代中国的宇宙观是如何被实践和紧迫情境下的要求所塑造出来的。

接下来的三篇文章讨论的均是儒家的死亡观。艾文贺（Philip J. Ivanhoe）教授的文章《〈论语〉中的死亡与临终》，对这部最为基本的儒家经典有关个体对自身必死性的忧虑，以及对挚爱之人离世的悲伤这两个相互关联问题的讨论进行了全面的分析。与孔子同时代的许多思想家认为，宗教与世俗在应对死亡问题上所作的努力可以使人们获得慰藉。因为一旦将死亡看作是可怕的和悲剧性的，我们便须依靠那些被精致构造起来的方式，力图成就"成功的""真正有意义"的人生，以对抗死亡所带来的恐惧。但孔子却未将死亡本身视为悲剧。在他看来，比精致的意义建构更为重要的，乃是与他人分享生命的乐趣。从这个意义上说，孔子赞同我们的直觉，即将一些人的死亡看作是可悲的，而死亡对于每个人而言都是一个合理且重要的问题。但他坚持认为，对该问题深刻而复杂的回答关联于并且必须奠基在一系列幸福生活的标准之上。奥伯丁（Amy Olberding）的文章题为《"我不懂什么叫'好像'"——〈论语〉中有关父母离世的哀恸》。该文对《论语》相当重视的一种独特的死亡类型——父母的去世——作了深入而细致的考察。这部经典显然赞同儿女应在父母去世后表现出极度的哀伤。但倘使父母的死亡是一种"善终"，这种态度就有点令人困惑。因为对善终哀恸，似乎就意味着我们坚信死亡本身是不可避免的，是恶的。奥伯丁的研究意在将这种信念同儒家所倡导的为父母之死而哀恸区分开来。在她看来，《论语》在父母之丧上的立场，更多的与一种在人际关系网络中对个体死亡进行定位的努力有关，而不单单是一种对待死亡本身的态度。父母的死亡之所以令人伤心，是因为父母处在人类自我认识与发展的最为核心的位置。据此，奥伯丁提出，《论语》既支持对父母善终的哀恸，也同时在避免着任何可能会促使人们将死亡绝对化为悲剧的思想框架。齐思敏（Mark Csikszentmihalyi）教授在《早期中国思想中的命运与死亡》中指出，"为何有些人的生命戛然而止""为何有些个体短命而亡"之类的问题显然引发了中国古代思想家的兴趣。他将论述的焦点集中在《论语》中的一个案例，即孔子高弟颜渊的英年早逝上。这件事对孔子触动极大。《论语》的注疏者尝试对颜渊的死以及孔子对此的反应给出一个合理的解释。但有的儒者认为命运本就是随意的，有的则赋予寿命以更加深刻的甚至是宇宙论上的意义，各种解释方案相互抵触。不过，在诠释多样性的背后，作者发现他们其实都诉诸一个共同的术语，即将"寿命"归因于"命"。齐思敏的这项研究表明，在儒家传统内部，人是否有能力影响和掌控死亡的问题曾引起激烈的争论。

　　道家对待死亡的态度与儒家迥然不同。伯克森（Mark Berkson）教授的文章《〈庄子〉中的死亡：心、自然与忘却的艺术》对早期道家代表人物庄子所给出的精神治疗方案进行了分析。在伯克森眼中，

庄子可谓是中国历史上最与众不同的思想家。庄子对死亡的言说方式
——他的幽默、嬉闹以及对死亡是件坏事的质疑——似乎表现出一种
罕见的轻松感。可实际上，其死亡观中的种种张力却明显反映出当时
社会的破碎与动荡。例如，庄子劝告众人，无论死亡何时来临都应当
坦然接受。但另一方面他又明确以"终其天年"为更高境界。伯克森
认为我们这样理解庄子：他的某些建议意在帮助人们在思考死亡时实
现自身心灵的转化，另外一些则直接提点我们应当理解自然，并与
之保持和谐、一致。两种不同的言说策略彼此支持，共同促成了一种
极不寻常的、轻松自在的死亡观。普鸣（Michael Puett）教授在论文
《圣人、过去与亡者：〈淮南子〉的死亡观》中指出，《淮南子》这部
道家经典充分证明，在早期中国，鬼神信仰广泛流行，且信仰的方式
多种多样。文中最值得注意的一个结论是：即便是圣人与凡人都认可
的鬼神信仰，他们的信仰方式或理由也不一定相同。圣人虽承认鬼神
的存在，却显然不对其持畏惧态度。相反，圣人将之视为维持社会秩
序的助手。又如，凡人希望自己死后可以像鬼一样继续存在。但圣人
则认为自己死后将归于无的境界，再无世俗烦扰。普鸣的这项研究清
楚地表明，有关死亡的经历、理解与意义，圣凡之间存在着差异。成
圣不仅意味着过不一样的人生，同时也代表着一种与众不同的死亡。

　　蒋韬教授在第十篇文章中对美国实用主义与禅宗之间的关系进行
了探讨，具体题目为《两种实用主义视域：临济宗与威廉·詹姆斯的
死亡观》。首先，他指出两家虽各有其独特之处，但都力图借助智识
和分析的方法实现人类的实际利益。在一定程度上，临济宗与詹姆斯
都对智识上的努力在最紧急、重要的时刻所提供给我们的帮助进行
了测量与评价。作者论述了这些务实的信念在詹姆斯与临济宗面对
人类永生问题的挑战时，是如何对他们的思想起到影响和塑造作用
的。其次，作者指出，除却上述这些相似性，二者对"永生"概念
所作的具体分析却是截然不同的。詹姆斯似乎赞同人类永生的信仰，

因为它具有治疗意义和慰藉作用。而临济宗则反对任何与此有关的信仰。在其看来，该信仰对精神发展具有极强的破坏力，会遮蔽人们对根本真理的认识。在此基础上，作者还对造成二者分歧的根源作了进一步的追问。

佛教对中国思想的影响之一，即激发了理学家对于死亡问题的兴趣。彭国翔教授的文章《宋明理学传统中作为终极关怀的生死关切——以阳明后学为例》即与此相关。作者指出，直至宋代，很多儒者在生死问题上仍秉持孔子以降不愿多言的态度，强调"未知生，焉知死"（《论语·先进》）。到了明代，阳明学者打破了这种相对缄默的局面。他们将生死关切作为焦点问题纳入自身的哲学思考中，在主动吸收佛教资源的基础上开创了一个极为丰富的思想传统。当然，除了儒释交融这一主要因素外，明代政治高压体制对儒者的残酷迫害，经常使其面临死亡威胁，也是生死关切成为阳明后学重要课题的一个原因。而在生死关头仍能保持寂然不动、泰然自若，更被儒者视为道德修养工夫所能达到的一种极高境界。

由此可见，古代中国的死亡观是一个极其复杂又极具吸引力且亟待发掘的重要课题。上述作者的研究工作都具有相当大的开创与启发意义，这使得《中国传统思想中的死亡问题》成为一部该领域无法绕过的著作。与此同时，论文集所折射出的问题的多元化与丰富性，业已引起海内外学者的广泛关注。相信未来会有更多优秀的研究成果涌现出来，以飨读者。

《儒家思想：心灵的积习》

董铁柱

（北京师范大学—香港浸会大学联合国际学院）

尽管从 20 世纪末开始，就有很多学者鼓吹儒家思想将在 21 世纪复兴。可是，在历史上长期影响中国以及东亚地区的儒家思想，在当今的中国社会究竟还具有什么样的意义？如果它要对世界上其他国家产生影响，那么又是否可以通过西方思想的视角，来审视儒家思想在当代社会的价值？这正是《儒家思想：心灵的积习》（*Confucianism: A Habit of Heart*，SUNY，2016）所探讨的主题。本书的编者和作者们对第二个问题给出了肯定的答案。他们所采用的西方视角，是著名社会学家罗伯特·贝拉（Robert Bellah）的"民间宗教"（civil religion）理论。他们希望通过这一理论，来寻找第一个问题的答案。

长期执教于美国加州大学伯克利分校社会学系的贝拉是针对越战后的美国而提出这一理论的。在他看来，所谓民间宗教，就是渗透于美国文化方方面面的理念与价值观。这些理念和价值观左右着人们的行为——从这一层面来说，它们带着浓郁的宗教色彩；与此同时，这些理念和价值观与传统宗教不同，并不是通过教会、政府或是其他政治的途径传播并被大众接受的——从这一角度来看，它们是"民间"的。

贝拉认为这些民间宗教极其重要，它们不需要等级、制度和其他手段的约束，就能自然而然地存在于人们的心中，成为大家"心灵的积习"。《儒家思想：心灵的积习》一书的主编金圣文和艾文贺借用这一概念来形容儒家思想在当今中国以及世界的地位，也的确很好地概括了儒家思想的特点：一方面它的影响无处不在，另一方面它的影响在一定程度上又是非官方的。

围绕着这一理论，本书包含了10位学者所写的论文。值得注意的是，本书所关注的并不是儒家思想本身，而是儒家思想的现状及其在当代的意义，因此这10位学者的研究领域非常广泛，从社会学、宗教学、政治学到哲学均有涉猎。从内容来看，这10篇文章大致可以分为三个部分。第一部分的焦点是儒家思想在当代中国。普度大学社会学教授杨凤岗、巴黎狄德罗大学汉学家毕游赛（Sébastien Billioud）、浙江大学哲学系教授彭国翔、Kenyon学院亚洲研究中心主任孙笑冬（Anna Sun）四位学者所探讨的都是这一话题。第二部分讨论的是儒家思想的全球化，主要以日本、韩国为对象，包括美国加州大学圣地亚哥社会学系教授赵文词（Richard Madsen）、中国香港城市大学公共政策学系教授金圣文、韩国学中央研究院的韩道铉和日本东洋文化研究所的中岛隆博四位学者对此作了阐述。第三部分则关于民间宗教理论本身，贝拉对此作了专门阐发，凯尼恩学院的哲学教授萧阳则对其理论作了进一步的诠释。

杨凤岗的《作为民间宗教的儒家思想》（"Confucianism as Civil Religion"）一文讨论了当代中国的新儒家运动。当代的所谓新儒家一方面强调儒家思想在当今社会道德重建过程中的关键作用，另一方面则积极推进儒家思想成为"国家"层面的意识形态。杨凤岗赞成前一主张，而反对后一观点。新儒家运动批评西方民主制度会导致个人主义，并使得社会一盘散沙，认为儒家思想才是让国家有凝聚力的关键。杨凤岗则指出儒家思想相反应该在民间保持其活力，如果能结合已经在中国有着相当基础的基督教思想，那么不仅对中国，甚至对东亚乃至全世界都会有极大的影响。很显然，杨凤岗对新儒家运动的批评是中肯的，而对中国的基督教现状则有些过于乐观。

毕游赛的《儒家思想在风俗习惯上的复兴与民间宗教争论在中国的恢

复》（"The Revival of Confucianism in the Sphere of Mores and the Reactivation of the Civil Religion Debate in China"）从实践上分析了儒家在当代中国的现状。他以两个个案为例，描述了身为商人和教师的普通中国人在他们的生活中如何身体力行地传播儒家思想。其中一位长期资助小朋友读儒家经典，而另一位则组织受过高等教育的年轻人研习儒家思想。毕游赛阐述了牟宗三、蒋庆等人对推动儒家思想的影响，并且也提及了台湾净空法师的作用。在此基础上，他描述了当今学界对儒家思想地位的争论，这场争论分为两方，以大陆儒家学者蒋庆等人为代表的一方主张儒家思想官方化，而以大陆学者陈明和美国学者杨凤岗等人为代表的另一方表示反对。毕游赛讨论了儒家思想官方化可能带来的负面影响，并指出儒家思想还是应该在社会层面——而不是政治层面——起作用。

彭国翔在《透视中国大陆的儒学复兴：以儒家经典在当代中国的兴衰为例》（"Inside the Revival of Confucianism in Mainland China: The Vicissitudes of Confucian Classics in Contemporary China as an Example"）同样对儒家思想在当代中国的政治化表示了忧虑。他考察了新中国成立以来儒家经典在中国的命运变迁：1949 年至 20 世纪 70 年代，儒家经典遭遇了低谷；在 20 世纪 80 年代开始复兴，到新世纪后则受到了广泛的关注。然而儒家经典的复兴同样带来了一系列的问题。同时，儒家思想还遭遇到商业化的危机。各种出版物、旅游机构都想通过贩卖儒家思想以获得经济效益。彭国翔认为，在政治化和商业化的双重冲击下，儒家思想在当代中国的真正复兴还有着相当大的挑战。

孙笑冬的视角比较独特，她在《当代中国的儒家政治》（"The Politics of Confucianism in Contemporary China"）中考察了三个与儒家有关的社会事件。根据这三个事件，孙笑冬讨论了三个问题：第一，什么是宗教？第二，当儒家被定义为宗教后，会如何定位儒家思想？第三，儒家思想和中国人的自尊紧密相连，在这样的情况下，如果将儒家思想官方化，会出现什么样的情况？她认为这三个问题都意味着儒家思想在当代中国的确可以被视为一种民间宗教。

这四位学者都从不同角度讨论了儒家思想在当代中国的影响，提出了存在的问题。而接下来的几位学者则将视野转移到了儒家思想全球化的问题。赵文词在《儒家思想全球化的阻碍》（"Obstacles to the Globalization of Confucianism"）中探讨了儒家思想不能像道教、佛教那样风靡欧美和其他地区的原因。赵文词指出：这首先是因为儒家思想在 19 世纪末被作为宗教介绍到其他国家后，其身上的神秘色彩被淡化，被强调的是其人文精神，这使得对它感兴趣的主要是知识分子阶层，而普通大众则觉得它缺乏吸引力；其次在历史上，儒家思想和统治阶层联系在一起，并且推崇个人服从集体，这与西方崇尚的个人主义相悖。他认为要改变这一局面，就要使儒家思想去政治化，以迎合西方的自由平等观念。在赵文词看来，只有从下而上——而不是从上而下——自发地推行儒家思想，儒家思想才有可能全球化。也就是说，儒家思想要全球化，就要拥有"民间"的特色。他指出儒家思想在韩国正是这样的情况。

金圣文是来自韩国的学者，他在《超越纪律社会：重新想象韩国的儒家民主》（"Beyond a Disciplinary Society: Reimagining Confucian Democracy in South Korea"）对赵文词的观点作了回应。他指出，韩国虽然可以说是目前全球受儒家思想影响最深的国家，但韩国人却不认为可以通过儒家思想来实现民主政治。他认为 20 世纪末 21 世纪初一些推崇儒家的思想家和社会活动家所发起的新儒家运动失败，失去了大众尤其是年轻人对儒家政治的信任。金圣文特别讨论了咸在凤的后现代儒家思想，认为他的政治理论是西方思想和儒家思想的结合，但是由于其过于强调纪律，从而会伤害韩国的民主制度。很显然，金圣文认为在韩国儒家思想的影响也应该保持在民间的层面。

韩国学中央研究院的韩道铉在《20 世纪 70 年代新农村运动中村

干部的经验：以男性干部的生活为焦点》（"The Experience of Village Leaders during the Saemaul Movement in the 1970s: Focusing on the Lives of the Male Leaders"）中考察了韩国前总统朴正熙在 20 世纪 70 年代所发起的新农村运动。新农村运动以朴正熙的"儒家权威主义"为指导，却获得了当地干部以及村民的大力支持。韩道铉认为，这一运动之所以成功，是因为当时的人民从内心支持儒家思想所引导的政治运动。在他看来，儒家思想在当时是韩国人民心中的一个"习性"，他们会自发地参与其中，而他们也将朴正熙视为儒家意义上的理想领导人。在此，作为民间宗教的儒家思想和政治得到了完美的结合。

来自日本的中国哲学专家中岛隆博则探讨了儒家在当代日本的繁荣。他在《从宗谱角度看当代日本的儒家》（"Contemporary Japanese Confucianism from a Genealogical Perspective"）中谈到了日本的儒家复兴和中国、韩国的异同。相同之处在于主张复兴儒家的日本支持者们也从精神的层面出发，将儒家思想视作一种宗教，并且将它提高到了"国家精神"的高度。而不同之处则体现在日本的儒家只推崇孔子和《论语》，而无视其他众多的儒家典籍。他们相信只有在《论语》中才可以找到"儒家"的真谛，他们希望通过背诵、学习和实践《论语》中的礼仪来提高"教养"。中岛隆博指出当前日本的儒家复兴和二战前的情况相似，都是为了强调日本自身的民族性，批评西方思想的影响。他表示这种保守的思潮并不可取，认为应该推崇"批判性的儒家思想"，而不是满足于将儒家思想树立为民间或是国家宗教。

本书的最后两篇文章关注的是贝拉的宗教理论。萧阳在《心灵的成长小说：罗伯特·贝拉"人类进化中的宗教"的浓重自然主义》（"The Bidungsroman of the Heart: Thick Naturalism in Robert Bellah's Religion in Human Evolution"）里，将贝拉的民间宗教理论和当代儒家的发展现状联系了起来。萧阳指出贝拉的民间宗教理论是一种广义的文化理论，在其中宗教占据着重要的地位。贝拉在书中认为宗教和生物学、儿童心理学等自然科学密不可分，而人们对宗教礼仪的热衷正是来自于生物本能。萧阳认为贝拉这一论断非常重要，不仅揭橥了宗教的特质，也触及了人的本性。既然人类是在不断进化的，宗教也就在不断地发展。这也是儒家思想可以在今天依然有生命力的理论依据。

贝拉在本书最后作了总结性的论述。在《我们能否想象一个全球性的民间宗教？》（"Can We Imagine a Global Civil Religion？"）中，他指出一个全球性的民间宗教也许听起来不现实，但是首先对美国来说，应该思考在这个世界中扮演什么样的角色，又需要如何去贡献自己的力量。在这个意义上，每个国家都有着共通点，因此也就可能需要一个全球共同的民间宗教，儒家思想也就有这样的需要和可能。但是如果这样的民间宗教是大家自己选择而不是被强加的，那么就意味着首先要有一个全球性的"公民社会"，而目前来说这依然只存在于想象之中。

10位学者的研究指出了一个事实：作为民间宗教的儒家思想正在复兴。同时也揭示了一个问题：在民间宗教与官方宗教之间，儒家思想究竟会如何发展？可以想见的是，这并没有统一的答案。即使我们完全接受贝拉的理论，儒家思想在当代社会的发展方向，依然是开放性的。而如何使用西方社会学理论来跨学科地探讨中国哲学的发展，或许才是这本书给我们的最大启发。

《孔子·孟子·荀子》

李 卓

（天津社会科学院）

《孔子·孟子·荀子：先秦儒学讲稿》（以下简称《讲稿》），陈来著，生活·读书·新知三联书店 2017 年 11 月出版。

这是著名中国哲学史家陈来先生多年前的一部"旧作"首次付梓。其缘起正如作者在"序"中所言：1999 年至 2000 年，作者应邀在香港中文大学哲学系教书一年，曾为哲学系的本科学生讲授"先秦儒学"课程，并写就讲义。书名《先秦儒学讲稿》，顾名思义，即是在这个讲课稿基础上整理而成。

此书由"序言"、"附录"和正文六章构成，正文部分以孔子、孟子、荀子三位思想家为主，中间插入了《礼记》中的《大学》《中庸》《学记》三篇，此外还在"郭店竹书"一章中讲述了《郭店楚墓竹简》的重要篇目。具体包括：

第一章"孔子"共六节，分别从"学论""德论""仁礼论""君子论""政论""天论"六个部分介绍孔子的思想，突出了孔子发展出的包括真善美在内的一套完满的人生理想。第一节"学论"通过分析文献指出，"学"与"好学"，"既是孔子思想的发生学的起点，也是他的思想生命的逻辑起点，是孔子思想的重要基础"。讨论了"学"的具体指涉所包含的不同面相，以及为学的目的。第二节"德论"主要分析了孔子伦理思想的特征。第三节"仁礼论"指出孔子是以仁统礼，以义贯礼，把仁所代表的道德精神注入"礼"中。第四节"君子论"讨论君子人格。第五节"政论"讲述孔子的政治思想。第六节"天论"则是考察孔子对天、鬼神、命的态度。

第二章"《学》《庸》"共两节，分别以"修身论"和"诚明论"概括《大学》与《中庸》的思想特征。"修身论"在修身之外，还讲述了《大学》的政治社会思想、"絜矩之道"的伦理原则以及《大学》的正心说。"诚明论"分别讨论了"中庸"之德与"诚"的哲学。

第三章"郭店竹书"分"性自命出说""求己反本说"两节，分别介绍郭店竹书中《性自命出》篇"以乐化民，以情感民"的思想，以及《成之闻之》篇"以求己用民，以修身率民"的思想。

第四章"孟子"共五节。第一节"仁政论"讲述孟子的经济民本主义思想。第二节"君民论"讲述孟子的政治民本主义思想。第三节为"性善论"，分析孟子对仁政之所以可能所作的心性论论证。第四节"仁义论"主要讲述孟子对道德原则的看法。第五节"修身论"讲孟子的"修身"观念和修养功夫。

第五章"《乐记》"分四节。第一节"心性说"讨论《乐记》对乐与人心的看法，分别考察了"心物说""性情说""性欲说""心情说"四个方面。第二节"乐气说"论述乐包含有气的属性，指出"乐在根本上来源于天地之气的协和运化，又符合人身之气的平衡和合，并能促进大地、社会、人身的和谐安宁"（第202页）。第三节"乐教说"阐发乐的社会教化功能。第四节"礼乐论"比较礼乐异同。

第六章"荀子"分四节。第一节"分群论"论证礼义的起源及其必要性。第二节"隆礼论"讲述荀子的礼治主义思想以及荀子的君民论。第三节"性伪论"按照荀子人性论展开的内在逻辑，考察荀子这一最有特色的思想。第四节"心君论"略讲荀子的心论，即心作为"天君"的主宰控制功能。

最后的附录"香港中文大学1999—2000年度科目考试"，是一份影印的试卷，即作者当年为此门课程的期末考试所命的测试题。

全书着重讲述了先秦儒学的主要代表人物（孔、孟、荀）和重要儒家文献（郭店楚简出土儒书和《大学》《中庸》《学记》）的核心观点与思想特色，揭示了先秦儒学传承发展的固有脉络与内在讨论，并对一些问题作了新颖独到的阐释。主要有三个特点：

一、史料精熟，选材精当。《讲稿》对史料运用精熟，文献选取精当，可推知书中的"辨名析理"建立在详细地、系统地爬梳文献的基础之上。论述时注重比较各家思想的异同，注重先秦儒学与宋明儒学的连贯性。可见作者深造自得，"目无全牛"而"胸有成竹"，在中国哲学史领域学识深厚。

二、比较的视野。在哲学诠释方面，作者注重使用一些西方哲学的相关因素，作为助缘来进一步诠释先秦儒学思想。例如在讲述孔子"德论"时，引入了亚里士多德、西季威克、麦金泰尔、罗尔斯等人的相关伦理思想作为诠释的资源。特别是通过与亚里士多德德性伦理（virtue ethics）的比较，来揭示孔子伦理思想、道德思想的特征。指出孔子思想中的仁既是"德"，也是"道"，从"金律"和忠恕一贯之道来看，孔子的"德论"显然不能全部归结为德性伦理（第 26 页）。再如借助奥托（Rudolf Otto）《神圣者的观念》中不确定神圣的他者（Holy other）的观念，来诠释孔子"天论"的思想特征，指出了郝大维和安乐哲内在论或事件本体论的不切之处（第 66 页）。于此可见作者广博的西学素养。

三、新颖独到的阐释。《讲稿》注重出土文献与传世经典相互发明。对于人人触手可得，却常常被忽略的文献材料，作者也能有所发覆，作出创造性的诠释。"尤其对孔子的'学论'、儒学与德性伦理学的比较以及对荀子的理解等有新颖独到的阐释"（封底简介语）。

此外，《讲稿》中加入了学术前沿最新的研究成果，这在当时是非常难能可贵的。1998 年文物出版社《郭店楚墓竹简》的出版，可谓重要的学术史事件。作者同年就做出了对《性自命出》《成之闻之》等篇的研究。这些战国竹简的内容在当时对学生而言非常新鲜。当然，由于此书的出版迟于讲义完成近20年，这个特点在今天看来已不明显，但学术研究当与时俱进，授课要及时向学生介绍学术前沿的做法显然并未过时。

作者曾谓"我当作教材来写的书，把叙述简明、介绍准确、分析清楚、体系完整、表达规范作为目标，并不追求研究本身的细致和深度"（《有无之境》后记）。此《讲稿》近于教材，由于讲义的形式所限，故所论不尽深入、全面。但揆之以上诸优长，冯友兰所谓"譬犹画图，小景之中，形神自足。非全史在胸，易克臻此。惟其如是，读其书者，乃觉择焉虽精而语焉犹详也"（冯友兰《中国哲学简史》自序），此书是当之无愧的。书中平实浅显的解说，实乃高屋建瓴的深入浅出、"极高明而道中庸"之论。《讲稿》大体呈现了先秦儒学的基本面貌，是极佳的入门导读，可供读者用以学习、了解先秦儒学，尤其适合不同知识背景的中国哲学爱好者自修。

《讲稿》提出了一些新的看法，后来作者在此基础上完成了精深的、专门的研究。正如"序"中所交代："如对孔子思想中'好学'的理解和关注，后来我曾以此稿为基础写出论文加以讨论；又如孔子部分较多考虑到儒学与德性伦理学的比较，后来我也曾以此稿为基础专门著文论述。其中对于荀子的讲法也为我后来做荀子的研究准备了基础。"这些进一步思考的成果，便是"论儒家教育思想的基本理念""古代德行伦理与早期儒家伦理学的特点——兼论孔子与亚里士多德伦理学的异同""《论语》的德行伦理体系""'儒'的自我理解——荀子说儒的意义"、"重订荀子《性恶篇》章句情""性与礼义——荀子政治哲学的人性公理"等专论。如今这些成果大部分都已收录到作者的近作《从思想世界到历史世界》（北京大学出版社，2015年8月）之中，阅完《讲稿》意犹未尽的读者，可进一步阅读此书。

《儒门内的庄子》

蔡岳璋

（新竹交通大学社会与文化研究所博士候选人）

　　《儒门内的庄子》（台北：联经出版事业公司，2016 年）系杨儒宾先生"庄子研究"（其他研究还有"理学与反理学""新经学""五行物学""理论翻译"等）之论文集，写作时间跨度长达四分之一世纪。除"第七章"与"结论"为新作外，其余包含"导论"与"附录"在内的八章，皆先后独立发表于海内外（具严格审查制度）的学术期刊或会议论文集。综观本书章节安排，分章次第并非按照各篇文章的原始发表时间胪列而成。由其集结序列不难发现，一切看似逶迤相属实则有意为之，充分反映作者对于庄子精神的根本理念的把握与发展构想：一开始为庄子思想定锚（导论），继而从庄子与"前历史"的巫文化联系出发（第一章），东有启明，自传记与道论的双重角度研庄探孔，借道明末大儒对庄子的再诠释（第二章）襄赞辅佐，递相传袭而续有进步；从而推导庄子哲学的特殊主体性格（第三章）如日中天，伴随在语言表现（第四、五章）、技艺物论（第六章）和超知觉统合的体知形态（第七章）等各层次的精神发展与表现理趣，先锋驱除而据有城池；各章相激相荡终于相合，最后落实于人文创造（第八章）之终极依归，承先启后。本书虽为论文"集"，却似天然凑泊，犹如先河之于后海。作为全书收尾之作的"附录"，似往已回，原来是前述所有篇章援以诞生的发轫种子，保留作者此一往昔"少作"以为对照，由此更可见一路走来剥蕉抽茧之迹：既见共同之轨辙，更不乏特殊之蜕变。古云："踵其事而增华，变其本而加厉，物既有之，文亦宜然。"从"附录"的角度来看，本集更可谓其现代见证。

综括本书要旨，不妨直接抽绎作者"结论"中之一段为代表展开介绍："当庄子的主体由宇宙心转向形气主体，其知由神秘的性体之知转向形体论的无知之知，逍遥论由抽象的绝对自由转向乘物游心的具体自由，语言、技艺由道之障碍物转向道之朗现载体时，我们看到的庄子就不再是，至少不仅是传统的文士、高道或艺术精神导向的哲人，而是可以和各种的帝国的政治秩序与当代的处境对话的知识人，也就是带有现代意义的'世界公民'。"（页 458-459）其中已然隐含本书所有主要的核心概念"形气主体"，及由此而来乘心游物的"物论"、语言"卮言"、"技艺"、无知之知的气学，以及面向自然同时游心人间世界的"人文精神"。

作者指出，庄子对于气的把握与理解，异于其他秦汉诸子，此气既是"立基于无名的主体之上的精微之动能，这种精微的动能被认为具有精神的属性"，同时与"超越之道也有奥妙的系连"，两者的一体连带，也引发"冥契之感的宇宙意识"（页 52）。基于上述的观察与判断，作者最终缩结出"形气主体"此一哲学概念。"形气主体"作为本书极为关键的基本预设，与之交叉出现使用的还有"气化主体"一词，前者系庄子哲学的展开基点（页 56），后者则被视为"进入庄子世界的锁钥"（页 50）。"气化主体"一词，于作者早期 1989 年撰作庄子的身体论述（即"附录"）时即已出现，此一概念在近年的台湾庄学界几成共识（此间容或有不同称谓者如"游化主体""身体主体"等，实则理一分殊）。它主要意指"主体的属性在气化，主体经由气化显现出来"（页 49），而一旦"'气化主体'落实到人身上，'身体'体现'气化'，遂有了'形气主体'一词，亦即'形气主体'是'气化主体'加上形体的作用"（页 49）。换言之，"形气主体"意谓"五官互融、形气神同化、认知与行动合一的作用体，它是落实于形气神构造中一种具有超知觉统合能力的创造力"（页 56）。另一方面，"'气化主体'是'形气主体'在宇宙论或深层意识面上的表现，'形气主体'则是'气化主体'的概念更完善的呈现形式"（页 50）。两者之中，作者重视形气主体甚于气化主体，因为前者用法更能够涵盖社会性的身体，发挥个体的实践作用与意义。（页 56-57）作者标举"气化主体"（或"形气主体"）之说意在对治（或云"补充"）心性主体，至于后来的"游之主体"（页 173）则更强调主体的流动性。

气化主体不同于传统心学的意识主体（或曰"心性主体"），它极力对抗限缩心性意识的整体化的风险，而意在表明主体意识的去个人化、去中心化、解疆域化、再"主体化"、再身体化、再形气化。如果"心性主体"视气为唯物，则"气化主体"之说则尖锐地冲撞"心性主体"，突破唯心与唯物的敌我对垒。也正因着"具有统合身心以及协调周遭环境的一种超自觉的能力"（页 55）的气化主体，方才有真正的语言"卮言"（页 225-264）及其根本性的隐喻（页 265-310）、无懈可击的技艺与技艺达人（页 311-352）以及鉴赏自然的游观（页 173-224）。也由于这样的"形气主体"，庄子的物论更留下了极具风格化的表现印记。庄子物论的特别之处，在于"物"并没有像其他冥契传统那样被吞噬或者模糊化于超越的主体之中，"而是在形气主体逆返到形—气—主体的深层依据时，物气四流，物即物化，也就是物更精致化，气化不已被庄子视为物之实相"（页 53），当然其主要根据并非来自知识论上的理由，而是源自体证哲学之上的自然结果。这样的气化—物论与创造，也彻底地反映在庄子不惮其烦地屡屡调动"由技入道"的技艺达人，所表现的出神入化的诸多寓言故事之中。另一方面，气化主体不仅只具有使自然世界意义化的气感阶段，更具彰显（非意识所及的）知觉事件，将之转译成语言叙述的能力与需求。其中隐含着呈现问题（语言与非语言的同一），而浑圆酒器式的语言（"卮言"）不再只是个人语言，更可谓之道言。

在"气化主体"的前提下，作者也对传统庄学的内部义理诠释展开批评。历史上常见两类关于庄子学的主流诠释，分别是：一、以向郭为代表的魏晋玄学的现象论解释模式"精致的气化论"；二、明中晚期以陆西星为代表的丹道论解释模式"精微的心体论"（页153）。此外，或许还可再加上以"明至人之心"为逍遥义绝对纲领，从而反对向郭现象论的支道林的心体自由论（页380）。虽然，面对这两种主流诠释模式，作者认为，"庄子说的气化流行既不是向郭的现象论模式，也不是陆西星的丹道模式"（页309）。原因在于，"庄子讲的气化流行虽遍布一切，但却有'不得其朕'的源头；反过来说，庄子虽也肯定对造化之源的体证是必要的，但这样的造化之源又不能孤守虚明，它流布于造化流行之中"（页309）。于是在老子、支道林，乃至陆西星的心体论，以及向郭的气化论之外，作者更倾心明末方以智与王夫之的（物论）注庄观点。

"气化主体"的各种人间表现，更导致作者对于庄子人文性格的"传统的发明"。庄学诠释史上具有三种不同形态的人文表现：一是常见具批判性，（包含积极反抗与消极逃逸儒家所代表的主流价值在内的）追求个体自由的解构"支离型庄子"；另一则是深谙冥契之道，以历代道士成玄英、褚伯秀、陆西星为代表的同一"冥契型庄子"。这两者是最为常见的庄子的历史形象（即反人文与超人文），不过此二者"坐落在意识运作的两端，一是以自外于主流价值的方式介入社会层，一是以自外于经验世界的方式退居无之意识层"（页453），虽各有理趣，却非作者所取。作者更着意能够"掌握创化之源"，重"有"而非重"无"（乃至佛教重"空"），能"以'有'证'无'"（页7）的天均创化的"积极型庄子"。这也是本书一开始的自我定位：在观点上"主要是呼应17世纪的天均哲学"（页9）。

若"以向秀、郭象为代表的魏晋名士学者做的是第一波的修正运动，明末以王夫之、方以智为代表的大儒则是第二波的修正者"（页

455）。在此之后，作者指出，"我们未尝不可在第二波修正运动的基础上，将庄子更精准地带返到一种创发性的、原初秩序的、心与物化的源头上去，这是个尚未结构化的场所，却是人文精神展现的源头，也是庄、儒共享的场域"（页226）。作者有意识地衔接以明末大儒为代表的第二波庄学修正运动，接着讲"第三期的庄子人文说"（页445、459）。而当代学者论及儒家的人文主义，至少有三种类型含义：一、由社会结构的礼乐与人群五伦所组成"礼乐伦理的人文主义"；二、以主体意识中的道德法则赋予人文秩序以价值根据的"道德意识的人文主义"；三、以主观精神与客观精神的发展形态为主的"体用型的人文主义"（页417）。庄子则是侧重第三型的"关心基本存有论的人文主义者"（页420）。这样的庄子，"给身体、世界、语言、技艺，都带来新的向度。此时的庄子恰好不是扮演文化世界中拆除大队队员的角色，而是扮演不断新化世界、理化世界的建构者"（页414）。而正是在恢复庄子的人文创造精神此一面向上，作者发现了庄子本具的原始儒家身份，或者说庄子被认为开始向儒家靠拢（以张载、王夫之为代表之一系），在儒家的面纱中显露。在拒绝荀子对于庄子"蔽于天而不知人"的千古定评之余（页421-424），作者笔下的庄子也成为"儒门内的庄子"，而儒门也成为"有了庄子的儒门"。皮毛落尽，洞见真实，在作者的"庄子儒门说"之后，庄子与儒家的固有形象反而开始变得模糊起来。儒家不再是传统意义上显而易见的儒家，而庄子也不再是历史上想当然而被归属于老子之道的庄子。这样的"儒家"与"庄子"无疑开启了某种保持距离的相互孕育的新关系，更新并复杂化早已僵固的重层内涵。即便作者更着墨于哲学上的理由，重新发明、澄清庄子所隐含的理论问题，而非思想史上的兴趣（重构历史上已然发生的影响），这会仅仅是作者个人对庄子思想所作出的"晚年定论"吗？"是非经久而论定，意气阅世而平心"（钱基博语），杀青付梓，褪蜕净尽之余，恐怕更是一场对于思想史的重新理解与对于难以抗拒的哲学赌注的书写。

作者坦言，本书的内在对话对象即新儒家，包括宋明新儒家与民国新儒家（页9）。而形气主体、卮言、物论、身体等等自庄子而来的创造性精神发展的人文活动侧面（绝对有的呈现），这些几乎看起来要与传统佛教对立的观点，与其说来自作者自身不同历史阶段的思想轨迹与合乎理性的必然发展及推移过程，毋宁也是作者自始至终的"判教精神"，壁立万仞，止争一线。外在的历史虽为杂多，内在性的历史却往往联系为一。在作者看来，台湾地区当代出现庄子学的第三波修正思潮，不再是像第一波那样以古典主义式的注疏方式出现的历史效应，或者像在晚明三教融合的格局下出现的第二波修正潮：出于对心学主轴的反动而借道庄子。毋宁说，这是以一百多年前的洋务运动、西潮冲击为历史背景的现代回应（页456）。台湾地区庄子学的发展，多大程度上算是晚清诸子学复兴的民国遗绪，或说五四以来未完成的现代性工程，学术上的衣冠南渡？这可能既是历史的产物，同时又是解释的结果。晚清以来的诸子学发展，在台湾地区究竟是遗产抑或债务？它与当代台湾地区庄子学研究群体的内在关系为何？更多知识社会学（个人知识与其社会和个人背景的关联）的历史梳理，犹待来者。而气化是否可能总是显得"不够气化"？不断例外、溢出的气化主体最后是否也有可能成为常规（问题或在真正的"外部"究竟是什么）？甚至气化主体是否也有朝反向发展的可能，并为实际上后来的历史政权与庸俗的社会形态提供难以克服的合理化的解释？换言之，如何规范化地理解具规范化的气化主体？检讨主体内部的吊诡潜能（里头可能含有实际的历史基础与社会需求）似乎也是不可少的程序。

《李梦阳：明代南北差异与士人学术》

王菲菲

（湖南大学岳麓书院）

关于李梦阳的认识，以往的研究大多集中于其在文学方面的成就，例如"前七子""文学复古运动"等基本成为对他的主要界定。然而2016年哈佛大学出版社出版的新加坡国立大学王昌伟（Chang Woei Ong）教授所著《李梦阳：明代南北差异与士人学术》（*Li Mengyang, the North–South Divide, and Literati Learning in Ming China*）一书，则另辟蹊径，从史学分析的视角，将其放置在明代思想史的脉络中进行考察，不仅仅形成了对其个人的全新认识，亦为我们重新窥探明代的士人学术打开了新的视野。

该书主要从明代中期的南北地区差异，以及士人学术分裂的背景中定位李梦阳的思想，以及后代对其思想的接受状态。所谓的南北差异，作者在本书中主要从三个不同的层面进行阐述：一种是南北地区在生态、地理、经济等层面存在的一般性差异；一种是指南北士人群体在思想方面的不同导向，尤其是关于国家的看法；另外一种是根植于明代士人思想中，为合理化现实的差异而建构起的南北差异。

本书共分为四部分，每部分包含两章内容，共八章。其中第一部分首先对李梦阳思想的形成提供一个历史和思想文化的背景。作者在第一章中，主要对李氏家族的历史、科举状态以及社会网络关系进行考察。李氏家族的成功，并非是历史必然，而是由于他们抓住了明前期国家在科举取士政策上向北方倾斜这一机会。永乐以后，明代政权从"南方政权"转为"北方政权",朝廷在科举上刻意压制江南士人,因此为北方士人提供了机会,也因此形成了关于南北问题的激烈讨论。另外,南北士人群体无论在家族成功模式上,还是思想的倾向上,都表现出了明显的差异。而李梦阳正是处于这样强烈的南北差异环境中,因此注定他的思想历程也会受到深刻影响。第二章主要梳理了宋明时期的思想潮流,为进一步理解李梦阳的思想提供一定的文化背景。宋代关于士人的"学",不同学派有不同的观点,北宋时期古文运动的提倡者认为文比较重要,南宋的道学坚持自我道德修养重要,浙东学派则试图建立起一个整合的系统,但最终的目标是恢复上古秩序。明代力图重新恢复道学的正统,主要通过科举考试控制文人的学,直到李东阳建立起了一个结合经、史以及文学各方面的知识体系,目的是为政权服务。而李梦阳则打破了这一体系,提出了新的看法,认为文学与政治是相互独立的。

接下来的三个部分,则从不同的层面,对李梦阳的思想进行具体分析。其中第二部分探讨李梦阳思想视野的形成,主要通过他关于宇宙及其与人类社会关系的看法进行考察,呈现出了其对于南宋道学的吸收与摒弃。在第三章中,李梦阳认为宇宙由"气"组成,多元且变化莫测,因此不可预测才是自然界的法则,不存在和谐统一的说法。人类亦非如道学所论的性本善,相反人性本恶。因此若想维护世界秩序,要靠国家政权,而非个人的德行进行维持。第四章主要分析李梦阳关于政权与法制的探讨,他认为君主不应尊崇道学,因为道学将人的道德权威从政治立法中分离出来,君主应该注重如何掌握政治权力,而非强调个人德行的培养。那么对于个人的发展,"情"的作用亦高于德行,个人应根据不同情况采取不同的学的方式。可见,李梦阳对道学的部分论说,已经提出了一定的挑战。

根据李梦阳对士人学术的划分,作者认为他的整体思想架构可分为政治与文学两类,因此第三与第四部分,则分别从这两方面展开论述。第三部分集中讨论在"文"的理论中李梦阳的政治视野，以及他所认为的理想的学的状态。第五章主要讨论与学相关的制度问题。李梦阳为官之时，经常改淫祠为书院或社学，因此他提倡建立起一个包容性的国学体系，有助于士人的学。他认为学而出仕是士人的职责，并且要保有政治忠诚，而学是成功出仕的基础。第六章集中探讨李梦阳所提倡的学的内容，他将仪式、历史、文学等不同类别的知识整合为一个整体，以教育士人为国家服务。关于皇权，李梦阳认为皇帝需要通过严格犀利的政策来维护权威，并且要学会招揽群才，而不是集中于培养自我德行。社会也要形成遵守秩序的习俗。关于历史，要从历史中汲取道德经验，因此关于历史的书写，不仅仅是纪事，更应该要能够以古鉴今。关于文学，社会要通过风气规范人的行为，观"风"包含观世界，而观世界可以通过观诗完成，因此诗是一种了解社会习俗的工具。

第四部分，主要探讨李梦阳关于散文和诗的理论和实践，以呈现出他的"文"的理论如何通过文学诠释自我。第七章是关于散文的探讨，李梦阳认为散文是用来记述事实的，作者应该是观察和记录者，而非思想者，因此不涉及美学以及自我情感的表达，而诗歌才是表达个人情感的形式。在第八章中，关于诗的讨论，李梦阳认为宋诗缺少了诗歌该有的韵律，诗应该具有情感和动听的特点，关于诗最好的时代，是其刚被创造的时候。可见，关于"文必秦汉，诗必盛唐"的说法，难以完全概括 16 世纪早期复古运动的复杂理论根基。李梦阳提倡的诗和文的文体，远超于汉唐时期。因此他将平民歌曲作为诗歌的基础，但是由于他对模仿没有作出进一步的修饰，经常被指责为纯粹的模仿。

借此可知，李梦阳关于宇宙、伦理、士人学术以及治国策略等都提出了一定的见解。但是他的这些思想，尤其是关于学的理论，并未受到后代的重视，而与其同时期的南部士人王阳明的思想，却得到了广泛的传播。如前所论，李梦阳对于南宋道学的部分论说已经提出了一定的挑战，尤其是他关于诗歌的讨论，注重个人情感的表达，近似于王阳明关于道德的讨论，而且王阳明曾借用了很多李梦阳的观点。但是二者在明代思想史中的地位，却呈现出了很大的不同，李梦阳基本未被后代纳入到儒学思想体系中，这主要是受到了明代中期南北地区差异的影响。李梦阳关于学的讨论，坚持学的目的就是为国家服务，这与南部士人注重个人德行的培养，忽略国家层面的意义，有着显著的差异。因此在 16 世纪中期南部士人掌握主要话语权的情况下，李梦阳这种"国家倾向"的思想很难引起他们的关注。但是，在程朱理学受到挑战的时候，李梦阳的文学复古，追求文学书写的艺术形式，使其独立于政治，为晚明思想提供了一个基于真情呈现出本我的理论。而这些正是南部士人的关注点，因此成就了其在文学上的地位。

作者从南北差异的视角，对李梦阳的学术思想进行探讨，重新界定了他在历史上的地位，及其对明代思想的贡献。李梦阳并不仅仅是一个文学家或者文学批评者，更是一个思想丰富的思想者。仅仅注重他在文学上的贡献，事实上会忽略其在思想领域的成就。对李梦阳的研究，也有助于我们从一种更新的视角去理解阳明心学在明代的兴起，以及由宋至明思想变迁的问题。另外，如作者所论，我们对于晚明思想状况的认识，大多是从南部士人群体的言论中获得，因此，在此语境下被忽略的北部士人的声音亟待受到重视。

《成圣与家庭人伦：宗教对话脉络下的明清之际儒学》

丘文豪

（台湾大学历史所博士生）

自梁启超以来，"明末清初"便是思想史学者甚为关注的时段，研究成果丰富。在此"难以攀越的高峰"中吕妙芬教授的《成圣与家庭人伦：宗教对话脉络下的明清之际儒学》（台北：联经出版事业公司，2017年）一书以较新的研究视角、史料，试图复杂化现有的思想学术史图像。作者认为此前的研究多以"理学衰微"为前提，探究明清之际之"新"思想典范的产生，研究架构多为"程朱 vs 陆王"，并常在现代化启蒙问题意识下进行，采用的史料则以著名学者之著作为主。本书的最大特色在于，它认识到程朱理学仍为17世纪的核心思想价值，因此以理学为主要研究范围，试图透过分析大量尚未被充分研究的理学文本来观察当时儒学的共识与趋向。作者也强调宗教的面向，注意到理学与佛、道、天主教之对话脉络，以及明清之际儒学的宗教意涵。在此方法论的反省下，本书以"成圣"和"家庭人伦"为主轴，讨论个人修身与家庭人伦在为学目标、工夫论、个人认同等方面呈现的辩证关系。除前言、结论外，全书共分为三部分七章，以下就各章简略介绍。

第一部分"成圣、不朽、家庭伦常"以"思想"为主，共三章。第一章"生死观的新发展"探讨明清儒学是否具有近似个体灵魂的概念，以及关于死后的想象和描述又是如何。作者指出明末儒者开始对宋儒"人死后气散无知""圣凡贤愚皆同归太虚"等说法提出质疑，当时有不少人相信人可以透过道德修养，达到死后神灵不灭的境界，他们对于人死后的想象，也有圣贤相聚"在帝左右"的描述。作者认为在生死观上，不仅可以看见从晚明到清初延续性的发展，也可以看到清初学者有别于宋儒的一面。第二章"儒门圣贤皆孝子"主要说明虽然延续儒学成圣的目标，但在工夫论方面清初儒学也批判、修正晚明学风，反对阳明学逆觉体证的本体工夫的倾向，转而强调日用人伦的重要性，主张人不可能离开家庭场域而修身成圣。第三章"圣人处兄弟之变"透过整理分析明清儒者对《孟子·万章》中舜象故事的不同诠释，说明士人心目中理想的圣人形象，而在他们寻求更圆满、更合理地诠释舜的心境与行为时，舜个人的道德成就亦与象的真诚悔悟紧密联系，唯有家人真诚感化才能成就舜之圣德。以上几章均说明17世纪儒者将家庭人伦视为个人修身求道的前提。

第二部分"道脉与血脉的双重认同"转入实际"活动"为主题，讨论儒者对父子之伦、圣贤道脉的重视，以及儒学宗教化、庶民化的倾向。第四章"万里寻亲的孝行"分析大量万里寻亲的故事，发现这些故事的叙事中有一定的结构，作者以孝思、艰困的旅程、天人相助、救赎四个主题来分析孝子传再现的意涵，并指出这类寻亲孝行显示，对17世纪儒者而言"家"是生命的永恒归属。第五章"在家拜圣贤的礼仪"说明在官方孔庙、书院祭拜圣贤的仪式外，17世纪的理学家也在家中祭拜圣贤。这样的礼仪行为除了展现个性化与私人化外，也体现了儒家士人对展现家庭人伦的血脉以及儒家圣贤道统道脉的双重认同。

第三部分"宗教对话语境下的儒学论述"共两章，主要重探理学研究中讨论甚多的人欲、人性问题。第六章"夫妇之伦"指出儒学文献中对于夫妇之伦有两个不同的论述脉络：在家训文本的脉络下，夫妇间的亲密与家庭秩序产生一定的紧张，因此必须被压抑；然而在辟二氏的发言语境下，理学家高扬夫妇之伦为天地宇宙生生、创生之始，强调男女之交的神圣性，并抨击佛道灭人伦。明清儒者论人欲并非反宋儒、提倡情欲解放，而是试图与佛老区隔，强调儒家为节欲而不绝欲，反私欲而不反欲的人伦之道。第七章"人性论述"由于人性论与当时气论的讨论有密切关系，因而作者特别透过气论说明，以"天"为本源、权威的看法也是明清之际思想延续性的展现，同时也尝试带入天主教的灵魂论进行比较。作者整理出明清之际人性论的五项特色：性为生成过程中天所赋予；品类各具其性；性善是指具有扩充学习的能力；气学仍以天为道德、存有的本源，同时强调人的道德能力与自主；辟二氏的宗教对话语境。最后，作者再以晚明到清初儒学思想的延续与变化、儒学的宗教关怀与庶民倾向、明清之际儒学转型在中国思想史上的意义三点，总结全书的论点。

思想之延续与断裂本是由学者观察的层次所决定，在多半以典范转移、忽略理学的明清之际思想史研究中，本书并重"延续"与"变化"。就其核心议题而言，以"天"为依据，以"成圣"为目标是清儒延续宋明理学理想的一面；而天人关系之改变，以及于"家庭人伦"中作工夫便是其变化的一面。具体的操作方式则是透过大量理学文本，同时兼顾了儒者之思想与活动，如第一部分便着重在成圣于家庭人伦的思想讨论，而第二部分则由"万里寻亲"与"居家拜圣贤"来观察儒者如何以实践来达成这一理想。由此作者打破过去程朱／陆王两极之钟摆的分析框架，挖掘晚明到清初，一个以家庭伦理为成圣场所的新思想倾向。另一方面，理学诞生之初即与佛、老有千丝万缕的关系，然而现有研究对于明清之际思想变迁的讨论多半将其视为对外在政治、社会环境的反应，或是儒学内部思想演变的过程，较少涉及儒佛道交涉的议题。然从本书，特别是第五章可见，不仅如宋明时儒学与佛教于思想义理上的争论，明末清初之争也反应在日常生活礼仪的实践上。此外，本书透过对宗教面向的重视，也描绘出当时庶民化、宗教化的明清思想史图像，并引入了天主教思想，作为进一步与儒家比较研究的基础。

　　本书最基本的贡献便是挖掘出一批过去学界甚为陌生的儒者，如是镜、杨屾、劳史、文翔凤等人。然而这类学者或许生平数据不完整，或许师承脉络难以探究，再加上作者为了探寻一些当时的新趋向而以"理学文本"为核心，便无法避免地忽略了这些人物彼此在思想内容、脉络、属性间的差异。此外，作者选取的都是宗教性、庶民性比较强烈的人物，若是选取另一批儒者作为研究对象，可能又会描绘出另一番景象。诚如作者所言，本书以复杂化现有的明清思想学术史图像为目的，然在明清大量的史料文本中，个别研究要如何展开对话，就是一个可进一步思考的问题。另外，如作者所言，学界长期以来以求新（新思潮、新方法、新学术社群）为问题意识，忽略程朱理学对日常生活中的明清思想发挥的作用。作者在呈现本书时虽重视延续性，但在讨论变化时不得不举出当时理学一些新的发展趋向，并以清代理学"推陈出新""具时代特色的儒学新思想"为关怀。因此对于思想上没有创新，而在生活实践中固守程朱者便注意较少。如作者在各大图书馆见到大量抄录先儒语录的"理学类"著作，便因与本书探讨之议题无关而被割舍。要透过怎样的方法与问题意识来探究这些"可能不会成为明清学术史研究的主要对象"的文本，挖掘其中包含的 17 世纪理学之历史意义，也是一个值得思索的问题。

《另类的佛学家——天台宗对牟宗三新儒学的影响》

姜明泽

（深圳大学哲学系）

牟宗三与佛教之间渊源甚深，这是学界所公认的。围绕这一课题展开的研究数量不可谓不多，但以一本书的篇幅来系统而全面地研究牟宗三与佛教之间错综复杂的关系，并不多见。因此，现任教于加州州立大学的美国汉学家柯文杰（Jason Clower）的专著《另类的佛学家——天台宗对牟宗三新儒学的影响》（*The Unlikely Buddhologist: Tiantai Buddhism in Mou Zongsan's New Confucianism*, Brill, 2010）就格外引人注目。

醒目的书名不仅泄露了这部书的主题，同时也告诉了我们展开这一主题的基本脉络，即由"另类的"（或译为"特别的"，从正文来看，其亦隐含有"被忽视的、被低估的"之义）一词与副标题所蕴含者。柯文杰并非单纯地聚焦于牟宗三对佛学的援用，亦非聚焦在单一的佛学内在脉络中，而是在一种立体的，具体表现在牟宗三身上的儒佛交涉、彼此激发、彼此赋能的综合语境中来展开其主题。柯文杰选定的脉络给他带来很大挑战，也给这本书提出了很高的要求。不过，这也正是此书值得重视的最重要原因，因为如此才能相应于"牟宗三与佛教"这一课题的复杂性。

关于这一选题的意义，柯文杰认为，被视为当代新儒家领袖的牟宗三却选择将他的"新儒学"建立在佛学的基础之上，足以说明牟宗三与佛教关系的复杂与深刻，也足以说明了解二者关系对于了解牟宗三哲学的基础性。牟宗三身上所表现的儒释交涉远比以往的儒家更为复杂。在柯文杰看来：牟宗三主观上对佛教著名高僧比如天台智者大师等的崇敬之情，与历史上其他大儒相比是史无前例的；其呕心沥血花费数十年工夫消化并系统梳理佛教圣典，其所建构的"道德形而上学"许多核心观念与方法援引自佛教或受到佛教启发；等等，这些都是以牟宗三对佛教的巨大投入为基础，这在儒家是罕见的。因此柯文杰认为，我们应严肃地追问这一问题："为什么一个从头至尾都在为儒学辩护的人，却如此地关注佛教哲学，并且使其成为其工作的核心？"进一步的问题是，牟宗三将佛教的观念与方法谨慎地挪用到儒教中，必要性何在，其最终目的又是什么？这一切即归结为：佛教对牟宗三究竟意味着什么，牟宗三对佛教又有何意义？

但是在柯文杰看来，对如此紧迫的问题，学界的投入远远不足。迄今为止，牟宗三的巨大付出并未获得来自佛教内部的等价的回应——更不用说来自佛教内部学者的公正评价；他被很多佛学家视为儒家沙文主义者，其贡献以往被忽视而其对佛教的批评也未得到充分的总结。柯文杰认为导致这一局面的原因很多。就牟宗三本人而言，他对同时代的重要佛学家给予了相当的关注，在他的工作中，不时表现出对这部分佛学家观点的重视，但他的主要身份和活动范围仍局限于儒家团体，这使得他的成果很难成为佛学进一步发展的客观基础。与他的老师熊十力不同，牟宗三对来自佛教内的批评缺乏反驳与辩护的兴趣，他无意与他们展开公开争论。因此在现实学术界牟宗三并未成为儒释互动的发动机。就儒家内部而言，其工作多被狭隘单一地理解为援用层面，儒释之间往复回环、交织勾连的复杂性并未得到正式揭示。

在充分认识这一问题复杂性的基础上，柯文杰解决这一问题的切入点与线索简洁明了：在简要展示牟宗三佛教史梳理的基础上，剖析牟宗三对佛教的批评以及对佛教的吸收。柯文杰对佛教自身的问题与脉络有一定的理解，因此他在梳理牟宗三的佛教史研究时并非亦步亦趋地跟在牟宗三后面，而是保持一个远观的姿态，而准确提炼出牟宗三佛教研究的特色之处——以存有论（保存万法）为核心视角。关于牟宗三对佛教的批评与吸收，柯文杰周到而细致的梳理与辨析给人深刻印象。本书充分严谨的论证使读者相信，牟宗三对佛教的批评并非只是一种狭隘的门户之见，而是表现在一种严肃的哲学运思过程中。同时，牟宗三对佛教的吸收并非只限于语言表述与方法论层面，深层次的佛教义理对他也产生了深刻启发。

在柯文杰看来，牟宗三从佛教中获得的最大收益是将源自天台宗的别教模型、圆教模型作为一般解释框架来使用，既依此来梳理儒学史，同时更上一层楼，依此来判释儒释道耶，产生了丰富的理论效果。可以说柯文杰非常扼要地把握住了佛教对牟宗三最重要的影响。

全书共分七章。其中第一章"牟宗三：他的时代与他的目标"主要从近代中国所遭遇的政治危机与文化危机、新文化运动对儒学的攻击、中西文化融合与新儒学的兴起等角度考察了牟宗三哲学创造的大背景。第二章简要考察了牟宗三的哲学观以及牟宗三哲学体系的基本结构。在柯文杰看来，牟宗三对"哲学"的理解与西方学界对哲学的一般理解有很大的不同。在牟氏这里，哲学本质上是生命的学问，哲学应在具体实践中被运用，并在这个过程中使我们的生活变得更美好。对学者来说，哲学工作是对精神生命的理论研究，它追求对精神运行的精确描述，以促进精神的提升与转化。佛教在历史上创造了关于人的精神活动的复杂而精致的理论，其对人的各层意识的分析比儒家更深入，对佛与众生、圣人与凡人之间心理状态差异的分析更严谨、论述更周密。柯文杰认为，基于此，我们便不难理解牟宗三为何如此重视佛教。

在第三章"佛陀的基本教诲——五时教"与第四章"佛教哲学家"中，柯文杰主要沿着牟宗三的思路，扼要梳理了牟宗三对佛教史的研究。在这部分，柯文杰也粗略地反思了牟宗三对佛教所作的重新判教。这两章可以说回答了"牟宗三对佛教的意义"这一问题。接下来的第五、第六两章，解决的是"佛教对牟宗三的意义"问题：牟宗三对佛教的援用与批判。在第五章"佛教之不足"中，柯文杰首先对牟宗三儒学史的梳理作了归纳与提炼。在他看来：牟宗三依据宋明儒学而将儒家核心观念提炼为天道创生万物的纵贯系统；同时，天道内在于人而表现于人的道德实践中；从道德实践出发而最终实现万物的存在。综合言之，即是一套道德的形而上学。以此为参照，牟宗三指出了佛教的不足——对道德法则重视不够、缺乏天道创生不已的精神，以及在实现终极价值上不如儒家直接等等。

第六章"佛教的意义"则集中探讨了牟宗三从佛教那里所获得的利益，这一章虽然所占篇幅不大，但实际上是全书的逻辑枢纽。柯文杰将这一问题聚焦在佛教判教对牟宗三的影响上——特别是"别教""圆教"被牟宗三转化为一种通用的解释模式。

在柯文杰看来，别圆二教为探讨一个中国哲学中最具普遍性的话题——如何处理佛与众生、天与人、圣人与凡人等等两层关系，提供了一个重要基础。而根源于这一问题的"两层存有论"又是牟宗三哲学体系的重要架构，因此别圆分判作为一种观念与方法受到牟宗三的极大关注乃是顺理成章的，它成为牟宗三从佛教那里所得到的最大利益也不难理解。进一步说，别圆分判——尤其是圆教模式，为何具有这样的意义？其对牟宗三的具体影响是如何发生的？柯文杰从圆教所处理的特定问题、圆教模式在表述上的优势、牟宗三对儒学的判教以及圆教理论的现实意义四个方面作了细致而精彩的分析。值得关注的是，在柯文杰看来，传统中判教所处理的特定问题——天人之间、佛与众生之间的关系，今天从哲学的角度来看，实际上是终极价值与万事万物之间关系的问题。宇宙万物与终极价值之间互相隔离，即是一种别教观；如果认为二者是相即的，则是圆教观——更直接的表述是，包括人在内的宇宙万物"即是"终极价值。总之，在柯文杰看来，牟宗三对将判教特别是圆教从佛教特定脉络中抽离的这一方法，赋予了新的意义，带来许多观念上的更新。

由"相即"所体现的圆教特殊的表述方式，在柯文杰看来，对牟宗三自身的哲学建构产生了重要影响。这种修辞技术，乃是特殊义理的自我要求，并非只是文字游戏。柯文杰称之为诗意地表达，认为它能产生一种警醒效果。

作为全书最后一章，柯文杰在第七章中集中反思了牟宗三的佛教史梳理、对佛教的批评与援用，以及在此基础上的哲学建构。柯文杰区分了作为哲学史家与作为哲学家的牟宗三，在他看来，《佛性与般若》即代表了牟宗三作为一名职业哲学史家的重要成就。不过柯文杰也指出，牟氏这部分工作仍有许多值得讨论的地方，比如对佛教，牟宗三是否真正做到了客观，是否有过度诠释的问题，用存有论的思路来解释天台宗的判教是否相应，等等。作为哲学家，牟宗三对佛教提出了许多新的议题，比如如何保住万法以及其意义何在。这一问题具有多重面向，既关涉在无分别智中法界无差而差的问题，佛圣人同样有感触直觉、拥抱现象世界的问题等等；同时，牟宗三对这一问题的提出与其哲学追求——两层存有论的建构——密切相关。因此，掌握了这一问题的全貌，才能真正了解牟宗三这一要求在佛教内在脉络中的意义。

关于两层存有论，柯文杰也提出了个人见解。关于"从哲学的角度来看，为什么既需要无执的存有论又需要执的存有论？"，柯文杰认为，这样的哲学系统更能"歌颂"物质世界与日常事物；他认为牟宗三在这里表现出一种认识论的乐观主义（epistemological optimism），以及对科学的尊重；物质世界和科学研究的对象不应被过度贬低，不应在追求成圣成佛的过程中以"假象"的身份被搁置起来。

牟宗三批评佛教缺乏一个创生的实体，柯文杰认为牟宗三并未指出从什么意义上这构成一种缺陷，因此佛教内部并不需要作出回应。站在儒家立场上，牟宗三认为佛教对道德法则的重视不够，佛教没有忧患意识，等等；从社会政治层面牟宗三也给予佛教诸多批评，比如他认为佛教在激励大众以服务社会与国家方面发挥的作用实在有限，他指责历史上佛教对于挽救唐代的衰落无能为力，而在柯文杰看来，对于佛教来说这种批评实际上也是非常微弱的。

柯文杰同时也认为，牟宗三对佛教的态度还有另一面，即他包容主义者的姿态：牟宗三承认，儒释各自揭示了同一真理的两个不同方面，儒释之间存在着"大通"；同时，儒释二教可以彼此教会对方自身所没有的东西。总而言之，在儒释之间存在会通之道，表现了牟宗三超越儒释两家特定立场与传统、寻找更高整合的追求。

柯文杰的这本专著，从立意与目标，到脉络与过程，可以说扣紧了"牟宗三与佛教"这一课题最核心的部分。他抓住"判教"这个最重要的线索，顺着它展示了牟宗三对佛教的贡献，也细致剖析了佛教对牟宗三的意义。其颇具哲学深度的剖析，周到而细致，引人入胜。更为难得的是，儒释两家在牟宗三这里的冲突与融合，在柯文杰有条不紊的复调式的叙述中，得到清晰的呈现，为我们进一步研究这一课题奠定了重要基础。

《思想的芦苇——黄进兴自选集》

冯一鸣

（华中师范大学历史文化学院）

帕斯卡尔在《思想录》中将人比喻为"会思想的芦苇"，人之存在虽脆弱如芦苇，却因能够思考而显现出强大和尊严。黄进兴先生的《思想的芦苇——黄进兴自选集》（上海：上海人民出版社，2017 年）虽然取帕斯卡尔"思想的芦苇"这一著名比喻为书名，但他自言取意与帕氏有别，"只不过要供出：个人微不足道的知识探索，说穿了，也只能是'思想的芦苇'的一己之见，盖难脱野人献曝、敝帚自珍的俗谛"。然而，在我看来，借用此喻更体现出一位思想史研究者举重若轻的智慧与学术生命的积淀。

黄进兴先生早年求学于台湾大学历史学系，受教于杜维运、陶晋生、林毓生诸位中西贯通的先生，以治中国史为志业，同时又广读西方经典名著，以"比较思想史"作为未来治学目标，他关于"历史主义"的论文即是台大求学时期的答卷。[1] 嗣后，进兴先生远渡重洋，赴哈佛大学历史学系攻读博士学位，受业于史华慈、余英时两位先生，在当年名师云集、有着"浓郁的智性氛围"的哈佛汲汲求索。这一阶段的经历，后来被写成数篇随笔，并结集为《哈佛琐记》，[2] 其中文字灵动有趣、率性天然，所记载哈佛往事、诸位前哲，跃然纸上，令人神往。哈佛求学的成果日后成为专著《18 世纪的中国哲学、

---

1 黄进兴：《历史主义与历史理论》（西安：陕西师范大学出版社，2002 年），第一部分。
2 黄进兴：《哈佛琐记》（北京：中华书局，2009 年）。

考据学与政治：李绂与清初的陆王学派》[3]，即是在比较思想史的视野下研究中国思想的产物。从哈佛学成归来，黄进兴先生入台湾"中研院"历史语言研究所工作，至今已逾三十载，其研究以史学理论、近世思想史、宗教文化史为主要方向，以国学之扎实根基融通西学的深厚涵养，问题意识与思考维度皆别开生面，不囿于传统。

不吝辞费述及黄进兴先生的学术生平，皆因《思想的芦苇》一书乃是他治学数十年来的第一本学术自选集，所收论文十四篇，以内容分为"思想""史学""作为儒教圣域的孔庙"三部类，撰写时间自1980年至2013年，基本上涵盖了他的哈佛时代至史语所时期的所有重要创获，从中可以体察一位研究者思考、成长以及自我砥砺的学术历程。

一

本书所呈现的学术特征首先是"比较思想史"的广阔视阈。黄进兴先生承续史华慈、余英时二先生之精神，以深厚的西学背景，立足于中国历史文化的探讨，反思批评西方理论的照搬套用。

如《所谓"道德自主性"——以西方观念解释中国思想之限制的例证》及《孟子的"四端说"与"道德感说"》二文，反思自清末西方哲学传入百余年来，学界热衷以康德"道德自主"之说或休谟、亚当·斯密之"道德感说"解释中国儒家思想，这种比附性的解释多有局限。儒家思想与康德道德哲学在某些部分固然可以相通，比如孟子"性善说"，然而同时，"康德与儒家伦理之差异不胜枚举，其间有些是纯粹道德层面的问题，有些则为特殊文化脉络所导致"。另一方面，

---

3 黄进兴：《18世纪的中国哲学、考据学与政治：李绂与清初的陆王学派》(*Philosophy, Philology, and Politics in Eighteenth-century China*：*Li Fu and Lu-Wang school under the Ch'ing*，英国剑桥大学出版社，1995年)。

初步的观察似乎表明孟子的伦理学与"道德感说"甚相近似，然而，"作为'道德感'的'恻隐之心'与作为'道德判断'的'仁'之间的确切关系，值得探究"，"孟子惯以'恻隐之心'与'仁'交互界定，其所呈现相互渗透性，似乎孟子并不分辨'道德情感'与'道德判断'的不同"，由此可见，"道德感说"与儒家思想亦并非能够互相解释。由这些较具体的比较可见，试图以西方哲学解释中国思想，在实际操作中已是处处捉襟见肘。

更深层的揭橥在于：比较研究的真正意义所在。"欲了解或重新解释中国文化，仅诉诸西方或任何外来文化都是不够的。不可否认，异文化的观点提供了许多认识中国文化的新角度，这方面的成绩极具启发价值；但如果不能逐步从自己的文化里爬梳出一些适切的现代语言和概念，恐怕很难真正把握传统文化的特征及其现代含义。""研究中国思想，我们首要的信念为：'返归原典'！"进兴先生指出，"返归原典"是研究中国文化的根基。与西学的比较研究是方法和视野的开拓，而不是阵地的转移。因此，要守住中国文化的"本体地位"，参考西学的方法与思想，从自身文化中生成现代意义的话语体系和概念系统，完成中国传统学术向现代学术的转变。

二

对中国近代史学及近代思想史的自觉反思，是本书另一个重要特点，以《中国近代史学的双重危机——试论"新史学"的诞生及其所面临的困境》一文为代表。在现代人文社会科学的门类中，仅"史学"一科为中国传统学术所固有，中国史学在清末民初面临两大困境：一方面是自身学科发展所遭逢的"内在危机"；另一方面是在社会思潮激荡变化的背景下，该学科面临新的生命力和现代价值的考验，是为"外在危机"。由此，以梁启超为首倡而"新史学"兴起，同时，传统史学进入了一个漫长的转化时期，求新求变。然而这场绵延百余年至今未已的变革可谓坎坷多艰，由"史学"而嬗变为"史料学"的进程中，史学自古奠定的权威地位已岌岌可危。如何避免史学沦为仅仅是资料提供者，如何定位中国史学自身的现代价值，是至今仍亟待解决的课题。对此，进兴先生提出建立"别有特色"的史学："要建立别有特色的史学必须'学有所本'。这个'本'即是历史自家的园地；必得勤于耕耘，方有所获。反之，光凭西学理论究竟只能糊口度日，并不足以成就大事。再多、再高明、再先进的西学，充其数只能将中国历史降为普遍的事例而已，实质上并无法彰显中国独特的历史经验；况且不意之中，也将消解了中国历史对世界史学可能的贡献。"这一思考以中国史学为主体而具有长足的发展眼光，强调"学有所本"，求新求变的同时扎根坚实，务令史学不为其他社会学科的仆从、中国史学不为西方史学的附庸。

这一反思作为研究者的学术自觉而贯穿全书始终，如《清末民初道德意识转化的几点观察》一文讨论近代道德思想从传统"理学"到现代"伦理学"的递嬗，这一过程是"清末知识分子企图利用西方知识系统重新架构中国的传统道德"的尝试，同时，"中国的道德思维也起了极大的转化"，这种格局下的近代道德意识，内有自身的转化，外受西学的冲击，如何建构新的道德伦理思想，尤以立足中国、兼纳西学为要。[4] 又如《论"方法"及"方法论"——以近代中国史学意识为系络》一文，反思西方近代以来对史学研究方法及方法论的探讨与重视，提出"史家不能迷信方法及方法论，因为它们既不是实际历史研究的充分条件，也不是必要条件"，而应"本着'求经溯源'的态度，去阅读更深刻的原典，同时本着'实事求是'的原则，从实际

---

4 关于理学与伦理学的研究与反思，见黄进兴：《从理学到伦理学：清末民初道德意识的转化》（北京：中华书局，2014 年）。

研究工作中去体会这些问题"。进兴先生时刻强调回归史学本身，以历史叙述、秉笔直书的精神进行史学研究，观照学科重建，处处显现着史家本色。

三

围绕孔庙展开的儒教与宗教文化史的研究，是黄进兴先生多年所致力的，相关成果已有专著《圣贤与圣徒》[5]及《优入圣域：权力、信仰与正当性》[6]等问世。在此部自选集中，又特列"作为儒教圣域的孔庙"一部分，收入五篇代表作品，足见对此项研究的格外看重。

这部分的研究，基础是廓清"执基督教作为宗教的基型，以此裁度儒教"的思维定式，认为："以西方界义来了解其他异文化的宗教，已处处窒碍难行"，"必须着手反思并修订传统以基督教为基型的宗教界义"。前人的研究往往先以基督教为范式定义"宗教"，再奉此定义为圭臬评判儒教，进而认定儒教并非宗教。进兴先生以平等观照不同文化的宗教的视角，采用"历史论述"的方法，真实还原了儒教在传统社会与其他宗教"并排齐观"的态势，提出儒教本为"国家宗教"与"官方宗教"的独特性质，其重要结论为："儒教于'三教鼎立'的状态，可以成为独立的宗教个体，其基本性格为官方宗教，但在'三教合一'的情状，因与释、道二教结成有机体，遂蜕变成民间宗教。毋论其为国家宗教或民间宗教，至19世纪末的传统社会，其宗教性质素受肯定。"他凭借宏观的文化视野和切实的历史论述，厘清了在传统中国，儒教具备宗教的特质、发挥宗教的功能这一客观史实。

黄进兴先生对儒教的研究，选取了能够"聚焦神圣空间与信仰者的互动"的孔庙作为独到的切入点，参考了人类学的研究理路，

---

5 黄进兴：《圣贤与圣徒》（北京：北京大学出版社，2005年）。
6 黄进兴：《优入圣域：权力、信仰与正当性》（修订版）（北京：中华书局，2010年）。

十分新颖。《权力与信仰——孔庙祭祀制度的形成》一文着重稽考了从私庙到官庙、从地方到全国的孔庙祭祀制度起源与演变之路，作为"圣域"的孔庙以及作为国家制度的全国性祭祀，凸显了儒教的宗教本质，在历史上绵延不衰地展现了"国家宗教"对权力和信仰的交互渗透。

清末以降，自梁启超始开启了儒教"去宗教化"历程，从此"儒教非宗教"之说逐渐成为主流观念。《研究儒教的反思》一文总结其原因有三：一是遵循"界义式"进路，以基督教为一切宗教的基型来衡量儒教，因其不同而认为儒教非宗教。二是"陷于教义的论辩，而忽略了帝制时期儒教所曾发挥的宗教角色与功能"。三是"宗教"一词已逐渐沦为贬义，"希冀儒教非为宗教，或予以改造为非宗教"成为主流价值判断。这三点原因的明确，为我们解答了近代以来儒教非宗教的观念之所自出，阐明了是外在因素蒙蔽了儒教的宗教性质。

这部名为"思想的芦苇"的自选集是一位研究者的自我呈现。黄进兴先生以大陆、台湾、海外三重维度的学缘，以中西比较思想史的视角，多年沉潜。他的治学告诉我们：研究中国思想文化，一方面要有全球视野和现代意识，另一方面要守住中文典籍文化的本体地位。立根扎实，放眼高远，方才是现代中国人文科学研究的开新境界。

图书在版编目（CIP）数据

人文学衡：汉文、英文 / 彭国翔主编. —杭州：浙江大学出版社，
2019. 7

ISBN 978-7-308-19326-9

I.① 人… Ⅱ.① 彭… Ⅲ.① 人文科学—研究—中国—汉、英

Ⅳ.① C12

中国版本图书馆 CIP 数据核字（2019）第 144152 号

人文学衡

彭国翔　主编

责任编辑	王志毅
文字编辑	吴昱璇　张兴文
责任校对	赵　珏　仲亚萍
装帧设计	周伟伟
出版发行	浙江大学出版社
	（杭州天目山路 148 号 邮政编码 310007）
	（网址：http://www.zjupress.com）
排　　版	北京大有艺彩图文设计有限公司
印　　刷	浙江印刷集团有限公司
开　　本	710mm×1000mm　1/16
印　　张	23.5
字　　数	294 千
版 印 次	2019 年 7 月第 1 版　2019 年 7 月第 1 次印刷
书　　号	ISBN 978-7-308-19326-9
定　　价	85.00 元

《人文学衡》稿约

一、《人文学衡》由浙江大学国际学衡人文研究中心主办，浙江大学出版社出版。暂拟每年出版一辑，欢迎海内外学界随时赐稿。

二、本书为中英双语文集，兼收中英文稿，旨在在全球学术思想共同体的范围内聚焦和推动中国人文学的研究。

三、本书征稿范围以研究性论文为主，兼及书评论文、书评及其他相关论述。

四、原则上中文论文每篇不超过三万字，英文论文每篇不超过二万字，书评论文每篇不超过一万五千字，书评五千字以内。

五、来稿中涉及版权的部分，由作者负责，本书不负版权责任。

六、来稿请用真实姓名，并同时提供作者的工作单位、通信地址、邮箱和电话，以便联络。

七、来稿收录并出版之后，编辑部将向作者支付稿酬并寄赠当期样书两册和作者单篇抽印本二十册。

八、来稿邮箱：chinesehumanities9@126.com.